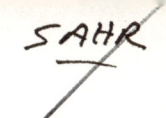

**PERGAMON INTERNATIONAL LIBRARY**
of Science, Technology, Engineering and Social Studies

*The 1000-volume original paperback library in aid of education, industrial training and the enjoyment of leisure*

Publisher: Robert Maxwell, M.C.

# Defense Manpower Planning

## THE PERGAMON TEXTBOOK INSPECTION COPY SERVICE

An inspection copy of any book published in the Pergamon International Library will gladly be sent to academic staff without obligation for their consideration for course adoption or recommendation. Copies may be retained for a period of 60 days from receipt and returned if not suitable. When a particular title is adopted or recommended for adoption for class use and the recommendation results in a sale of 12 or more copies the inspection copy may be retained with our compliments. The Publishers will be pleased to receive suggestions for revised editions and new titles to be published in this important international Library.

# Pergamon Titles of Related Interest

*Cannizzo* THE GUN MERCHANTS: Politics and Policies of the Major Arms Suppliers
*Douglass* SOVIET MILITARY STRATEGY IN EUROPE: An Institute for Foreign Policy Analysis Book
*Edmonds* INTERNATIONAL ARMS PROCUREMENT: New Directions
*Hunt/Shultz* LESSONS FROM AN UNCONVENTIONAL WAR: Reassessing U.S. Strategies for Future Conflicts
*Keliher* NEGOTIATIONS ON MUTUAL AND BALANCED FORCE REDUCTIONS: The Search for Arms Control in Central Europe
*Owen* BRASSEY'S INFANTRY WEAPONS OF THE WORLD
*Owen* INFANTRY WEAPONS OF THE ARMIES OF AFRICA, THE ORIENT AND LATIN AMERICA
*Owen* INFANTRY WEAPONS OF THE NATO ARMIES
*Owen* INFANTRY WEAPONS OF THE WARSAW PACT ARMIES
*RUSI* BRASSEY'S DEFENSE YEARBOOK
*Sarkesian* BEYOND THE BATTLEFIELD: The New Military Professionalism
*Simpkin* MECHANIZED INFANTRY
*Yost* NATO'S STRATEGIC OPTIONS: Arms Control and Defense

# Related Journals*

ADVANCES IN SPACE RESEARCH
LONG RANGE PLANNING
NUCLEAR TRACKS
PROGRESS IN PLANNING
REGIONAL STUDIES
TECHNOLOGY

*Free specimen copies available upon request.

**PERGAMON POLICY STUDIES ON SECURITY AFFAIRS**

# Defense Manpower Planning
## Issues for the 1980s

Edited by
William J. Taylor, Jr.
Eric T. Olson
Richard A. Schrader

**Pergamon Press**
NEW YORK • OXFORD • TORONTO • SYDNEY • PARIS • FRANKFURT

Pergamon Press Offices:

**U.S.A.**  Pergamon Press Inc., Maxwell House, Fairview Park, Elmsford, New York 10523, U.S.A.

**U.K.**  Pergamon Press Ltd., Headington Hill Hall, Oxford OX3 0BW, England

**CANADA**  Pergamon Press Canada Ltd., Suite 104, 150 Consumers Road, Willowdale, Ontario M2J 1P9, Canada

**AUSTRALIA**  Pergamon Press (Aust.) Pty. Ltd., P.O. Box 544, Potts Point, NSW 2011, Australia

**FRANCE**  Pergamon Press SARL, 24 rue des Ecoles, 75240 Paris, Cedex 05, France

**FEDERAL REPUBLIC OF GERMANY**  Pergamon Press GmbH, Hammerweg 6, Postfach 1305, 6242 Kronberg/Taunus, Federal Republic of Germany

Copyright © 1981 Pergamon Press Inc.

**Library of Congress Cataloging in Publication Data**
Main entry under title:

Defense manpower planning.

(Pergamon policy studies on security affairs)
Bibliography: p.
Includes index.
Contents: Conscription and the all-volunteer army in historical perspective / Robert K. Griffith -- Women, combat, and the draft / William J. Gregor -- People, not hardware / Melvin R. Laird -- [etc.]
  1. United States--Armed Forces--Recruiting, enlistment, etc.--Addresses, essays, lectures. 2. Military service, Voluntary--United States--Addresses, essays, lectures. 3. Military service, Compulsory--United States--Addresses, essays, lectures. I. Taylor, William J. (William Jesse), 1933- . II. Olson, Eric T. (Eric Thorne), 1950- . III. Schrader, Richard A. (Richard Allen), 1950- . IV. Series.
UB323.D43   1981       355.2'2362'0973        81-4462
ISBN 0-08-027561-3                             AACR2
ISBN 0-08-027560-5 (pbk.)

The views and conclusions expressed herein are solely those of the authors and do not purport to represent the policy of any government agency of the United States

All Rights reserved. No part of this publication may be reproduced, stored in a retrieval system or transmitted in any form or by any means: electronic, electrostatic, magnetic tape, mechanical, photocopying, recording or otherwise, without permission in writing from the publishers.

Printed in the United States of America

*To Louise, Vicki, and Eileen*
Whose support and understanding
made this effort possible.

# Contents

Preface .................................................... ix

An Overview: Military Manpower into the 1980s
    *Robert B. Pirie, Jr.* ....................... xi

A Military Manpower Chronology ..................... xix

Chapter
   1. Outline of Manpower Issues and Debate ............ 1

## PART I: ACTIVE DUTY FORCES

Introduction to Part I ............................... 19

2. Conscription and the All-Volunteer Army in Historical Perspective
    *Robert K. Griffith, Jr.* ........................ 21

3. Women, Combat, and the Draft: Placing Details in Context
    *William J. Gregor* ............................ 34

4. People, Not Hardware: The Highest Defense Priority
    *Melvin R. Laird* ............................. 61

5. "Dumb" Soldiers and "Smart" Bombs: Precision-Guided Munitions and the All-Volunteer Force
    *Bruce E. Arlinghaus* ......................... 80

6. AVF vs. Draft: Where Do We Go From Here?
    *Richard V. L. Cooper* ........................ 88

## PART II: RESERVE FORCES

Introduction to Part II ............................... 109

7. Historical Continuity in the U.S. Military Reserve System
    *Robert L. Goldich* ........................... 111

8. U.S. Army Selected Reserves: Incentives/Disincentives to Join/Remain
   *William J. Taylor, Jr.* .......................... 133

9. Are We Really Serious? A Critical Assessment of Manpower Policies in the Army Reserve Forces
   *Kenneth J. Coffey* ............................ 148

10. Future of the Army Reserves: Plans, Policies and Programs
    *John R. Brinkerhoff* .......................... 163

## PART III: ALTERNATIVES

Introduction to Part III .............................. 177

11. Selective Service Program Overview and Results of the 1980 Registration
    *Bernard D. Rostker* .......................... 179

12. The Market Model of Military Labor Procurement: A Survey of Current Issues
    *Robert C. Kelly* .............................. 194

13. National Service: An Alternative to the All-Volunteer Military
    *William R. King* ............................. 217

14. Making the All-Volunteer Force Work
    *Charles C. Moskos* .......................... 228

15. National Service Program
    *Adam Yarmolinsky* .......................... 237

16. If the Draft Is Restored: Uncertainties, Not Solutions
    *Kenneth J. Coffey* ........................... 250

17. Conclusion ....................................... 266

Glossary ............................................. 271

Index ................................................ 273

About the Authors and Editors ....................... 275

# Preface

This book focuses on a critical set of national security issues for the 1980s, all related to defense manpower. Will the nation to able to attract and retain sufficient numbers of quality volunteers to perform the increasingly complex tasks of the nation's armed forces? What are the major incentives and disincentives involved in military recruitment and retention in the All-Volunteer Force (AVF)? Are there viable alternatives to the current system for military manpower acquisition?

The contributors attempt to provide perspectives on the issues and to answer some of the relevant questions. They bring to bear diverse disciplinary backgrounds and different experiences shaped by service to civilian government, business, the armed forces, and academia.

The genesis of this volume was the U.S. Military Academy Senior Conference which brings together each year a distinguished group of senior people from government, the military, business and academia for an informal and "off the record," two-day seminar on national security policy topics to stimulate discussion of as many ideas and alternative courses of action as possible, rather than to outline specific proposals.

The topic selection for 1980, "Defense Manpower Management," was based on the conclusion that manpower acquisition and retention had become one of the nation's most critical defense problems—a problem likely to continue throughout the decade of the 1980s. Several papers were distributed in advance to the participants to serve as a partial basis for discussion. Many of the articles herein are based on those papers. The concluding section is based in part upon the general thrust of two days of discussion.

All royalties from this publication are paid to the Dean's Faculty Research and Development Fund, a non appropriated fund at the U.S. Military Academy.

> Colonel William J. Taylor, Jr.
> Captain Eric T. Olson
> Captain Richard A. Schrader

# An Overview: Military Manpower Into the 1980s

## Robert B. Pirie, Jr.

Few subjects demand as much continual questioning, appraisal, and review as do our policies and performance with regard to manning the armed forces. This is as it should be. In a time when sophisticated technologies, forward deployments, and rapid responses are indelible facts of national security, military preparedness depends critically on forces-in-being. We can augment those forces rapidly in time of emergency, but a credible defense begins with our ability to steadily attract and retain the men and women who would assume the initial burden of a fast breaking war.

At the same time, few subjects inspire as much debate, or require such patient discourse, as our capacity for maintaining the first line of defense. This, too, is as it should be. In manning the nation's armed forces, we contend with an enormously subtle, ever shifting, supply/demand relationship—one that defies easy analysis and ready-made remedies. It is a stubbornly complex matter for three reasons.

First, our manpower requirements themselves are never beyond dispute, and always subject to adjustment. The links among foreign policy, the capabilities and intentions of allies and adversaries, national defense strategy, and force levels are invariably imprecise, often shifting. The balance of any one year may be awkwardly unsuited for another, and force levels have risen or fallen in the past thirty years in reaction to changing perceptions of need. In this sense, establishing manpower requirements is as much an art as it is a science. History cautions that turbulence in the international arena can be anticipated, but rarely can its demands be predicted with any precision.

Second, we meet these requirements with a manpower organization that is linear in construction, long in shaping, and delicate as a matter of internal balance. Ours is not a system of lateral entry. With few exceptions, we recruit people, not developed skills. We manage a manpower flow that emanates from two points of entry—our junior enlisted and junior officer grades—and branches into multiple points of exit or retention. Size is in the overall numbers, but strength is in the balances, in retaining the proper mix of experienced personnel as much as in acquiring new people. These balances are long in the building. Both errors and accomplishments in the management of such a system tend to be cumulative. Missteps along the way can leave substantial legacies that yield to no quick fixes. It is a structure that long remembers, and that rarely forgives.

Third, we strive to match resources to requirements within a tangle of external influences. Except perhaps during major wars, military accessions have seldom been indifferent to the vagaries of the economy, whether we have drafted or not. We are dependent on the size of the youth population and, in this sense, on demographics that were set in motion eighteen to twenty years ago. We bear the fruit or the brunt of the quality of high school education. We develop highly valued skills in our people, but we do not contract them for life. We must, accordingly, compete for their continued service in a marketplace that often offers extraordinary lures. And, of course, we are always dependent on how America feels about itself and about its military.

It is within this context that I will review the principal lines of correspondence between where we have been and where we are headed in manning the force in the 1980s. Our manpower experience of the past decade has been controversial and rich with difficulties, but not every mishap is a trend, and not every trend is terminal. The art, as we peer over the horizon, is in figuring out which is which, because we will select our strategies no more wisely than we characterize our problems. In this respect, it is important that we carefully distinguish between difficulties that are unique to an all-volunteer force, and those that will be with us regardless of how we fill the first-term ranks. It is equally important that we be steadfast in emphasizing manpower productivity—that we cherish what we get, and manage it accordingly—and not become too distracted by schemes that would only increase its supply or offset the losses that we invariably must incur.

## CIRCUMSTANCES OF THE 1970S

We enter the 1980s with considerable legacies from the past ten years. The most prominent, if not the most consequential, manpower change of the first half of the 1970s was the substitution of a wholly volunteer organization for one that had been partly conscripted. Other things were at work as well: our involvement in Vietnam ended; our requirements were adjusted downward, from a two and a half war planning scenario to a programmed capability to fight one and a half wars simultaneously; a policy of total force planning—in which the reserves took on a pivotal, early role in manning the defense—replaced an earlier, almost exclusive, reliance on the active forces. Our manning performance in the remainder of the decade has been mixed, soft in some important places, always a bit controversial, but, on balance, quite resilient.

Despite some periodic shortfalls in enlistments, the active forces have been generally successful in meeting recruiting goals, and, since 1974, have never been more than 1.5 percent below authorized strength. (That authorized strength is not insubstantial: we field today one active duty military member for every 100 Americans.) First-term reenlistments have remained strong. The all-volunteer enlisted ranks are demographically different than those the draft produced. The proportion of black and other minority males has increased, notably in the Army, as has the proportion of women. Longer terms of enlistment have given us a longer average term of service for new recruits, and problems with such things as drug abuse and disciplinary infractions are only a whisper of what they were a decade ago.

At the same time, we have experienced a significant, almost chronic, slippage in retention of our more experienced enlisted members. Career reenlistment rates dropped from 81 percent in 1974 to 68 percent in 1979, a slide that has been only partially compensated by first-term reenlistments. The problem is particularly serious in the Navy, where second-term reenlistment rates have fallen 15 points over the last five years.

Reserve manning has lagged notably behind the active force—mostly in the Army Guard and Reserve. A five year decline in reserve strengths was arrested only last year, when strengths increased by some 19,000. A similar shrinking of the pool of Individual Ready Reservists was also only halted as the decade ended. It is too early to tell whether we have finally turned the corner on either score, although we view with confidence the management steps that produced these recent upturns.

While we continue to reject large numbers of people who fail to meet enlistment standards (in 1979, we recruited 316,000 and turned away another 200,000), we took far fewer high school graduates at the end of the decade than in its early years. While we have made some dents in first-term attrition, the wash-out rate for new members is still more than one in four.

We closed the decade with a force that is remarkably strong in a number of respects, and notably shy of our expectations in others. This mixed yield has taken place in a context that circumstantially favored our manning needs in two ways, but which otherwise was not very sustaining. We benefited through the greater part of the decade from two things in combination. First, demographics—the baby boom legacy worked to our advantage. By the time it peaked in 1978, the prime recruiting pool of males between 17 and 21 topped 10 million. Second, we met a smaller manpower requirement in the post-Vietnam 1970s, than we had at any time since 1950. In addition, the recession of 1975, the worst since the 1930s, gave a temporary boost to enlistments, although economic recovery rapidly took away whatever passing benefits the recession had bestowed.

But other factors were not favorable, and more than offset these cushions. First, a key assumption of all-volunteer manning—that we maintain the force at competitive levels of compensation—has not materialized. The relative value of military compensation eroded notably in the 1970s. Since 1972, the differential in pay raises between the military and civilian sectors has ranged between 7 and 20 percent. In recent years, it has been on the order of 11 percent. Junior enlisted pay is a poignant illustration. We began all-volunteer manning with a starting basic pay well above the minimum. For both our career force and our junior members, the harsh fact is that military personnel have not shared equally in the growth of salaries and wages experienced by most other segments of the American economy, although they have shared the distress of inflation.

This erosion is all the more pronounced in our armed forces, one-quarter of which are stationed outside the continental United States at a given time and, thereby, more exposed to the twin vagaries of inflation and dollar devaluation. Unlike the case with most federal departments and major businesses, a lion's share of the people we assign overseas are junior personnel at the lower pay grades who are least able to absorb the decline of the dollar in relation to other currencies. Decent off-base housing, both overseas and in the United States, has inflated to levels beyond the reach of many military families.

A compounding factor has been a similar erosion in the uniqueness of the advantages that military service had long offered our youth. As the 1970s ended, no longer was the military a major source of initial jobs and training for America's young people, nor the principal stepping stone to higher education. Entitlement programs, which historically had not greatly affected the population that we sought for military service, now compete with us for recruits. New programs such as the Basic Educational Opportunity Grants have made education beyond high school possible for large numbers of students who might otherwise have chosen to enlist first. We compounded the difficulty by replacing the G.I. Bill with an educational package that is seen by many young people as less attractive. We compete with a rapidly expanded (and, for awhile, much more generous) Public Health Service medical school scholarship program to acquire future doctors. Government-funded programs such as CETA have created additional competition for potential recruits.

Lastly, we embraced all-volunteer manning with a compensation and incentive structure that is long on tradition but short on flexibility, ill-suited in key respects as a manpower management tool, and poorly tailored to meet the needs of many of our members. Our retirement system is a notable example; it is a structure built on perverse incentives, such that a person has little inducement to stay after twenty years, and no incentives to stay for less. We have no rewards to offer the young man or woman who would give 10 or 15, but not 20, years of service to country. In the reserves, we contend with outmoded personnel laws and policies that were put into effect in the draft era—a time of reserve manpower abundance—and that were designed to make it hard to get in and easy to get out. We pay military members the same 10 cents per mile travel reimbursement allowance for moves between duty stations that we paid in 1949.

## THE DECADE AHEAD

Those cushions that we did have in the 1970s offer little comfort as the 1980s emerge. The prime recruiting pool will decline steadily. By 1987, that population will be 15 percent smaller than its 1978 level; by 1992, it will be 20 percent smaller. Were our requirements to remain relatively constant, we would have need for one in four of that population. Put another way, we will need to recruit one of every three male high school graduates who is not bound for college. Moreover, in light of the current turbulence in the international arena, we cannot assume that those requirements can remain constant. The demands on our military forces may be much greater in the years ahead than in the 1970s.

We enter the 1980s then, with a significant legacy, a generally resourceful but mixed record of manning performance, and serious concerns about maintaining our career force as we simultaneously face a more difficult time in enlisting new people. In many respects, our philosophies have changed faster than our structures; our programs have not kept stride with the promises that ushered in an all-volunteer force.

## DIFFICULT CHOICES

What do these things portend? Not necessarily the demise of the all-volunteer force, unless one is already predisposed to favor that outcome. But certainly not fat and happy times either, as the decade matures. Our difficulties are much more stubbornly structural and societal than a simple debate over conscription versus voluntarism could do justice to.

Three strategies suggest themselves. First, we can reduce demand, principally by managing the force in ways that permit us to require fewer recruits from the marketplace. We are already firmly embarked on such a course in three respects: reversing the trend toward higher attrition of first-term personnel, pruning manpower requirements in weapons systems acquisition and design, and improving our long-term retention of those who do join us. We have made some headway, but certainly not enough, in reducing attrition. We think that, with appropriate attention to maintenance concepts, consolidation of functions, and easier trouble shooting through automated testing equipment, we can save manpower over current levels even as we embrace ever more sophisticated weapons and technology. We can, at the same time, make high technology less skill-demanding while we simultaneously enhance its readiness through maintenance. A case in point is the Pershing II (a medium range ground-to-ground missile system) which saves on the order of 750 people out of a total of 5,100 for its predecessor.

Reducing attrition and the manpower demands of modern weaponry are matters of better management. So, too, is career force retention; but, in addition, it requires a forceful act of national resolve: to compensate our career force more equitably and change archaic compensation structures so that military service can respectably compete in the economy. Our retirement proposals would, over the long haul, hold down the rising cost of retirement benefits while balancing equities between members who serve a full 20 years and those who serve less, and increasing the attractiveness of service for personnel with 5 to 15 years of service. We think a better way to determine military pay increases is to link them to private sector pay increases, while freeing them of the artificially restrictive connection with civil service pay increases.

None of these will come easy. Attrition has been a stubborn problem; the dynamics of the weapons acquisition process are not naturally attuned to be cognizant of down-the-road manpower demands; in the short run, compensation and retirement reform will cost money. To maintain a balanced and productive force, however, we probably need all three.

As a second strategy, we can expand supply, by embracing policies that would make more people eligible for military service, and would make service more attractive to those who are eligible. We are doing the first of these by increasing the enlistment of women for noncombat positions. From less than 1 percent of the force in 1970, they will constitute 12 percent by 1984. We are also studying whether some of physical entrance standards—many of these adopted in the draft era when supply was virtually unlimited—bear a sound relationship to required performance. But, without increasing the attractiveness of service, one should not be sanguine about our long-term prospects. Military service is not now competitive in the civilian labor market, surely not enough so for many young people whom we would hope to attract. It will be less so as the eligible population declines and the competition stiffens. When we pay less than the local supermarket or gas station, we should not be surprised that we don't always draw from the top of the talent pool. But we need to do more than reverse the downward trend in the comparative value of pay benefits, bonuses, and other incentives for first-term personnel. We need also to critically reexamine our educational assistance incentives in light of the heavy competition from other federal programs that require no service obligations. In effect, we now have the G.I. Bill without the G.I. Either we must build some *quid pro quo* into these other programs, or we must revise the military package to make it more nearly competitive.

These things, of course, cost money, but so does the third strategy: a return to conscription, with or without a full-fledged program of national service. Indeed, the difference between the second option and the third is not so much a matter of cost, as it is of who will pay. With a shrinking eligible population, a draft would solve some problems, create others, and entail a wholly different set of costs. It would guarantee both the supply of active force accessions and the flexibility to make quick-order changes in the sizing of the force. By moving more people through presumably shorter periods of active duty, it would spill more people for longer periods into the individual ready reserve. On the other hand, it would be, at best, indifferent; and may well be counter-productive, as regards our career force concerns—concerns that we should view as much more critical than accessions over both the short and the long haul. Depending on the ratio of conscripts to volunteers, a draft may degrade the military "value" of the first-term force, by merely substituting a number of two-year conscripts for some current number of three and four-year enlistments. At the same time, a draft such as that in 1971-1972, one in which only nineteen year olds with high lottery numbers were vulnerable to its call, might be totally indifferent to the accession problems of the organized reserve, lacking the inducements to join that earlier drafts with greater uncertainty had possessed.

It is certainly conceivable that we will not make sufficient headway with the first two of these strategies, that the nation will choose not to pay the political and budgetary price of either, and that we will have no choice but to revert to the third. It is also conceivable that all-volunteer manning cannot be sustained in the 1980s no matter how dedicated we might be to it, either because requirements will increase beyond our capabilities to enlist volunteers or because the adverse demographic trend and competition from schools and employers will be too much for it. We should be mindful, however, that our military strength is not a matter of raw numbers but of balance; that we can conscript people to enter service but not compel them to stay beyond an initial tour; and that our future preparedness no less than our current readiness depends most critically on men and women who are willing to give us 8, 10, 15, or 20 years of service.

These are not matters that permit easy choices. In adjusting to the stern demands of the decade ahead, we cannot afford ignorant resistance to change. By the same token, we cannot afford ignorant change either.

# A Military Manpower Chronology

| Date | Event |
|---|---|
| May 8, 1792 | Enactment of the Militia Act of 1792; established legal precedent for universal male (white, able-bodied) obligation for state militia service. |
| Sep. 1794 | Whiskey Rebellion in western Pennsylvania; first call of state militia drafts for federal service. |
| Dec. 1814 | First National Conscription Bill; despite strong support of President Madison, Congress failed to pass bill. |
| April 16, 1862 | Conscription Act, Confederate States of America; approximately 300,000 (⅓ of confederate total) drafted into military. |
| July 17, 1862 | Militia Act: supplemented enlistments with state militia drafts, reaffirmed universal military obligation of able-bodied white males, aged 18-45. |
| March 3, 1863 | Enrollment Act; implemented registration of all white males between 20 and 45. Federal Government assumed conscription authority based on Constitutional powers of legislature, 170,000 subsequently drafted for civil war (includes 118,000 substitutes). |
| May 1916 | National Defense Act; reaffirmed use of state militia for federal service, empowered President to conscript up to 1 million. |
| May 18, 1917 | Selective Service Act; 2.8 million men inducted into Army during World War I. |
| June 4, 1920 | National Defense Act; ended conscription, reorganized peacetime regular army. |
| Sep. 16, 1940 | Selective Service and Training Act; 45 million men registerd, 10 million drafted, extended conscription authority to March 31, 1947. |
| June 10, 1948 | Selective Service Act, extended before outbreak of Korean War, various extensions to July 1, 1973. |
| June 1951 | Universal Military Training and Service Act; mandated a universal male obligation for military service. |
| July 1, 1973 | Draft Extension Act of 1971 expires, (last actual conscription in Dec. 1972); authorized peacetime registration and classification under the Selective Service System. |
| April 1, 1975 | President Ford ended requirement to register with the Selective Service System. |
| July 21, 1980 | Selective Service System resumed mass registration. |

# 1
# Outline of Manpower Issues and Debate

The casual observer perusing the current literature on military manpower is bombarded with a bewildering array of issues, problems, and polemics. At first glance, the reader of this volume seems to face the same predicament in this collected assortment of papers, speeches, and articles. Moreover, neither the analyses nor the solutions herein fall into neat categories. The methodological approaches and the variables cited in those approaches exhibit differing degrees of overlap. The task of this introduction is to assist the reader by preparing an overall analytical framework which can be used to compare different authors. While this framework is by no means exhaustive, it will identify the salient issues, classify alternative solutions, and hence provide a fairly comprehensive compendium of the manpower situation.

## SALIENT ISSUES

### The Problem of Quantity

Certainly, the most critical problem underlying and shaping manpower policy is that of maintaining the requisite number of people in the armed services. Indeed, it is the questioned ability of the All-Volunteer Force to produce the necessary numbers of military personnel which has sparked the current debate over reinstitution of some form of conscription. One could even assert that this criterion provides the most necessary condition for evaluating the adequacy of various alternative manpower systems.

To borrow an economic analogy, this issue can be further subdivided into demand-side problems and supply-side problems. Rationally, desired manpower levels should derive from force level requirements; or, in other words, personnel requirements are governed by the numbers and types of military forces deemed necessary to meet national security objectives. More often, however, it is the prevailing manpower policy which tends to influence (and some would say determine) the overall force structure. Therefore, while established armed forces strength goals constitute the overall demand for manpower, it must be recognized that these goals are subject to political and budgetary vagaries and analytical incongruities.

Manpower demand is further affected by the efficiency of manpower management and the establishment of personnel standards. Mismanagement logically results in higher demand. Examples of policies that are usually investigated include personnel usage, job rotation, promotion, and specialty designation. Standards established for validated positions disaggregate overall demand into subcategories of skill, experience, education, and mental ability. For example, the demand for officer-level positions is normally filled only by the college graduate pool of a particular age cohort.

Supply-side problems are concentrated in the areas of recruiting and retention and reflect the impact of several exogenous factors. The adjustment of standards of qualifications for entry-level personnel entails a corresponding adjustment in the size of the available manpower pool. Recruitment, constrained by these standards, must then develop successful marketing strategies to meet demand quotas. Entry-level supply is thereby affected by individual incentives to enlist: monetary and in-kind compensation, skill training, career orientation, public service, or adventure. Since responsiveness to these incentives exists in the general population, recruiting strategies must focus on the margin, on those individuals who perceive good alternatives to military service.

In the personnel structure above entry-level, supply varies with rates of first-term attrition (the failure of an enlistee to complete the first term of service) and reenlistment (retention of careerists). While raising entry-level goals can compensate for higher first-term attrition, it cannot satisfy demands for experienced professionals. The focus here, then, must be on career incentives such as promotion opportunity, assignment flexibility, and the quality of family life.

Among the important exogenous or near-exogenous factors identified by the authors are demographics, economic conditions, and public attitudes. Obviously, these variables cannot be controlled by policy; rather, policy will be constrained by them. Thus, high unemployment will increase the supply of individuals seeking jobs and the armed services will benefit as an available alternative. Similarly, a tendency toward narcissistic traits in several age cohorts might require a shift in marketing strategy to deemphasize national service.

## The Problem of Quality

Second only to quantity in analytical effort expended is the "bugaboo" of quality—the quality of personnel entering and remaining in the armed forces. The difficulties inherent in establishing appropriate standards have been compounded by doubts about the validity of measuring those standards. Quality measurement traditionally has been expressed in terms of education level (particularly the "high school diploma graduate") and entry-level tests—the Armed Forces Qualification Test (AFQT) and Armed Services Vocational Aptitude Battery (ASVAB). Far less attention has been directed at the quality of personnel retained in service. There is a presumed confidence that "up or out" promotion systems and Quality Management Programs (QMP eliminate the less desirable. This presumption bears closer scrutiny in future analyses.

## Socioeconomic Factors

With the increasing proportion of minority groups, particularly in the Army, racial and socioeconomic representativeness have become contentious issues. Should blacks, even considering the free choice inherent in enlistment, be allowed to bear an unfair exposure to casualty-producing action in future combat? Is it desirable to have an armed force in which the enlisted segment overwhelmingly comes from deprived backgrounds? To some observers such a system is just as inequitable as selective service. Women, also an ever-increasing proportion of the services, constitute another minority problem—what percent should be women and to what degree should women be exposed to combat? Will the services become socially isolated from the mainstream of American society? Would social and philosophical in-breeding lead to problems of civilian control of the military? Apart from the representativeness problem, there is the question of the general compatibility of manpower policies with other collective social goals. For example, should these policies deliberately foster a spirit of public service, national pride, or patriotism? At the micro-level, one can examine such issues as the proper economic relationship between military and civilian communities or employer support of Reserve involvement by employees.

## The Issue of Cost

In a general sense, cost becomes an issue when the public (or Congress) examines and evaluates national security requirements in relation to other slices of the national budget pie. However, the more specific issue raised by the All-Volunteer Force is its own benefit/cost ratio. Secondly, what impact does increasing the proportion of personnel costs have on other defense expenditures? At what point, for example, does readiness for war suffer more from lack of operation and maintenance funds than it benefits from enhanced personnel readiness? These issues have naturally come to the fore because of the absolute and relative increases in personnel costs of the All-Volunteer Force.

## Combat Effectiveness/Readiness Factors

Obvious issues in the category of combat effectiveness/readiness are the impairments on overall readiness because of total manpower shortages and, more specifically, the shortages of critical jobs or specialties. Related to the issue of quality is the trainability of entry-level personnel for designated skills. For example, if X percent of tank crewman positions require personnel of a certain quality (mental qualification), can more training time be allocated to use less qualified personnel; or are some people unsuitable altogether? On another plane, how does manpower policy support the overall readiness objectives of the armed forces? Is national mobilization (for example, reinforcement of NATO) better served by one type of system? Does the All-Volunteer Force provide a more effective or reliable overseas intervention force than other alternatives? Lastly, how does a particular manpower policy affect small group dynamics and, hence, small unit cohesion? Because of the nature of combat operations, cohesiveness of small groups is of vital concern to an effective military force.

## Other Factors

Lumped together are the infrequently examined but, nevertheless, important points about historical, philosophical, and political precedents in the U.S. experience. These precedents form a type of national style or tradition. Manpower policies which are not in the mainstream of that style may face public opposition or indifference. Consequently, manpower policies must take into account the political feasibility of implementation based on public receptiveness and perceived social benefits and costs.

# SOLUTIONS

## Variants of the All-Volunteer Force

Advocates of the all-volunteer solution tend to be market-oriented; that is, they feel the problems can generally be solved by enhancing the incentives to join or remain. A frequent argument, for example, will state that wages should be maintained at levels comparable with the civilian sector. Bonuses and other benefits are used to fill critical and shortage specialty areas. In-kind benefits, such as better housing or post-service education, will increase the attractiveness of career service. Peacetime registration and classification of eligible males satisfies the requirements of mobilization while recognizing political realities. Policy packages vary with the number and type of proposed benefits.

## Variants of Conscription

Proponents of the conscriptive solution usually highlight the failure of the market-oriented approach to satisfy key goals of quantity and quality at a reasonable cost. Moreover, the market approach only fortuitously fulfills socioeconomic objectives such as racial representativeness and economic class balance. The market approach may be further criticized as emphasizing individual or personal values to the detriment of collective or public values. The most common solution proferred is selective service, in which only the shortfalls in desired force levels are filled with conscriptees. More radical proposals (at least for the United States) call for universal military training or universal military service in which all eligible, able-bodied males would be compelled to participate. The most all-encompassing program is universal national service or public service. Here, military manpower is incorporated into a larger program of job alternatives.

## Combining Volunteers and Conscripts

Some analysts propose various creative combinations of conscripts and volunteers. For example, conscripts might be used to man a citizen soldier reserve army while volunteers form the peacetime regular army. The chapters by Professor Moskos and William King entail such options.

## A DEFENSE MANPOWER DEBATE

Within the framework of the major issues and solutions addressed in this introduction, there are countless positions advanced by statesmen, soldiers, scholars, and other analysts and observers. Literally every position advanced is debatable, and a nationwide debate on defense manpower is a certainty in the early 1980s. The final section of this introduction provides such a debate.

By definition, there are at least two sides to every debatable issue. The following represents what trained debaters would call the "first affirmative" and "first negative" of a resolution to abandon the AVF and return to conscription. Each side seeks to push its position to the extreme. The first presentation advocates a change from the status quo; the second presentation seeks to defend the status quo. In a full, formal debate, there would be six additional presentations, three by each side attacking the specifics of each other's arguments. In this case, we hope simply to raise questions in the readers' minds—questions to be addressed in various ways in the chapters that follow. It is up to readers to make up their own minds and to develop their own positions.

All other issues of military manpower notwithstanding, the fundamental issue Americans have a right and duty to explore is whether or not the armed forces of the United States can, with a volunteer force, deter or fight wars effectively. The answer hinges not only on the adequacy of weapons systems but also on the readiness and responsiveness of the men and women in uniform who, in tandem with weapons systems, constitute military units.

As suggested throughout this book, the issue of the impact of manpower on military effectiveness is replete with debatable points. It is important to keep in mind what debate in a democratic society is all about. Those who argue for a fundamental change in the status quo always have the "burden of proof." The status quo for the American military does not include conscription or national service alternatives. The burden of proof demands demonstration of the following arguments:

1. The present system is so bad that change is clearly necessary;
2. The problems of the present system can be resolved only by the institution of a specific alternative system such as conscription or a variant of national service, and the alternative would solve the problems of the present system without creating other problems worse than those in existence; and,
3. Not only would the specific alternative solve the problems of the present system, but would lead to additional advantages in the public interest which the present system does not yield.

A draw or standoff over debatable issues means that the proponents of change lose. In other words, in the context of the basic issues treated in this book, a proposed alternative would have to solve the defense manpower problems identified without diluting military effectiveness, and leave the national security of the United States in better condition than it is now—in fact, in better condition than any other alternative policy proposals might yield. If the reader is not convinced that alternative defense manpower acquisition schemes would accomplish all this, the logical conclusion is obvious.

# DEBATE: RESOLVED THAT THE UNITED STATES ABANDON THE AVF CONCEPT

## Affirmative Argument

*Science* magazine observed in September 1980 that: "Tank gunners who don't know where to aim their battle sights, mechanics who can't repair anything, missile firers who can't tell the difference between a Soviet and a U.S. fighter plane—the evidence is piling up to indicate that there is a disturbingly high number of such individuals in today's armed services."[1]

Since the mid-1970s there has been a growing concern about the quality of the All-Volunteer Force (AVF), which has constituted America's defense manpower since the draft was abolished in 1970. This concern grew large indeed in late 1980 in the wake of a public revelation that almost half of the Army's new recruits belong in the lowest mental category accepted in the armed services. As a result of these trends and their impact on national security, one can reasonably conclude that the AVF concept is not working, and should be abandoned. In support of this position one might offer the following three lines of analysis.

**Contention I.** The AVF has been getting a much lower quality soldier than anticipated and, even more significantly, quality continues to decline.

The first indicator of this decline is that Army entrance test scores are falling. Particularly discomfiting for the Army were the results of a study released in July 1980 recalibrating the results of entry-level Armed Forces Qualification Tests (AFQTs) which are administered to all potential recruits. The AFQTs bear some similarity to standard intelligence tests, measuring reading skills, ability in arithmetic, and spatial perception. the AFQT (part of a larger test called ASVAB for Armed Services Vocational Aptitude Battery) was introduced in 1950 as a measure of *general trainability.* The test content has changed over the years, but each new AFQT has been calibrated so that its results would be comparable to those tests given the armed forces during World War II.

The accuracy of the 1976 AFQT began to be suspect in 1977 when the Marine Corps noted that recruits arriving at boot camp appeared to be less able than their scores indicated. This led to studies by the Center for Naval Analyses, the Army Research Institute, and the Educational Testing Services in Princeton, N.J. A panel of academic experts asked to evaluate the results of these studies reported their findings in July 1980. They found that the methods used to convert raw scores into percentiles had resulted in overestimates of the scores of recruits in the lower range of the five mental categories into which scores are assigned. Categories I and II are above average, III is average, IV is below average (the 10th to 30th percentile), and V is "out of the question."

The Army had been using test scores to defend the quality of the All-Volunteer Army, pointing out that the percentage of recruits in category IV (called "Cat Fours") was around 9 percent, considerably lower than the 21 percent who participated in World War II. However, the corrected scores showed that a very significant 46 percent fell into that category.[2] This large number of category IV recruits is disturbing, and the declining trend is even more so. Regardless of the validity of any base year criterion, there does appear to be a declining level of quality in the volunteer soldier.

A second indicator of the declining quality is the declining number of high school graduates who volunteer. A high school diploma is an indicator not only of educational level but also of the presence of the dedication and persistence required to complete the program successfully. Studies during the Korean War also show that high school diplomas are positively correlated with combat effectiveness.[3] Yet, here too, we find a declining trend in educational achievement, with the Army getting the worst of it. In 1979, the Army managed to achieve a 70 percent rate of high school graduates among its recruits; the rate by March 1980 (halfway through the fiscal year) was 38 percent, and the Army would be fortunate to end up with 55 percent.[4]

Now, the impact of these trends is only adverse if the quality of the AVF recruit is not *good enough* to train as a soldier, to man and maintain the Army's equipment, to deter aggression, and, if needed, to fight and win America's wars. Unfortunately, there are indicators that these requirements are not being met. First, let us turn to training. One Army training study, reported in 1978, indicated severe problems with the large number of category IV recruits. The report stated that one and one-half times as much training (both in duration and in frequency of repetition) is required for a category IV recruit as a category III recruit, and that the cost of training materials, such as ammunition, was 40 percent more.[5] The study zeroed in on a selection of 1,288 tank crewmen in the United States and Europe and found that most indicated a need for more and better training. They found low performance levels in both tank commanders and gunners, aggravated by high personnel "turbulence" (which means turnover of people and general lack of job stability); they also noted that "performance decay" was "significantly greater among lower mental groups."

Specifically, the study found that 17 percent of the tank commanders in Europe and 21 percent of those in the United States "did not know where to aim when employing battlefield gunnery techniques." Among the gunners, 21 and 28 percent, respectively, did not know where to aim when using battle sights. On the whole, tank crew proficiency was found to be 40 and 50 percent below what should be expected. Of the 1,288 tank crewmen, 20 percent of the commanders and 25 percent of the gunners "did not know some of the essential basics of battlefield gunnery."[6]

Turning from tanks to air defense soldiers, a survey of men in charge of shooting Redeye surface-to-air missiles revealed that most of them felt inadequately trained. What is more, the study found that the gunners in the lower mental category appeared to be incapable of learning the "Range Ring

Profile," which entails the ability to differentiate between the silhouettes of Soviet and American planes. In the area of equipment maintenance, the situation was also reported to be less that adequate. The study found that tank repairmen's chances of correctly diagnosing a repair problem were between 15 and 33 percent; and chances of fixing the problem, once correctly identified, were between 33 and 58 percent, i.e., less than 1 in 5 repair problems get fixed *at best,* or 1 in 20 in the worst case.

Tests in other areas appear to confirm these findings. Army Skill Qualification Tests were inaugurated in 1977 and are administered to enlistees after they have been trained in their Military Occupational Specialties and have some field experience. They are intended as a feedback device to gauge the effectiveness of training. Army records show that Skill Qualification Tests in 1977 and 1978 were failed by 90 percent of nuclear weapons maintenance specialists and 98 percent of tank turret and artillery repairmen. In 1979, a reported 91 percent of aviation maintenance personnel and 51 percent of military intelligence personnel failed. In a list of Army Skill Qualification scores for 370 Military Occupational Specialities, there was a 40 percent or higher failure rate in 179 of them.[7]

One must conclude, then, that the quality of the AVF has declined to the point where it already may not be good enough to train its manpower and maintain its equipment.

**Contention II.** The distribution of the burden of service in the AVF is falling disproportionately on the poor and on minorities, especially in the enlisted combat forces.

As Professors Morris Janowitz and Charles Moskos reported in 1979, the proportion of blacks in the enlisted ranks has continued to increase over the course of the All-Volunteer Army. Blacks comprised 30.1 percent of male Army recruits in fiscal year 1977, and 33.9 percent in the first three quarters of fiscal year 1978. Likewise, the reenlistment rate of black first-term personnel was about 1.7 times that of first-term whites. Within Army enlisted ranks, racial content varies by branch and career field. Blacks tend to be concentrated in low-skill fields whereas whites are disproportionately found in technical specialties. Although the number of other minorities in the Army is not as reliably tabulated as are blacks, a figure of at least 6 percent, principally Hispanic, would be a cautious estimate. In other words, close to four out of ten men now entering the Army's enlisted ranks are from minority groups.[8]

Professors Janowitz and Moskos go on to explain that the shift in the social composition of the Army's enlisted ranks reflects increasing reliance on two discrete streams: one from minorities, principally blacks but also Hispanics, and the other from white youth with modest educational attainment. The All-Volunteer Army, that is, attracts not only a disproportionate number of minorities, but also an unrepresentative segment of white youth who, if anything, are even more uncharacteristic of the broader social mix than are the minority group soldiers.[9] What makes the problem especially sensitive is the fact that blacks now constitute about 30 percent of the armed forces, whereas they make up 13 percent of the general population. This puts political liberals in a particularly uncomfortable position. It was they who brought to the nation's attention the fact that blacks were being sacrificed disproportionately in Vietnam. Certainly, the disproportion will be much greater if another war occurs.[10]

In addition to unbalanced representativeness from this perspective, we also find a higher proportion of lower income groups in the AVF. It has been found that those who joined the military, compared with those who did not, are 1.5 times more likely to have fathers with less than $9,000 annual income. These ratios were encountered despite the fact that the sample did not separate recruits according to which service they entered. We can almost surely assume that, within the U.S. Army and Marine Corps, the status background would be even lower for those who were assigned to the combat arms and heavy labor tasks.[11]

The reason many of these soldiers join the AVF has been reported: "Informal surveys have shown that most soldiers join the Army because they cannot find other work, and they often come from economically underprivileged and undereducated groups."[12] One must conclude, then, that the AVF is also inequitable in its impact upon the population. This same conclusion was reached by Professors Janowitz and Moskos in 1979: "The all-volunteer force is smaller, more expensive, of lower quality in selected but crucial segments, and less socially representative than the economists anticipated."[13] It is inherently undesirable in a democracy to allow the burden of defense—and that of casualties in combat—to acquire such a pattern.

**Contention III.** We must now consider the future, and here we find it likely that the parameters facing the AVF will if anything, become more constrained. Professors Janowitz and Moskos further point out that, in terms of numerical recruitment goals, inescapable demographic constraints appear. In 1978, some 2.14 million males reached age 18; in 1980, the figure declined slightly to 2.13 million and will drop precipitously to 1.82 million by 1985, and 1.61 million by 1992. Only after 1999 will the youth cohort increase to over 1.9 million. In other words, the services over the next decade will confront a drop of close to 20 percent in the available pool of male youth. It is impossible to anticipate, moreover, the level of youth unemployment in the United States during the second phase of the AVF. But it is neither reasonable nor desirable to assess the future of the AVF on the basis of the high levels of unemployment. An aging population may also increase the demand for youthful workers. But, more directly, the President and the Congress have embarked on youth training and employment generating schemes which will compete with military recruiters for personnel.[14]

To summarize the future of the AVF, if no changes are made, problems will only become more severe. Low birthrates in the 1960s mean the manpower pool will continue to shrink, while Scholastic Aptitude Test scores of the best in that pool continue to decline. Low retention rates of senior enlisted men and mid-career officers will exacerbate the loss of supervisors needed to prevent further deterioration of combat readiness. Yet, this low education, low performance, and low trainability force will be required to operate a host of newer, highly technical weapons systems.

The AVF is not coping successfully today. It cannot reasonably be expected to do so in the future. Clearly, the AVF concept should be abandoned.

## Negative Argument

The elimination of the draft in 1973 and the adoption of a voluntary system of military manpower management has resulted in continuous debate on the merits of the market approach to meeting military labor requirements. While the voluntary method has generally been able to keep the active force filled, questions surrounding the entry level characteristics of active force enlistees and the ability of the volunteer system to retain skilled careerists have led to a continual debate on whether the volunteer method has proven successful.

Despite the arguments made by some AVF critics, the AVF should be retained. To support this thesis, one need briefly examine only three variables: (1) the accomplishments of the AVF to date; (2) the quality of the current force; and, (3) equity and social representation.

**Contention I.** On balance, the AVF has been a success. The institution of a voluntary military in the United States in 1973 was one of the most ambitious social policies implemented by the United States in the past few decades. Starting in 1973, the military services totally met accession requirements with volunteers and replaced a manpower system which five years earlier had required almost a quarter of a million draftees to fill the ranks.[15] Since 1973, the volunteer system has kept end strengths of the military within 1.5 percent of congressionally-mandated objectives.[16] Because the military services must compete with the private sector in a high-technology economy, meeting this objective has led to some benefits for those entering the force. These include more choice in training and occupations, improved living standards, and better opportunities for women and minorities.[17] These opportunities have arisen because the military services in a volunteer environment have begun to realize that labor is no longer a free resource as it was during the draft era, and that competition for human resources requires that the work environment and initial occupational choice be attractive enough to turn young men and women away from other occupations and toward military service.

**Contention II.** Entry-level characteristics have been adequate when placed in the proper context of cost-benefit analysis. Although the AVF has met total strength requirements, the main criticism of volunteerism has been that it has led to entry level characteristics which, in some sense, are not perceived to be conducive to military effectiveness. While many critics of the AVF argue that the "quality" of the force as declined, their criticisms usually never define an "adequate" level of quality, only that it always seems to move in an adverse direction. However, it should be noted that some measures of quality have increased. High school diploma graduates, for example, were 68 percent of accessions in FY 1964, 69 percent in FY 1976, and 73 percent in 1979.[18] In the area of mental categories, however, one could argue that the data indicate a recent declining trend, particularly in the accessions of mental categories I and II, and a rising trend in accessions of those in mental category IV.[19]

While definitive conclusions on the relationship between military effectiveness and entry level characteristics remain to be proven, it should be noted that whether the trends are up or down begs the real issues. The real issues are: (1) what specific goal should be established; and, (2) if we have not achieved it, how one can best get there. No one would argue only that more quality is better. Clearly, the nation does not need, and could not afford, a military composed solely of Ph.D.s from mental category I. Thus, the issue of quality must be defined in terms of whether the additional resources society is willing to spend on obtaining additional enlistees are worth the benefits in terms of military effectiveness.

This raises an issue concerning which factors affect accession and retention and what alternatives to the market mechanism exist. The volunteer force necessitates that the military services compete in a market for labor. To compete, the services must be able to offer incentives for joining that will make a sufficient number of young men and women freely choose military service over civilian alternatives. Yet, for the past several years, the primary incentive (pay and allowances) has significantly deteriorated in terms of real purchasing power and in relative terms compared with civilian alternatives. Between 1974 and 1978, for example, real wages per workers in the overall economy rose from $6,961.00 per year to $7,031.00 per year (increases in 1967 dollars), while per capita military compensation declined from $6,924.00 to $6,233.00.[20] Thus, between these years, not only did the average service person experience a significant decline in real income, but the decline was experienced during a period when real earnings in the private sector were going up.

The incentive issue was put in more concrete terms in a recent *Wall Street Journal* editorial:

> As a concrete example [of declining pay incentives], a plane handler on the carrier Nimitz—recently rushed to the Indian Ocean—works about 100 hours a week on $25 million F-14 aircraft. Yet he makes less per hour than a

cashier at McDonalds', lives below the poverty level, is eligible for food stamps and probably has not seen his family for six months.[21]

The conclusion is obvious. One will not get a quality force without offering incentives that compete with often less-demanding, civilian employment.

What can be done? The first step in solving perceived problems in this area is to define exactly the quality composition the force needs. More quality is not always better, especially if it entails society foregoing alternatives in terms of other government programs or in private expenditures that have greater benefits. Assuming for the moment that a solution to this problem can be found, and that it implies that the military increase its intake of personnel with entry-level characteristics such as high school diplomas or mental categories, one can then turn to the two oft-debated solutions for acquiring military manpower: the market system (AVF), of the draft.

The issues involved in the choice between the draft and the AVF as methods of increasing the quality of the force really boil down to the single issue of who pays the bill for the cost of manpower. Under the AVF, the cost of increased manpower is borne by the general taxpayer; under the draft, the cost is borne jointly by taxpayers and those drafted. Essentially, draftees pay a conscription tax which amounts to the difference between what they could earn in alternative civilian employment (with hours and working conditions equivalent to those of the military) and their draft wage. What is the difference in these two methods of taxation? First, the AVF distributes the burden of paying the cost of increased quality to all Americans earning income. Second, assuming the general income tax system is progressive, the AVF requires those with greater incomes to contribute relatively more to the effort than those with lower incomes.

The draft, on the other hand, is much less equitable. Given the current level of manpower requirements, it is clear that the military services do not need to draft the entire male and female 17-year-old age cohort to provide sufficient first-term enlistees. In 1980, for example, there were approximately 4 million men and women 17 years old;[22] the services will take in approximately 400,000 persons.[23] Only about 10 percent of the draft-age cohort will be required to serve. This means that 90 percent of those will not serve. Thus, the conscription tax is borne by only 10 percent of the entire population.

Some argue that a lottery system would give everyone a fair chance of serving and this would solve the equity problem. It certainly makes the *chances* of paying the conscription tax equal before the fact, but does not reveal that, after the lottery is conducted, only 10 percent of the relevant population would carry the burden for the other 90 percent. There is, of course, considerable historical evidence indicating that the draft system would not be strictly an equal-chance lottery in the sense that all those physically and mentally qualified would not participate in the lottery. The draft, during the early years of the

Vietnam conflict, essentially resulted in deferments that led to a conscription tax which was paid disproportionately by those youth from the segments of society with lower incomes, and was essentially regressive.[24]

Importantly, there is no way of evaluating the cost to society of the loss of individual freedom involved in the draft. Certainly, the compulsory nature of the service requires young citizens to forego a most precious resource—their ability to choose their life styles freely. This cost, of course, is not borne under the volunteer system.

A final word about the draft is that, in one sense, it would not deal with the most critical current issue of military manpower, that is, retaining *skilled* careerists. One cannot draft citizens for 20 or 30 years of service. The only solution to the careerist problem is to make the choice between leaving the service and staying in more favorable toward the military. One method of increasing incentives is increased compensation. The draft is not an alternative in this case.

In the light of these arguments, it is clear that society can have the quality it deserves in the military by paying the cost. The real question is not whether the cost will be paid, but by what method. In this regard, the AVF is a much more progressive alternative.

**Contention III.** The AVF is equitable and sufficiently representative socially. The increased percentage of black Americans and those from families with low incomes serving in the military is also a cause for concern to some AVF critics. The major arguments here are that too large a black force would result in too many black casualties in future wars, and that the unrepresentative force leaves the burden of defending the country on the poor. These issues are related to the issue of quality in terms of both the "problem" and it solution. If an unrepresentative force is assumed to be inferior due to some quality dimension, then the preceding contention II arguments apply. If the entry-level skills of an ethnically-unbalanced force and a balanced force were to be the same, however, it does not make sense to have representativeness solely for its own sake. No other occupation or vocation requires such a distribution of races and income groups, and it does not make sense to saddle the military with such a constraint.

The argument that an overly large percentage of blacks would suffer disproportionate casualties somehow implies that blacks, as opposed to whites, do not realize individually the risks associated with the voluntary choice to serve in the military, and that government somehow must correct this inability to properly evaluate occupational risk. This degradation of the sensibilities of black Americans is irresponsible rhetoric. Black Americans, as well as white Americans, are assumed to make rational choices in selecting an occupation based on available opportunities. If the follow-on argument is that the choice of the military is a form of economic conscription, it hardly makes sense to rectify the situation by placing quotas on low-income groups and blacks to cure the problem, thus excluding them from a major opportunity only to pursue some nebulous objective based on racial and socioeconomic balance.

If, for some abstruse reason, a broader spectrum of society is desired as an objective of military manpower management, then the incentives in a voluntary system simply must appeal to the broad spectrum. As noted in the previous discussion on quality, this can be done under the AVF by making incentives to join more attractive through changes in composition. It could also be accomplished by conscription, but this has all the disadvantages argued previously.

## CONCLUSIONS

The current debate about whether or not the AVF has failed is misleading. The real issues are: 1) whether American society is willing to pay the cost of increasing the effectiveness of the force, and 2) the preferred system for financing the increased costs.

The country will get what it pays for in terms of military capabilities; the old cliche that "there is no free lunch" applies well here. If society chooses a more effective military, it must be willing to pay the cost of increased effectiveness. The AVF implies that these costs are paid through the general revenue system and leaves the choice to serve voluntary. The draft leaves the burden on a small segment of society and employs coercion. When viewed in this light, the AVF provides a superior method of implementing any political decision to upgrade the force and clearly should be continued.

## NOTES

1. Excerpted from "Doubts Mounting About All-Volunteer Force," *Science* 209 September 5, 1980: 1095.
2. Ibid.
3. A. Hoiberg and N. H. Berry, "There's No Doubt About It, A Diploma Goes a Long Way for Combat Efficiency," *Marine Corps Gazette,* September 1977, quoted in Morris Janowitz and Charles C. Moskos, Jr., "Five Years of the All-Volunteer Force: 1973-1978," *Armed Forces and Society 5* (Winter 1979): 192.
4. *Science,* September 1980.
5. Ibid., p. 1096. This and all other statistics mentioned from the Army Training Study reportedly come from a copy of the summary of the report leaked to Representative Robin Beard (R. Tenn).
6. Ibid., p. 1095.
7. Ibid.
8. Janowitz and Moskos, "Five Years of the All-Volunteer Force," p. 196-97.
9. Ibid., p. 197-98.
10. *Science,* September 1980, p. 1099.
11. Janowitz and Moskos, "Five Years of the All-Volunteer Force," p. 199.
12. *The New York Times,* September 24, 1980, p. B-4.

13. Janowitz and Moskos, "Five Years of the All-Volunteer Force," p. 177.
14. Ibid., pp. 180-81.
15. Data on percentages of draftees in 1968 are from Bernard Karpinos, *Male Chargeable Accessions: Evaluation By Mental Categories (1953-1973)*, Defense Manpower Data Center Report No. MR-77-1.
16. Department of Defense, *America's Volunteers—A Report on the All-Volunteer Armed Forces*, December 1978, p. 3.
17. Ibid.
18. Ibid., p. 199. 1979 Figures on high school diploma graduates are from Department of Defense, *Military Manpower Statistics,* June 19, 1979.
19. See the preceding arguments to abandon the AVF.
20. See in this volume Robert C. Kelly, "The Market Model of Military Labor Procurement: A Survey of the Issues," tables 12.1 and 12.2.
21. "The Retention Problem," *The Wall Street Journal,* March 19, 1980, p. 24.
22. Population data is from projections given in *Current Population Reports,* U.S. Department of Commerce, Series p-25, No. 601, October 1975. Series II projections.
23. The projected total accessions for 1980 are given as 430,000 in *America's Volunteers,* p. 190.
24. Richard Cooper, *Military Manpower and the All-Volunteer Force* (Washington, D.C.: The Rand Corporation, 1977).

# Part I:
# Active Duty Forces

# Introduction to Part I

As the nation enters the 1980s, there is a growing awareness that the active duty military forces of the United States are confronting serious problems. Despite the occasional defense of the forces in a particular service by a serving advocate in uniform, the general thrust of public commentary has indicted the low state of readiness of U.S. units deployed around the world. Problems in recruiting people of sufficient mental capacity, problems of retaining the skilled officer and noncommissioned officer specialists required for an increasingly technical armed force, morale problems, and more are becoming common headlines.

Many of the criticisms come from retired professional officers who elect to speak out under the immunity of retirement. Occasionally, a serving officer speaks out to describe the inadequacies of his service and to seek budgetary support needed to redress the situation—always with the risk that his civilian or military supervisors will react adversely.

Few knowledgeable observers would argue that the armed forces are totally unprepared for their deterrent and war-fighting missions; nor would they deny that existing manpower problems are insignificant. Probably the best judgment comes from small unit commanders in the field who think they are "coping" fairly successfully, doing the best they can at the margin with scarce but quality manpower resources.

The chapters in Part I attempt to place the AVF in historical and contemporary perspective, pointing to problems both old and new and examining current and proposed solutions. On balance, the authors are not optimistic, given a projection of the manpower situation in 1980.

# 2
# Conscription and the All-Volunteer Army in Historical Perspective*
## Robert K. Griffith, Jr.

Despite the fact that the President, the Secretaries of Defense and the several uniformed services, the Chiefs of Staff, and leaders of Congress have declared the all-volunteer force viable and are committed to making it work in peacetime, some Army officers continue to insist that the volunteer Army is not working. These officers argue that before the Army can ever begin to perform its assigned functions adequately the active and reserve components must be filled to authorized strength with quality soldiers and that the replacement system cannot be left to the whims of voluntary enlistments. The consensus of this group is that the experiment has not produced sufficient forces at an acceptable cost and should be scrapped.[1]

The unwillingness of some officers to consider an alternative to conscription is unfortunate, for it places these military professionals in an adversary relationship with the government, the Army, and the society which they serve and to which they are subordinate. Furthermore, those within the military who yearn for a return to the draft or some form of universal service as a "quick fix" to current manpower problems overlook the fact that peacetime compulsory military service in any form is an aberration in the United States. An all-volunteer force is the norm in American history. Only during periods when

---

*"Conscription and the All-Volunteer Army in Historical Perspective" by Robert K. Griffith, Jr., has appeared previously in Volume X (September 1980) of *Parameters—Journal of the U.S. Army War College,* pp. 61-69, and is reproduced here with their permission.

there was a broad popular consensus of a "clear and present danger" to society have the American people resorted to conscription.

## POPULAR OPPOSITION TO CONSCRIPTION

Only as colonials of Great Britain did the American people ever come close to experiencing universal military service. Yet even in the 18th century, as the frontier moved west and men found profit more appealing than military service, the settled and secured regions along the Atlantic coast modified the universal service implied by the militia system. As the threat receded, active participation in the militia became voluntary and the units themselves became increasingly social in nature. During the Revolution volunteers made up the backbone of both the Continental Line and those units that served beyond their states' borders. By the 19th century, the volunteer system had triumphed, despite the fact that the Militia Act of 1792, which formed the basis of US military manpower policy for over 100 years, reiterated the principle of universal military obligation. Even during the Civil War, when both the Union and Confederacy resorted to rudimentary state-controlled forms of conscription, volunteers formed the bulk of the contending armies.[2]

World War I brought the first truly modern draft (modern in the sense that it permitted no hiring of substitutes and was centralized at the federal level) in the American experience. The draft supplied two-thirds of the manpower needed for the war, but it was strictly a wartime measure. The Selective Service Act of 1917 explicitly stated that conscription would end with hostilities; no one was inducted after 11 November 1918.[3]

In the summer of 1940, Congress enacted the first peacetime draft in American history. Alarmed by the rapidity of the German sweep into the European low countries and France, an organization of eastern businessmen with international connections organized a well-financed lobby effort that capitalized on the uncertainty of the times to overcome deepseated isolationist tendencies and pushed a selective service bill through Congress. Interestingly, the Chief of Staff of the Army, General George C. Marshall, and the General Staff initially opposed the measure. Marshall preferred a more gradual and balanced buildup of the Army based on the volunteer principle. Only when the new Secretary of War, Henry L. Stimson, a prominent member of the organization favoring a draft, scuttled the Army's planned volunteer effort did Marshall throw his support behind peacetime conscription. A year later, in 1941, after the hysteria attending the fall of France died down and England still stood, the Army and the Roosevelt Administration experienced great difficulty in extending the draft in peacetime; the House approved the continuation of conscription by only one vote. The subsequent total involvement of the United States in World War II and the ultimate victory obscured the prewar hostility to peacetime selective service and justified the apparent wisdom of that extraordinary move.[4]

Following World War II the United States initially pursued its familiar postwar tendencies. The mass army was quickly dispersed. By mid-1947 the strength of the Army, which still included the Air Force, had dropped from 8,267,958 to 1,070,000. The Selective Service Act expired 31 March 1947.[5]

The developing Cold War brought a resumption of the draft in 1948. Despite widespread opposition to both selective service and universal military training, the draft continued into the 1950's. After the Korean War, opposition to the draft diminished. Congress renewed the Selective Service Act with little debate every four years beginning in 1951—notably in off-election years. During the height of the Cold War military leaders enjoyed a far greater role in formulating defense policy than they had ever experienced before. The realities of facing up to fascism and communism had silenced most of the opponents of a large peacetime military establishment and the draft.

American involvement in Vietnam ended an era of bipartisan agreement on foreign and defense policy. As Americans began to question the assumptions behind their foreign policy, they also began to examine the instrumentalities by which those policies were sustained. In one sense the draft was a natural casualty of the longest, most unpopular war in American history. Inductions from 1954 to 1964 averaged 100,000 a year. As American involvement in Vietnam escalated, so too did conscription. (Voluntary enlistments also increased, but certainly many of these were draft-motivated.) In 1966, 400,000 were called. Casualties also increased, especially among draftees. Draftees, who constituted only 16 percent of the armed forces, but 88 percent of infantry soldiers in Vietnam, accounted for over 50 percent of combat deaths in 1969, a peak year for casualties.[6] Little wonder that the draft became the focus of anti-Vietnam War activism.

But more than the war in Vietnam ended in the early 1970's. By officially embracing the policy of detente, normalizing relations with China, and enunciating the Nixon Doctrine, the United States (perhaps prematurely) effectively proclaimed the end of an ever longer war—the Cold War. Thus, in a larger sense, the end of the draft simply represented a return to the status quo antebellum.

## PAST EXPERIENCE WITH VOLUNTEERS.

Unfortunately for the military services, the draft had in their eyes come to represent the natural state of affairs. By 1973 only a few of the most senior officers still on active duty could remember having served in a truly all-volunteer force. The services had neither institutional memory nor experience related to recruiting or retaining peacetime volunteers in an environment free of conscription pressures. Thus it was natural that when the all-volunteer force of the 1970's failed to live up to expectations—when higher pay and better working and living conditions failed to attract either the required quantity or quality of recruits—critics would declare the experiment a failure and demand a return to the draft. In fact, the record of the contemporary peacetime volunteer Army is about the same as those of its predecessors. Volunteers have rarely been representative of the large society; dependency on volunteers has often left the Army understrength; and officers have been less than satisfied with the quality of peacetime enlisted volunteers in the past.

Enlisted men in the 19th-century Regular Army came largely from the disadvantaged or disaffected elements of society. Some few were educated men, often professionals, who had fallen on hard times. In 1850, the *United States Journal* reported that in one company of 55 men, "nine-tenths enlisted on account of female difficulty; 13 . . . had changed their names, and 43 were either drunk, or partially so, at the time of their enlistment." By mid-century, immigrants constituted over half of the volunteer Army.[7] In the 20th century the proportion of immigrants in the Army began to decline. Legislative restriction cut the flow of immigrants to a trickle in the 1920's, and Congress restricted enlistment to citizens or men who had declared their intent to become citizens. Most enlisted men in the Army of the 1920's and 1930's came from urban working class backgrounds. Except during the depths of the Great Depression, few possessed more than an eighth-grade education. These soldiers served the pre-World War II Army's needs well enough, and after 1931 "quality" recruits were not an issue. As late as 1940, high school graduates made up only half of the 17-year-olds in the country.[8]

Conditions of service in previous all-volunteer American armies were often harsh. Low pay, slow promotions, and arduous fatigue duty did little to attract men to enlist. Before the Civil War, privates received five or six dollars a month, compared to about $30 a month earned by non-farm workers in 1860. They enlisted for five years and could not expect a promotion before their second or third enlistment. When they were not campaigning, soldiers on the frontier laid out and constructed roads, built their own forts and barracks, and grew and harvested most of their food and forage. One soldier complained in 1838, "I never was given to understand that such duties were customary in the Army, much less that I would be called on to perform them, or I never would have enlisted. I enlisted to avoid work, and here I am compelled to perform three or four times the amount of labor I did before my enlistment."[9]

Desertions plagued the peacetime armies. Nearly half the men who enlisted in 1825 deserted before the end of the year. In 1891 the Adjutant General reported that one-third of the 255,712 men who had enlisted since 1867 had deserted. Not surprisingly, the army found that reenlistments tended to be lowest when desertions were high.[10]

Throughout the 19th century, the Army accepted high annual losses philosophically. The conventional wisdom of the era seemed to be that conditions inducing desertions and low reenlistments—low pay compared to prevailing civilian wages, for example—were beyond the ability of the service to control. Furthermore, the recruiting service usually proved able to enlist enough men to keep the small Regular Army reasonably up to strength. After World War I, when for the first time the peacetime strength of the standing force exceeded 100,000, the War Department began a determined effort to reduce losses, improve the quality of inductees, and establish "scientific" recruiting practices.

## REORGANIZATION OF THE RECRUITING SERVICE

Modernization of the recruiting system began in 1919. Faced with the task of replacing virtually the entire enlisted force after the World War I Army was demobilized, the Adjutant General conducted a review of the existing recruiting service and its practices. Major Irving J. Phillipson, who prepared the report, concluded that the established practices of getting recruits, which relied heavily on uniformed recruiters canvassing local districts throughout the country, supplemented by periodic recruiting drives, would not be adequate in the future. He proposed a flexible organization that could expand or contract to meet the Army's manpower needs. Phillipson also recognized the potential of advertising and urged the Adjutant General to exploit all aspects of the news media.[11] At about the same time, Colonel Charles Martin, the Chief of the General Recruiting Service, commissioned an undercover investigation of recruiters and their activities. Martin sent Lieutenant Harry G. Dowdell on an inspection tour in the guise of an unemployed drifter. Dowdell found that most recruiters concentrated their efforts on unemployment lines and railroad stations frequented by itinerants. He reported that throughout the country recruiters enthusiastically enlisted him despite his ostensible medical disabilities, criminal record, and illiteracy. Martin made energetic use of the information; he dismissed about one-third of the recruiting sergeants and officers.[12]

While the Adjutant General and Colonel Martin busied themselves with building an effective recruiting system for obtaining the higher number of requisite volunteers for the postwar Army, others in the War Department considered what to do about enlisted losses. In 1920 Colonel Edward L. Munson, Chief of the Morale Branch of the General Staff, ordered a study of the desertion problem. Munson believed that desertions were but a symptom of a broader internal problem affecting Army manpower procurement and retention—in short, poor morale. Munson identified seven general causes of manpower loss: discharges without reenlistment, discharges by courts-martial, discharges by order, desertions, disability discharges, retirement, and death. The last three he considered legitimate; the first four could be affected by low morale. Only improve the morale of the service, Munson said, and reenlistments would go up while desertions, courts-martial, and directed discharges would go down.[13]

Major Edward N. Woodbury, an infantryman detailed to the Morale Branch, conducted the study on desertions ordered by Colonel Munson. The final report ranged well beyond the immediate issue, exploring the relationships among recruiting, reenlistments, and desertions. Reenlistments, Woodbury found, varied inversely with desertions, because "the causes which produce lack of contentment with the service undoubtedly increase desertion and prevent reenlistment." Woodbury also identified conditions in society which appeared to affect losses. The most significant outside influence was the economy. He discovered that desertions decreased sharply during every economic panic in American history. Conversely, he found that when employment was high desertions rose and reenlistments declined.

Woodbury recognized that the Army could not control the outside influences. He concentrated on the internal influences, such as pay, length of the enlistment period, increases or decreases in strength, and condition of service. Decreases in pay or increases in the length of the enlistment contract had a negative impact on morale, while the opposite adjustments had a positive impact. Any sudden changes in strength created personnel turbulence and uncertainty, which also affected morale adversely. But conditions of Army life affected soldiers most. These conditions included state of barracks, quality of food, pass and furlough privileges, recreational facilities, and guard and fatigue duties. All of the conditions named, Woodbury said, fell under the control of the local commander. The commander who looked after his soldiers' health, welfare, and living and working conditions could appreciably hold down losses.[14]

Not everyone agreed with Woodbury's conclusions. His report received wide circulation in the Army and generated considerable comment. Few of the 156 responses to the study directly challenged Woodbury's contention that leadership was crucial to holding down losses, but fully half of the replies mentioned recruiting practices and the poor quality of recruits obtained during peacetime as central to the Army's manpower problem. Brigadier General Henry Jervey, the Assistant Chief of Staff for Operations, complained that the problem resulted from unenlightened recruiting—taking men who were "mentally deficient or ignorant, irresponsible, young, unstable or easily influenced, addicted to drugs or excessive use of intoxicants, physically weak, ill or physically deficient, degenerate or of weak character, of known bad or criminal civil record, discontented or disgruntled, given to excessive association with or victims of immoral women." Jervey recommended tightening recruiting requirements to weed out the undesirables even if it meant accepting fewer men. Above all, he wanted an end to recruiting drives which induced recruiters to accept the dregs in order to meet quotas. Major General Charles P. Summerall, Commander of the First Division, felt that "the fundamental cause of desertion is instability of character, a thing that is, I think, beyond the power of the military to remove." Summerall, a future Chief of Staff, suggested an additional study of individual deserters to enable the Army to identify potential deserters before they enlisted. Brigadier General Douglas MacArthur agreed with Summerall, whom he would succeed as Chief of Staff in 1930, but he also agreed with Woodbury that desertions were a function of dissatisfaction with the service. However, rather than eliminate sources of discontent, MacArthur urged that malcontents be discharged. "In all business enterprises, except that of the military or naval establishment," MacArthur wrote, "men who do not fit the positions for which they are hired are discharged almost immediately." MacArthur was only one of the most eloquent who thus blamed the recruit, the enlisted men, or the Recruiting Service for the Army's problems.[15]

Most of the officers who commented on Woodbury's study listed causes and conditions within the Army which affected losses. The question of outside factors received scant treatment. One officer, however, Major C. W. Harlow, Commander of the Tenth Field Artillery at Camp Pike, Arkansas, recognized the external economic factor and addressed it candidly. Harlow felt that the brunt of the blame for high losses fell on poor recruits. Although he did not hold the Army or the Recruiting Service blameless, he believed that all "causes simmer down to one. Protracted peace produces genuine economic prosperity which in turn, by increasing the pay of industrial workers, relatively reduced the pay of the soldier, whereupon the recruiting service, compelled to fill the Army, accepts men below a good standard. . . ." It is in periods of depression that the Army gets good men, Harlow said: "Industry's extremity thus becomes the Army's opportunity." Harlow recommended that the Army cease recruiting drives in good times and concentrate on picking up good men in hard times.[16]

## THE VOLUNTEER ARMY BETWEEN WORLD WARS

The ideas and recommendations embodied in Phillipson's and Woodbury's reports and the comments generated by Woodbury's report set the tone for the Regular Army's approach to manpower procurement and retention problems for the next 20 years. In February 1921, Congress reduced the enlisted strength of the standing Army from 150,000 to 125,000. The War Department halted all recruiting and disbanded the Recruiting Service as an economy measure. When enlistments were allowed to resume in September, a reorganized Recruiting Service, designed according to Phillipson's proposal, took to the streets. The system remained under the supervision of the Adjutant General but was decentralized and extremely flexible. A General Recruiting Service officer, attached to the headquarters of each of the nine Army corps areas, monitored the strengths and losses of the units in his area. The number of men assigned to recruiting duty could be expanded or contracted to meet the Army's needs, while the General Recruiting Service could be supplemented by recruiting teams drawn from local units or posts. A Recruiting Publicity Bureau, located in New York City, was established to coordinate advertising, advise recruiters of the Army's monthly personnel needs, and keep members of the widely dispersed recruiting service informed. By the end of 1923, this reorganized procurement system was functioning smoothly and, except when Congress made sudden changes in the enlisted strength, enabled the Regular Army to maintain its authorized strength throughout the interwar period.[17]

Recruiters had to work hard to keep the ranks filled during the 1920's. Starting pay for an enlisted man was $21 a month, an amount which, owing to the general prosperity of the decade, unskilled laborers frequently earned in a week. The Army understood the influence of pay on both attracting and retaining soldiers, and lobbied hard before Congress for a raise. The effort was to no avail, however, so that recruiters had to find other ways to appeal to potential recruits. A Recruiting Publicity Bureau handbook of the period stressed the theme "earn, learn, travel." Recruiters countered the disadvantage of low pay by pointing out that the Army offered job security and excellent retirement benefits to enlisted men at a time when only a few skilled blue collar workers enjoyed similar advantages. The Army also appealed to that sense of adventure it was sure lurked in the hearts of all young men. Finally, the Army offered itself as a vocational school for those men seeking to develop marketable skills. An effective canvasser determined what his prospect was interested in and then sold the Army accordingly: if the civilian was out of work the recruiter offered a steady job; if he was filled with wanderlust, the recruiter talked of faraway places like Hawaii or Panama; if he seemed interested in bettering himself, the recruiter might suggest enlisting in the Signal Corps, which promised assignment to radio school. Little or no mention in printed literature was ever made of patriotism or preparing for war.[18]

Beginning in the mid-1920's, War Department efforts to improve the quality of recruits and cut down on enlisted losses made the recruiter's task more difficult. The Army initiated a program of fingerprinting all applicants for enlistment, checking these against discharge records and Justice Department files in an effort to prevent criminals and former soldiers discharged under less than honorable circumstances from enlisting or reenlisting. For the first time, youths were required to furnish authenticated proof of age. The Army also insisted that applicants under the age of 21 produce notarized consent papers from parent or guardians before they could sign up. But the major effort focused on preventing potential deserters from enlisting. Between 1924 and 1926, the Department of Psychiatry and Sociology of the United States Disciplinary Barracks at Fort Leavenworth, under the guidance of Brigadier General Edward Munson, developed a series of examinations designed to identify misfits and malcontents.[19] When Charles P. Summerall became Chief of Staff in 1926, he ordered the tests administered to all applicants for initial enlistment. The Army also developed intelligence tests for applicants and established minimum standards of basic literacy for enlistment. At about the same time, the General Recruiting Service adopted the slogan "quality not quantity."[20]

The stock market crash of 1929 followed by the onset of the Great Depression changed the social and economic context in which the interwar all-volunteer Army operated. Whereas during the 1920's the Army struggled for every man it got, during the early 1930's recruiters enjoyed a seller's market. The Army lost no time in taking advantage of the situation. The official publication of the General Recruiting Service admonished canvassers:

> Now is the time when every application for service with the colors must be scrutinized with unusual care. . . . The good man must be shown every consideration. . . . But the Army has no place for the individual who is merely seeking "three squares and a flop." The "quality not quantity" idea must be kept always in mind.[21]

As applications for enlistment began to increase dramatically in 1930, desertions predictably fell and reenlistments rose. The Army responded by tightening reenlistment standards. Beginning in 1931, the Adjutant General directed that "no man discharged from his first enlistment with character less than 'very good' will be reenlisted." The Adjutant General also raised the minimum acceptable score on the intelligence test for original enlistment from 34 to 44 (a score "which corresponds to the completion of the eighth grade in school"), and required applicants for enlistment to furnish letters from citizens of known reputation attesting to the good character of the applicant.[22]

From 1930 to 1933, canvassers did not have to look far to find recruits. Lower annual losses meant that the Army needed fewer recruits at a time when more men sought to enlist. By the end of 1930, most recruiting districts had waiting lists. In 1932 the Adjutant General reported that "Employment conditions throughout the country were such that recruiting resolved itself into a matter of selection." In 1933, however, the situation changed. The inauguration of work relief programs by the New Deal, such as the Civilian Conservation Corps, offered unemployed youths an alternative to military service. By 1934 the waiting lists were gone and canvassers returned to the streets on a full-time basis.[23]

Douglas MacArthur, who became Chief of Staff in 1930, took an active interest in the program to upgrade the enlisted ranks. A year after the highest enlistment and reenlistment standards went into effect, he asked all major commanders to comment on the results of the program. The replies were gratifying. Unit commanders throughout the Army declared that "a much higher type of recruit is being obtained at present, both physically and mentally." MacArthur insisted that the higher standards remain in effect even after the Depression eased and recruiting again became more difficult.[24]

MacArthur also gave his personal attention to attempts to purge the ranks of inefficient soldiers. The principle effort focused on married enlisted men. The Army prohibited soldiers below the top three enlisted grades from marrying, on the premise that the pay for the lower ranks was insufficient to support families. The families of these men thus constituted a "burden on the service" and the men were deemed inefficient. In 1931 MacArthur ordered men who married without permission or who could not support their families on Army pay barred from reenlistment.[25]

When Congress began to increase the strength of the volunteer Army in response to the deterioration of peace in Europe, the programs established for enlisted procurement functioned adequately at first. In 1936 Congress increased strength from 118,750 to 147,000 and the next year to 165,000. The War Department responded by increasing the size and budget of the Recruiting Service, so that the new enlistments were obtained with relative ease. But in 1939 and 1940, Congress raised strength so rapidly that the system could not keep pace with the demand. For example, in September 1939 Congress approved an enlisted strength of 227,000. The Army responded by doubling the size and budget of the Recruiting Service. The new strength was attained in July 1940, but by that time Congress had enacted an additional increase to 370,000 men. The Army again prepared to double both the budget and strength of the General Recruiting Service, but by the summer of 1940 events overtook the peacetime volunteer Army, and it was scrapped in favor of a draft.[26]

## LESSONS LEARNED FROM THE PAST

The experience of the volunteer Army between the World Wars suggests several lessons for the contemporary force. The individuals charged with both obtaining and keeping volunteers went to great lengths to understand the problems they faced. The different Army agencies involved with personnel procurement studied virtually every shred of available data on voluntary enlistments, desertions, and reenlistments. They did not confine their inquiries to recent experience, but carried their investigations as far into the past as reliable records permitted. Recruiters clearly understood that more than pay brought men to the service. The volunteer Army of the 1920's, albeit smaller, obtained the men it needed without the benefit of competitive pay or enlistment bonuses. It did so in an atmosphere of congressional and societal indifference to the size of the Army, and, except during the worst years of the Depression, during an era when few men showed interest in military service except as a last resort. In the early 1930's, the Depression enhanced volunteer Army recruiting beyond the wildest expectations of recruiters of the day, but by the late 1930's recruiting had become a full-time job again. To overcome these significant obstacles the War Department involved all levels of the Army in the programs to understand and solve manpower problems. The General Staff frequently circulated proposals to unit commanders for comment. Officers were encouraged to express their opinions on all matters directly to the Chief of Staff or appropriate General Staff directorate. By doing so, the War Department tacitly condoned loyal dissent and encouraged full and open discussion of Army policy. Finally, and perhaps most significantly, the pre–World War II Army "succeeded" because there was no alternative. When the recruiters failed to maintain strength or when losses became embarrassingly high, there were no "good old days of the peacetime draft" to look back on. Officers before World War II possessed a better appreciation of the subordination of the Army to society. They knew that in peacetime social, economic, and political priorities took precedence over purely military considerations. General Summerall clearly recognized the principle of military subordination to society when he asked President Hoover for an increase in both the Army's strength and budget in 1929 (Hoover had asked Summerall to propose areas for a budget cut). "It is recognized," Summerall wrote, "that the establishment of military policy is not a function of the Army."[27]

The error of those who seek a return to the peacetime draft is that they define the problem in purely military terms. They want society to conform to the military and cannot understand or have little patience with the notion that the military is and appropriately must remain subordinate to society. In my opinion, it is unlikely that in the absence of "a clear and present danger" society will tolerate a return to the draft. Indeed, even stand-by registration for a draft has caused the kind, though not the measure, of divisive debate occasioned by the draft itself. Critics of the shortcomings of the contemporary volunteer Army should redirect their attention from seeking alternatives to making the system work. A number of sociologists and political scientists have proposed schemes to enhance the attractiveness of military service to volunteers without prohibitive expense.[28] History does not offer solutions. But it does offer a past rich with experience in maintaining an all-volunteer force under a wide variety of conditions. Especially in the area of manpower procurement and retention, policymakers can ill assume that present problems are unique and that there are no useful ideas to be gained from past successes or failures.

# NOTES

1. This is the author's subjective conclusion based on impressions gained in discussions with students at the US Army Command and General Staff College and based on CGSC student reponses to statements concerning the validity of the volunteer-force concept. Further evidence

of continuing dissatisfaction with the all-volunteer force can be found almost weekly in the letters to the editor of such unofficial publications as the *Army Times*.
2. For a discussion of the Colonial Militia see Douglas Leach, *Arms for Empire: A Military History of the British Colonies in North America, 1607-1763* (New York: Macmillan, 1973), pp. 8-40. A good treatment of the decline of the militia is found in Richard H. Kohn, *Eagle and Sword: The Beginning of the Military Establishment in America* (New York: The Free Press, 1973). The figures on draftees during the Civil War are taken from *The Report of the President's Commission on an All-Volunteer Armed Force* (Washington: Government Printing Office, 1971), chap. 13.
3. For a brief overview of the World War I draft, see Russell Weigley, *History of the United States Army* (New York: Macmillan, 1967), pp. 356-58.
4. The organization referred to is the National Emergency Committee of the Military Training Corps Association. A comprehensive study of the World War II Selective Service System that includes an analysis of its origins is found in the Selective Service System's Special Monograph No. 2 series, *The Selective Service Act, Its Legislative History, Amendments, Appropriations, Cognates, and Prior Instruments of Security* (Washington: Government Printing Office, 1954). The Army's plans, including Marshall's views, are summarized in Mark S. Watson, *Chief of Staff: Prewar Plans and Preparations* (Washington: Government Printing Office, 1950), pp. 184-89.
5. Weigley, pp. 486, 529.
6. John W. Chambers, *Draftees or Volunteers: A Documentary History of the Debate Over Military Conscription in the United States, 1783-1973* (New York: Garland, 1975), pp. 359-71, 428-31. Chambers provides excellent introductions to each period covered in his documentary history.
7. This coverage of the composition of the 19th-century Army is drawn from Marcus Cunliffe, *Soldiers and Civilians, The Martial Spirit in America, 1775-1865* (New York: The Free Press, 1968), pp. 111-20. See also Francis Paul Prucha, *The Sword of the Republic: The United States Army on the Frontier, 1783-1846* (Bloomington: Indiana Univ. Press, 1977), especially pp. 319-30, and Robert M. Utley, *Frontier Regulars, The United States Army and the Indian, 1866-1890* (New York: Macmillan, 1973), pp. 22-28.
8. The decline in the number of foreign-born enlisted men can be traced in the *Annual Report of the Secretary of War.* Information on educational levels is sketchy. See for example *U.S. Army Recruiting News,* 5 (January and March 1923). Comparative educational levels are found in *Historical Statistics of the United States, Colonial Times to 1970* (Washington: Government Printing Office, 1975), p. 379.
9. Prucha, p. 170; *Historical Statistics,* p. 165.
10. Prucha, p. 324; Utley, p. 23.
11. Phillipson's study "Report on Recruiting" is in the National Archives, Washington, D.C. See file 341.1, Central Files of the Adjutant General's Office, Record Group 407.
12. "Excerpts of the Report of LT Harry G. Dowdell," AGO 341.1 (Confidential), RG 407, National Archives.
13. Edward L. Munson, *The Management of Men* (New York: Henry Holt, 1921), pp. 564-65.
14. E. N. Woodbury, "A Study of Desertions in the Army," Mimeograph, Morale Branch General Staff, Washington, D.C., 1920. A copy of Woodbury's report may be found in the Military History Institute, Carlisle Barracks, Pa.
15. Woodbury reviewed and compiled the replies and wrote a cover letter for them. They are in AGO 251.1 (10-12-20) Bulkey, RG 407, National Archives.
16. Ibid.
17. "Proposed Plan for Resumption of Active Recruiting," Memo, Adjutant General to Chief of Staff, 18 July 1921 AGO 341.1, RG 407; "Recruiting Situation," Memo, Adjutant General to Chief of Staff, AGO 341.1, RG 94, National Archives.

18. Based on an analysis of articles on recruiting published betwen 1923 and 1930 in *U.S. Army Recruiting News,* the monthly publication of the Recruiting Publicity Bureau. A fairly complete collection of *Recruiting News* is located at the Military History Institute, Carlisle Barracks, Pa.
19. For a good summary of recruiting restrictions during this period see Captain Reyburn Engles, "Recruiting Problems and Possibilities," *Quartermaster Review,* 6 (January-February 1927), 29-31. The development and institution of mental and intelligence tests for recruits is documented in the files of the Adjutant General's Office. See AGO 220.8 and 319.12, RG 407, National Archives.
20. The development and implementation of literacy and suitability tests for recruits is documented in records at the Adjutant General's Office for the period. See file numbers 220.8, 319.12, and 702; Record Groups 407 and 94, National Archives.
21. "Parting the Sheep from the Goats," *U.S. Army Recruiting News,* 12 (April 1930), 2.
22. *Annual Report of the Secretary of War, 1931* (Washington: Government Printing Office, 1931), pp. 213-15; Memo, Assistant Chief of Staff, Personnel Division to Chief of Staff, "Improvement in Calibre of Recruits," 23 October 1931, AGO 341, RG 94, National Archives.
23. *Annual Report of the Secretary of War, 1932,* pp. 237-39. For a more detailed discussion of this subject see Robert K. Griffith Jr., "Quality Not Quantity: The Volunteer Army During the Depresssion," *Military Affairs,* 43 (December 1979), 171-77.
24. The replies were addressed to the Adjutant General. See for example the replies of the Commanding Generals of the Second and Fourth Corps Areas, 21 and 10 February 1933, respectively, AGO 341, RG 94, National Archives.
25. The issue of married enlisted men cropped up periodically during the 1930's. In this instance see "Marriage of Enlisted Men," a lengthy staff study with supporting documents filed under AGO 220.81, RG 94, National Archives.
26. These statistics are derived from a number of sources, principally *Annual Report of the Secretary of War, 1939,* p. 64; *Annual Report of the Secretary of War, 1940,* p. 40; Special Report, Statistics Branch, General Staff, 1939, 1940, File 198-A, Military History Institute, Carlisle Barracks, Pa.; *The New York Times,* 17 February 1940, p. 6; and Letter, Adjutant General to Commanding General, First Corps Area, 6 February 1940, AGO 341, RG 94, National Archives.
27. Report of the Survey of the Military Establishment by the War Department General Staff, Washington, D.C., 1 November 1928, AGO 333 E.P., RG 407, p. 124.
28. See for example Jerald G. Bachman, John D. Blair, and David R. Segal, *The All-Volunteer Force: A Study of Ideology in the Military* (Ann Arbor, Mich.: Univ. of Michigan Press, 1977), especially chap. 7; Morris Janowitz and Charles C. Moskos Jr., "Five Years of the All-Volunteer Force: 1973-1978," *Armed Forces and Society,* 5 (February 1979), 171-218; and William L. Hauser, "A Smaller Army? Adapting to the All-Volunteer Situation," *Parameters,* 9 (September 1979), 2-7.

# Chapter 3
# Women, Combat, and the Draft: Placing Details in Context

William J. Gregor

After seven years of the all-volunteer armed forces and almost as many years of debate over the role of women in the military, one might properly ask why anyone would seek to add a single additional syllable to this deeply emotional, frequently acrimonious, discussion. By now the antagonists have walled in their positions and it seems unlikely that any new discussant can carry these stout ramparts. However, though many have thrown brick upon brick to produce these walls of words, there nevertheless is neither a coherent design nor mortar to bind the details together. As is characteristic of most political debates, the positions taken by the adversaries have been dictated more by expediency than by clearly defined concepts. The opponents have sought victory through depth of conviction rather than clarity of thought. The consequence is that, despite the volumes of arguments, the fundamental questions have been either assumed or ignored. Our purpose here is to illuminate those questions, and to sift through the existing arguments to discover the underlying assumptions of both the proponents and opponents of women in combat.

## THE ESSENTIAL QUESTION

What is the essential question and how shall we find it? It may seem arrogant to suggest that the question is obvious. Nevertheless, it has been an implied part of almost every discussion of women in combat. For example, the Department of Defense background study, *Use of Women in the Military,* in its introductory paragraph suggests the question whose answer has been universally assumed. This paragraph is quoted in length because it is rich with assumptions.

> To put this study in context, one must remember that the overriding issue is maintaining the combat effectiveness of the armed forces. Within that context, the use of women in the military is a question of increasing importance, for two reasons. First is the movement within society to provide equal economic opportunity for American women. Second, and more important, use of more women can be a significant factor in making the all-volunteer force continue to work in the face of a declining youth population.[1]

The first question that arises is what is a combat effective unit and how does one measure combat effectiveness? Without a clear description of the model for a combat effective unit, how it functions as well as how it is organized, one cannot hope to define a method by which to assess existing or proposed combat formations. Those who have investigated the issue of women in combat and those who have argued for and against this innovation must have had some paradigm in mind in order to proceed. It is impossible to collect data without a model to direct attention to the important variables. The chaos in the debate over women in the military is partly the result of allowing these paradigms to be implicit rather than explicit.

## THE ARMY'S MODEL

The opening paragraph in *Use of Women in the Military* lists two reasons for considering the question of the use of women in the military. These reasons suggest both how the issue of combat effectiveness is approached and, in part, how combat effectiveness is defined. The phrase "making the all-volunteer force continue to work in the face of a declining youth population" implies that effectiveness is primarily an issue of recruitment. The phrase, "provide equal economic opportunity for American women," implies that recruitment is largely a question of social norms. This approach is emphasized a few paragraphs later in the introduction in the following statement: "Women and low quality men are cheaper to recruit than high quality men because they are attracted at no additional cost by the recruiting and advertising effort. . . ."[2] This is obviously a market approach to personnel requirements and it places the following constraints upon the underlying model of an effective combat organization: individuals willingly join because it meets their personal pecuniary expectations; and the organization is attractive only if it conforms to the individual's norms of social legitimacy.[3] The market approach strongly suggests that organizational effectiveness results from placing qualified people into positions which permit them to fulfill their personal expectations.

If we examine the *Use of Women in the Military* further, we find that the assessment of organizational performance is largely a question of task accomplishment. In its simplest terms; was the position filled, the individual present, and the task performed? This concept is manifest in the study's concern for rates of individual attrition and retention, absenteeism, and task accomplishment. The discussion found in this study of army tests of "Women Content in the Army" displays a similar concern for task accomplishment by focusing upon measures of unit and individual performance and by placing emphasis upon the findings that the presence of women in combat support and service support units did not adversely affect unit performance.[4] It should be noted that this particular concern for task accomplishments is not peculiar to the army's study of the use of women. The Army's Training and Doctrine command as well as the Amy War College text on command and management view the issue of organizational effectiveness in similar terms: training + tools + technique = effectiveness.[5] Although we have not yet inquired into the nature of combat effectiveness, we can safely say that, in general terms, the Army views organizational effectiveness to be having sufficient persons with the necessary skills in the proper positions completing certain discrete operational tasks. Effectiveness is task completion.

An organizational model which focuses primarily upon outcomes of organizational activity, that assesses effectiveness solely upon the completion of specified tasks, might be properly labeled an instrumental model. The term instrumental serves to highlight the model's emphasis upon what gets done. The instrumental model is also simple. It is simple in the sense that it considers organizational effectiveness the result of a single relationship; that relationship being the application of individual skills to the accomplishment of individually assigned tasks. Hence, the entire organization can be represented by the sum of the organization's autonomous components and their associated functions. In essence the army's model for its organization assumes that the performance of the army is simply the sum of all tasks performed; the whole is the sum of its parts.

## THE NORMATIVE MODEL

Although the army's critics would agree that the accomplishment of tasks is important for any organization, they, nevertheless, would assert that task accomplishment is not achieved solely by providing skilled individuals to perform required tasks. Instead, organizational effectiveness may be achieved through the interrelationship and mutual dependence of the organization's members. This organizational quality might be referred to as bonds. James Webb, in "Women Can't Fight,"[6] calls this interdependence camaraderie. Quite understandably, the concept of bonds is subjective and stresses that bonds are less a function of what soldiers do and more a function of who they are and how they perceive each other. Therefore, those who comprehend military organizations by this model are very much concerned with the norms and values of the individual service members and the way they interact. Measuring task accomplishment is less important than examining how tasks are performed. Process (individual relationships and interactions) is more important than objective measures of outcomes. This paradigm suggests that the whole is not simply the sum of its parts.

There is a tendency in organizational literature and particularly in the debate over the effectiveness of the all-volunteer army to dismiss the notion of bonds and the model it describes because it is subjective and, therefore, difficult to measure quantitatively. Though that is certainly true, it does not necessarily follow that the essential qualities of any organization, let alone a military organization, can be adequately represented by quantitative measures. A quantitative rather than qualitative model assumes that the essential aspects of an organization can be portrayed by statistical measures. Many may argue that the statistical measures depict reality, but that assertion is still no more than an assertion and in no way diminishes the plausibility of the competing model.

To illustrate the differences between these two organizational concepts, consider a situation in which the Army needs the services of an expert marksman to perform the duties of a sniper. An expert marksman from a National Rifle Association team might perform the objective tasks of a sniper as well as a trained infantryman. The instrumental model would suggest that the only difference between the two marksmen would be the NRA member's lack of familiarity with the other tasks a soldier performs. An observer concerned with the subjective dimension of the military would be forced to conclude that the NRA marksman, though individually skilled, was not a soldier; and the performance of the unit would reflect that fact. The difference between these concepts can be perceived although it may not be modeled mathematically.

Because the concept of bonds is subjective and defies quantitative measurement, it seems appropriate to label the model normative. The normative model stresses the relationship between organization members and the process by which they interact to accomplish the organization's tasks. Changing the character of the organization's members and shifting soldiers from one position to another changes the set of interrelationships among unit members and, consequently, alters the unit's performance. Measures of task accomplishment may remain the same but, nevertheless, the unit is different. The normative model is, therefore, constitutive because the model holds that military organizations are larger than the sum of their parts. The normative model is also distinguishable from the instrumental model because it is complex rather than simple. The relationships between organizational members are not the same and are the result of a large number of personal as well as organizational variables. Additionally, the relationships constantly change and, therefore, the organization itself changes organically. Altering any aspect of the organization alters in some inscrutable way the whole organization. If the normative model accurately depicts the nature of the army, then military units are highly differentiated, pluralistic, and in some ways beyond full comprehension.

## THE NATURE OF COMBAT

At this point, we have identified at least two distinct organizational models and their associated concepts of organizational effectiveness. We have yet, however, to explore the way in which these models influence their supporters' views of combat. What we do know, and what is not surprising is that an observer's theory or model of an organization dictates the variables he considers significant in evaluating an organization. Thus, the discussion of combat units and the effects of placing women in combat is largely the result of applying the observer's underlying model to the investigation of combat units. The specific details of the debate over women in combat are a reflection of the organizational models or theories the discussants use to analyze the nature of combat. Though combat and combat organizations have an independent character of their own, the essential task is to determine which theory best depicts the important aspects of that reality. Unfortunately, the actual debate has focused more on the details emphasized by the antagonists than on the underlying theoretical perspectives they represent.

## COMBAT AND THE INSTRUMENTAL MODEL

The instrumental model is both simple and rational and, hence, directs its adherents to those aspects of combat organizations which seem most subject to reason. Foremost in the minds of these observers is the question of whether women can perform the tasks assigned to combat units. In response to the usual objection that combat is too physically demanding for most women, advocates of expanding the military's use of women cite data related to tasks. For example, it is frequently noted that women are assuming new roles in the civilian labor force and are now performing jobs formerly dominated by males. It is noted, too, that female enlistees have had higher education levels than their male counterparts and, therefore, are more easily trained and, once trained, personally more efficient. M. Kathleen Carpenter, Deputy Assistant Secretary of Defense for Equal Opportunity, in an interview with George Gilder remarked that tests show that while men have greater upper body strength, women have greater midsection strength so that tasks might be restructured to make better use of this capacity.[7] A far more sweeping comment which emphasizes the special importance the instrumental model assigns to tasks is the frequent observation that modern combat no longer entails the use of physical force, that technology has changed the nature of combat and has, thereby, made physical prowess less significant, if not totally irrelevant.

The details of the arguments for expanding the use of women in the military reveal that, for its advocates, combat is essentially the completion of assigned tasks. If you place in a position a person capable of performing the tasks assigned to a position and train the person in those critical tasks, those tasks will be performed and the unit will be effective. Jill Wine Vollner, in an interview with Raymond Coffey, was quick to cite army tests that units with a composition of up to 35 percent female showed no loss of efficiency.[8] The tasks were accomplished. Additionally, these arguments assume that all the essential tasks required of combat unit members are identifiable and that, through either education or training, unit members can acquire these skills. If need be, the tasks can even be redefined. The instrumental model strongly suggests that combat is rational and comprehendible, and that it can be organized to suit the requirements of the protagonist who will conduct the war.

## COMPLEXITY AND COMBAT

The opponents of women in combat cannot be identified solely with the normative model. This is true because some of the opponents base their position solely upon their assessment of combat tasks which suggests to them that women cannot fulfill the task requirements of combat. The emotional commitment of these opponents of women in combat, however, betrays a deeper objective than merely a concern for the task accomplishment. There are others—for me, more thoughtful opponents—who strongly hold that combat and its essential requirements are to some extent inscrutable, that proficiency in battle is in part dictated by irrational, subjective elements not subject to human invention. These are the adherents of the normative model and they comprise only a portion of those opposing women in combat.

Because the normative model is constitutive, images and the nature of personal interactions play an important part in the description of combat and combat effectiveness. Although adherents might emphasize physical prowess, it is less a matter of strength than a subjective image of a warrior. For example, the dismissal of Sergeant Bambi Lin Finney from the Marine Corps after her photograph appeared in the April 1980 edition of *Playboy* magazine suggests that the U.S. Marine Corps finds image an important element of performance. Certainly, the photograph did not in any way affect the job skills Sgt. Finney possessed or the training she had received. If organizational performance is simply a matter of completing discrete, quantifiable tasks, then there is no reason to believe Sergeant Finney would be any less competent after the publication of the photograph than before. Therefore, indirectly, her dismissal indicates the view that personal qualities and subjective images do impact on organizational performance, that tasks alone do not completely depict the essential aspects of a military organization.

One problem in unraveling the debate is the unavoidable tendency of political opponents to interpret their opposition's arguments. The subtle distinctions made by adherents of the normative model are frequently lost in the interpretations created by their opponents. Thus, such items as physical prowess and aggressiveness are frequently stripped of the subjective meanings and reduced to a set of objective performance goals. For an adherent of the normative model, whether a woman can scale an eight-foot wall is less important than how a woman scales the wall. Process is more important than outcomes.

It is perhaps necessary to pause a moment here to investigate the importance of examining process, not outcome. Concern for process automatically produces objections. The instinctive response is, who cares how a job is done, what matters is whether it is done; and perhaps most Americans would agree. That reaction, however, begs the question. The normative model suggests that it does matter; and, thus, that proposition ought not be dismissed without investigation. To dismiss it is to declare that there exists but one view of reality, the instrumental model. Our purpose here is to explore the opposing concepts and to do that we must necessarily assume that the concern for process is reasonable.

To assume the plausibility of the normative model does not, however, require us to abandon usual standards of credibility. Indeed, it is quite easy to illustrate these subjective distinctions, even if it is not possible to quantify the impact of these distinctions upon the results. Consider, for example, the barroom scene in the film version of *From Here to Eternity* in which Ernest Borgnine confronts Burt Lancaster. In response to Ernest Borgnine drawing a knife against Private Pruit, Burt Lancaster (Private Pruit's first sergeant) breaks a liquor bottle against the bar and threatens Ernest Borgnine saying, "Come on Fatso, if there's killin' to be done, start with me." Physical prowess plays a subjective rather than functional role in that scene. It is difficult to imagine, indeed it would be ludicrous to suggest, that Cheryl Ladd or Private Pruit's girlfriend (Donna Reed) could play Burt Lancaster's part in that scene. Now, it is possible to suggest that the violence in this scene could have been averted in other ways or that confrontation between these soldiers was a result of poor socialization or a male-dominated violent environment. Such observations, however, obscure the purpose of this illustration. The manner in which Burt Lancaster subdues Ernest Borgnine is less a matter of what was done, than how he did it. It is the process that makes the essential, albeit subjective, distinction.

What the normative model and the concern for process mean when it comes to describing combat and combat effectiveness is that the intangible qualities of combat are emphasized. For writers such as James Webb and George Gilder, combat is an uncertain environment in which the relationships between unit members produce the intangible element known as cohesiveness which, in turn, produces the unit's ability to respond to uncertainty and the unit's staying power. Understandably, this complex view is built upon discussions of military history, anthropology, and perhaps sociobiology. In any case, the thrust of this argument is that the relationships between unit members cannot be contrived, that the process by which these bonds are created is not totally scrutable; and that the nature of combat is largely beyond man's capacity to shape his world.

## THE CLASH OF COSMOLOGIES

What one sees in the debate of women in combat is the clash of two world views. The advocates of women in combat place faith in man's ability to reason and his ability to shape his environment to suit his will. The opponents of women in combat find the nature of combat and combat performance to be largely beyond man's control. Nowhere is this fundamental conflict better illustrated than in Jill Wine Vollner's reaction to George Gilder's article, "The Case Against Women in Combat." Reacting to Gilder's article, Ms. Vollner fumed, "It's absurd, very biased, based on assumptions of the grossest kind. The whole tone of the article is blatant sexism."[9] Commenting on the suggestion that the majority of men and women are repelled by the idea of women in combat, she said the solution lies not in barring women from combat, but in breaking stereotypes, and in training men to accept women as fellow combat soldiers.[10] What Ms. Vollner had, in fact, said was that we can apply our reason to reshape attitudes to meet our social, as well as performance goals. What Mr. Gilder had written was that we are limited by our biological nature and the nature of combat. Mr. Gilder's complex world wars with Ms. Vollner's simple world. Mr. Gilder's suggestion that we are limited by our nature is interpreted by Ms. Vollner as sexism, the irrational attempt to limit our ability to shape the world. These are irreconcilable differences.

## CONFLICTING OBJECTIVES

Despite the fact that two opposing models of combat organizations are evident in the fabric of the debate over women in combat, identifying the objectives of the opposing groups is not as easily discerned or organized. The confusion and proliferation of objectives stems in part from the need of the participants in the debate to define new objectives to justify their continuing commitment. Additionally, an individual's model of military reality does not instruct that individual on what goals ought to be pursued, although it does tend to color his opinion of what may be reasonably achieved. The more complex the view, the less optimistic will be its advocate concerning the propects for change.

To avoid confusion while sorting through the various military, social and political objectives found in the debate, we shall temporarily set aside considerations stemming from our discussion of the instrumental and normative models, and concentrate on identifying and organizing the proffered salutary and deleterious effects of placing women in combat units. We shall return to considering the implications of the conflicting perspectives once we have ordered the goals.

## THE SALUTARY EFFECTS

Perhaps foremost in the minds of those advocating placing women in combat units is the extension of political and social equality. If, as M.D. Feld has argued,[11] "the right to bear arms has been symbolic of the extension of citizenship to new groups," then permitting women to serve in combat units would be a logical step in admitting women as full participants in American citizenship. It is further argued by John D. Blair and Nora Scott Kinzer that women serving in these nontraditional roles will develop personal attitudes of self-esteem and confidence which they will bring to civilian society and the civilian work force.[12] Dr. Susan Mansfield has suggested that introducing women into combat units will produce more sweeping beneficial changes. Specifically, she asserts that full integration of women into combat organizations will produce a drastic reorientation of training and leadership which will eliminate the hierarchic distinctions of this now male-dominated game and, thereby, transform the nature of combat itself. The result will be a democratic defensive instrument of peace rather than an aggressive instrument of war.[13]. Dr. Naomi Heller's optimism in this regard is somewhat more reserved but extends to the suggestion that placing women in combat units might result in "fewer atrocities against civilians and less random violence by groups of soldiers."[14] In contrast to these civilian advocates of women in combat, members of the military, such as Lieutenant Colonel Mitzi D. Leibst, confine their comments to purely functional issues of providing the military with the required numbers of trained personnel. It would appear that the goals of the military are more immediate and functional.

Sorting through the alleged benefits of women in combat from the most limited goal of providing trained personnel to the most visionary, the transformation of combat itself, an observer readily recognizes a common aspect of the proffered goals. The most vigorous advocates of women in combat see the issue in internal or domestic terms. For example, Dr. Kinzer suggested that introducing women into combat positions would promote the self-esteem of these women. Dr. Heller argued that women in combat formations would restrain the American use of violence and prevent war atrocities. Dr. Mansfield urged that this innovation would create a defensive American force for peace. These perspectives are all inward looking. Neglected is any evaluation of the perceptions of America's enemies or the manner in which our enemies train and organize for war.

## CONTRARY VIEWS

In contrast to the proponents of women in combat, the opponents tend to emphasize goals that are oriented toward external military considerations. Additionally, where they touch upon domestic issues, their purposes are collective rather than individual. If the purpose of an army is to deter war, then the army must appear terrifying to the enemy and show its prowess to America's allies. Since the Soviet Union excludes women from its combat formations, conscripts its male recruits, provides military training in its secondary schools, and even accepts training deaths as a necessary cost of sound combat training, observers such as George Gilder or James Webb argue that introducing women into combat for domestic social reasons necessarily diminishes our allies' confidence and our enemy's dread of our combat potential.

Critics of women in combat also do not agree about the humanizing effects such an innovation will bring to the battlefield. Their criticisms fall into two planes: one is its effect on small unit cohesion and aggressiveness; the other the effect upon social norms and limits on domestic violence. In the first objective, male bonding and combativeness are seen as essential elements for developing commitment and intensity among small groups engaged in battle. For these observers, combat, visiting death and terror upon an enemy, is a primoral act of savagery. Savagery is essential for victory and, for people like George Gilder, eliminating this aspect, civilizing combat units, is a prelude to combat failure.

The second objection that is raised concerning the humanizing effect of introducing women in combat attacks is the assertions we noted earlier about the reduction of atrocities and the pacification of the use of force. If introducing women into American combat units shall lessen the possibility of American units attacking civilians, these observers would argue that it will have the opposite effect upon the enemy. This will be true because, by arming women, the United States will eliminate the easy distinction between combatant and noncombatant. For example, why should the enemy spare unarmed women when these women may be combat soldiers who have melted into the civilian population to escape capture, or who tomorrow may be armed to fill new combat formations? It may be argued that the policy of the North Vietnamese of arming women and children during the Vietnam War or the current armed militancy of Iranian women and children has made the historical distinction between combatant and noncombatant obsolete and, therefore, irrelevant to the decision of arming women. Nevertheless, opponents to women in combat find it disingenuous to suggest that arming women and blurring the easy distinction between combatant and noncombatant shall have a humanizing effect on warfare. Opponents of women in combat contend that returning to the rules of engagement reminiscent of the Thirty-Years War shall only serve to sanction ravages reminiscent of the Thirty-Years War.

An additional objection to arming women deals with the impact that policy may have on domestic violence. Dr. Nora Kinzer asserted that the participation of women in combat training will heighten a woman's self-esteem and permit her to transmit these attitudes when she returns to civilian life. George Gilder orienting on the collective character of society counters that training men and women for combat legitimizes violent physical competition between the sexes and undermines the social norms which have existed to restrain men and to prohibit the use of physical violence against women.[15] In other words, if a male soldier may pommel a female soldier with a pugil stick during the day, why should he make a distinction when he feels like punching her in a barracks fracas that night?

In the arguments against women in combat, we see, once more, contrasting perspectives. Proponents of introducing women in combat units emphasize goals which are essentially domestic and individual. Their arguments emphasize individual choice, individual economic opportunity, political equality, and feelings of self-worth. The opponents, on the other hand, speak of collective social goals and the perceptions of the nation's enemies. Advocates of women in combat assert that if you create an army that reflects the social values of America, it will necessarily be effective. Their adversaries are convinced, as Machiavelli was, that a nation which abandons what is done for what ought to be done will learn to bring about its own ruin rather than its preservation.[16]

## RETURNING TO THE MODELS

A review of these opposing objectives suggests that they can be logically subsumed within our previous models. Since the instrumental model is summative and focuses upon the individual elements of a functional organization, it would follow that, if individuals profited personally, then the organization would profit collectively. More simply, the effectiveness of the organization is merely the sum of its individual parts. Placing skilled women into new functional roles will contribute to that person's individual sense of well-being and competence; and, therefore, that spirit should be reflected in the work actually performed. The emphasis by opponents of women in combat on collective social goals and their attention to perceptions of the Army might logically be encompassed by the normative model. If, as supporters of the normative model assert, military organizations are constitutive, then the advancement of personal goals need not contribute to the collective success of the Army. From this perspective, permitting individuals to fulfill their personal aspirations at the expense of traditional male comradeship means that though these individuals may obtain their personal goals in peace, the organization will fragment in war and, hence, fail in its collective social purpose. It is possible, therefore, to deduce the competing objectives in the debate over women in combat from underlying models of the military organization.

Logical consistency, however, is not always found in political discourse. It cannot be concluded that the antagonists in this struggle are conceptually well organized. There is a tendency among participants in this debate to use details in their arguments which are drawn from both the competing models. Thus, one finds opponents of women in combat, especially retired and active military leaders, who will discuss issues of physical strength and individual skills and who will also show considerable concern for the impression such an innovation will make upon America's enemies. Individual and collective perspectives are easily and frequently mixed in the heat of political battle.

## THE INADEQUACY OF SCHOLARSHIP

More than one article has been written which smugly reports that it will eliminate the confusion found in this debate by eschewing emotionalism and developing factual information upon which rational choices can be made.[17] Unfortunately, in the study of social phenomena, data do not emerge and facts do not explain themselves. The study of social phenomena requires that certain data be selected from the complex set of details which comprises everyday life. The facts that are selected reflect the researcher's preconceived concept about what data are significant. Therefore, the scholar is no less prone than the polemist to select data that is congruent with the models which he uses to understand military organizations. If he understands military organizations through an instrumental model, then he will inevitably collect data that is individualistic, quantifiable, and related to tasks or personal attitudes. Thus, the method the researcher uses proceeds from his underlying model and the facts that are selected are no less biased.

A useful illustration of the importance of research models and their relationship to method is the differing interpretations of the Army's test of the impact of women on unit performance during an annual NATO "REFORGER" exercise in September 1977. The study, REFWAC 77, conducted by the Army Research Institute for Behavioral and Social Sciences, reported that unit and individual performance were not adversely affected by the presence of women in service support and combat support units.[18] That is, individual and unit tasks were adequately completed. However, that same report also contains statements by supervisors and subordinates that the presence of women increased friction within their units and adversely affected morale. Some first-line supervisors suggested that men frequently assisted or performed the tasks of women in addition to fulfilling their own duties.[19] A researcher who wishes to emphasize organizational outcomes and quantitative data will highlight the functional conclusions of this study which finds no degradation in unit performance. The same researcher will also be skeptical of the qualitative observations of soldiers and supervisors, arguing that these observations are either isolated and inaccurate or simply irrelevant because the desired outcomes were achieved despite unit disturbances. A researcher concerned with organizational process and unit cohesion would quite naturally be more interested in the qualitative data; and would be prone to conclude that, though the unit's tasks were completed during the peacetime exercise, the discord found among these units would cause the units to disintegrate in actual battle. The scholarly attempt to produce illuminating facts has only served to reproduce the competing paradigms and their particular explanations and conclusions.

## PROBLEMS OF CAUSALITY

Just as the scholar's paradigm influences his methodology and his conclusions, his model also influences his explanation of the causes of observed phenomena. If the researcher supports a constitutive model of the military, he essentially finds his explanation for observed phenomena in the nature of the military organization, the nature of combat, or the nature of man himself.[20] Supporters of the instrumental model are much more impressed by man's ability to structure organizations and to shape social relations. Thus, the explanation of observations can always be found in human failing, insufficient application, or environmental or educational shortcomings. It must follow, therefore, that, regardless of a study's design, the researcher's commitment to his original model is always reaffirmed.

The problem of causality and the researcher's commitment to his model is evident in a good many studies on sex integration. Take, for example, the report by Lois B. DeFleur, David Gillman, and William Marshak of their study of sex integration at the Air Force Academy. These researchers expected that the attitudes of upperclass and fourth class males would become less traditional after initial interaction with female cadets. However, their findings showed that the attitudes of the males became more traditional.[21] The explanation of these results proceeds from the design of the study. Since they expected that bringing men into contact with women at the Air Force Academy would result in a favorable change in male attitudes, the failure to obtain that result led them to conclude that the distance between housing areas and the hierarchical status differences between upperclass males and fourth class women did not permit enough close personal contact. Since these researchers expected close contact to favorably alter male attitudes, the finding that attitudes were not favorably altered necessarily meant that there was not enough close contact. The original paradigm remained unchallenged.

The fundamental problem in producing causal explanations in the social sciences cannot be avoided. As Harry L. Miller noted recently in *The Public Interest,* explanations in the social sciences display the familiar conflict between those who are confident that we can change people by malipulating their social and small group environment and those who assert that there are natural limits to human change.[23] This dualism is seen in the discussion of pregnancy among military females. The assertion is made that a large number of pregnancies occur among enlisted women because they are ignorant of human sexuality and contraception. The army has, therefore, prepared as part of its new training program instruction dealing with sex education and contraception.[24] It is equally arguable, however, that adolescents, particularly those among the lower status social groups, are indiscrete in their sexual conduct and that the opportunity for such conduct exists in the close and somewhat isolated society of the army. One holding this view would find sex education classes in the military an ineffective means to combat what polite society formerly called promiscuity. Sexual indiscretion may be a product of the nature of adolescence and military life, not the soldier's ignorance.

# THE NEED FOR CONTEXT

Having examined, albeit briefly, the competing perspectives, diverse objectives, and causal explanations common in the discussions of women in combat, what can we conclude about the debate? Apart from the emotional commitment and intractability of the participants, the debate is dreadfully tedious. The debate is particularly fatiguing because the content of most of the arguments is platitudinous and abstract. We are seldom treated to an assessment of the social and organizational realities of an American combat battalion. Instead, proponents of women in combat stalwartly defend individual choice and conjure pictures of future warfare which resemble episodes from *Buck Rogers;* scenes in which Colonel Wilma Dearing, through charm, intellect, technology, or jujitsu, manages to subdue the physically robust but mentally deficient invader. Opponents of arming women do little better. Drawing their images from the past, they envision battle much like Hannibal must have known it. Yet, if the perspectives of these antagonists cannot be reconciled, we can at least assess the ability of their models to depict present organizational realities. Though we cannot determine whether their goals are desirable, we can at least measure the capacity of the all-volunteer army to take upon it these new tasks. The debate over placing women in combat occurs inside a broader political debate concerning the all-volunteer army's success. It is in that context that the issue obtains some substance.

## MAKING SOLDIERS

The attention paid to the expanding role of women in the military is not solely the result of political pressure to extend concepts of social democracy. Another cause for concern is the declining manpower and skill level of the all-volunteer army. In fiscal year 1979, the army met only 90 percent of its recruiting goal.[26] Clearly the all-volunteer force is having difficulty finding the necessary recruits to meet its manpower needs.

A related manpower question, more directly associated with the proposal to integrate women into combat formations, is the issue of retention. It was supposed by many that the institution of an all-volunteer army would necessarily provide the military with people more adaptable to military discipline and the unique requirements of army life. This was assumed to be true because the new recruits would all be volunteers. It was also suggested that these volunteers would be more interested in extended military careers, so that retention rates would increase and so would the army's general level of experience and competence.[27] This, however, has not been the case. Out of every 100 recruits, only 58 actually complete their initial enlistment and only 17 reenlist for a second term of service.[28] Attrition rates are even higher for those males and females who enter nontraditional job specialities, e.g., administrative specialities for men and heavy equipment maintenance for women. It might, therefore, be concluded that the power of the Army to transform civilians into professional soldiers, even among willing volunteers, is indeed weak.

This may not be a cause for alarm. Morris Janowitz has noted with some delight that the fears of some that an all-volunteer army would be an isolated professional military force have not been realized. Dr. Janowitz argues that despite some evidence of increased homogeneity and a stronger "absolutist" outlook, the contemporary military has become more like the larger civilian society, rather than less.[29] Whether this is a positive situation is debatable. Nevertheless, Dr. Janowitz's observation should create some doubt about the military's ability to alter the perceptions and behavior of those it recruits.

There is reason to doubt whether the army can even educate and train new soldiers in their individual skills. Since the inception of the present system of Skill Qualification Tests (SQT), the performance of the soldiers has been exceedingly poor. In 1978, 85 percent of the army's wheeled vehicle mechanics and 89 percent of the tracked vehicle mechanics failed their skill qualification test.[30] Recently published SQT results report that 86 percent of the artillerymen and 98 percent of the turret mechanics have failed their tests.[31] Additionally, the army has taken upon itself the task of teaching basic math and verbal skills to a large number of its soldiers. The Basic Skills Education Program (BSEP) is designed primarily to raise the soldiers' skills to the ninth grade level. This is a considerable task because the army continues to recruit a large portion of its new soldiers from among high school dropouts and individuals with below average intelligence. In October 1978, one division had 2,400 soldiers who were eligible for BSEP because of low reading skills and 2,500 other soldiers without high school diplomas.[32] The suggestion that women might provide increased educational skills has been proven unfounded. Since the expansion of occupational specialities open to women and the lowering of female enlistment criteria, the army has recruited 50.1 percent of its female enlistees from the lowest two authorized mental categories, IIIb and IV.[33] Thirty-one percent of these new female recruits are without high school diplomas. It would seem that the army has a considerable education and training task to perform even without attempting to undertake transforming male attitudes toward women.

## SOCIAL COMPLEXITY

The discussion of women in combat also neglects the social complexity of the all-volunteer force, reducing individual identities to a single dimension—sex. Yet, it is not altogether clear that the social difference between a white male high school graduate and a white female high school graduate is wider than that between a white male high school graduate and a black male high school dropout. Reducing the conflict over the role of women in the army to sexual terms is convenient, but fails to adequately display the social complexity of the all-volunteer army.

A more complex, but more accurate, picture of the social tensions within a unit would recognize the potential difficulties of integrating a combat force which is increasingly drawn from the lower strata of American society, both white and minorities. In fiscal year 1979, 36.3 percent of all enlistees were black. Among those black recruits, 65 percent held high school diplomas but only 12 percent ranked in the top three mental categories.[34] Although white enlistees scored somewhat higher on their mental tests, a larger proportion of the white enlistees had failed to complete high school.[35] Additionally, at least 6 percent of the army's soldiers are Hispanic or members of other minorities. The increasing proportion of females in the military does not directly affect the social composition of the combat battalions. Yet, if they are considered and if we also recognize that approximately 42 percent of the females are members of minority groups, one begins to appreciate the social complexity of the army's units. It is difficult to imagine that the only significant social cleavage in the military is sexually defined.

## SUPERVISORS

If overcoming racial, sexual, or other social tensions is a function of sound leadership, then the army's shortage of company grade officers and noncommissioned officers gives cause for concern. The army is presently short approximately 5,000 company grade officers, mostly captains. To compensate for this shortage the army is attempting to coax 1,000 reserve officers to volunteer for active duty.[36] It has also decided to retain officers who have twice failed to obtain promotion and who otherwise would be separated.[37] These temporary measures are tied to numerous other proposals designed to stem the loss of middle grade officers (captains and majors). These other proposals are, however, tied to incentive programs dealing with military compensation and, therefore, require congressional approval in a period of national budget restraints; a doubtful prospect.

The noncommissioned officer situation is perhaps even grimmer. The Army is losing its trained specialists in the grades of E-5 through E-7 and has proposed an incentive program to help retain these skilled individuals overseas.[38] Soldiers in these three middle grades are refusing overseas movement at a rate of 5,000 per year.[39] However, shortages are not restricted to overseas units. Recently, voluntary overseas extensions in some areas were curbed because many of the units in the United States were short 40 percent of their authorized number of noncommissioned officers.[40] Yet, numbers may be only a part of the leadership problem. Many of the army's master sergeants are refusing to take assignments as company first sergeants. Many of the first sergeant positions are now filled by sergeants first class and platoon sergeants, E-7. The shortage of first sergeants is particularly serious in field artillery batteries, and the army has begun to assign master sergeants without artillery experience to these units. Thus, not only are noncommissioned officers leaving the service in large numbers, but senior noncommissioned officers are refusing the top noncommissioned leadership positions within the combat companies. It would seem something is seriously amiss.

## A COMBAT BATTALION

Up until now, we have been concerned with developing a broad picture of the educational, social, and supervisory problems that the army faces. Combat battalions represent a relatively small portion of the army's units, but it is this small portion which justifies the Army's existence and which is the focus of attention for those wishing to expand the role of women in the military. The combat battalion is less representative of the army as a whole because its positions may be filled by soldiers with lower levels of education. Nevertheless, most of the general problems faced by the Army are manifest in its combat battalions.

Drawing from data obtained from a single tank battalion located in the United States, we find that education levels are similar to those already described; namely, 40 percent of the unit's enlisted personnel are eligible to enter the Army's basic skills education program. Approximately 30 percent of the soldiers are black and 10 percent are Hispanic. Additionally, the battalion is short 20 percent of its officers, mostly captains, and many of the captain positions are filled with second lieutenants. Despite the fact that the battalion's enlisted personnel strength exceeds the authorized level, the battalion is short 40 armor-qualified NCOs in grades E-5 and E-6—fully half the authorized number. Additionally, two of the five companies have no first sergeant; two have no supply sergeant; and only one company has a communications sergeant. Thus, a large number of junior enlisted soldiers are relatively unskilled and these soldiers are trained, led, and supervised by fewer and fewer experienced officers and NCOs. That is not an organization particularly suited for radical social innovation. Some might even suggest that it is difficult to understand how such a unit can reach any degree of combat proficiency at all. At any rate, barring some unforeseen miracle in the army recruitment and retention program, this is precisely the organization in which women will have to be integrated if the nation chooses to put women in combat units.

## CONTRACTS AND OTHER CONSTRAINTS

It might be argued, perhaps even convincingly, that there have always been practical obstacles to social reform and, had man waited for favorable conditions, most social change would never have occurred. The particular predicament of the all-volunteer army, therefore, ought not be seen as an insurmountable obstacle, especially if reforms are executed with vigor and dispatch. There is, however, reason to believe that vigor is wanting.

An interesting incident occurred in February 1980 which suggests a radical change in the relationship between the army and its soldiers. LTG Robert G. Yerks, Deputy Chief of Personnel, sent to Congress a proposal that would permit the army to amend enlistment contracts. It seems that nearly half of all the army's soldiers are serving on guaranteed stabilized tours. That is, they have enlistment or other guarantees that state that they must remain in their present assignment at least 12 months before they can be moved. Although General Yerks believed that no congressional action was needed to move these soldiers, the legislative proposal requested that Congress provide the army the authority during national emergency to alter the soldier's enlistment agreement to permit his involuntary movement. The shift to the all-volunteer army and contractual inducements has diminished the discretion the army exercises in dealing with its soldiers if it must seek authority to use its personnel for their intended purpose. The army recruiting slogan, "Serve Your Country While You Serve Yourself," has created some ambiguity as to which comes first.

The shift from a collective perspective to an individual perspective is seen in other areas of recruiting. For example, M. Kathleen Carpenter, Deputy Assistant Secretary for Equal Opportunity, has noted that black enlistees are not getting their fair share of enlistment bonuses. This is apparently true because blacks are increasingly attracted to military service and consequently do not need any additional personal inducement to join. To remedy this situation, Ms. Carpenter has urged the National Association for the Advancement of Colored People to provide preenlistment counseling to insure that black enlistees know what bonuses are available.[41] This may be politically and socially desirable, and certainly personally profitable for the individual enlistee, but, nevertheless, it changes the purpose of enlistment incentives from the collective goal of attracting hard-to-recruit, specially skilled individuals, to that of individual government entitlements which should be dispensed according to some socially desirable formula. The collective goal is obscured.

What these last two examples serve to illustrate is a market recruiting policy which generally assumes that, if the military can accommodate the individual's preferences, then individuals will not only join but will also reenlist. Such a policy is apparently wise so long as the range of social expectations are limited and those expectations are not at odds with the organization's purpose. The problem may be that neither is true. Comments by black officers at the first *National Conference on Race in the Military* indicate that white officers are suspicious of minority officers who gather to discuss their own particular problems. Presumably, the gathering of black officers is seen as a threat to discipline.[42] Similarly, the army has been questioned several times about restrictions it places upon soldiers who speak Spanish. The army walks a very tight line, permitting the use of Spanish in all military contexts except duty-related conversations. Minority groups are, thus, pursuing their own concept of self-fulfillment in the once Anglo–Saxon-dominated military. It is increasingly unclear what actions the army may take to produce a homogeneous outlook among its soldiers or whether impressing any particular set of norms on the soldiers is permissible at all.

## PUBLIC VS. PRIVATE

Restrictions placed upon any attempt by the army to impose an institutional set of norms on its soldiers come from a wide variety of sources. For example, Senator Strom Thurmond and the Senate Armed Services Committee have successfully opposed the army's recent values clarification program. Besides denouncing the alleged moral relativism in the program's design, the distinguished senator from South Carolina said emphatically, "It is not the role of the government to intervene in the soldier's political, religious or social attitudes."[43] Congress' reluctance to support the military's efforts to alter its soldiers' values is probably less significant, however, than the gradual changes that have occurred in the military legal and administrative systems.

Although the legal norms of civilian society have been gradually extended to the military legal system since World War II, the 1969 Supreme Court decision in *O'Callahan v. Parker* has significantly altered the nature of military law. In that case, the Supreme Court ruled that service members could not be tried in military court for crimes that are not service-connected. Despite the vagueness of the term service-connected, this decision clearly intended to separate the actions of a soldier into two spheres; one dealing with his public role as a soldier and the other with his essentially private role as a citizen. The effect, however, was to obscure both. For example, if a soldier uses illegal drugs on a military installation it is a matter of legal concern to his commanding officer. If that same soldier uses those drugs somewhere away from the military installation, his commander is indifferent or at least legally impotent. It might be difficult to develop adherence to the strict military norms when the soldier is isolated from the influence of his commander should he pursue his pleasures elsewhere.

The trend in military law to separate public from private is manifest in other legal and administrative changes. The decisions of the Military Court of Appeals have consistently sought to limit the role of commanders while simultaneously extending individual constitutional protections to military defendants. Due process standards have been extended to administrative discharge hearings to ensure the protection of individual rights. Reflecting the notion that the performance of an individual as a soldier does not reflect on his character as a citizen, there have been repeated efforts in Congress to eliminate less than honorable administrative discharges. Even though these proposals have not been adopted, 97 percent of all discharges from the military are classified as honorable,[44] despite the fact that 42 percent of the soldiers never complete their initial enlistment. The military legal system, though now more congruent with civilian legal practices, is no longer a means to enforce conformity within the military.

## SEXUAL HARASSMENT AND FRATERNIZATION

Nowhere is the separation of public and private norms and the ambiguities of military policy more evident than in the area of fraternization and sexual harassment. A significant number of men and women in the military find the army's traditional strictures against fraternization a serious infringement on individual rights, since for most Americans the choice of with whom to associate is a private matter. It is, therefore, no surprise that one woman interviewed by Sandra Boodman for *The Washington Post* said, "I don't think what you do off duty is the army's business," and another senior enlisted woman who is secretly dating an officer found Army policy harmful to her relationship.[45] The army's purpose in maintaining a fraternization policy supposedly is not to dictate morality but only to avoid the appearance of impropriety. That position, however, underscores the difficulty of separating public roles and private conduct. The Army seeks to permit individuals to make private choices but, at the same time, seeks to ensure that those private choices do not conflict with the organization's collective purposes. Without creating a set of organizational norms and consciously indoctrinating its soldiers, the attainment of such a goal may be extremely difficult.

Complaints of sexual harassment are another manifestation of the ambiguities inherent in attempting to achieve collective goods without imposing the organization's will upon its members. When an incident occurs that is clearly a violation of military and criminal law, offenders, both male and female, may be sharply disciplined. However, the most prevalent complaints of sexual harassment or sexism involve conduct which falls short of criminality; unsolicited or unwelcome advances, mess hall stares, and male resentment or hostility. In an interview with *The Washington Post,* William D. Clark, Acting Assistant Secretary for Manpower and Reserve Affairs, asserted that controlling sexual harassment was a command problem at base level,[46] but is it? If we review just briefly the complaints about the fraternization policy and those concerning sexual harassment, we find that both involve command intervention into the relationships between individuals. The problem is not controlling the public statements of key officials, but controlling the private statements of soldiers when they meet in the dayrooms and barracks of the army. Whereas some would prohibit the commander's involvement in their private relationships, others commend it in order to alter the organizational environment to suit their preferences. Having denied the institution's authority to dictate morality with regard to fraternization and sexual conduct, the institution is expected to impose another, albeit secular, version of morality whenever those private interactions are offending. Authority is limited by the soldier's preference.

One sees, in the term institutional sexism and institutional racism, the essence of the policy struggle. Individual members of the army and minority groups, variously defined, are locked in a struggle to alter the structure of the military organization to promote their definition of self-fulfillment, either by eliminating existing institutional constraints or by invoking the institution's authority on their behalf. M. Kathleen Carpenter's statement before the NAACP reveals the thrust of one attack. The real barriers to equal opportunity for minorities are "wrapped up in our traditions, our directives, regulations, operating procedures, and way of doing business."[47] However, if the army's traditions and regulations have been biased and are, therefore, suspect, what new orthodoxy shall take its place and from whence shall this model come? The difficulty lies in the assertion that the goals of women or minorities in the military are the same. That assertion ignores the essential plurality of their interests.[48] It is certainly arguable that the army has traditionally been an organization which reflected the values of Anglo-Saxon, protestant, white males. In contrast, the proposed replacement is essentially undefined. Those attacking the institution have a clear idea of what must be struck down, but there is no single view and, therefore, no vision at all of what shall take its place.

The elimination of institutional sexism is seen by many as analogous to the elimination of racism and many, such as Donald Gray, Director of the Department of Defense, Equal Opportunity in the Military,[49] argue that the persistence of sexual harassment is a result of indifference on the part of military leaders. There is, however, another explanation. When the army initiated racial integration in the 1940s and early 1950s, racial integration meant sameness. The military not only compelled service through conscription, it used the institutional structures to force black and white alike into an institutional mold. That mold was probably culturally biased but it was distinct. The goal of integration is the 1980s is not homogenization. It is individuation and self-fulfillment. The army is asked to proceed without a mold. The army repeatedly reports to Congress that it does nothing to discourage a soldier's use of Spanish and permits Hispanic soldiers to maintain their separate cultural identity. Can a company commander in such an environment assume he has the license to repress the Hispanic soldier's conquistador heritage in the name of androgeny? Can a local commander administer punishment to a Mormon soldier who firmly believes that the traditional role of women is in accordance with God's ordinances? Who will support the company commander who punishes a Catholic female soldier for expressing openly her disgust when her female coworker has an abortion? In an organization which has adopted the contractual norms of civilian society and has redesigned its legal system to protect individual rights and to promote cultural diversity, the exercise of institutional authority to create conformity is ambiguous in its effect, if not arbitrary in its application. It is at least arguable that the use of coercion to drive people together in an organization in which the members have been encouraged to express their individual identities results not in integration, but fragmentation. It is quite possible that, in small groups of individuals holding conflicting personal values, conflict is avoided only through a general indifference to one another.

## A DIFFERENT REALITY

Earlier in this chapter we noted the fundamental differences between the concepts of those advocating women in combat and those opposing it. Yet, in our subsequent discussion of the social character of the military and of the changes in the military legal system, we noted little evidence of competition between well-defined concepts of military organizations. If there is any connection between the two sections of this chapter, it is that the essential struggle concerning women in the military is an internal political struggle for the control of social policy. The evidence we have thus far examined shows that the authority of the Army to use legal and administrative sanctions to compel compliance with its collective purposes has been increasingly circumscribed and generally diminished. It would seem that, were the Army to decide to integrate women into its combat units, the military's leadership would have difficulty even impressing a uniform set of norms upon its female members, let alone upon unwilling or unenlightened males. Yet, given the cultural pluralism found in the all-volunteer army, it is equally difficult to image that male combat units will display solidarity. The army may well be—as critics have already charged—just another work place which functions only because most members maintain their distance from one another.

The data also reveal something else. The adoption of contractual norms, the separation of public roles and private preferences, and the institutional changes to protect individual rights and to promote individual autonomy suggest that the army has unconsciously—though nonetheless surely—altered its organizational structure in such a way as to resemble what we earlier described as the instrumental model. The instrumental model essentially argued that an organization is the sum of its individual tasks and functions. If the tasks are accomplished, what matter the individual's private activities, diverse values, or individual associations? The Supreme Court's distinction between service-connected crimes and other crimes is a decision which holds that the military may only be concerned with that conduct which directly relates to a soldier's work. Assistant Secretary William D. Clark's statement that the objective of the army's fraternization policy is protection against impropriety, not the imposition of morality, is another manifestation of the notion that the army is concerned with promoting job performance, and not with building a collective community, a corporate identity. It would seem the army has already adopted the organizational model that is most supportive of the arguments favoring the inclusion of women into combat units.

The army's military leadership has apparently been persuaded to pursue policies that are derivatives of the instrumental model. The charges by civilian elites in the Department of Defense and Department of the Army Offices of Equal Opportunity that the army's traditions and procedures are inherently biased and, thus, poor guides directly assaults the military leader's claim to expertise. The claim by advocates of women in combat that the nature of combat has changed and that the history of war displays sexual bias further undermines an old soldier's pretentions of competence. The issue of incorporating women into combat units is, therefore, not raised as a conflict between two competing concepts of military organization. Instead, this issue is raised as a technical question to be solved through scientific research. For the leaders of the American military, the issue of women in combat is not a political struggle of opposing philosophies. It is a matter of technique. A fundamentally political issue has been converted to a technical issue, and the practitioners of war have thereby been excluded from the debate.

## THE DRAFT

When the representatives of the Department of Defense went before Congress to request resumption of draft registration, they did not resolutely state—as General Leonard Wood did in 1916—that Congress ought to place the resources of the nation in the control of the federal government. They did not declare that the Republic had a right to impress upon its citizens whatever obligations it deemed necessary to ensure national survival. Instead, they proposed the registration of men and women as a matter of equity. Representative Marjorie S. Holt asked what was the need.[50] Like the beaten egg white used to clarify a fine wine, the proposal to resume draft registration has clarified the position of those who would place women in combat. Equity suggests that the government must fulfill the expectations of those it conscripts. It is a foolish nation indeed that, in times of danger, does not bend its citizens to its requirements for survival, to its collective purpose. Those who support women in combat, such as the National Organization of Women, oppose the draft in principle and would deny the authority of the government to bend its citizens to its will. These same advocates support a woman's right to choose to serve in a combat position. This position denies the authority to impress upon the volunteer the army's norms. Upon what compulsion would the army enforce conformity to its purpose? The Department of Defense's call for equity indicates that either the need for conscription is lacking or the army acts only at the sufferance of the soldier.

At a meeting in May 1980, of the Defense Advisory Committee on Women in The Service (DACOWITS), Navy Commander Patricia Gormley argued that existing laws and military regulations which prohibit women from assignments in combat units are the barriers that must be eliminated to achieve full integration. Eleanor Smeal, president of the National Organization of Women, has told Congress that, were women permitted to enlist for combat positions and all sexual barriers eliminated, the ranks of the army would be full and there would be no need for draft registration. But, when all barriers have been leveled and Sue Mansfield's democratic force for peace has been created, where would the Army find the authority with which to mold its members to the will of the state? It seems that these social visionaries are the same theoretical politicians of whom Madison wrote:

> [They] have erroneously supposed that by reducing mankind to a perfect equality in their political rights, they would at the same time be perfectly equalized and assimilated in their possessions, their opinions, and their passions.[51]

The goals of the advocates of women in combat are principally individual and pluralistic. The traditional goals of the military have always been collective and authoritarian. The authoritarian character of the military makes it appear that it can serve as a dynamic force for social change. In promoting pluralism, the army may tear down more than it builds up, creating ambiguity throughout its organization.

If there are still military leaders in the Army who oppose women in combat, their voices are largely silent. Those who enact policy at the senior levels of the army are instituting changes which promote pluralism and which, therefore, make it difficult to define what a soldier is. If tradition and history are inappropriate references because they stand contrary to our present social goals, then what reference shall we use to define the meaning of the term soldier? A recent issue of the Army personnel newsletter noted that the Army had adopted a maternity uniform because commanders had complained that pregnant service members could not present a soldierly appearance in civilian maternity clothes. A pregnant woman, regardless of her garb, has never been the image of a soldier. Frances FitzGerald, writing about the draft in *The New York Times* commented: "To draft women is necessarily to diffuse [a soldier's] collective identity—to change the very idea of what a soldier is."[52] The idea of what a soldier is has already changed. The essential problem may be that no one yet knows the new definition, nor is anyone willing to impose one.

# NOTES

1. Headquarters, Department of Defense, Office of the Assistant Secretary of Defense (Manpower, Reserve Affairs, and Logistics), *Use of Women in the Military,* 2d ed. (Washington, D.C.: September 1978), p. 1.
2. Ibid.
3. Legitimacy is defined as the judgment of those affected that the exercise of authority is right or appropriate. Legitimacy is always problematic because the conferral of legitimacy reposes with those subject to the authority rather than those ostensibly in control.
4. *Use of Women in the Military,* p. (b).
5. U.S. Army War College, *Army Command and Management: Theory and Practice* (Carlisle Barracks, PA: U.S. Army War College, 1977), p. 97.
6. James Webb, "Women Can't Fight," *The Washingtonian,* November 1979, p. 144.
7. George Gilder, "The Case Against Women in Combat," *The New York Times Magazine,* January 28, 1979, p. 30.
8. Raymond Coffey, "Should Women Go Into Combat: Yes, Because U.S. Needs 'Manpower'," *Chicago Tribune,* February 18, 1979.
9. Ibid.
10. Ibid.
11. M.D. Feld, "Arms and the Women: Some General Considerations," *Armed Forces and Society* 4 (Summer 1978): 558.
12. Library of Congress, Congressional Research Service, *Women in the Armed Forces: Proceedings of a CRS Seminar Held on November 2, 1979,* by Robert L. Goldich, CRS Report No. 80-27F (Washington, D.C.: February 14, 1980), pp. 9-11.

13. Ibid., pp. 46-47.
14. Ibid.
15. Gilder, "The Case Against Women," p. 46.
16. Niccolo Machiavelli, *The Prince and the Discourses* (New York: Random House, 1950; The Modern Library), p. 56.
17. For example, on page 1 of *Use of Women in the Military* its authors state:

    Most of the other arguments favoring both more and less women in the military have centered on emotionalism and have been supported by unsubstantiated generalities or isolated examples. It is the intention of this paper to report where the Defense Department stands on the use of women in the military and what factual information is available as to where we can expect to be in the next five years

18. *Use of Women in the Military,* p. (b).
19. Jay Finegan, "Female Troops Spell Trouble to NCO's," *Army Times,* July 10, 1978, p. 4.
20. For those who would object to my choice of words as a reflection of fundamental bias, I wish to acknowledge that I choose to use standard English as it has evolved with all its nuances and subtleties rather than any bureaucratically derived, androgenous forms.
21. Lois B. DeFleur, David Gillman, and William Marshak, "Sex Integration of the U.S. Air Force Academy," *Armed Forces and Society,* 4 (Summer 1978): 617-18.
22. Ibid., 618.
23. Harry L. Miller, "Hard Realities and Soft Social Science," *Public Interest* 59 (Spring 1980): 69.
24. Department of the Army, Office of the Deputy Chief of Staff for Personnel, "Comprehensive Evaluation of Total Integration of Women in the Army," (Washington, D.C.: 4 February 1980), p. 4.
25. Library of Congress, Congressional Research Service, "Military Manpower Policy of and the All-Volunteer Force," by Robert Goldich, Issue Brief No. IB77032 (Washington, D.C.: February 11, 1980), p. 23.
26. "Army 2000 Short of Recruit Target," *Army Times,* February 11, 1980, p. 26.
27. U.S. Congress, Senate, Committee on Armed Services, *Volunteer Armed Force and Selective Service, Hearings Before the Subcommittee on the Volunteer Armed Force and Selective Service,* 92nd Cong., 2d sess., March 10 and 13, 1972, passim.
28. U.S. Congress, Senate, Committee on Armed Services, *Department of Defense Authorization for Appropriations for Fiscal Year 1979, Hearings Before the Subcommittee on Manpower and Personnel of the Committee on Armed Services on* S.2571, 95th Cong., 2d sess., 1978, part 3, p. 1976.
29. Morris Janowitz, "The Citizen Soldier and National Service," *Air University Review* (May-June 1980), pp. 10-11.
30. Larry Carney, "Auto Mechanics Failed on SQT's," *Army Times,* May 14, 1979, p. 3.
31. "Volunteer Army Hurt By Drop in Test Scores And Cuts in Training," *The New York Times,* April 6, 1980.
32. Extracted from an Annex to minutes of a Division Staff Meeting.
33. "Comprehensive Evaluation of Total Integration of Women in the Army."
34. Jay Finegan, "Blacks Join Army at Record Rate," *Army Times,* January 21, 1980, p. 6.
35. This is a continuation of a trend which was noted by Charles Moskos in Morris Janowitz and Charles Moskos, "Five Years of the All-Volunteer Force: 1973-1978," *Armed Forces and Society,* 5 (Winter, 1979): 196.
36. "Boards to Recall Reserve Officers," *Army Times,* March 3, 1980, p. 27.
37. Andy Plattner, "Needed O-3's, 4's to Stay Despite Passovers," *Army Times,* December 17, 1979, p. 3.
38. Larry Carney, "Incentives Urged for O'Seas MOS's," *Army Times,* April 21, 1980. p. 6.
39. Larry Carney, "5000 a Year Leave Army Rather Than Go Overseas," *Army Times,* December 17, 1979, p. 3.

40. Larry Carney, "Tour Extensions Barred in 5 Areas," *Army Times,* April 21, 1980, p. 3.
41. Tom Philpott, "Carpenter Says Blacks Shortchanged on Bonuses," *Army Times,* September 24, 1979, p. 2.
42. Don Mace, "Panel Says Racism Still a Problem," *Army Times,* February 25, 1980, p. 4.
43. Jay Finegan, "Troop 'Values' Study Blasted," *Army Times,* January 21, 1980, p. 4.
44. James B. Jacobs, "Legal Change Within The United States Armed Forces Since World War II," *Armed Forces and Society,* 4 (May 1978): 413.
45. Sandra G. Boodman, "Women GIs Cite Sexual Harassment at Army Bases," *The Washington Post,* January 29, 1980, p. A6.
46. Ibid.
47. Philpott, "Carpenter Says Blacks Shortchanged on Bonuses."
48. There are even military members now championing the rights of single persons against an institution which favors those who are married. "Single Soldiers Complain of Discrimination," *Army Times,* March 10, 1980, p. 20; and M.L. Craver, "Women's Group Hits Singles Housing," *Army Times,* April 23, 1979, p. 7.
49. Karen McKay, "Legal Bars, Sexism Hurt Servicewomen's Progress," *Army Times,* May 12, 1980, p. 7.
50. Richard Halloran, "Registration of Women Meets Obstacle in Congress," *The New York Times,* February 20, 1980, p. A16.
51. James Madison, "Federalist 10," *The Federalist Papers* (New York: The New American Library, 1961; Mentor Books 1961), p. 81.
52. Frances FitzGerald, "This Man's Army," *The New York Times,* February 17, 1980, p. E19.

Chapter 4
# People, Not Hardware: The Highest Defense Priority*
Melvin R. Laird

## INTRODUCTION

In January 1973 one of my last acts as Secretary of Defense was to end draft calls. With that step, the United States embarked on one of the more important ventures in its recent history: we would endeavor to become the first nation in modern times to maintain a large standing military force on an all-volunteer basis, comprising about 2.5 percent of the total labor force and relying completely on the equitable considerations of the competitive market place.

My confidence that this undertaking would succeed in the best interests of the United States was based on the expectation that the President, Congress, and the American people would honor a commitment to provide a decent standard of living and meaningful quality of life for men and women who volunteered for duty in the armed services and for their families. The Gates Commission (The President's Commission on the All-Volunteer Force, headed by Thomas S. Gates, Jr.) which laid the foundation for our transition from selective service to the All-Volunteer Force, put the matter this way: "The viability of an all-volunteer force ultimately depends on the willingness of Congress, the President, the Department of Defense, and the services to maintain . . . competitive levels of military pay. . . ." The commission defined "competitive" as that earned by civilian workers of comparable age and education.

Today, we have reneged on this commitment and are failing to provide this

---

*"People, Not Hardware: The Highest Defense Priority" by Melvin R. Laird is reproduced here with the permission of the American Enterprise Institute for Public Policy Research, which holds the copyright.

decent and competitive standard of living for personnel in the armed forces, especially at the lower enlisted levels from E-1 to E-5. This explains many of the current problems with the All-Volunteer Force and its threatened collapse.

In the early 1970s, there were three courses of action available to maintain adequate military manpower levels in the armed forces of the United States.

1. Continue to fulfill military manpower requirements by using conscript labor through a selective service system that had been used since 1939. The need for manpower (young men and women) required for the military services was no more than one out of fifteen young people between the ages of eighteen and twenty-four. Even using this system, pay scales would have to be established and maintained at least equal to the compensation paid young people in civilian occupations. This system provided, without proper military compensation, the most regressive type of reverse taxation on these young military people ever devised in a free society.

2. Establish a national Universal Federal Service, which would provide for conscript service for all young people between the ages of eighteen and twenty-four. This system, although costing the military less, would cost our Government a great many tax dollars in finding millions of young people proper service employment at low wage rates in hospitals, schools, urban and rural slums, and other areas. This program would have been fair because all our young people not choosing military service would have been required to serve from a year to two years in federal service on a comparable pay basis. The universal service approach has been and continues to be used by the U.S.S.R. and other countries. It had little support in our country in the early 1970s, although as a member of Congress I had advocated universal service.

3. Establish the All-Volunteer Force, which pays the small percentage of American young people needed for military service on a competitive basis with other jobs in our society. The Executive Branch, the Congress, and especially the young Americans of our country chose the third alternative. Thus was born the All-Volunteer Force for the peacetime manpower requirements of our military establishment. It was never anticipated that the All-Volunteer Force would meet emergency requirements or military mobilization requirements. For that reason, registration and the lottery system which I started in 1970 were continued on a standard pay basis along with the Volunteer Force.

Faced in early 1980 with new threats to national security as a result of Soviet action, the Administration belatedly is advocating increased funds for national defense. But as we embark on increased levels of national defense spending, we had better make sure we understand where the essence of our national defense lies. It is the quality of our combat and combat support personnel, officer and enlisted, which undergirds our entire defense effort. Attracting and retaining persons of quality in sufficient numbers should be our number one priority in the fiscal year 1981 budget, commencing October 1, 1980. This means increased pay and benefits at all levels, with special attention to the lower enlisted ranks. The Carter budget for 1981 does little to meet this problem. Until such time as Congress is ready to establish a new conscript military establishment at lower pay than that currently tendered the All-Volunteer Force—and I strongly oppose such action—we must keep pay and allowances for our military personnel competitive with civilian workers of comparable age and education in the economic marketplace. The imperative is clear for the 1981 defense budget: put first things first, people ahead of hardware. We need *both* people and advanced technology but in that order of priority.

There is a strong tendency in the civilian bureaucracies of the Department of Defense, not unknown in the military services as well, to seek out technological solutions for tough problems in the application of deterrence and defense; we all hear talk about the growing vulnerability of large carriers or heavy armored divisions or marine amphibious forces or airborne units or bombers because of new technologies. This talk is another way of saying we can cut back on the numbers of people traditionally needed in the major combat arms. Yet where do Presidents turn in time of crisis when military force may prove vital? Suddenly the question of high-quality personnel in sufficient quantity to carry out missions across the globe—on carriers, in tanks, in amphibious and airborne units—becomes paramount.

In this analysis of the present, deplorable state of equitable compensation for the All-Volunteer Force, I would like to outline the major problems today, address the condition of present compensation, assess the impact of poor compensation on our national security, and present practical solutions for these problems.

## PROBLEMS IN TODAY'S ALL-VOLUNTEER FORCE

Seven years after I ended draft calls and as we enter the dangerous decade of the 1980s, the All-Volunteer Force is beset with severe and growing problems of both quantity and quality.

Recruiting and retention targets have been revised downward each year. The Gates Commission was confident we could maintain a volunteer force of 2.5 million qualified people. When we ended the draft, the size of our force stood at 2.3 million, but we had confidence that this level or higher could be maintained. Today, it stands at about 2 million, 16 percent below the level of seven years ago. Each year, at least one of the services has missed these declining targets, and last year, for the first time, all four of our armed services failed to meet their recruiting goals. The Army fell almost 12 percent or 16,000 people below its target. Even the Air Force, normally in good shape in attracting high quality men and women to its enlisted ranks, missed its goal by 2,000 people. Overall the Department of Defense came in under its reduced recruitment goals by 25,000.

Most importantly, the armed services have experienced not only quantitative but qualitative shortfalls as well. Last year, the percentage of high school graduates joining the military declined by 10 percent. Only a little more than 50 percent of those enlisting in the Army were high school graduates, while the Navy, with its increasingly demanding technology, was forced to accept one person below high school graduation level for every three high school graduates who entered. Nearly 50 percent of the new male volunteers in fiscal year 1979 tested mentally in the lower half of the U.S. population. Five years ago the figure was 32 percent. The quality problem is so bad that, even with a 16,000-person shortfall, 60 percent of the men recruited in fiscal year 1979 by the Army were below the national average in intelligence and required additional training time. For fiscal year 1980, the Army has lowered its standards even further. Pressure for recruitment has become so intense that last year 324 recruiters were charged with various types of malpractice.

It is important to note that the vast majority of quantitative and qualitative recruiting shortfalls came in those areas of the military service for which no civilian counterpart exists, the all-important realm of combat arms—armor, artillery, and infantry. While it is easy to understand why combat branches might be somewhat unattractive, we should not forget that these are what the military is all about. These are the people on whom we are now relying to build the newly organized Rapid Deployment Force.

Recruiting people is only half of the personnel difficulty in today's military. Retaining qualified people is an acute problem and will get worse unless remedial action is taken. Approximately 30 percent of males enlisting do not even complete their first term of enlistment. Since 1976 the services have been losing an average of more than 75 percent of those completing their first enlistment. In fiscal year 1979 the Marine Corps was able to keep fewer than 10 percent of its first-termers, while the Air Force dropped below 20 percent in its first term retention rate for the first time in five years.

While the failure to retain an adequate number of those completing their first term is a severe problem, it is not nearly as important a national defense issue as the failure to retain the requisite number of those who have completed their second and third terms of service. These individuals, who form the backbone of the non-commissioned officer cadre and provide the reservoir of technological skills and experience necessary to operate and maintain our sophisticated weapon systems, are irreplaceable. It takes at least a decade for a military novice to gain the training and experience possessed by these individuals. Yet, the defense establishment is losing them in record numbers. None of the services is currently retaining more than 60 percent of its second-termers. Moreover, except for the Army, which has experienced a slight increase over the past two years, the second term retention rates of the services are dropping rapidly. Over the past few years, the second term retention rate in the Air Force declined from 75 to 59 percent; in the Navy from 64 to 45 percent; and in the

Marine Corps from 47 to 45 percent.

Retention rates for third-termers—people who have completed approximately eleven years of service—are also in decline, now averaging less than 70 percent. The rates range from a low of about 66 percent in the Marine Corps to a high of approximately 90 percent in the Air Force. Two years ago, third term retention rates in those two services were above 70 and 95 percent. When one considers that these third-termers, on the average, are more than half way toward retirement, a dropout rate of over 20 percent per year is significant and alarming. Most of those who leave are in critical skill areas such as submarine technicians, electronics technicians, air traffic controllers, aviation repair specialists, and computer programmers. For every one of the mid-career petty officers and senior noncoms who stays past his or her third term, the services need four fewer recruits to be trained in their places.

Not even the reinstitution of the draft would solve this severe retention problem. In fact, it would probably make the situation worse. Previous experience has demonstrated that conscripts rarely stay beyond their term of obligated service. Moreover, even if sufficient numbers of the draftees did stay on, it would be more than a decade before they reached the experience level of the third-termers who currently are resigning.

As a result of declining reenlistment rates among second- and third-termers, the armed forces have a shortage of more than 70,000 noncommissioned officers. The Army alone has a shortfall of more than 46,000, the Navy 20,000, the Marine Corps 5,000, and the Air Force 3,000.

There are shortfalls among selected categories of officers as well. The Department of Defense, faced with a 10 percent shortage of doctors and a far greater shortage of qualified specialists, cannot provide adequate care for a peacetime military, let alone in time of emergency. Retention rates for pilots in the Navy and Air Force are less than half of the required number. The Navy is also experiencing serious difficulties in retaining adequate numbers of nuclear submariners and surface warfare officers, while the Air Force cannot keep the required numbers of engineers and navigators. At the present time, the Air Force is short 2,500 pilots, 1,000 engineers, and 500 navigators.

When we ended conscription and accepted an active force smaller than during our Vietnam involvement, we did so on condition that this nation would adopt a Total Force Concept—that is, it would maintain (1) an effective reserve component of approximately one million trained people that could be mobilized immediately, and (2) a viable standby selective service system that could provide scores of thousands of personnel within a few months. Neither condition has been met.

The reserve component has a shortage of over 350,000 people, 75,000 in the selected reserve and 275,000 in the individual ready reserve. And, as the Nifty Nugget Exercise conducted in the fall of 1978 convincingly demonstrated, this shortage makes it virtually impossible for the ground forces to sustain a conventional war in Europe for any length of time.

Moreover, our Selective Service System is now nonexistent. When I left office in 1973, the Selective Service System's budget was nearly $100 million and it employed 2,500 people. Last year, the budget had been slashed to $7 million, and only 100 people were on the System's payroll. Peacetime registration ended in April 1975, and classification was terminated in January 1976. I think it was a serious mistake and a false economy of the Ford Administration to end registration and classification. The Carter Administration and this current Congress saw problems but refused in 1979 to reinstate even registration. Current mobilization plans require the Selective Service System to provide the first inductees within thirty days, 100,000 people in sixty days, and 650,000 within six months. Only the most optimistic and uninformed person could imagine that this system, in its present condition, would be responsive to national needs in an emergency. As a minimum, it would take the present Selective Service System over 125 days just to provide the first 100,000 people to the armed forces. Simply put, an American capacity to draft sufficient numbers of men for a major war—even with some advanced warning—does not exist today.

Our military forces have other problems as well. We have underfunded the defense investment area for over a decade. The military balance vis-à-vis the Soviet Union is deteriorating in the strategic, theater and tactical nuclear, and conventional areas. Our operating forces are woefully short of funds for spare parts, training weapons, and fuel oil. Yet, ironically, the small amount of growth in the investment category during the past two years has come at the expense of the personnel area.

While shortcomings in the Selective Service System, reserve components, and certain officer categories are serious, the main problem for the Department of Defense continues to be its inability to attract and maintain the required numbers of qualified enlisted personnel. When and if military force is used in the future, the brunt of the fighting will have to be borne by our active forces, that is, forces in being. Even the most advanced, capable, and numerous weapon systems are only as good as the people operating them.

Fortunately, the solution to the problem of recruiting and retaining the required number of qualified enlisted people in the active force is comparatively simple. The United States must provide these individuals and their families with a quality of life commensurate with the sacrifices we demand from them, and the primary ingredient in providing that quality is competitive pay and related benefits.

## THE COMPENSATION SITUATION

Shortly after assuming office as Secretary of Defense in 1969, I was appalled to discover that approximately 50,000 military families were eligible for welfare. With the assistance of the President and Congress, we succeeded in enacting pay increases of over 35 percent between July 1969 and November 1971. As a result, the number of military families who could qualify for family assistance was reduced to practically zero. In January 1973, as I left the Pentagon, I was confident that military compensation not only was adequate to provide a decent standard of living for even the lowest ranking enlisted person, but also was reasonably competitive with relevant sectors of the private economy. Today, the situation is drastically different. Military pay, particularly for enlisted people, is no longer adequate nor is it, by any standard, competitive with those sectors in the private economy with which it must contend. My judgment is based on the following facts:

- Since 1972, the Consumer Price Index (CPI) has risen by 76 percent, while the level of miltary compensation has increased by only 51 percent (see Table 4.1). This represents an average decline of over 14 percent in purchasing

Table 4.1. Percentage Change in Pay and Purchasing Power in Various Wage Systems, 1972-1979

| Year[a] | Consumer Price Index | U.S. Wage System | Manufac- turing Workers | Unionized Workers | Regular Military Compen- sation |
|---|---|---|---|---|---|
| 1973 | 6.2 | 3.7 | 7.6 | 7.0 | 7.3 |
| 1974 | 11.0 | 9.7 | 6.2 | 9.4 | 5.5 |
| 1975 | 9.1 | 10.6 | 7.9 | 8.7 | 5.0 |
| 1976 | 5.8 | 11.6 | 9.7 | 8.1 | 4.8 |
| 1977 | 6.5 | 8.8 | 9.4 | 8.0 | 7.1 |
| 1978 | 7.6 | 8.8 | 8.9 | 8.2 | 5.5 |
| 1979 | 13.0[b] | 7.0 | 9.9[b] | 10.0 | 7.0 |
| Cumulative change | 76.2 | 77.8 | 77.1 | 76.8 | 50.6 |
| Cumulative purchasing power change | — | +0.9 | +0.5 | +0.3 | −14.5 |

[a] Change from previous calendar year.
[b] Estimated.
**Sources:** U.S. Department of Defense, *Report of the Pay Adequacy Study,* October 1979, Appendix A, pp. 3, 4, and 8; and *Congressional Record,* Senate, November 9, 1979, p. S 16377.

Table 4.2. Loss in Average Military Disposable Income, January 1972-May 1979 (in percentage points)

| Rank | Under 2 | Over 2 | Over 3 | Over 4 | Over 6 | Over 8 | Over 10 | Over 12 | Over 14 | Over 16 | Over 18 | Over 20 | Over 22 | Over 26 |
|---|---|---|---|---|---|---|---|---|---|---|---|---|---|---|
| O10 | | | | | | | | | | | | | | −24.6 |
| O9 | | | | | | | | | | | | | | −21.9 |
| O8 | | | | | | | | | | | | | −19.5 | |
| O7 | | | | | | | | | | | −19.0 | | | |
| O6 | | | | | | | −18.2 | −18.9 | −18.1 | −18.4 | −18.4 | −18.4 | −18.5 | −18.7 |
| O5 | | | | | | −18.1 | −18.2 | −18.5 | −18.8 | −18.8 | −18.8 | −18.9 | −18.9 | |
| O4 | | −16.8 | −17.7 | −16.9 | −17.9 | −17.9 | −18.3 | −18.6 | −18.8 | −18.9 | −19.0 | | | |
| O3 | −15.1 | −15.7 | −16.1 | −17.4 | −17.6 | −17.4 | −17.8 | −18.1 | −18.2 | | | | | |
| O2 | −16.1 | −16.1 | −16.8 | −16.9 | −17.2 | | | | | | | | | |
| O1 | −15.7 | −15.8 | −15.9 | −17.0 | −17.2 | | | | | | | | | |
| O3E | | | | −17.2 | −20.5 | −19.7 | −20.0 | −20.3 | −20.5 | | | | | |
| O2E | | | | −22.3 | −20.8 | −21.0 | −21.3 | −21.6 | −21.8 | | | | | |
| O1E | | | | −20.1 | −20.1 | −20.2 | −20.4 | −20.6 | −20.8 | | | | | |
| W4 | | | | | | | | −18.2 | −18.0 | −18.3 | −18.4 | −18.7 | −18.8 | −19.1 |
| W3 | | | | | | −17.5 | −17.9 | −17.9 | −18.2 | −18.3 | −18.5 | −18.7 | −19.0 | −19.2 |
| W2 | | | −17.2 | −17.2 | −17.2 | −17.2 | −17.3 | −17.4 | −17.6 | −17.8 | −18.0 | −18.2 | −18.4 | |
| W1 | −16.1 | −16.8 | −16.9 | −17.2 | −17.1 | −17.1 | −17.2 | −17.1 | −17.2 | −17.3 | −17.4 | −17.3 | | |
| E9 | | | | | | | | −15.5 | −15.2 | −15.2 | −15.4 | −15.6 | −16.0 | −16.7 |
| E8 | | | | | | −13.5 | −14.4 | −14.4 | −14.5 | −14.6 | −14.9 | −15.0 | −15.4 | −16.2 |
| E7 | | | | −13.9 | −14.1 | −14.2 | −14.2 | −14.3 | −14.4 | −14.4 | −14.5 | −14.5 | −14.7 | −15.6 |
| E6 | −11.5 | −12.4 | −12.6 | −12.9 | −13.2 | −13.4 | −13.7 | −14.1 | −14.2 | −14.3 | −14.3 | | | |
| E5 | −19.7 | −11.2 | −11.4 | −11.7 | −12.1 | −13.4 | −13.7 | −14.1 | −14.2 | | | | | |
| E4 | −10.9 | −11.1 | −11.3 | −14.6 | −14.8 | −12.4 | −12.7 | −12.9 | −12.0 | | | | | |
| E3 | −11.9 | −12.0 | −12.1 | −12.2 | | | | | | | | | | |
| E2 | −12.5 | | | | | | | | | | | | | |
| E1 | −13.5 | | | | | | | | | | | | | |

**Source:** U.S. Department of Defense, *Report of the Pay Adequacy Study*, October 1979, Appendix A, Table 10.

power for all military personnel over the past seven years. As indicated in Table 4.2, for some grades the decline in disposable income approaches 25 percent. (For those who would contend that the CPI is distorted because of the rapid rise in housing costs, bear in mind that the average enlisted person is forced into the housing market anew every couple of years.)
- The average compensation for an enlisted person, including pay and allowances, currently is $9,900. According to the Bureau of Labor Statistics, the minimum amount necessary to maintain a "lower" standard of living for a family of four is $11,546, while a "moderate" standard of living costs just over $20,000. This means that the typical enlisted family has a standard of living 17 percent below a minimum standard of living, and 50 percent below a moderate standard.
- At least 100,000 and possibly as many as 275,000 military families may be eligible for public welfare assistance. The exact numbers are difficult to calculate because many military people are too proud to apply for public assistance; in fact some people resign from the service when they discover that they are eligible. Military commissaries take in over $10 million a year in food stamps. In effect, we are hiding part of our defense budget in appropriations of the Departments of Health and Human Services and Agriculture. When considering the number of military people on welfare, it is important to note that, in contrast to the draft era, large numbers of enlisted people are married. Today, about 50 percent of all E-4s are married. For E-3s the figure is close to 30 percent.
- As of May 1979 the basic pay for all personnel in grades E-1 to E-4 was at or below the minimum wage level. This translates into 32 percent of the entire enlisted force and means that approximately 580,000 military personnel, regardless of skills or educational background or length of workweek, are paid no more, and in most cases far less, than the minimum permissible level for any work performed in the private sector in a 40-hour workweek. This situation has occurred because, since 1972, the minimum wage has increased by 81 percent while basic pay for the E-1 to E-4 grades has increased only 43 percent. A comparison of basic military pay to the hourly minimum wage is found in Table 4.3.
- The average enlisted person qualified for a home loan of only $25,000. Less than 1 percent of the available homes in most areas of the United States where enlisted personnel are stationed are in this price range.
- Five years ago, the Army was able to pay a bonus of up to $2,500 to those men who joined the combat branches. As a result, it could attract the required quantity of men into this area and ensure adequate quality as well. For example, in fiscal 1974 over 25,000 of those receiving the bonus were high school graduates in mental categories one, two, or three. Presently, the bonus level, despite the ravages of inflation, remains at $2,500, and consequently is less attractive. As a result, the number of men eligible for a bonus

**Table 4.3.** Service Pay and Federal Minimum Wage, 1970-1981

| Fiscal Year | E-1 Basic Monthly Pay | E-1 Hourly Wage[a] | Federal Minimum Wage[b] | Military Pay as a Percentage of Minimum Wage |
|---|---|---|---|---|
| 1970 | 115.20 | 0.66 | 1.60 | 41.5 |
| 1971 | 134.40 | 0.78 | 1.60 | 48.5 |
| 1972 | 288.00 | 1.66 | 1.60 | 103.8 |
| 1973 | 307.20 | 1.77 | 1.60 | 110.8 |
| 1974 | 326.10 | 1.88 | 2.00 | 94.1 |
| 1975 | 344.10 | 1.99 | 2.10 | 94.5 |
| 1976 | 361.20 | 2.08 | 2.30 | 90.6 |
| 1977 | 374.40 | 2.16 | 2.30 | 93.9 |
| 1978 | 397.50 | 2.29 | 2.65 | 86.5 |
| 1979 | 419.40 | 2.42[d] | 2.90 | 83.4 |
| 1980 | 448.80 | 2.59 | 3.10 | 83.5 |
| 1981[c] | 480.30 | 2.77 | 3.35 | 82.7 |

[a] Hourly wage (for member with less than two years of service) is calculated as twelve month basic pay divided by fifty-two weeks at forty hours per week.
[b] Data are from Table 11a, "History of Federal minimum wage under the Fair Labor Standards Act," published by the Wage and Hour Division of the Department of Labor.
[c] Assumes a fiscal year 1981 pay raise by 7 percent.
[d] Hourly wages in 1979 for grades E-2 to E-4 equal $2.70, $2.80, and $2.91, respectively.
**Source:** *Congressional Record,* Senate, November 9, 1979, p. S 16376.

has declined by 33 percent, and the number of high school graduates joining the combat areas is down by 50 percent. Bonus costs in current dollars for fiscal year 1979 were actually 46 percent less than five years ago. In constant dollars, they are down almost 60 percent.

While these facts are appalling enough in the abstract, a few concrete examples are even more shocking. An E-4 plane handler on the nuclear-powered carrier *Nimitz,* currently deployed to the Indian Ocean during the Iranian crisis, normally works sixteen hours a day or about 100 hours per week. In the course of his duties, he handles F-14 aircraft which cost $25 million per plane and helps operate a $2 billion ship. Yet he makes less per hour than a cashier at McDonalds, lives below the poverty level, is eligible for food stamps, and probably has not seen his wife and child for six months. A chief petty officer, E-7, on that same ship with seventeen years of service makes the same salary as a janitor on union scale and puts in twice as many hours. An individual who joined the service after the end of the draft in 1973 was making about $6,200 as a single man. Today, with almost eight years of service behind him, he is probably an E-5 with a wife and child. Yet with four promotions, four longevity increases, and increased dependents' allowances, his real income has increased by less than 3 percent a year over the past seven years. The average foreign employee in an overseas U.S. embassy makes 40 percent more than the Marines who risk their lives to guard those embassies. Of the thirteen Marines taken hostage in Iran, four earn $7,250 per year; eight receive $8,200; and one just over $12,000. Thus, only 8 percent of these guards has been paid what the Bureau of Labor Statistics says is necessary to maintain a lower standard of living; their average salary is $8,200 or nearly 30 percent below this lower standard, and their hourly earnings for a typical sixty-hour workweek are less than the $3.10 minimum wage.

Given situations like this, it is not surprising that the services cannot meet recruiting quotas and that career people are leaving the armed forces in record numbers.

While the pay situation for enlisted people is poor when compared with the economy as a whole, it is even worse when compared with those areas in the public and private sectors with which the armed forces must compete for scarce manpower. For example, since 1972, production and other nonsupervisory workers in the manufacturing category have experienced a real growth in earnings of about 0.5 percent; federal wage system employees or blue-collar workers who work side by side with military people at depots and bases across the country have seen about 1 percent growth in real earning levels in that same period; and unionized workers have experienced no loss in average purchasing power over the past seven years. Since 1974, the median incomes of male high school graduates in the civilian sector in the 18-24 and 25-34 age groups have actually grown 10-15 percent more than military pay. Thus, the typical enlisted person has seen a loss of more than 15 percent earning power over the past eight years vis-à-vis some of his contemporaries in the non-military sector. The difference is even more pronounced in certain high skill areas. A mid-career non-commissioned officer earns approximately $12,000 per year. If he or she is a computer programmer, comparable civilian earnings would be at least $25,000. For a boiler technician at $12,000 the civilian comparison is $23,000; for an electronics technician $21,000.

While it is nothing short of a national disgrace that our military people are losing purchasing power rapidly through a precipitous decline in their salaries, these same people are also being unfairly gouged in other areas as well. Each year military people who are transferred must spend over $1 billion out of their own pockets to accomplish the move. The average cost to an E-7 with three dependents to move himself and his family 1,500 miles is approximately $3,835. (This does not include the costs of buying and selling a home or advance house hunting trips.) Presently, he is reimbursed only $644 by the government and thus must come up with over $3,000 to defray the cost of a move which is undertaken for the good of the service. This amount represents over 20 percent of his annual compensation. A GS-9 asked to execute the same move would be reimbursed approximately $4,500, plus the cost of buying and selling a home should he choose to take advantage of this benefit.

Similarly, it costs the 650,000 active duty personnel who must live in off-base housing over $1 billion above their housing allowance to provide this civilian shelter for themselves and their families. For example, an E-7 with three dependents currently draws a housing allowance of $248 per month. If he is stationed in the San Diego area, the average rent for a three-bedroom home is $420 per month. Thus, the E-7 is forced to spend over $5,000 per year (or about $2,000 above his allowance), or 32 percent of his annual compensation, to provide housing for his family. An E-4 with the same number of dependents draws a $185 per month housing allowance and must dip into his pocket for nearly $3,000 above his allowance if he is stationed in San Diego. It is estimated that the average military person stationed in the United States spends over $1,000 per year more for housing than he or she receives in quarters allowance.

Single military personnel living in the barracks also suffer financially if they are stationed outside the continental United States in high cost areas like Germany, Japan, or Alaska. Married people or service members living in nonmilitary housing in those places are authorized a cost-of-living allowance to maintain their purchasing power at the level of their contemporaries stationed in the United States. Those residing in the barracks are not. Yet these individuals spend about 35 percent of their pay in the local economy for such items as recreation, transportation, clothing, food, and gifts. It is estimated that the typical single junior enlisted member spends an additional $1,500 more per year for higher prices associated with the economic environment of areas like Germany, Alaska, or Japan.

The final place where military personnel are forced to spend extra money out of their own pockets is in the area of medical care. Theoretically, free medical care and supplies are supposed to be provided to all service personnel and their families. Because of the lack of medical facilities and the shortage of doctors, the Department of Defense cannot provide this service to most dependents. These individuals must rely on the Civilian Health and Medical Program of the Uniformed Services (CHAMPUS). This plan has a number of features which force the service member to bear some expenses for his dependents' "free" medical care:

- $100 deductible.
- 20 percent cost sharing on outpatient medical care and supplies after the deductible limit has been reached.
- a fee schedule that keys benefits for medical services in a particular year to the seventy-fifth percentile of the nationwide costs of those services in the previous year. Thus, in a high cost area like Washington, D.C., the service member must pay 25 to 35 percent of the cost of most surgical procedures out of pocket. Even in lower-cost areas, CHAMPUS fees are often overtak-

en by the rapidly escalating costs of most medical procedures. A typical enlisted person with dependents normally pays several hundred dollars per year out of his own pocket for medical services and supplies for his family's allegedly free medical care.

In addition, the Department of Defense no longer provides dental care to the dependents of service personnel. Those expenses, therefore, must be borne entirely by active duty personnel since they cannot participate in dental plans available to an increasing number of their civilian colleagues in private industry.

Essentially, there are four reasons why the present military pay situation has developed.

First, over the past seven years, changes have been made in the method of calculating the comparability increases for federal employees on the GS scale. These changes were necessary to correct certain inequities in the Civil Service pay system. Since the military pay system is linked to the GS system, however, military pay levels were automatically depressed without sufficient reason. These changes alone resulted in a 7 percent decline in purchasing power in the pay of armed services personnel.

Second, in 1974, 1978, and 1979 the President imposed pay caps on raises for all government employees to hold down inflation and reduce the size of the federal deficit. Together, these three pay limitations cost the military another 7.2 percent in purchasing power.

Third, in October 1976 and October 1977, the President reallocated portions of a military person's pay increase into the Basic Allowance for Quarters. For those living in government housing, this meant that the increase in their take-home pay was about 25 percent less than the amount of the raise.

Fourth, an extraordinary and unprecedented rate of inflation has, in the past two years, compounded the effects of the first three actions and has diminished the purchasing power of the military in relation to the CPI by an additional amount.

## IMPACT ON U.S. NATIONAL SECURITY

Whatever the reasons for the present situation, they do not diminish the negative impact on defense readiness. The failure of American society to keep its commitment to maintain an adequate level of pay for the members of the armed forces has and will continue to have a number of serious effects. Every study done on the subject confirms that there is a direct correlation between the erosion of pay and the decline in levels of retention. An Air Force study conducted in August 1979 revealed that future financial security is a daily concern to 90 percent of its airmen and that pay is the factor that is most influential in persuading an individual not to make the military his only career. Over the past two years alone, the importance of pay as a factor in career decisions has doubled for typical airmen. Navy studies conducted in the fall of 1979 reveal that the number one reason for leaving the service is better employment opportunities in civilian life. More than half of those who resign from the service cite the unavailability of housing as a factor in their decision to resign. A simulation conducted by the Office of the Secretary of Defense last summer, using the retention model developed by Dr. John Warner of the Center for Naval Analysis, concluded that a 6 percent decline in real pay over the next three years would result in about 30,000 more people leaving the service than would do so without the decline. Studies done by such groups as Rand and the Defense Advanced Research Projects Agency indicate that a 1 percent decline in military pay relative to civilian pay will lead to a decline in retention of between 1 and 3 percent.

If pay continues to drive high quality people out of the service, it cannot but undermine our national security. No matter how sophisticated, weapons cannot be effectively operated and maintained without sufficient numbers of qualified people. The size of our active duty force continues to decline slowly but steadily each year. Absent a specific policy decision or a reduction in commitments, the number of people on active duty has declined by 300,000 since the creation of the All-Volunteer Force. Many operational units are woefully short of personnel. For example, none of our five Army divisions in Europe is up to its wartime strength. Some training units in the United States are 50 percent below their authorized strength. Some naval ships deployed to the Mediterranean and the Indian Ocean have a manpower shortage of 15 percent, and over 30 percent in certain key areas like boiler technicians. Frequently, those people who remain on active duty are forced to work extra hours to make up for the deficiencies; sailors on the *U.S.S. Concord,* a Navy supply ship operating in the Mediterranean, for instance, are working 110 hours per week, while radiomen put in their normal shifts and then substitute as cargo handlers. This is not only dangerous but demoralizing. Submarines are in even worse shape; these vessels go to sea with only 65 percent of the required training and man-hours of experience.

Equally serious is what this decline in pay is doing to the image of our military and the quality of their family life. When more than 10 percent of our enlisted force is eligible for welfare, when hundreds of thousands of enlisted men make less than the minimum wage, and when an E-6 with eleven years of service receives less compensation than a unionized grocery check-out clerk in San Jose, California, the image of the military is not helped. It has become fashionable in some circles to lament the fact that for many people in the armed services the military profession has degenerated from a calling or vocation, with the emphasis on service, to a mere occupation, we have only ourselves to blame. When we allow military compensation to fall 15 percent below the cost of living and even further short of wages in comparable industries, when we compel enlisted people already living below the poverty line to dip into their own pocket to pay for excess costs in moving, housing, and medical services, and when we ask enlisted people to work unpaid overtime to make up for personnel shortfalls, then we should not be surprised that these people have pay and benefits as their primary concern. They act this way, not because they are mercenaries, but because they are being exploited.

A second and possibly more profound effect of declining pay on those individuals who are in the service is the impact on the quality of their home lives. In order to make ends meet, increasing numbers of enlisted people and their spouses are forced to seek outside income. At the present time, approximately 20 percent of our enlisted personnel have a second job which consumes from 11 to 30 hours per week, while more than half of the spouses of enlisted people work full or part time. As a result, thousands of enlisted people, whose home life is already under an abnormal strain because their own workweeks at the base or on the ship often amount to seventy hours and because operational commitments frequently keep them away from home for prolonged periods, put an even greater strain on their family lives when they take on other jobs requiring an additional twenty or thirty hours per week outside the home. Similarly, more than half of the enlisted wives, who frequently must act as both father and mother because of the husband's prolonged absences from home, are forced to perform both roles while working full- or part-time outside the home. What kind of home life can the family of a Navy boiler technician have when the father must spend three out of every four years on sea duty, which involves 50 percent of the time on deployment and fifty to sixty hours per workweek while home, and the mother is compelled to work just to provide a minimum standard of living?

The necessity for husbands to hold second jobs and for wives with children to work just to make ends meet produces a number of side effects which also lessen the appeal of a military career. Many enlisted people with second jobs often earn more money from these part-time jobs than from full-time military jobs while working fewer hours. For example, an E-5 at the Moffett Field Naval Air Station in California, whose annual military compensation is about $10,000 per year, can make $12,000 by moonlighting sixteen hours per week. If he can work thirty-five hours per week, his outside income can rise proportionally. Conversely, the wives of military people who have a second job usually make less and have higher unemployment rates than their counterparts in civilian life. This occurs because of the frequent moves which the military family must make. Normally, the working military wife is forced to obtain a new job every three or four years and thus repeatedly starts over at the bottom as a new employee. Not surprisingly, studies show that the mean earnings of the working wife of an enlisted man are 20 percent below those of her civilian counterpart in the same age bracket and with a similar educational background. In addition, her unemployment rate of 16 percent is more than double that of her civilian colleagues. Thus, it is not startling that an enlisted person who can make more outside of the service than in would not want to reenlist and accept a transfer which would mean that he would lose his outside income while his wife would have to accept a reduction in pay and temporary unemployment at their new duty station. The real surprise is that some do accept the transfer!

# SOLUTIONS

What is needed to solve our current military pay muddle is a national commitment to maintain an acceptable standard of living and meaningful quality of home life for those who are willing to dedicate their lives to the defense of this country.

We need no repetition of political campaign rhetoric of 1976 that the defense budget could be reduced billions of dollars by reducing personnel costs. That has hurt national defense as we are paying a stiff price for this misguided economy. As the Gates Commission noted, we need a commitment "to maintain and improve the effectiveness, dignity, and status of the Armed Forces so that they may continue to play their proper role." As a minimum, upholding that promise involves ten specific actions which must be taken now.

*First,* military pay must be restored to its 1972 real income levels immediately. This would involve a 17 percent across the board increase for all grades in order to make up for the loss in purchasing power which has occurred since 1972.

*Second,* legislation indexing military pay to future changes in the Consumer Price Index must be enacted. This step would protect the future purchasing power of active duty people in the same way that the compensation of military retirees is protected. It is rather ironic that the nation is more concerned with safeguarding the purchasing power of those who have served than those who are now serving. This step would have the added benefit of inducing more people to remain on active duty after becoming vested in the retirement system at the twenty-year point. Only the most noble person would remain on active duty when his or her pay will rise more rapidly if he or she retires. Finally, indexing active duty military pay to the CPI would remove the ever-present temptation from the executive and legislative branches to use military pay to support specific economic and monetary polices. The cost or savings for each percentage point change in military pay is $300 to $400 million.

*Third,* mandate that changes in military pay levels be applied to all forms of military compensation. Hence, if in a given year the CPI rises by 10 percent, then basic pay, the housing allowance, and subsistence would each increase by the full 10 percent. Under the present system, if the President applied part of the raise to the quarters or subsistence portions of compensation, then the basic pay does not increase by the full amount.

*Fourth,* military pay must be decoupled from that of civil service workers on the GS scale. Such a step is implicit in the first two recommendations and is eminently reasonable because the situations of the two work forces are quite different. The demand for jobs in the federal civil service far outweighs the supply, and civil servants generally are not subject to long hours of unpaid overtime, frequent moves, and family separation.

*Fifth,* establish a variable housing allowance keyed to the local area. It makes little sense to pay the same housing allowance to enlisted people stationed in Fort Rucker, Alabama, and the Presidio of San Francisco. As a corollary to this recommendation, the Department of Defense should undertake a crash program to increase the amount of military housing available to members of the armed services. At the present time, housing is available to only 20 percent of the enlisted force. At a minimum, it should be available to 50 percent. We cannot tolerate the type of neglect which occurred during fiscal year 1980 when no funds were appropriated for the construction of new family housing.

*Sixth,* reimburse military families for the full cost of their moves. This would involve the adoption of the same standards as those in existence for civilian employees of the federal government. It would mean establishing reimbursement for activities before and after moving such as temporary housing allowance and increasing the mileage and per-diem rates to reflect actual costs for the military person and dependents. For example, the present change of station entitlement for a service member is 10 cents per mile, while the actual expense is about 21 cents per mile. President Carter's new proposal to provide members on permanent change of station orders with $35 per-diem is a step in the right direction, but does not go far enough.

*Seventh,* provide annual special-skill pay to those enlisted and officer ratings where severe shortfalls are experienced. These payments would be over and above the reenlistment bonuses paid to people in such areas and would mean extending to the entire force the monetary inducements currently provided to doctors. Such a step would help narrow the gap between the pay that an enlistee receives and the pay he or she could be earning on the outside in such areas as computer programming.

*Eighth,* adopt the Blue Cross and Blue Shield fee schedules for CHAMPUS. These schedules are much more current and realistic than the present system. Such a step will reduce the cost to the military person of providing medical care for dependents and thus increase the availability of medical services.

*Ninth,* increase the bonus for those joining the combat arms branches to $5,000 in fiscal year 1980 and index future bonuses to reflect increase in the CPI. This will restore the bonus level to what it was five years ago and should help the quantitative and qualitative shortfalls in the key area of combat arms.

*Tenth,* provide a cost-of-living allowance for personnel stationed overseas in high cost areas even if they live in the barracks. Since these individuals spend about 35 percent of their pay in the local economy, approximately 35 percent of their pay should be on the same scale as that of people living off post.

These ten initiatives will be expensive. Their total costs could amount to billions of dollars a year. Restoration of comparability will involve a one-time jump of at least $5 billion. Implementing a variable housing allowance and paying the full cost of moves will involve $2 billion in additional costs annually. Indexing military pay will add some $750 million per year over the normal pay raise. Meeting the 50 percent target for family housing will require an additional $1.5 billion each year. Special-skill pay for 10 percent of the enlisted force would amount to $2 billion annually. Increasing CHAMPUS benefits will add some $300 million per year to the cost of the system. Restoring the bonus to the level of five years ago will add $40 million per year, and COLA for those in the barracks will come to $47 million. Some will say, understandably, that devoting more money to compensation could increase the percentage of the defense budget absorbed by manpower costs to over 60 percent and make it more difficult for us to compete with the Soviets, who spend a scant 17 percent of their military budget on personnel.

When compared with the fiscal 1981 defense budget total of $157 billion or with a trillion dollar five-year program or the $4 billion that the federal government spends each year on youth jobs programs, the costs of improving the quality of life of the men and women in the military services are not immense or unreasonable.

Moreover, these expenditures could save money in the long run. Each year billions of dollars go down the drain when people leave the service for lack of pay. For example, the cost of training a pilot is in excess of $700,000 while an electronics technician costs almost $100,000 to train. On the average, the Department of Defense could save $25,000 for each additional first-termer it retains, $60,000 for each second-termer, and $125,000 for each third-termer. Additional billions could be saved by not having inexperienced personnel operating and maintaining sophisticated weapon systems. Finally, the Pentagon spends about $10,000 for each person it recruits, and about $2 billion per year to recruit, train, separate, and pay benefits to individuals who do not complete their first term. These military "dropouts" also cost the government $50 million per year in unemployment compensation. Competitive pay would help attract a high-quality person and would lead to higher retention.

Even if these additional expenditures do not save money in the long run, there are three compelling reasons why they must be borne no matter what the cost. First, they are necessary to uphold the commitment that other leaders and myself in the nation made to the youth of America when we embarked on the All-Volunteer Force and ended the hidden tax of conscription. Second, during this new decade maintaining the All-Volunteer Force will be more, not less difficult. By the end of the 1980s the number of males reaching age 18 will decline from its present level of 2.14 million to 1.6 million, a drop of 25 percent in ten years. Currently, because of the turbulence in the international arena, the demands upon our military forces will be much greater than in the 1970s. I *am* afraid that the seizure of our embassy in Iran and the invasion of Afghanistan are only harbingers of things to come.

I recognize that increased compensation alone will not solve the problems of the All-Volunteer Force. Such innovative steps as reducing the length of deployments and restoring the G.I. Bill are also necessary. Reinstituting registration for a standby draft will be essential. I am certain, however, that unless we compensate our people adequately the All-Volunteer Force will not work and we will do irreparable harm to the prestige of military service and to the military family. The choice confronting us is simple: either we pay salaries high enough to retain skilled people or we settle for a military less ready to fight in the future.

Chapter 5

# "Dumb" Soldiers and "Smart" Bombs: Precision-Guided Munitions and the All-Volunteer Force

Bruce E. Arlinghaus

One of the recurring criticisms of the all-volunteer force is that it has failed to attract, recruit, and retain sufficient numbers of "quality" personnel.[1] While there exists little agreement on how to define or measure quality,[2] a commonly used index is the alleged inability of those personnel to operate, maintain, and employ increasingly sophisticated equipment—that they are simply too "dumb" to use "smart" bombs.[3] Implicit in this criticism is the notion that their being unequal to the technological demand of modern warfare is somehow their fault, or that of society, and that if they came from the proper social and economic background, and were properly educated, they would master their weapons and constitute a truly professional, competent, volunteer force.

I would suggest, however, based upon a review of the literature concerning both the all-volunteer force and precision-guided munitions, and a series of interviews with individuals both in and out of uniform,[4] that the focus of concern should not be so much on the quality of the personnel in the force, but on the quality of the weapons which we expect them to use. Soldier quality has improved, but at a rate unequal to that of technological innovation in weapons development, such that the all-volunteer force will most likely never be able to recruit or retain personnel of sufficient quality. Put another way, our soldiers are not too dumb; rather, our weapons have become too smart. This research has focused on this dilemma and its impact on the land battle, where precision-guided munitions will hopefully permit small numbers of our "dumbest" to defeat numerically superior Soviet forces and "win the first battle."[5]

In the recent past, there have been contradictory claims, usually made by senior military officers and government officials,[6] that the all-volunteer force is the best educated and motivated group to ever serve in uniform. Under scrutiny, these claims have been repudiated, and have resulted in a serious credibility problem for those who once complimented, and now complain about, the quality of personnel serving in both the active and reserve forces. Discussions of the possible reinstitution of the draft, revitalization of the GI Bill, or increases in pay and benefits focus upon the need for higher quality personnel to keep pace with technological innovations.[7] Yet, many balk at the estimated costs, both monetary and political, that such actions would require. Manpower has always taken a back seat to "the principal preoccupation of the U.S. Military [which] has been the acquisition of more, and especially more expensive, hardware."[8]

There is a pronounced tendency in the Department of Defense to seek technological solutions for difficult defense problems.[9] It is a logical development out of the experience of two world wars, where American industrial might was manifested permitting military forces to expend firepower rather than manpower on the battlefield. This tradition forms the cornerstone of our defense policy, and is the direct opposite of the course followed by the country which constitutes the primary military threat to our national interest: "The United States has never attempted to match the Soviet Union in either ground force personnel or material, relying instead on technology."[10]

In the past decade, this "technological advantage" has more and more come to mean the development and fielding of precision-guided munitions (PGMs)—terminally guided, "smart" direct and indirect fire weapons.[11] While PGMs are indeed technological marvels representing quantum increases in both accuracy and lethality on the battlefield, their advent has had a dramatic impact on the manpower needs of the forces using them:

> The process of rapid technological substitution has not only led to enhanced capabilities but also has gradually turned Western armed forces into technocracies where a declining ratio of combat to support personnel has meant that, though firepower has increased, a decreasing number of individuals are actually involved in combat.[12]

But a fatal assumption usually is made regarding this shift from a manpower-intensive to firepower-intensive military force; namely, that there is no need for the quality of personnel operating and maintaining these systems to improve as well:

> One specific advantage that seems likely to accrue to countries possessing such weapons is the possiblity of substituting highly accurate weapons

systems for manpower. Many of the new weapons are comparatively easy to operate, and thereby require fewer skilled military personnel in the field.[13]

PGMs, in particular the anti-tank guided missile, are "an excellent example of the American military's unregenerate faith in the capacity of technological innovation to determine outcomes on the battlefield"[14] which many have heralded as revolutionizing the battlefield.[15] The BGM-71 TOW (Tube-launched, Optically-tracked, Wire-guided missile) and its shorter-range counterpart, the M47 DRAGON, are second-generation, optically-tracked, wire-guided missiles which are far superior in performance to their Soviet equivalents.[16] The increased accuracy and lethality which they possess have made them the apparent solution to the problem of Soviet armored vehicle superiority, and they have proliferated (over 275,000 TOW systems alone) both in the United States Army and Marine Corps, and in the services of over 32 other nations. Yet, several critical limitations exist which make their introduction to the contemporary battlefield less than revolutionary.

The system under which we test these new weapons is a major variable in the weapons acquisition process. Clearly, if new weapons are to be employed by "average" soldiers, they should be tested in the hands of average soldiers, not by hand-picked soldiers or by specially-selected or organized units. This principle is easy to understand, but somewhat more difficult to execute. There is a traditional "can do" ethic[17] in the military (an admirable trait, especially in combat, though much-maligned by some observers) which translates into herculean efforts to get the mission (a set of assigned tasks) accomplished. Commanders of many, if not most, units would have a natural tendency to exert every effort to train their men to the utmost so that any failure in testing a new weapon system would be a reflection of the system's design, not of their own inadequacies or those of people in their units. The problem here is obvious, is not easily overcome, and has a direct bearing on the central problems raised.

A second and related problem concerns the natural tendency among weapon systems designers/manufacturers in a highly-competitive market to influence decisions on contracts to purchase weapons. Among the many "access points" in the research, development, testing and evaluation process is the test itself. Systems to be tested come with corporate representatives who "look after" and initially teach people how to use them. These "tech reps" know their system, can keep it working, and can teach and train people how to use it better than anyone else. If the system is adopted, very few in the military will be able to match their knowledge, maintenance ability, or standards of training. In this case too, the weapon system test is somewhat divorced from the eventual realities of its deployment in the hands of soldiers worldwide.

Once the system is adopted and fielded, unrealistic conditions still persist. Normally, units are provided one live round per launcher per year for training and to assure that systems function properly. Unfortunately, these live fire exercises are such critical events that often only the best gunners are given the opportunity to fire a live missile, an experience which they consider unforgettable and perhaps the best training in proper gunnery that they will ever receive. A similar situation exists in Advanced Individual Training, when only one gunner—the honor graduate—has the chance to fire a live projectile. Cost of a live missile precludes more personnel having this opportunity, and few commanders would risk such a scarce resource in the hands of a marginal gunner. In addition, prior to live fire exercises, contact teams and technical representatives are present to inspect the systems to assure that they are functioning properly.

Finally, unrealistic and unjustified optimism in the combat effectiveness of these systems has become fully integrated into our force planning and gaming. As General William E. DePuy (ret.), former commander of the Army's Training and Doctrine Command, has recently stated:

> War games are notorious for playing at too fast a tempo. Few of the games take into account such dampening mechanisms as troop-leading times, friction in execution such as errors, stupidity, fear and incompetence. All weapons are manned by perfect crews; that is, they extract the full design potential from weapons. Small-unit tactical leaders are assumed to be able to deploy all their weapons during all engagements so that every one bears upon the enemy.
>
> In fact, crews in war are lucky to realize 50 percent of their weapons potential and tactical leaders would be unusually skillful if they could bring half their weapons to bear. And, as we all know, Murphy's law runs rampant.[18]

Despite their technological superiority, these weapons are dependent upon the humans operating them—a factor that has largely been ignored in both their design and their anticipated employment.

The recurring theme, however, in advertisements and promotional films developed by their manufacturers, is the ease and simplicity of PGM operation and maintenance, and this has been reflected in much of the literature assessing their impact on American and other military forces:

> To operate TOW, a gunner merely has to keep the cross hairs of his optical sight on the target, while an infrared sensor in the sight tracks the missile.[19]
>
> Many (PGMs) can be operated by average soldiers.[20]
>
> For automatic systems like the TOW, crews may be trained quickly, and there is no great problem in selecting potentially expert individuals.[21]

The impression that one gets from reading these descriptions is that literally any soldier can learn to operate and maintain these systems quickly, and to the maximum effectiveness of the weapon's capabilities.

Yet, these are facile descriptions, suitable for a powerful marketing strategy, but which ignore the realities of actual operator procedures. For example, maintenance of the TOW necessary to ensure reliable performance requires the gunner to conduct an 11-step manual test (not automatic) anytime the system is moved crosscountry, is installed in its carrier, or has experienced a significant change in ambient temperature (±10 degrees). Otherwise, the test is required every four hours. The steps must be performed in proper sequence to ensure accurate readings, and that the missile guidance system and optical sight are properly synchronized.[22] This is a complicated procedure, requiring either intensive study or use of a reference manual. If the system malfunctions, there is little the gunner or crew can do to fix it on the spot—the defective component must be evacuated to a corps-level maintenance unit for exchange or repair. While such units normally provide forward contact teams, it is highly unlikely that they would be readily accessible to frontline units.

In addition, there is increasing evidence that firing such weapons is actually a complex task consisting of both continuous and procedural motor responses. The latter type tasks are easily forgotten within a matter of weeks or even days, and many gunners cannot achieve qualification after as little as 30 days between training sessions. There are indications that gunner success may be correlated to higher aptitude test scores and cultural background, but it is doubtful that the volunteer army can require sufficient numbers of such individuals to man these rapidly proliferating systems.[23] Even if they existed and could be recruited, as systems become even more sophisticated, there simply may be cognitive limits[24] to how much even a "quality" soldier could learn and retain. Even with a draft, there is no assurance that higher-aptitude, achievement-oriented soldiers will be found in the combat units which will employ TOW and DRAGON.[25]

The attitude that PGMs are too complex and sensitive is denied by their developers and manufacturers, who see the problem as inadequate training or selection of personnel. In their experience, "All tests . . . fired at a static target from a rigid mount met accuracy and reliability requirements . . . selected personnel trained by the developers achieved acceptable first-ever live round hit rates after training. . . ."[26] But such conditions, both for the weapons systems and the personnel using them, are unrealistic. As one defense official put it, "Anyone who likes the TOW has never seen a battlefield."[27] Perhaps the foremost authority on the reactions of men in combat, S.L.A. Marshall, has commented that: "Expecting the infantryman to stand firm and die hard simply because he has a superior weapon in his hand that can kill tanks at heretofore undreamed ranges is no good. Men are not made that way and training will not make them over."[28]

Attempts to provide more protection for PGM gunners, with such systems as the Improved TOW Vehicle (ITV) and the Infantry Fighting Vehicle, exacerbate rather than relieve this situation. Individual user and support tasks increase in number and complexity, requiring additional training and retraining. For example, gunners on the ITV lose their tracking ability faster than on the previous system.[29] Further, training them has become much more expensive: some training ammunition costs have increased by 40 percent;[30] and the introduction of more sophisticated systems, such as the replacement of the LAW (Light Antitank Weapon) with the VIPER, can more than triple the costs of training.[31] While less costly training devices which simulate launch effects and tracking requirements exist for both the TOW and the DRAGON, they are not without fault either; they are highly susceptible to equipment failures and may, in fact, teach gunners improper rather than proper gunnery techniques.[32] These devices were originally intended for use in selecting potential gunners who already possess naturally the continuous motor skills necessary to be successful, rather than for training.

Higher training costs must be funded, and can only be eased slightly by improving personnel quality. It is easy to recommend that this situation be relieved by recruiting more higher-mental-category soldiers, instead of Category IVs who are unable to remember complex firing sequences and who require more repetitive training.[33] But already our allies provide over four times the training we currently give our soldiers, and even more for those assigned to operate complex weapons systems such as TOW. Personnel training constraints have both immediate and long-range effects. While the ability of present soldiers to master and maintain new systems may be the principle limiting factor to incorporating new technology into the force, these individuals also form the pool from which future noncommissioned officer trainers and supervisors will be drawn.[34]

This situation has arisen because technological innovation has occurred without reference to the mental and physical limitation of the humans expected to operate, employ, and maintain the resulting weapons systems. In other words, the dominant philosophy has been to provide systems which represent the latest state of the art, to which the military and its people must adapt. What has come to be known as the "man-machine interface" must be considered, and "hardware and procedures must be operable by the soldiers anticipated to be available to the army without adding significantly to the difficulty or cost of training."[35] Recent attempts have been made to correct this problem. Research to determine the characteristics of a "Strawman Infantry Soldier Profile" has been undertaken,[36] to provide human engineers a better understanding of the "biggest variable" in operational testing—the individual soldier. Coping with the man-machine interface will most likely be considered in the design of future weapons systems. But, since it takes approximately ten years to design, test, produce, and field a new system,[37] it is unlikely that such studies will have much short-term impact.

In the interim, more funds *must* be dedicated to identifying human capabilities for future weapons systems specifications, and for the training needed to narrow the gap between human abilities and weapons capabilities—the man-machine interface. Force planners must reevaluate their combat estimates and plans to reflect a realistic assessment of what precision-guided munitions will contribute in the hands of real soldiers, instead of those of a mythical, ill-defined, "quality" force. Finally, the most telling consequence of the "dumb" soldier-"smart" bomb controversy is the growing realization that technology is not a panacea to our defense problems. As General S.L.A. Marshall has admonished: "New weapons . . . do not of themselves revolutionize warfare, though they may seem for a time to have that effect, which history attests as a recurrent illusion."[38]

# NOTES

1. John J. Fialka, "A Question of Quality," *Army* 30, (June 1980): 29-32; "Who'll Fight for America?" *Time,* June 9, 1980, pp. 24-30.
2. "Army Blames Exam, Not the Exam-Taker," *New York Times,* August 10, 1980, p E2.
3. "Doubts Mounting About All-Volunteer Force," *Science* 209, September 5, 1980; 1095.
4. Conducted with members of the Department of Social Sciences, United States Military Academy, West Point, New York; the United States Army Infantry Board, Fort Benning, Georgia; and the Third Infantry Division, Wurzburg, West Germany. In addition, I have served for 14 months as a TOW-equipped anti-tank platoon leader and 22 months as a DRAGON and TOW-equipped mechanized infantry company commander in Europe.
5. FM 100-5, Operations, (1976) p. 1-1. See also Robert Kennedy, "Precision ATGMs and NATO Defense," *Orbis,* Winter 1979, pp. 897-928.
6. "Army Drops Test Scores that Categorize Soldier's Mental Ability," *New York Times,* August 9, 1980, p. 5; and "Menetrey Says Soldiers Today of 'Uniform' IQ," *Colorado Springs Sun,* March 7, 1980, p. 8.
7. James Webb, "The Draft: Why the Army Needs It," *The Atlantic,* April 1980, p. 34.
8. "Philosophers at the Pentagon," *Science* 210 (October 24, 1980), 409-11.
9. Melvin R. Laird, "People, Not Hardware, The Highest Defense Priority," American Enterprise Institute for Public Policy, 1980, p. 2; and Jack N. Merritt and Pierre M. Sprey, "Negative Marginal Returns in Weapons Acquisition," in *American Defense Policy,* 3d ed., edited by Richard G. Head and Ervin J. Roppe, (Baltimore: The Johns Hopkins University Press, 1973), pp. 486-95.
10. "Department of Defense Appropriations for 1976," statement by General George S. Brown, USAF, Chairman of the Joint Chiefs of Staff (Feb. 27, 1975) in Hearings Before a Subcommittee of the Committee on Appropriations, House of Representatives, 94th Congress, 1st Session (Washington, D.C.: U.S. Government Printing Office, 1975), p. 167.
11. Clifford D. Bradley, "Regain the Technological Advantage," *National Defense,* 65 (October 1980): 40.
12. Richard Burt, "New Weapons Technologies: Debate and Directions," *Adelphi Papers,* No. 126 (1976), p. 1.
13. Amos A. Jordan, Introduction to Geoffrey A. Kemp, Robert L. Pfaltzgraff, Jr. and Uri Ra'anan eds, *The Other Arms Race: New Technologies and Non-Nuclear Conflict* (Lexington, Mass.: D.C. Heath) p. xlv.
14. Jeffery Record, "The Fortunes of War," *Harper's* 9 (April 1980): 19.

15. James Fallows, "Muscle-Bound Superpower, The State of America's Defense," *The Atlantic,* October 1979, p. 61; and Robert Kennedy's "Precision ATGMs and NATO Defense," *Orbis* 22 (Winter 1979): 897-99.
16. John Weeks, *Men Against Tanks: A History of Anti-Tank Warfare* (New York: Mason-Charter, 1975).
17. Sam C. Sarkesian, "An Empirical Reassessment of Military Professionalism," in *The Changing World of the American Military,* edited by Franklin D. Margiotta Boulder, Colo.: Westview Press, 1978, pp. 37-56; William L. Hauser, *America's Army in Crisis* (Baltimore: Johns Hopkins University Press, 1973) pp. 173-88; and Richard A. Gabriel and Paul L. Savage, *Crisis in Command: Mismanagement in the Army* (New York: Hill and Wang, 1978), pp. 99-101.
18. General William E. DePuy (ret.), "FM 100-5 Revisited," *Army* 30 (November 1980): p. 14. See also Seymour J. Dietchman, *New Technology and Military Power: General Purpose Military Forces for the 1980s and Beyond* (Boulder, Colo: Westview Press, 1979), pp. 73-82.
19. Jacquelyn K. Davis, Robert W. Helm and G. Phillip Hughes, "An Inventory of New Weapons Systems for Non-Nuclear Combat," in *The Other Arms Race: New Technologies and Non-Nuclear Conflict,* edited by Geoffrey A. Kemp, Robert L. Pfaltzgraff, Jr. and Uri Ra'anan (Lexington, Mass.: D.C. Heath, 1975), p. 156.
20. James F. Digby, "Precision Guided Weapons," *Adelphi Papers,* No 118 (1975), p. 4.
21. James F. Digby, "Precision-Guided Munitions: Capabilities and Consequences," in *The Other Arms Race: New Technologies and Non-Nuclear Conflict,* edited by Geoffery A. Kemp, Robert L. Pfaltzgraff, Jr. and Uri Ra'anan (Lexington, Mass.: D.C. Heath, 1975), p. 10.
22. TM 9-1425-470-12, Operator's and Organizational Maintenance Manual for TOW Heavy Antitank/Assault Weapon System.
23. Major Stanley H. Holgate, U.S. Army, "The Dragon Dilemma: Why Low First-Round Hit Rates?" *Military Review,* September 1980, pp. 25-30.
24. James G. March and Herbert A. Simon, *Organizations* (New York: Wiley, 1958), pp. 137-71.
25. Richard Reeves, "Suppose There Was A War . . . ," *Esquire,* May 1980, p. 13; James Fallows, "The Draft: Why the Country Needs It," *The Atlantic,* April 1980, pp. 44-47; and S.L.A. Marshall, *Pork Chop Hill* (New York: Morrow, 1965), p. 19.
26. Holgate, "The Dragon Dilemma," p. 27.
27. Fallows, "Muscle-Bound Superpower," p. 61.
28. S.L.A. Marshall, "Man Against Armor," *Armor,* January-February 1980, p. 31.
29. TRADOC Battlefield Development Plan (u), 1979, pp. 2-18.
30. Fialka, "A Question of Quality," p. 33.
31. MG Thomas P. Gorman, address given at the U.S. Military Academy, West Point, New York, April 1980. LAW/VIPER gunners must be requalified quarterly since the skills associated with these weapons are "forgotten" within three months (see TRADOC Bulletin No. 5, "Training with the LAW"). The cost of a live LAW round is $114, compared to $397 for the VIPER. Quarterly training is accomplished using ten less-expensive, subcaliber rounds per gunner. For the LAW, each subcaliber round costs $9, for the VIPER, $37.
32. Holgate, "The Dragon Dilemma."
33. Fialka, "A Question of Quality," pp. 30-31.
34. TRADOC Battlefield Development Plan (u), pp. 1-4.
35. U.S. Army Administration Center, "The Battlefield Development Plan and Division 86: Human Dimensions," 1980.
36. Andrulis Research Corporation, Alexandria, Virginia, 1980.
37. TRADOC Battlefield Development Plan (u), pp. 1-4.
38. Marshall "Men Against Armor," p. 30.

## Chapter 6
# AVF vs. DRAFT: Where Do We Go From Here?
### Richard V. L. Cooper

## INTRODUCTION

The All-Volunteer Force (AVF), now more than seven years old, is coming under increasing scrutiny. This can be seen in the Congress, the media, and, indeed, in everyday conversation. Although the AVF-draft debate has continued on an on-again/off-again basis for most of the AVF period, there has been a noticeable change in the tone of the debate during the last year or two. Concern about the future of the volunteer force would appear more widespread than at any time since the draft was ended.

Fiscal 1978 marked the first time since the draft was ended that all four military services fell short of their recruiting goals. Recruiting picked up in fiscal 1979, but still not enough to match all objectives. There has been growing concern about attrition, and about the quality of new troops. Reenlistment rates among career personnel have fallen during the last several years, and readiness problems in the military have become more visible. Moreover, all this has occurred while the Soviet Union has expanded its military capabilities and presence.

While some of the above factors are largely, if not totally, unrelated to the volunteer force, they have been viewed by many as AVF problems. They have occurred since the AVF was begun, and are thus associated with the AVF. Indeed, some have gone so far as to blame the failure of the 1980 ill-fated hostage rescue mission on the volunteer force.

The capstone to this most recent surge in the debate was, of course, President Carter's decision to reinstitute peacetime registration. Although not really an AVF issue—indeed, the President's Commission on an All-Volunteer Armed

Force (under President Ford) recommended that an active registration system be retained for emergency standby once the draft was ended—the recent call for registration certainly has served to heighten interest and concern. Whereas the draft debate had been largely limited to policymakers, policy implementers, and academicians, President Carter's decision brought the issue back into the home of every family with military-aged children, and back onto every college campus.

Given this platform, AVF critics have become more open and vocal in their opposition to the volunteer force, and some individuals once solidly behind the AVF have begun to express their doubts and concerns. Part of the reason for this change in mood is undoubtedly a result of the more general change in attitudes about defense. With the Vietnam legacy and Soviet ambitions once again more evident, the public and the politicians are becoming increasingly concerned about our national defense. Combined with the now more frequently expressed concerns about the "success" of the volunteer force, this has given much greater prominence to the AVF-draft issue.

It is most unlikely, however, that there will be a draft in the next few years. Despite the possible introduction of some form of draft legislation in the 97th Congress, the President has been (at least during the election campaign) opposed to a return of conscription, as are a majority of the present members of Congress. But, there appear to be a growing number of "fence sitters" who, though unlikely to support a draft in the near future, may be far less opposed several years hence. Thus, the practical result of any near-term efforts to return to the draft will likely be to lay the foundations and set the stage for the "real" debate, which, at this conjuncture, can probably be expected to occur about the mid-1980s.

This gives us the time to think about the issues, problems, and alternatives, for the options available to us then will, in a large part, be limited by what we do during the next several years. It is in this regard that I have found myself most frustrated, for it seems to me that the AVF debate has focused far too little on the alternatives. Rather, the debate has been negative in tone; the focus has been on what is wrong with the volunteer force rather than on what can be done to improve it or on how alternatives stack up against the volunteer force across the board. This is not to say that the volunteer force is without problems, for that is clearly not the case. Rather, it is to say that too little attention has been given to determining the extent to which criticisms of the AVF address valid problems, to what extent these problems are fixable, and to what extent alternative military manpower procurement policies could solve them. For example, the AVF has been criticized as being too costly by many of the same individuals who propose a much more costly alternative: universal national service. Similarly, the volunteer force has been criticized as being unrepresentative, when, in fact, a return to the draft would probably have no effect on the racial composition of the armed forces.

The purpose of this chapter is to take a broad look at the kinds of military manpower procurement alternatives that there are, and what the implications of each would be. To do this, it is important to first outline some general criteria for selecting such a policy; this is done in the next section. We will then examine the three main categories of military manpower procurement policy options: universal service, selective service, and volunteer service. Conclusions are presented in the final section.

## CRITERIA

Defining the criteria according to which the various military manpower procurement alternatives will be judged is an important first step in the process. In this regard, there would seem to be four major types of criteria that need to be addressed: (1) national security, (2) efficiency and cost, (3) equity, and (4) objectives. These are briefly discussed below.

### National Security

A nation has an armed force for the protection of its interests—i.e., national security. In this country, that means defense against other nations, since internal security is left primarily to the various civilian law enforcement agencies (except for the use of the National Guard for certain emergency and disaster situations). Thus, our armed forces must be able to provide a sufficient level of national security: to deter war if possible and, that failing, to wage and win a war.

Translating this general concept into operational requirements is, of course, the regular responsibility of the individual military services, the Secretary of Defense, the President, and the Congress. For the purposes of this chapter simply note that these agents have translated national security requirements to mean in the neighborhood of 2 million uniformed members of the active forces, around 900,000 members of the Selected Reserves (SR), and several hundred thousand members of the Individual Ready Reserves (IRR). The point of this is not whether the active forces, for instance, should be 2.1 million, 2.4 million, or 1.8 million. Rather, the purpose of the above is to establish general "ballpark" figures with respect to military manpower requirements. These ballpark figures, in turn, mean that the military will have to obtain in the neighborhood of 300,000 to 500,000 new recruits (or inductees) each year (active and reserve, officer and enlisted) in order to meet these military manpower strength requirements.

As important as these numerical requirements is the kind of defense effort that is envisioned for the United States. In particular, the U.S. Armed Forces are structured primarily as an "expeditionary" force, not to provide territorial defense of the U.S. mainland. Combined with the highly sophisticated technology embodied in our military this means that it is not a home guard or militia that is sought but, rather, a large standing army capable of fighting both on quick response and for an extended period on foreign soil.

If not already, it will become clear later how this general statement of defense requirements affects the appropriateness of the various potential military manpower procurement policy options. For the present, let me simply note them as what defense requirements are expected to be in the future. To the extent that future defense requirements vary markedly from these assumptions, evaluation of the particular policy alternatives must accordingly change, though it should also be noted that the general approach presented here should also be appropriate to such an evaluation.

## Efficiency

Efficiency, or cost, is the second important criterion for judging the various military manpower procurement policy options. Less expensive is obviously preferable to more expensive. In this regard, though, while budget costs are the most visible measure (and are, in fact, an important policy variable), it is the "real resource" cost that is of the most importance from an overall public policy perspective. For example, it is generally acknowledged that the real resource cost of manpower during the draft was much greater than the budget cost of military personnel, both because the wages paid to draftees understated the economic value of these individuals in alternative civilian pursuits and because military personnel costs did not capture the large amounts of resources expended for draft avoidance. The discussion here will focus on budget costs and, to the extent that they differ from budget costs, the real resource costs of the different policy options.

## Equity

The "fairness," or equity, of various policy alternatives is always an important criterion. Defining precisely what is "fair," and what is not, is of course impossible. Nevertheless, society must regularly make judgments of this sort with respect to a variety of different issues. It is not that society should not impart "burdens" on its citizens, for it must, usually in the form of taxes. Rather, the issue is one of trying to distribute these burdens equitably.

In the case of military manpower procurement, the issue of equity arises primarily when a draft is used, especially when it is a selective service draft. (Though perhaps less of a problem, equity is also an issue with universal service, since, for example, a desk job in the military is not the same as the infantry.) No matter how "fair" the selection process itself is, by its very nature, a selective service draft is inequitable after the fact. That is, those who are selected are forced to bear a burden that those not selected do not have to bear. This does not necessarily preclude a selective service draft, since there are other criteria that must be taken into account, as described above. It does imply, though, that, whatever policy is employed, efforts should be made to reduce the degree of inequity.

## Economic and Social Policy

To the extent possible, military manpower procurement policy should be consistent with the nation's other economic and social goals. In fact, one can go one step further and argue that, to the extent possible and reasonable, military manpower procurement policy ought to further the nation's economic and social goals. For example, the military paved the way for racial integration in the 1950s. Today, driven by cost and efficiency concerns, the military has begun to make much greater use of physician extenders in the provision of health care to its personnel. This has potentially important benefits for the civilian sector in the future.

At the same time, we must be very careful to avoid having "the tail wag the dog." For example, adopting a policy of universal service solely to encourage a "socialization" of American youth would seem to be a great waste of the nation's resources. Alternatively, if such a policy was useful for military purposes, then this "socialization" might be a useful and positive by-product.

Thus, it must be remembered that the primary purpose of military manpower procurement policy must be to provide the needed manpower to the military. It should not conflict with the nation's broader economic and social policy objectives, but it should also not be the primary agent to achieve social or economic change. Except in some few instances, military manpower procurement policy is simply a very inefficient way for affecting social and economic change. Moreover, using it in this fashion may have very undesirable military effects. To illustrate, it may be very sensible from the military viewpoint, and from society's viewpoint more generally, to attempt to enlist successful "graduates" of various social and economic action programs, such as the Comprehensive Employment and Training Act (CETA). At the same time, using the military instead of CETA is likely to be both inefficient and detrimental to national security.

## Peacetime versus Wartime

The above discussion has been cast largely in the context of maintaining a peacetime military force. All four criteria discussed are important during wartime as well, but the relative emphasis must shift in such circumstances. For example, a selective service draft may be rejected for peacetime as unnecessarily inequitable, but may be the only feasible alternative during a war. On the other hand, the World War I policy of drafting those of "least value to society" would rightly be rejected today for equity reasons, should war break out today. The remainder of this chapter is presented in the context of a peacetime military, but a peacetime military that must be prepared to go to war.

## Population

Although not a criterion per se, the population base from which the military must draw its manpower is an important factor that must be taken into account when choosing a military manpower procurement policy. At any point in time, the "relevant" population base is typically thought of as all able-bodied males (although military service may also be required for women). This is generally males aged 18 to 24, or 18 to 35, or some such age range. Using this population base, for instance, the United States was able to mobilize from less than 500,000 uniformed members in 1940 to more than 12 million in 1945.

While the military can draw from a large population base of the sort described above on a one-time basis, the fact that it is an up-through-the-ranks system means that the military is generally (and practically) limited to a narrower age window when the issue is one of sustaining a military force. In this regard, then, it is useful to think of comparing the military annual accession requirements with the number of young men who turn 18 or 19 years old each year, this being the "relevant" population base.

For the United States, the numbers of 18 year old males increased from about 1.1 million in the mid-1950s to more than 2.1 million by 1980. Indeed, given the relatively large forces maintained in the 1950s, this explains why such a large fraction of the 1950s military aged males and such a small fraction of the 1970s military aged males were required to serve. Because of the "baby bust" in the late 1960s and the 1970s, the number of males turning 18 years old each year will decline to about 1.8 million in the mid-1980s, and to 1.6 million or so during the early 1990s. By the mid to late 1990s, however, the number will once again increase, to somewhere in the neighborhood of 1.8 to 2 million. Thus, the population potentially available to the military will range between 1.6 and 2.1 million for the remainder of this century.

## POLICY OPTIONS

There are essentially three categories of military manpower procurement policies from which to choose: volunteer, selective service, and universal service. A volunteer system is self-descriptive. Selective service and universal service are both forms of conscription, but differ with respect to who is required to serve. Whereas all (or nearly all) of the eligible population is required to serve under a policy of universal service, this is not the case with selective service. With the latter, when the eligible population exceeds the military's requirements for conscripts, only some will be required to serve—hence, the "selective" nature of selective service.

There are, of course, many variations on the three basic military manpower procurement models just outlined. The discussion that follows first describes some of the main variants, and then proceeds with an evaluation of the different kinds of systems potentially available to the United States.

## Military Manpower Procurement Alternatives

To begin with, three types of universal service immediately come to mind: universal military training (UMT), universal military service (UMS), and universal national service (UNS). Under UMT, all qualified individuals in the eligible population (usually male youth) are required to receive military training, except for conscientious objectors who are generally assigned to alternative service. This training can range from just basic military training, to basic training plus individual skill training, to both of these plus some unit training. Upon the completion of such training, those individuals who do not remain in the military would be assigned to the reserve forces (in the case of the United States, the SR and/or the IRR). The period of active service (i.e., training) under UMT could thus range anywhere from as little as 8 or 10 weeks to as much as nine months to a year; the period of reserve service could range from as little as a year to perhaps many years. There are at least two variants of the UMT model: UMT-draft and UMT-volunteer. Under the latter, individuals would be conscripted only for training; the standing forces would be filled by volunteers from the trained conscript pool. Under the UMT-draft model, some of the trained conscript pool could be drafted into the standing forces. This approach is thus a combination of UMT and selective service.

UMS goes one step beyond UMT, in that all qualified eligibles not only receive military training, but also must serve in a substantive capacity in the active military. In order to make productive use of these conscripts, the active duty tour for UMS (including training) probably cannot be less than a year, with two years representing a more reasonable minimum tour length. After this period of active service, UMS conscripts will generally be assigned to some form of reserve service that could last anywhere from one to several years.

UNS is like UMT and UMS in that all qualified eligibles must serve, but differs from these two in one important respect: whereas UMT and UMS conscript individuals to serve in the military, UNS conscripts individuals to perform other public service as well. Individuals can satisfy their obligation by performing either military service or some other public service that is designated as being in the "national interest." The tour length for UNS is typically envisioned as one to two years.

Selective service represents the other main form of conscription. It differs

## AVF vs. Draft: Where Do We Go From Here?

from universal service in that not all eligibles are required to serve. It is the form of conscription used when the size of the qualified and eligible population base exceeds the military's requirements for manpower. In other words, when this situation prevails, the military or its agent (the Selective Service System in the case of the United States) must select only a portion from among the qualified eligibles to serve in the military.

As with universal service, there are many possible variations of the basic selective service concept. We can think of these variations in two dimensions: (1) for what purpose individuals are to be conscripted; and (2) the method of selection used. With respect to the former, conscription can be used to fill (or help fill, as with America's postwar mixed draft-volunteer system) the active forces, the reserve forces, or both. It is typically not necessary to have a reserve draft if a draft is used for the active forces. The reason for this is simply that, when an active forces draft is used, there are usually long queues of individuals waiting to join the reserves (since reserve service typically excuses them from further obligation). There have also been proposals to use selective service to conscript for both the military and public service jobs.

There are, likewise, many different kinds of selection methods. A random process, such as the lottery instituted by the United States in 1969, can be used to select which individuals will be conscripted into the military. Alternatively, deferments and exemptions can be used to channel which individuals will ultimately serve, as was implicitly the case in the United States before the 1969 lottery.

Despite these many possible variations, all selective service systems have one thing in common: they conscript only a portion of the qualified eligibles. Specific versions of selective service differ according to where conscripts are to be used and according to what type of selection process is used.

Finally, volunteer systems, as the name implies, rely on individuals joining the military voluntarily, not because of the threat of punishment. Rather than rely on coercion, volunteer systems rely on other motives, such as monetary incentives, educational incentives, patriotism, job training and experience, a sense of adventure, a chance to "travel and see the world," and so forth.

Although not generically different in the sense of the different conscription models described earlier, three variants of the volunteer force will be examined here: the current AVF, an "improved" AVF, and a "modified" AVF. By current AVF, I mean that the services will proceed along the lines of their present manpower policies, whereas an "improved" AVF means that the military would better adapt itself to the AVF environment. What I mean by a "modified" AVF is a substantial alteration in the basic way that the services operate, such as greatly expanded use of women or civilians or both, or by reduced force sizes. As such, the difference between my "improved" AVF and "modified" AVF is really one of degree, with the changes required for the "improved" version being desirable (at least, from my perspective) as opposed to the less desirable but potentially necessary changes for the "modified" version.

The remaining discussion here focuses on the implications and reasonableness of the various military manpower procurement alternatives just described.

## UMT and UMS

In many ways, there is something intuitively appealing about the concept of universal military service (or training). It would appear to go hand in hand with the notion of the "citizen soldier," which has long been a hallmark of the American system.

For all this, though, UMS and, to a lesser extent, UMT are highly impractical for the United States today. The issue in both cases is simply that there does not appear to be the need for the numbers of military personnel that would be generated by either UMT or UMS. This is most obvious for UMS, but is also probably true for UMT as well.

In the case of UMS, two years is probably the minimum active duty tour length that would be acceptable from a military standpoint. Exclusive of *any* female participation in the armed forces, UMS would thus lead to an armed force of some 3.5 to 6 million members.

The basic question, then, is "what would the United States do with a military force of 4 to 6 million individuals?" Moreover, such a force would be expensive: another $10 to $20 billion per year for manpower alone, not counting the additional expenditures that would have to be made for equipment to effectively use and support this manpower. (This is based on the assumption that only a subsistence wage would be paid to conscripts. The real resource cost would probably be about twice as much.) Given the questionable need for an armed force this size, UMS would appear to be highly wasteful of the nation's resources.

Like UMS, UMT does not appear to be practical for the United States for the foreseeable future. Under UMT, all able-bodied males (and females?) would receive some military training, after which some would be routed to the active forces, some to the Selected Reserves, and the remainder to the IRR. To be effective, such training would, at a minimum, have to include both basic military training and some individual specialty training, which would mean 12 to 16 weeks of training for each UMT conscript. Assuming that the active forces would take about 400,000 new recruits each year, and the Selected Reserves about 100,000, UMT would thus put 600,000 to 1 million newly trained UMT conscripts in to the IRR each year. Assuming a one-year obligation in the IRR for each UMT conscript, and recognizing that 300,000 or so active duty separatees would enter the IRR each year (for one or two years), the IRR would have between 1 and 1.5 million members at any point in time, exclusive of any female participation.

The first question, then, concerns the usefulness of an IRR this size. Even under the most demanding scenarios considered by the Department of Defense (DOD), there does not appear to be a justification for an IRR this large. Moreover, unlike many European countries where territorial defense is paramount, the United States envisions largely an overseas war. The American public historically has not been favorably disposed to overseas military service, and the use of conscription primarily for overseas action would be even less justifiable. Thus, it is precisely for this type of expeditionary force that UMT conscripts (serving in the IRR or its equivalent) are of the least use. Thus, because the greatest value of UMT conscripts lies in territorial defense, UMT does not provide the kind of manpower needed by the U.S. military.

In general, UMT would not appear to be strictly "needed" according to military requirements, but it should be recognized that UMT would help to shore up two areas where the present volunteer force has had some difficulties: the Selected Reserves and the IRR. (It should be noted, though, that there are probably other ways of solving these problems.) Moreover, some would also see UMT as having desirable social consequences insofar as it might act as a way of better integrating military and civilian life.

Finally, although not as expensive as UMS, it should be recognized that UMT would be costly. Training costs alone would probably add another $3 to $6 billion to the defense budget, not counting the additional capital expenditures that would be required to develop the military installations and facilities required to train this volume of new recruits.

In sum, UMT is probably not "needed" in terms of U.S. military requirements, although it can be argued that it could serve some military and social objectives. In the end, the what would appear to be less than entirely convincing advantages must be weighed against the very real shortcomings of UMT.

## Universal National Service (UNS)

As envisioned by its supporters, a national service draft would serve two principal purposes. It would help to supply the manpower required to staff the nation's armed forces; and it would provide a means for utilizing the remainder of young men (and possibly young women) in nonmilitary functions designed to benefit the national purpose.

Philosophically, national service is seen by some as a vehicle for encouraging a new "sense of commitment" to the country—a hoped for result of the direct labor contribution that each young national service participant would make. Ideally, this would be accomplished in part through the "meaningful" activities that would comprise a national service program. Youth would be brought into the mainstream of American society more effectively; and society in general would become better acquainted with the aspirations, needs, and ideas of youth. National service is also seen as a means for encouraging a certain "socialization" process among the nation's youth—specifically, a mixing of individuals from different backgrounds and with different interests that might not otherwise take place under a strictly market economy. Moreover, participants in a national service program would perform a number of tasks and duties that would presumably benefit society as a whole.

National service is also seen by its advocates as having certain practical advantages. Specifically, one only has to look at the very high youth unemployment rates—approaching 30 percent or more for certain minority groups—to see the economic rationale for compulsory national service. Not only would a national service draft reduce youth unemployment rates directly, but a possible side benefit would be decreased future unemployment rates for national service participants—a result of the skills and maturity presumably gained during their period of service. Thus, compulsory national service is seen as a tool for making youth more "employable."

Although the above objectives are clearly laudable, it is important to recognize that they are only a possible outcome of compulsory national service, not a certainty. Indeed, a national service draft could do far worse than the current system in achieving these objectives. For example, resentment among those subject to a national service draft might reduce rather than increase their "sense of commitment" to the country.

Not only are these supposed benefits uncertain, but compulsory national service has some severe shortcomings. First, there is the equity question concerning how national service workers would be distributed among the various national service jobs—especially between military and nonmilitary assignments—given that the distribution of individual preferences would be unlikely to match the distribution of jobs. In general, an excess supply of applicants for nonmilitary assignments would be expected.

Second, a national service draft would be enormously expensive. Total program cost would depend on a number of factors, including the number of young Americans serving in the program (which, in turn, depends on disqualification rates and the extent to which young women would participate), the length of the service commitment, the pay for national service, the costs of accession and training, and the costs of administering the program. Although it is difficult to pinpoint exact costs, in a 1977 essay entitled "A National Service Draft?," I suggested that a men-only national service program of this sort would add an estimated $15 to $25 billion to the federal budget. Including both men and women would about double this figure.

Third, a national service draft would be likely to displace some currently employed workers. Moreover, because national service workers would tend to be less educated, less trained, and less experienced, the individuals most likely to be displaced from their current employment would be the black, the poor, and the undereducated—those with the most difficulty in finding alternative employment offers.

Fourth, the removal of 1.5 to 3 million young men and women from the workforce and/or student rolls for one or more years each could cause possibly severe economic dislocations. For example, since about half of all graduating high school seniors go on to college each year, compulsory national service would create difficult transition problems for the nation's colleges, universities, and trade schools. In addition, the high youth unemployment rates during the 1970s are clearly cause for concern, but the fact that 80 percent or more of those in the youth workforce find employment means that a national service draft would deprive the economy or many productive workers.

Fifth, finding and managing the 1.5 to 3 million jobs needed to support universal national service would be an administrative nightmare. Many, if not most, of these jobs would likely be "make work," since the fact that government and industry do not presently support these kinds of jobs suggests that the value to society of the tasks that would be performed by national service members is less than their cost.

Sixth, there is considerable doubt about how well a program of compulsory national service would work, since the "need" for this type of conscription is unlikely to be seen by many of those subject to this type of conscription. One only has to look back to the Vietnam War to see the effects of an "unpopular" conscription or the lack of a national commitment on the ability to successfully maintain conscription. Whereas the importance of defense may be well recognized by the American public—thus providing a certain credibility for a military draft when needed—drafting for "nonessential" purposes might seriously dilute support for a nonmilitary draft. In other words, the same arguments used to support a military draft—e.g., a youth fighting force and the necessity of defense—cannot be used to justify conscripting young men and women for nonmilitary purposes.

Finally, compulsory national service would also seem to directly contradict the long-held principle of individual freedom. Indeed, for this reason, it is not clear whether a nonmilitary draft is even constitutional.

## Selective Service

From a military perspective, a selective service draft is probably the preferred form of conscription for the United States. By not being forced to accept all (or most) eligibles, the military is able to effect longer average tours than is the case under universal service, thereby increasing the readiness and capabilities of the force relative to universal service. Except for losses due to attrition, selective service typically has had a two-year minimum tour length. Moreover, in order to avoid induction, many individuals who would otherwise not join the military "volunteer" for longer enlistment tours. The reason, of course, is that the individual can have more say about the service he joins, the job he will get in the service, and when and where he will serve. For many, it is worth the additional year or two to realize these benefits. Thus, although a selective service draft is likely to result in higher personnel turnover rates than would be the case for a "well run" volunteer force, its implied turnover rates will be substantially lower than for most types of universal service. This translates directly into improved readiness and a more capable and less expensive force.

A selective service draft also has certain advantages, relative to a volunteer force. First, it is easier to manage, so that military managers are able to devote more attention to matters other than personnel problems. (It should be noted, however, that this frequently results in neglect of personnel problems that are important irrespective of the form of military manpower procurement.) Second, the military is assured of an adequate supply of manpower since it is not subject to the uncertainties of the marketplace. Third, the military is able to realize almost whatever level of quality it believes necessary. Again, it should be noted that this can result in unnecessarily high quality standards that, in reality, benefit neither the services nor the general public.

This assurance of a sufficient quantity and quality of manpower is important, not only for the active forces, but especially so for the reserves, since it is the reserves where the volunteer force has had some of its greatest difficulties. At the same time, it should be emphasized that the reserves are not quite the clearcut "winners" under selective service that some would suppose. Because the reserves become a gentlemanly way to dodge the draft, they have historically been populated by large numbers of affluent and well-educated personnel whose principal reason for being there was to avoid military service. This has made the reserves a less flexible policy option for the President, except under extreme emergency conditions when patriotism would be expected to prevail.

For the most part, though, a selective service draft is more than adequate from a U.S. military perspective—and is certainly preferable to universal service. Indeed, this explains why selective service has been the form of conscription employed when this nation has gone to a draft.

A selective service draft is not without problems, however—and some of them are severe. The problems with this form of conscription center on the equity and economic consequences associated with selective service.

The equity issue was perhaps the most important factor leading to the demise of the postwar draft, and will continue to be a key concern whenever a peacetime draft is seriously considered. There were, and are, two parts to the equity issue: the burden of conscription and the selective way that the burden was (or would be) applied. Those individuals subject to a draft are forced to bear a burden that other members of society are able to avoid. They include, among others, low pay, risk to life and limb, personal hardship, arduous working conditions, and disruption in their personal and working lives.

The issue of inequity arises when these burdens are applied selectively, with the result that only some have to pay, while others escape altogether. In the case of a selective service draft for the U.S. military, the problem is particularly acute, for the vast majority of military-aged youth would never have to serve. For every individual drafted, three or four would not be. No matter how fair or random the selection process itself is in an ex ante sense, there is no escaping the fact that selective service is inequitable ex post—i.e., to those unfortunate enough to be drafted.

A selective service draft turns out to be even more inequitable than implied above, since "who serves when most do not serve?" turns out to be those least able to avoid induction—that is, the poor and the black. Results presented in a 1979 study which I wrote and presented to the Hoover-Rochester Conference on the AVF show that even after the draft reforms implemented in 1969, lower income persons had a much greater chance not only of serving, but of being drafted than did their more affluent counterparts ("Military Manpower Procurement Policy: Equity, Efficiency, National Security"). Thus, selective service runs directly counter to some of this nation's most important social goals.

In addition to being inequitable, selective service is also inefficient. Although a selective service draft appears less expensive in budget terms than a volunteer military, a draft is actually more expensive. The reason for this deceiving appearance is, of course, that many of the costs of a drafted force are hidden from public view, while those of a volunteer force appear in the budget.

A selective service draft has a larger real resource cost for three reasons. First, individuals who have higher valued uses outside the military end up serving in the military. My estimate is that, if we had a lottery selective service today, these "excess economic costs" would amount to between $2 and $3 billion per year. Ironically, the fairer the selection process, the greater is this excess economic cost of the draft. It should be noted, though, that some would argue that the value of having a broader cross section of the population serve would be worth this excess economic cost. Second, enormous resources were (and would be) spent on draft avoidance. Again, my estimate of these "costs of collecting the conscription tax" would amount to several billion dollars today if we had a draft. Third, a draft encourages the military to misallocate its resources, i.e., to use too much labor, relative to capital; too many uniformed personnel, relative to civilians; and too many junior personnel, relative to more senior and productive service members.

Not only is a draft more expensive than a volunteer force in terms of real resource costs, but it provides considerably less leverage over manpower budget costs than is commonly assumed. Even if those in their first two years of service were paid a zero money wage, manpower costs would fall by only about $3 or $4 billion—less than 5 percent of total defense manpower costs. The reason manpower costs are so high is not because of the competitive wage paid to first termers, but because of the large costs of other personnel: career military, civilians, and retired military. Indeed, the draft provides only limited leverage over costs that total 2 or 3 percent of the defense budget, and no leverage over the remaining 97 or 98 percent.

In sum, while a selective service draft is clearly acceptable from a strictly military viewpoint, and would help solve some potential AVF problems, it has severe social and economic problems. And, moreover, it would not help at all (and, in fact, might exacerbate) other manpower problems, such as low retention among the career military.

The same results apply, but not to the same extent, for a reserve-only selective service draft. From a military viewpoint, such a draft would guarantee adequate manpower for the Selected Reserves, and would probably foster some increase in the numbers of recruits "volunteering" for the active forces. But, it would also have adverse economic and social consequences, although not as severe as under a draft for the active forces. The burden would be less for those forced to serve under a reserve draft than under a draft for the active forces and, thus, the inequity would be less. The real question would seem to be whether the minimal gains resulting from the imposition of a reserve draft would be worth the political and social turmoil that such a policy would entail. It would seem not, at least until we gain a better understanding of the role of the reserves, how they are to be trained and managed, but what the options are for manning them.

## Volunteer Force

Despite some specific problems along the way, the first seven years of the All-Volunteer Force generally have proved to be successful. The armed forces have, for the most part, met or came close to their recruiting goals and strengths objectives throughout this period. And, they have done so with reasonably high quality troops that are generally representative of American society.

This success has not been uniform, however. The reserves, for instance, have had more problems than the active forces, and the Army has had more problems than other branches of the armed forces. More significant, and more important, are the problems that lie ahead, for unless the military makes some important improvements and adjustments in the relatively near future, the volunteer force will face some possibly severe problems during the next fifteen years. These potential future problems are mainly attributable to the declining numbers of young men that will reach military age each year until the mid-1990s.

Before addressing these problems, though, let me first outline the present status of the AVF, especially since this in itself has been a source of considerable controversy during the AVF debate. To begin with, despite some modest recruiting problems during the first year of the volunteer force, and again in 1978 and early 1979, the military services have done quite well in meeting their quantitative recruiting objectives for the active forces since the end of the draft.

Quality has been a more controversial issue, with some claiming that quality has fallen off under the AVF, while others claim that quality has improved. An examination of the statistics suggests that quality is about what it was under the draft: the numbers of high school dropouts have increased somewhat since the end of the draft, while the numbers of personnel scoring below average on the mental aptitude exam have decreased. (There is some question about the validity of previously reported test results. Even correcting for possible bias in those earlier reports, the numbers of Mental Category IV entrants is still less than those experienced under the draft.) For the most part, though, quality seems to have held up reasonably well under the volunteer force. It is almost certainly better than it was during the worst part of the Vietnam era, and probably about the same as the pre-Vietnam period. Moreover, quality is certainly better than what the Gates Commission forecast it would be. Their original forecast was that the services might have to accept up to 20 percent category IV personnel.

Perhaps the most controversial AVF issue, however, has been social representation in general, and the racial composition of the forces in particular. Whereas blacks comprised about 10 percent of new recruits during the draft, the figure is now about 20 percent for the armed services as a whole (and about 30 percent for the Army). It is far from clear that the present situation is a problem.

The present racial composition of the forces is largely unrelated to the AVF. Rather, it is due to the fact that larger numbers of blacks are qualifying for military service and to the unusually severe economic prospects faced by blacks in the civilian job market. In other words, the number of blacks in the service would be about the same whether we had a draft or volunteer force, unless, of course, blacks were deliberately discriminated against and not allowed to join.

In addition to race, there has been concern that too few middle and upper class youth are serving in the volunteer force. Here, some of the evidence is contradictory. In December, 1979, Charles Moskos, for example, reported to the Hoover-Rochester Conference on the AVF that while young black recruits appear to be broadly representative of the black population, young white Army recruits tend to come in disproportionate numbers from lower income and less well educated families. My analysis in *Military Manpower and the AVF* (Rand Corporation, 1977) indicates that there is little difference between the draft and volunteer force with respect to the family incomes of those joining the military.

In sum, whereas I would argue that the active forces have fared reasonably well under the AVF in terms of quantity, quality, and representation, there are some important problems with the volunteer force. The three most notable are high attrition among enlisted volunteers, manpower shortages in the reserve forces, and a shortage of physicians. Attrition has improved since 1974, when about 30 percent of all new recruits failed to successfully complete their first tour of duty; nonetheless, this remains a serious problem. The reserve forces likewise appear to have turned the corner, as 1979 marked the first time in nearly a decade that reserve strengths increased (this is because 1978 marked the exit of the last draft-motivated cohort of reservists). Each of these problems has eased somewhat, but each is far from being solved.

The above problems appear small, though, when compared with the broader problems that the military is likely to face in the next fifteen years. The prime recruiting pool will decrease by about 15 percent in the next five years, as noted earlier, and by another 10 percent or so in the 10 years following that. Thus, the military services, which are only just making their recruiting quotas now, clearly face difficult prospects ahead, unless they now take corrective action. Without taking such action, there will be only three choices: (1) substantially reduce quality standards, (2) reduce force sizes, or (3) reinstitute the draft.

How the service might instead respond to these known future recruiting problems is the subject of the discussion below.

**"Modified" AVF.** One way of responding to these impending problems is to substantially alter the composition of the military, by using increased numbers of women and/or civilians. Both "solutions" would enable the military to reduce its enlisted recruiting requirements, but both present possible problems.

In the first instance, the armed forces have, in fact, already increased the numbers of women to a considerable extent. Women made up less than 2 percent of total strength in the early 1970s, but now comprise more than 5 percent, and further increases are planned. Before going much beyond these current plans, though, it will be important to reflect on and learn from the experiences to date.

A greatly expanded use of women implies substantial change in the military and considerable adjustment on the part of those women who would serve. That is, the key to successful use of more women in the armed forces rests in the so-called nontraditional skills. A number of studies have pointed to the potential for increasing the use of women in these areas, but we still have too little experience to understand fully the implications of such change or whether much larger numbers of women will volunteer for these assignments. The last five years clearly have been, and the next five years will be, a period of transition and adjustment with respect to women in the armed forces. The experiment needs to continue, but it would also seem too soon to make major policy change beyond the plans currently envisioned.

An alternative way of solving the problem is to substantially increase the use of civilians in the armed forces. Yet, this too has severe shortcomings. First, the services have, in fact, greatly increased the use of civilians during the past decade. While the services have, perhaps too often, used rotation requirements as an excuse for not civilianizing more military billets, there is a real validity to these arguments. The armed forces, especially in certain occupational specialties, are presently faced with severe rotation base problems—problems which would be made even worse with a wholesale substitution of civilians for uniformed personnel. Second, civilians are about as expensive as military personnel, so there is little to be saved by such an expansion of the DOD civilian workforce. Thus, although there are almost certainly specific areas and functions where an increased use of civilians is probably warranted, the large-scale increase in the use of civilians that would be necessary to offset the military's likely future recruiting problems would probably only exacerbate its present problems, not solve them.

In conclusion, it would seem to be a mistake at this point to base the future success of the volunteer force on a substantial increase in the use of either women or civilians. A substantial increase in the civilian component of the DOD is unlikely to be cost effective. Substantially increasing the use of women, on the other hand, may be wise in the long run, but the actual extent on any such increase must await further knowledge and experience.

**"Improved" AVF.** Whereas the two approaches described above would "solve" future recruiting problems essentially by reducing the numbers of male enlisted personnel, there is an alternative approach that would solve the problem while maintaining male personnel strengths. This solution I refer to as the "improved" AVF. Briefly, the approach is to reduce recruiting requirements by reducing personnel turnover rates, which, in turn, would be accomplished by relying to a greater extent on more senior personnel.

There have been a number of studies over the past five years which indicate that the military still relies far too heavily on first termers to man the forces. Increasing the career force would reduce the size of the first-term force, thus reducing annual recruiting requirements. Both the military and the Congress would seem to be at fault: the military for not adopting the kinds of policies needed to successfully accommodate larger numbers of career enlisted personnel; the Congress for not providing the pay and grade relief needed to affect such a change.

This solution, which I regard as the single most important AVF issue, would also help to solve what I regard as the single most important manpower problem—the shortage of experienced enlisted personnel in today's armed forces. In this regard, it is interesting to reflect back on the original AVF debate. As I read the literature, it seems that one of the principal concerns was whether enough individuals would volunteer for the combat arms. This, in general, has not turned out to be the problem that some originally forecast.

Rather, today's most pressing manpower problem, which would certainly be present under a draft as well, is the shortage of petty officers in the Navy and sergeants in the other services. These are the backbone of our armed forces. Thus, to solve both our future recruiting problems and our present manning problems, greater attention needs to be focused on reenlistments, not just on initial enlistments.

The list of improvements needed, of course, goes beyond this issue. The Services clearly need to be more successful in reducing attrition, for instance. The shortage of personnel in certain areas, and the resulting very long working hours, is clearly detrimental to morale. And there is probably some validity to the concern about recruiting more upper-middle class youth and more individuals with at least some college into the military.

On the whole, these "problems" can probably be solved, or at least the undesirable effects reduced. However, they need to be attacked to be solved.

## CONCLUSIONS

We seem to be at a crossroads now with respect to the volunteer force. Little will likely be done in the near future to change official public policy since, although the draft is likely to be an issue during the next few years, the real debate probably will not occur until the mid-1980s. The options available at that time, however, will be a result of what is done now. For the first eight years, the AVF has muddled through more or less on a "business as usual" basis. Demographics, however, tell us that that will not work as well for the next seven years.

Where do we go from here? To answer this question, we need to make a realistic appraisal, not only of the volunteer force, but also of the alternatives to it. Too much of the recent debate has focused on problems with the AVF, and not enough on the solutions to these problems or on how a return to the draft would "solve" them. To cite an extreme example, the volunteer force has been criticized by some for leading to an IRR that is too small. Yet, are we to reinstitute a draft simply to shore up the IRR? I think not. It is true that a draft would solve certain manpower problems now confronting the Services, such as reserve strength shortages or the shortages of medical doctors. But, a draft would also create new problems—many of them worse than the problems that were solved. Going back to peacetime selective service, for instance, would once again mean all the inequities of that policy. The inequities could be reduced with a universal service draft, but that would be both too costly and not suited to our present military needs.

In short, the volunteer force needs to be examined in the context of what the other alternatives are. From my perspective, the other alternatives do not look as attractive, taking *all* things into account. Yet, we may well be driven to one of these other alternatives since, unless positive steps are taken now to improve the AVF, the volunteer force may have only two possible futures: smaller force sizes or reduced quality. Neither of these may be acceptable.

While this country may well decide to return to a draft at some point in the future, it would be a shame to see that decision forced on us because the volunteer force was mismanaged. Yet, that would appear to be the implication of failing to exact now the improvements needed in present manpower policy.

# Part II:
# Reserve Forces

# Introduction to Part II

Since the end of the Vietnam draft era, the primary focus of force structure policy has been on the problems of the active Army in the establishment of the AVF. Relatively less attention has been given to concomitant problems in the reserve services. The guiding policy of the "Total Force Concept," as enunciated by the Defense Department, asserts that the Active, Guard, and Reserve forces are to be synthesized into "a homogeneous whole." However, the status of Total Force homogeneity and unity today is problematical.

Why are the capability and role of reserve forces vital to the success of the "Total Force Concept" and consequently national security? In concert with current two-contingency planning (one major conflict in Europe and, simultaneously, one minor conflict elsewhere), reserve forces—constituting nearly half of total available forces—must be ready for immediate overseas deployment. Not only must these units mobilize successfully, they must also be adequately trained, equipped, and led to accomplish assigned wartime missions. These units must perform at a standard equivalent to active duty units so that maximum flexibility of employment can be attained.

Given the problems of the AVF presented in Part I, the correlative question centers on the capability of the reserves to perform assigned tasks. In attempting to answer that question, the authors in Part II present an excellent overview of the reserve forces as well as a provocative contribution to the growing literature on reserve readiness. In providing perspectives on the historical background of reserve forces, on current programs to address reserve manning and training problems, and some judgments on the capabilities of these forces, they offer a variety of methodological approaches and proposals. The core issue is the critical shortage of personnel in the Individual Ready Reserves and, in particular, the Selected Reserves. While more recent trends indicate some prospect of meeting quantitative goals, meeting and defining other goals appears uncertain and complicated.

Chapter 7

# Historical Continuity in the U.S. Military Reserve System*

Robert L. Goldich

This chapter sketches the historical continuity of major aspects of the U.S. military reserve structure from its English antecedents to the present, and seeks to relate this continuity to post-World War II policy proposals for major restructuring of the reserves. It is oriented toward army reserves and militia and makes no mention of naval and air reserves, since the personnel requirements of the manpower-intensive army have always determined the overall military manpower policy of the United States. Reserve manpower, per se, is more important for armies than for navies and air forces, whose resources are measured primarily in terms of ships and aircraft, and which are equipment-intensive rather than manpower-intensive.

## THE ENGLISH MILITIA TRADITION

U.S. military reserve policies and the attitudes which led to them are outgrowths of England's military tradition of manning its armies with locally-raised contingents commanded by the local nobility or gentry. This system was a direct result of feudal relationships and responsibilities, when nobles maintained their own armed forces to serve in royal military ventures as part of their theoretical obligations to the Crown (and to expand and protect their own political and economic interests as well). The great nobles' subordinate vassals,

---

*"Historical Continuity in the U.S. Military Reserve Systems" by Robert L. Goldich is reprinted from *Armed Forces and Society* Vol. 7, No. 1 (Fall 1980) pp. 88-112 by permission of the Inter-University Seminar on Armed Forces and Society and of the Publisher, Sage Publications, Inc.

themselves nobles, were in turn subject to service in their own right.[1] Concurrent with this type of obligatory military service was the idea of the feudal levy on all freemen for home defense purposes. This was a militia (more and more bourgeois in nature as medieval gave way to early modern times) led not as much by great nobles as by lesser members of the nobility and the bourgeois gentry classes. Its purpose was home defense against invasion (it was an army of such militia that Elizabeth I reviewed at Tilbury in 1588, brought together to resist an invasion of England threatened by the approach of the Spanish Armada), coupled with some liability for expeditionary service abroad, depending on the temper of the times (and consequent interpretation of statutes and responsibilities and the extent to which manpower was needed).[2] The compulsory service that was irregularly levied on militia members and others—almost always members of the lower classes and, frequently, those not gainfully employed or who were otherwise indigent—did not vitiate the basic principles of de facto voluntarism and de jure localism in militia recruiting and service.[3]

These principles had the effect of providing both the "regular" and "reserve" forces of England with a political and social base and structure virtually independent of the central government. The "regular" forces were made up of those on active service for the purpose of prosecuting military ventures of the Crown. Standing regular forces were first maintained—other than a few royal household troops and guards—after the Restoration, 1660 during the reign of Charles II. Those forces on active duty in the service of the Crown could only be raised with the cooperation of local civilian leaders who often filled all but the highest military offices as well. The reserves—or militia—were commanded, trained, and frequently armed through the efforts of those same local elites.[4] These elites in turn secured their power more through their own status and achievements in their communities—primarily through ownership of land—than through the beneficence and patronage of the Crown. In an institutional sense, therefore, military power flowed from individual communities to the Crown, rather than from the Crown to the individual communities.

As the course of English military and political history resulted in a militia whose power was independent of the central government, the course of English constitutional and social history resulted in a civilian population largely independent of, and often hostile to, even the constrained and community-based military institutions that had developed in England. By the latter half of the sixteenth century, England already had powerful traditions of local autonomy and civil and political liberty underpinned by the incorporation of these traditions into the Crown's own attitudes and political instruments. Tudor and early Stuart autocracy was greatly tempered and restrained by pluralistic institutions whose role in English society was not to become fully apparent until the English Civil War and later. The security from invasion guaranteed by England's island status freed the Crown, and the English people, from the pressure of maintaining large standing forces backed up by large militias manned in large part by compulsion, and hence enabled the liberal-democratic tradition of voluntarism and localism in military affairs to flourish.[5] These feelings were exacerbated, as so many historians have pointed out, by Cromwell's military dictatorship, but they were integral to English popular belief and conventional wisdom long before the Commonwealth and Protectorate of 1649-1660.[6]

The effects of all this on the militia were mostly undesirable from a technical point of view. There was no structural integration of standing regular forces with the militia. Recruiting, command, organization, and training (such as it was) were separate. The results of this separation for the militia included inadequate individual and unit training proficiency, incapacity of officers to lead and men to follow, and casual attitudes toward discipline—among both officers and men—related directly to the popularity of the cause for which the militia was under arms, and the vigor and rigor of any regular commanders present. Particularly pernicious, from the point of view of military efficiency, was the entrusting of military command to civilian leaders whose political qualifications included little military training and often involved corruption. Their adjudicatory, get-along-by-going-along attitudes, so appropriate for a (comparatively) liberal society, usually precluded the toughness and ruthlessness necessary in war, whether on the battlefield or behind a desk.[7]

The military inadequacy of the English militia system is not subject to much dispute. The period from the ascent of Elizabeth I to the throne through the Restoration—i.e., of early American colonization—is replete with examples of the inability of the English militia system to meet the military demands placed on it, and of the enormous waste and inefficiency with which it met those demands. Examples can be drawn from English armies sent to Ireland or the Continent,[8] those raised to meet threats from Scotland,[9] or those assembled to repel possible seaborne invasion.[10] That this system survived and was not supplanted by the beginnings of a standing army supplemented by a conscription-supported militia system was due mostly to the lack of sustained land-based military threats capable of direct assault on the independence and territorial integrity of the British Isles. Only the large manpower requirements for both standing and militia forces generated by such threats would have been capable of creating a climate favorable to a reexamination of England's traditional belief in the local organization and mostly voluntary recruitment of military manpower.

# THE COLONIAL AMERICAN MILITIA TRADITION

English colonists came to North America with the concepts of local militia recruitment and voluntary military service firmly implanted in their minds. However, the initial military threats they faced were far greater than those of the mother country. The initial increments of colonists were few in number, their ignorance of their new land profound, and their vulnerability to assault from native inhabitants great. The militia concept, actively implanted and rigidly enforced, was healthy and vigorous during the first decades of colonization after 1607. It may be that an effective militia ensured the survival of European colonization in North America during the early years, saving the tiny European communities from total annihilation in the most ferocious (in terms of casualties as a percentage of total population) Indian wars in American history.[11]

American colonial militia were structured in accordance with three major concepts: local recruiting, frequently including the election of officers; short active duty for immediate threats only; and territorial restrictions on service when called to active duty. Militia units were theoretically composed of all able-bodied men in a particular settlement of jurisdiction, but were subsequently divided into two classes—this larger manpower pool; and a more specialized group who out of special interest, capacity, or ability were able to spend more time on both military training and on active duty. Officers were civilian leaders occupying positions of trust, responsibility, and authority in the community. The drastic social and economic consequences of mobilizing the militia—both the entire adult male population *and* the smaller pool of more vigorous volunteer militia—prevented its use in active service for long periods of time or for purposes other than meeting short-term threats to the immediate welfare of the community, with a few wartime exceptions. The profound attachments of the colonists to their local regions and individual colonies, plus the above mentioned unwillingness to serve for a long period of time, resulted in considerable territorial restrictions on militia active duty. Units were generally not subject to compulsory service outside their own colony (some colonial militia statutes made exceptions "for stipulated periods in special circumstances"); and some were frequently fractious when forced to venture far from their own jurisdictions within a colony.[12]

The colonial militia was thus strong during the first part of the seventeenth century because the immediacy of the threat made organizational shortcomings comparatively unimportant. As the frontier was pushed farther inland, the militia system atrophied in the major population centers of British North America. Compulsory military drill became less and less frequent, finally becoming either a dead letter or a mostly social occasion in many settlements far behind the line of contact between white man and Indian. These same population centers were little inclined to provide military or financial assistance to more threatened peoples on the edge of the westward expansion of European colonization, save when actual emergencies occurred.

At the core of this popular attitude—and the willingness of political leaders to abide by it—was the instinctive recognition that the Indians, no matter what the effects of their depredations on individual settlers and frontier communities, could no longer make English colonization as a whole untenable. Even King Philip's War of 1675-1677, called New England's "worst Indian war of the seventeenth century" by one historian, illustrates this.[13] Although "Under the pressure of Indian attack the whole outer line of English settlement had crumbled,"[14] the majority of New England colonists were inside this line and were never touched directly by the war. The balance of population shifted permanently and decisively in favor of the colonists very early in the colonial period—probably no later than 1650, and certainly no later than 1765.[15] The favorable population balance was supported by superior technology and organization, plus the relative unity of the colonies when compared to the Indian tribes.

Similarly, the various Franco-British wars fought in North America during 1689-1763, although they brought great suffering to some British frontier settlements, in no way threatened the survival of British North America. Even the halfhearted and usually-bungled colonial and joint expeditions against Canada pressed the French to the utmost; the superior leadership, strategy and organization of the French barely sufficing to check the lumbering and inefficient forces of Britain and her colonies. It was the British and their colonies who mounted efforts, no matter how inept, against New France. They finally succeeded in 1763; allowing no major French expeditions to drive into the heart of British North America by land, or to assault the major cities of the eastern coast by sea. In failing to create a standing force and corollary militia system with more potential, therefore, the British colonists were, in fact, demonstrating a clear, if unconscious grasp of the extent to which British North America was secure from serious threats to its survival.[16]

A further reason for the decline of the militia system was the social structure found in the colonies. Transplanted Englishmen and immigrants from other nations felt bound by few of the obligations and traditions of class that their predecessors in Britain and the Continent felt. America rapidly evolved a national social ethos under which the majority of the population defined itself as middle class and maintained the political and social attitudes of members of that class in Britain, regardless of the actual extent of social and economic stratification in American society. Americans exercised suffrage, enjoyed freedoms and options broader than those found anywhere else in the world, and fortified traditional British concepts of liberty with frontier exuberance and egalitarianism. Accordingly, they appropriated as the rights of all men the choices and privileges regarding military service that had belonged to only a minority of the population, and lacked a class concept to continue the noblesse oblige basis of much military service performed by the British nobility and gentry.[17] The only obligation to perform military service that remained intact was that of necessity, and their strategic situation guaranteed that necessity would arise only infrequently after the mid-seventeenth century—in the Continental European sense, it would arise hardly at all.

In opting for a military manpower system under which they sacrificed military efficiency (the American militia suffered from the same ills as its English predecessor) and the military security of some of their fellows (those on the edge of the frontier) for what they perceived as general liberty and freedom from unnecessary military coercion and military presence in society, the residents of British North America were blending their own English heritage with colonial circumstances. The former gave them belief in autonomous local militias and basically voluntary recruiting for both standing forces and regularly-trained reserves. The latter reinforced these traditions in a radical direction through near-absolute security from direct attack for most of the population and a militant egalitarianism. Almost all of these qualities and results, if not the geopolitical circumstances, remain part of the American military tradition to the present day.

# THE EXPULSION OF EUROPEAN POWER, 1775-1815

If the legitimacy of the militia system described in the preceding section was enhanced by surviving the colonial wars of 1607-1763, it is not surprising that it was burned into the military fiber of the new nation after surviving the tumultuous period from 1775 to 1815. It is instructive to enumerate the military actions of the United States during this period. They include the successful waging of the Revolutionary War during 1775-1783; the civil disturbances which ultimately led to Shays' Rebellion in 1786-1787; the Whiskey Rebellion of 1794; the quasi-war with France in 1798-1800; the War of 1812, during 1812-1815; and numerous Indian wars and campaigns during this entire period. When actual fighting or deployment preparatory to fighting was not taking place, the infant U.S. government had to worry about the British presence in Canada and the Mississippi and Ohio valleys; the Spanish presence in the Southwest and Florida; and the Spanish and French presence in territories that became known as the Louisiana Purchase. At the conclusion of the Revolution, we were surrounded by at best indifferent and often hostile powers. Forty years later, we had not altered one iota our steadfast adherence to local militia, voluntary recruiting, and rigid restrictions on time and geography in terms of the militia's active service. We had won one war (the Revolution) and drawn another tactically and emerged victorious strategically and geopolitically (the War of 1812). There were no European powers left in positions of strategic importance in North America save the British in Canada and an impotent Spain (soon to lose Florida in 1819). We had broken the back of any Indian tribes east of the Mississippi capable of threatening the major patterns of European westward expansion.[18]

The American militia system was codified in the militia-related clauses of the Constitution in 1789, at the beginning of this formative period of American military history. It is worth quoting at length Russell F. Weigley's interpretive summary of these clauses:

> [Congress] might call the state militias into federal service "to execute the laws of the union, suppress insurrections and repel invasions." It might "provide for organizing, arming, and disciplining the militia, and for governing such part of them as may be employed in the service of the United States." ...
>
> ... the Constitution also divided military power between the federal government and the states. The states retained their historic militias, with authority to appoint their officers and conduct their training (although Congress might prescribe the system under which training was to be conducted, and although no state might keep up troops without the consent of Congress). The militias might be called into federal service only for limited purposes, "to execute the laws of the union, suppress insurrections and repel invasions." The Second Amendment further guaranteed the status of the militia by declaring: "A well-regulated militia being necessary to the security of a free state, the right of the people to keep and bear arms shall not be infringed."
>
> ... the Constitution . . . retained the dual military system bequeathed to the United States by its history: a citizen soldiery enrolled in the state militias, plus a professional army of the type represented by the British army or, more roughly, the Continential Army.[19]

The Militia Act of 1792 (1 Stat. 271, ch. 33; Act of May 8, 1792) provided implementing legislation for these constitutional provisions. It provided that all free white males between 18 and 45 who were physically fit be members of the militia; required militiamen to equip themselves with personal weapons and equipment; prescribed tactical units from company to division; stated that no militia members could be called to federal service by the President for more than three months in any one year; and required that all members must be called in "due rotation with every other able-bodied man of the same rank."[20] The strict interpretation of the limits of Federal power in training the militia and time and geographical limitations on service ensured that the militia would be poorly disciplined, trained, and organized. The constitutional provision reserving appointment of officers to the states ensured that civil leadership and political connections—rather than any kind of proven military or executive capability—would remain the primary qualifications for militia officer status. Inevitably, the universality of militia obligations soon became a dead letter, and organized militia units were those who voluntarily trained and drilled. These volunteer militia units were better than nothing, but fell far short of what even strict implementation of the loose provisions of the 1792 Act would have resulted in.[21]

"Judged by standards of military efficiency, the act indeed lacked much," even if judged by standards of what was realistic in the American political and social context of the 1790s, it may have been all that was possible.[22] The central question, therefore, is how the United States managed to eliminate or neutralize the military threats it faced during 1775-1815 without altering its loosely organized, minimally-effective militia system. It is not enough to note the powerful force of traditional Anglo-American military ideas; tradition bows to circumstance if enough pressure is applied.

The pressure in this case would have been military pressure. That enough of it was not applied—that the Republic was never in enough danger to warrant the creation of a more centralized and rigorous militia system—was due to circumstances having little to do with events and ideas within the United States. First there was the overwhelming distance between North America and Europe and between points in North America. When all other factors are removed, it is hard to avoid the conclusion that if North America had been as close to Great Britain as the Continent, or North America as small as a European nation, the rebellious colonies (or, in 1812-1815, the United States) would have been defeated regardless of domestic opposition within Britain, technological limitations of the era, or European co-belligerents of the Americans.[23]

Second was the preoccupation of Europe in general and Great Britain in particular with the wars of the French Revolution and Empire during much of the period in question. Had Great Britain been able to bring its full military power to bear against the United States during the entire War of 1812, instead of only its last few months (after the abdication of Napoleon and defeat of France in April 1814), a drawn conflict could easily have been a lost one. Furthermore, both France and Spain might have been inclined toward more involvement in North American affairs were it not for their preoccupation with their own wars of 1793-1815.

This lack of military pressure, combined with traditions and beliefs, made the Revolutionary War and War of 1812 experiments with a more systematic and compulsory use of the militia feeble indeed. The lack of effective central authority, the resurgence of antimilitary sentiment engendered by the events of 1763-1775,[24] and probably the presence of sufficient neutralists, Tories, and practical apathetics prevented the effective imposition of systematic conscription of all available able-bodied men into the militia during the Revolution. Eventually, however, the pressures of war forced most states—at the request of the Continental Congress—to conscript men serving in the already-existing state militias into the Continental Army, according to state quotas assigned by Congress, but through conscription machinery administered by the individual states. Response to this system was unenthusiastic and spotty, and it did not solve the never-ending recruiting and strength problems of the Continental Army.[25] Revolutionary War conscription, such as there was of it, represented a continuation of Anglo-American militia traditions—and their ineffectuality in time of major emergency—in the face of harsh realities, rather than a new and more forceful response to those realities.[26]

During the War of 1812, after the fall of Washington in 1813 and the realization later in that year that the impending defeat of Napoleon would free British forces for use in North America, the Madison administration proposed that the militia—defined by the Act of 1792 as all able-bodied white males ages 18-45—be classified according to age and condition and be subject to conscription for two years. The Congress accepted different versions of Madison's legislative proposal, preserving and actually strengthening its basic thrust. It died in House-Senate conference committee in late 1814, however, when the 1814 campaigning season was over and American forces had successfully muddled through due to time, space, and luck. Peace a few weeks later, in early 1815, ended consideration of the matter. "The topic of conscription disappeared with it, for half a century."[27]

It is hard to avoid the conclusion that the United States avoided establishing more rigorous militia mobilization procedures and obligations by the skin of its teeth during 1775-1815. Certainly the United States, by adopting the Constitution, had shown itself capable of adopting a more rigorous, powerful, and centralized civil authority than that which had ever existed before in British North America or during the first thirteen years of independence. In addition, although the United States showed little inclination to establish national military institutions before, during, and immediately after the Revolution, this attitude changed drastically during the late 1780s and 1790s. The country, which, after the conclusion of peace with Great Britain, had reduced the Army to 80 men at one point (raising it to 700 a day later), had established by 1803, in response to generally perceived national security requirements, the following military infrastructure.:

> A chain of forts along the northern and western frontier manned by an army of 2,500-odd officers and men; frigates, navy yards, and a marine corps; arsenals at Springfield, Massachusetts, and Harpers Ferry, Virginia, as well as storehouses for supplies at various other locations; coast forts along the seaboard from Maine to Georgia; a newly-formed military academy at West Point, New York; and a group of agencies in Washington to administer the whole.[28]

The extent to which this miniscule military establishment represented a radical departure from previous American conditions is itself indicative of North America's isolation from real military threats and the United States' preceding 180 years of military history. That it had been established at all, however, represented a major adaptation to the circumstances of national independence by a newly-formed nation. It can be posited, therefore, that, had more trying times warranted it, more centralized control of the militia and compulsory military service (active or reserve, depending on circumstances of peace or war) could very well have been established. The nation's political and military institutions and constitutional interpretations were inchoate enough that miltary pressure threatening the very survival of the country could easily have enshrined compulsory military service in time of war, and a nationally-uniform and centrally-administered militia, as parts of the American military tradition, rather than their opposites.[29]

By 1815, geographical isolation and a good deal of luck had provided the United States with 40 years of history which appeared to validate the continuation of the local militia tradition and of voluntary military service. If the militia system worked in the face of numerous wars, smaller fights, and military-diplomatic conflicts with the Great Powers of Europe, why change it? The local militia tradition and voluntarism had survived the formative years of the Republic, and it would be almost a century before that tradition was bent even slightly to accommodate changing circumstances.

## STRATEGIC ISOLATION, 1815-1898

If a better-organized militia less dependent on local and popular whims would have been useful indeed during 1775-1815, a case can be made that such a militia was almost totally unnecessary during the rest of the nineteenth century. The subjugation and pacification of major Indian tribes east of the Mississippi removed almost completely, in the post-War of 1812 period, the need for military reserves capable of rapid response to immedate internal threats.[30] Militiamen were needed only on the frontier, if at all; since most of the population was well in the rear of the danger zone. The major Indian tribes west of the Mississippi never seriously threatened settlement of the frontier; the floodtide of westward expansion had grown too large by the mid-nineteenth century to do anything but overwhelm the Plains, Northwest, Southwest and Pacific tribes, regardless of the hardships inflicted on individual settlers.[31] Furthermore, the Regular Army had grown in size and capacity—regardless of theoretical inadequacies in strength, training, and funds—and was much more capable of assuming Indian policing duties than the incredibly tiny pre-1812 force.[32]

European military power had either been expelled or voluntarily withdrawn and European ambitions in North American effectively neutralized by 1812 (even though the extent of this European retreat was not yet fully apparent to the Europeans, especially the British, at the time). After 1812, there was increasing accommodation with Britain/Canada, despite occasional war scares and periods of tension. This accommodation resulted essentially from a progressive acceptance by Great Britain of the strategic superiority of the Unites States within the North American continent and periphery. The growing population and industrial power of the United States made potential American military power very substantial, given the geographical obstacles faced by European powers in conducting effective military and naval operations against the United States. The replacement of disunited provinces with a cohesive central government also removed the basic organizational and institutional obstacles that had prevented the colonies of British North America from seizing Canada before and during the Revolution. No longer could Canada feel relatively secure because of the internal disunity of its intrinsically far more powerful southern neighbor.[33] Mexico never posed a real threat to the United States and was reduced to total impotence by the war of 1846-1848.

In general, therefore, the overwhelmingly favorable effects of geographical isolation on the American strategic situation were no less operative in the nineteenth century than they had been before. Effective deployment of European expeditionary forces to North America was still very difficult (as the French incursion into Mexico in 1863-1867 demonstrated). Shielded by the oceans, American military institutions continued in their established pattern after 1815, interrupted only by two foreign wars against grossly inferior opponents, campaigns against neolithic tribes the prosecution of which suffered as much from the lack of real ruthlessness on the part of the government and the Army as from Indian fighting skills, and by one cataclysmic civil war whose unique nature and obvious never-to-recur status made it a poor model, in the eyes of the public, for military institutions.[34]

Accordingly, the United States had no pressing need for a large military establishment, including effectively mobilizable reserves, during the nineteenth century. A quasi-police force to deal with the Indians, a small cadre for border control, and the retention of military-institutional memory was sufficient. Throughout the nineteenth century, the United States military mobilization system proved fully capable of meeting whatever military requirements the international or domestic situation levied on it—in the Indian wars, in the Mexican War, and in the Spanish-American War. The Civil War, by definition, was almost impossible to plan for in any way. The problems caused by the smallness of the nation's regular forces, and the ineffectuality and smallness of its militia in 1861 would merely have been replaced by new ones had we possessed a larger standing army and a centrally-controlled militia. Both would probably have done little more than provide the Union and Confederacy with greater initial military capacity, as the standing army disintegrated along regional lines and local militia contingents gave their allegiance to the active Union or Confederate forces, depending on their location.[35]

The United States, therefore, was occasionally hampered in its military efforts throughout the nineteenth century due to the continued existence of the local militia tradition, the practical atrophy of the organized militia by the middle of the century, and the maintenance of an extremely small and voluntarily-recruited regular force. It would be difficult to argue that the country was threatened by its lack of effective militia and its voluntary service tradition, or by its small standing force, as could have been argued for the 1775-1815 period. As far as coordinating military policy with geopolitical realities is concerned, the United States would be fortunate if its military policy always accorded so well with its strategic situation.

## FROM 1898 TO THE PRESENT

The Spanish-American War of 1898 and the colonial acquisitons that it engendered are often cited as providing the impetus for major reforms in U.S. military organization and structure during the first two decades of the twentieth century. Actual impulses for such reform came earlier. During the latter part of the nineteenth century, the growth of American economic power and the increasing efficiency of transportation and communications led military analysts and other observers to realize that the United States would become more involved in international politics whether it wanted to or not. Many such analysts and observers, as well as segments of the public, were caught up in prevailing ideologies of imperialism, social Darwinism as a model for international politics, and racial/ethic/national superiorities so prevalent among justifications for European military institutions. It was felt that without similar institutions, the United States could not be a true world power.[36] In social terms, also:

> The era of insouciant wastefulness, planlessness, and *laissez faire* was about to die, and public reaction to the management of the Spanish War heralded the approach of muckraking and progressivism. A middle class that would soon grow intolerant of the wasting of human lives in slums, tenements, and anthracite fields was already unwilling to tolerate a waste of lives in which its own sons were involved, as they were in the regiments of the [Spanish-American War] volunteer army.[37]

Specifically, there was a desire on the part of military reformers to emulate the massive conscription systems and reserve obligations that the Continental European powers had developed (under Prussian tutelage, example and involuntary pressure) in the post-1871 era. Under these systems, men were drafted into the active army and involuntarily assigned to specific reserve mobilization billet upon release from active duty, with their reserve training obligations varying according to the needs of the army. This ensured that the reserves were filled exclusively by persons with prior active military service. It provided an orderly, manageable flow of trained personnel into the reserves; generated large numbers of individual reservists available for use upon mobilization; and fully integrated the active army with the reserves. To provide partial or complete American equivalent capabilities, suggestions were made by interested Americans during the pre-World War I period for universal military service and/or training; large-scale and possibly compulsory reserve officer training of college men; and comprehensive unification of the state militias with the Federal armed forces and/or the reduction in the importance of the former through the creation of large, purely Federal reserve forces.[38]

All of these proposals came to nothing for a variety of reasons. Perhaps the most important was that the United States faced few if any threats in North America requiring such massive army reserves and a concomitant radical restructuring of the militia system—possibly one with major constitutional problems. In addition, there was no indication before World War I that we would be called upon to deploy a truly massive military force overseas on short notice—i.e., one which could not be duly assembled and trained in the usual fashion of volunteerism perhaps supplemented by some form of conscription, all put into effect after the outbreak of war—and no survival-related strategic need existed for such a deployment.

The state militia—by now known as the National Guard—had an independent political and social base and was not about to be totally subsumed into, or completely bypassed by, the federal military structure. The Civil War state volunteer system—although probably more analogous to the conscript forces raised by the United States during both world wars—had been appropriated by the National Guard as a validation of its organization premise. The victories of the Spanish-American War (no matter how ineptly won) had done so more recently in the eyes of the National Guard. Finally, the need of the country for a force capable of supressing civil disturbances was apparent in the face of the industrial violence of the late nineteenth and early twentieth centuries, as was the continuing antipathy of the American people toward any kind of domestic paramilitary force maintained exclusively for such purposes.

Finally, the United States had not shed its intense distrust and dislike of a major military presence in American society and of compulsory military service, nor had its comfort with the dual state-federal nature of the National Guard abated.[39] The arrival of large numbers of immigrants from European countries where onerous conscription policies had existed reinforced these feelings.

Clearly, however, the colonial acquisitions of the post-1898 era, and the greater American involvement in international politics resulting from the nation's greater industrial potential and the improvements in transportation and communications, required a larger and more effective military force and a somewhat more centralized and rigorous reserve system than that of the pre-1898 army and militia. Consequently, two decades of intermittent controversy after the Spanish-American War saw a compromise reached between the advocates of a Continental European system and those of the status quo. The basic framework was provided by three statutes enacted by the Congress over a 17-year period: the Dick Act of 1903 (33 Stat. 775, ch. 196; Public Law 33, 57th Congress; Act of January 21, 1903); the National Defense Act of 1916 (39 Stat. 166, ch. 134; Public Law 85, 64th Congress; Act of June 3, 1916); and the

National Defense Act of 1920 (41 Stat. 759, ch. 227; Public Law 242, 66th Congress; Act of June 4, 1920). The results, in broad terms, of these three public laws for the reserve forces were the following:[40]

- A large voluntarily-recruited standing force, in terms of proportion of the total population of the United States, but smaller than those of Continental Europe.
- The establishment of wholly federal reserve forces, primarily with support, specialist, and technical missions, while ground combat reserve forces remained almost wholly the responsibility of the National Guard.
- Increased federal control of and involvement in, as well as financial support for, National Guard training, organization, and equipment, and increased National Guard liability for federal service, without lessening the state militia responsibilities of the National Guard.
- Establishment of a Reserve Officers Training Corps program with a stated mission of producing reserve commissioned officers, but not a program for all colleges and universities on a completely compulsory basis.

When superficialities are stripped away, it can be seen that this system, firmly established by 1920, has survived to the present day. The United States has a large standing army, but one much smaller than might be expected, given our role in international politics and the military strength of potential adversaries. We have a peacetime all-volunteer force. We have an Army Reserve composed overwhelmingly of combat support and combat service support units, and an Army National Guard composed of combat and front-line combat support units, and containing almost all of the combat units of brigade size or larger in the Army Reserve components.[41] We have close federal control over the personnel management, organization, training, and equipment of the National Guard, but no diminution of its availability and responsibility for state militia service.

The 1948-1973 period of post-World War II "peacetime" conscription in the United States in no way fundamentally changed this system. The draft was superimposed on the traditional militia and volunteer system, not integrated into it. Volunteers continued to be recruited for both the active forces and the reserves; all services and components continued to compete in the marketplace for recruits. The draft was used only to make up a deficit of volunteers, rather than to systematically allot national manpower resources according to the needs of the armed forces. Consequently, neither the introduction nor the end of peacetime conscription in the United States materially affected the basic nature of the U.S. reserve structure.[42]

The system described above retained the same deficiencies that had plagued the militia system, albeit to a lower degree. Reserve forces remained quantitatively and qualitatively inadequate in terms of training and equipment, particularly in the case of an adequate number of physically fit and professionally competent middle-grade and senior officers.[43] That the system survived both world wars was, once again, the result of time and space. Rapid and effective mobilization was not required for national survival and the maintenance of the territorial integrity of the United States against ground invasion; the country faced no direct threat to the homeland. The United States also sustained light casualties during the initial stages of both world wars, obviating the need for a large pool of trained individual reservists to replace casualties and support initial force expansion before enough draftees and/or volunteers could be made available.

## THE POST-1945 ANOMALY IN U.S. RESERVE STRUCTURE

After World War II, for the first time in American history, the probability of the immediate engagement of massive U.S. ground forces in the event of general war—a NATO/Warsaw Pact conflict in Europe and adjacent areas—became an integral part of U.S. military doctrine as the result of U.S. forward deployments in Europe. These deployments were deemed necessary to enable U.S. and other NATO forces to successfully defend Western Europe without being forced to escalate to a strategic nuclear exchange, and to prevent Soviet seizure of Western Europe and consequent dominance of the North Atlantic, with the major threat to North America that such Soviet acquisitions would pose.[44]

A corollary of this scenario is that a major war between NATO and the Warsaw Pact in Europe, the Mediterranean, and the North Atlantic, with ancillary air and naval action worldwide, would require massive and rapid manpower mobilization, principally to meet the Army's requirements for ground combat replacements and force expansion. Without such rapid mobilization, NATO would have insufficient theater-based warfighting capability to hold Western Europe against a Soviet assault.[45]

There is little doubt that the traditional Continental Europe conscription-based reserve system is much better suited to rapid mobilization than the Anglo-American locally-based, voluntarily-recruited, and separately-managed and structured reserve system. Such systems have a proven capability of delivering immense numbers of trained reservists to replacement depots and cadred units under desperate circumstances and at high speed. Thus, for the first time, there is an apparent contradiction between the military policy of the United States and the country's fundamental strategic situation. Given this contradiction, one might assume that the United States would have at least seriously considered shifting to some features of a Continental European conscription-based reserve system, particularly during the 1948-1973 period of conscription, and especially at the height of the Cold War.

The basic underlying reason why the United States did not change its military reserve policies in this manner—or even come close to doing so—is the general unwillingness of nations to change their military manpower policies overnight just because their geopolitical situation changes. This is particularly true in a democracy where interest-group politics and a free exchange of ideas are allowed to take place on national defense as well as all other issues. The United States has survived several major wars with a local militia system based wholly or substantially on voluntary recruitment in peacetime. Consequently, a national belief in a social contract expressed, on one side, in the form of compulsory military service has not developed; and the independent political and social base of the reserves has survived enormous social, economic, and technological change.[46] This might have changed somewhat during the 1775-1815 period or the Civil War, but it did not. The wars of those periods were won or drawn with variations of the militia system. Without a *sustained* threat in both peace and war requiring more rapid and extensive mobilization than the militia system could provide, a more rigorous reserve mobilization system probably would have atrophied anyway, once the immediate threat that engendered it had abated.

In any case, the current U.S. reserve system is by no means such a complete liability as some of its more extreme critics state. Even if many if not most reserve units cannot mobilize and deploy as quickly as current strategy requires, this does not mean that the current reserve force structure is useless. Reserves are a vital edge as a mobilization cadre for a long-term conflict; any trained military member is more useful than an untrained civilian. Planned short wars often, if not usually, become unplanned long ones. Furthermore, substantial incremental improvements in the responsiveness of the reserves have been made in recent years, within the broad framework of localism and voluntarism this chapter has described.[47]

In particular, the National Guard as a state militia meets a continuing requirement for powerful armed forces capable of coping with civil disturbances and disorders within the United States, such as the racial conflicts and political demonstrations of the 1950s through the present. Such a force is essential in a geographically large, ethnically and racially diverse, and heavily privately-armed country such as the United States. Equally essential, in the eyes of the American people, is the avoidance of a national police of paramilitary force maintained solely for this purpose. Public attitudes favor the use of the National Guard for control of civil disorders. Use of the active Army is a much more drastic measure and viewed as such, although uniforms, procedures, weapons, and organizations are absolutely identical. Despite the transition of the United States from agrarian ministate to industrialized superpower, the Guard remains the local militia, and the active Army the force of the central government, as was the case 200 years ago. The blending of the two for national defense purposes and their continued separation for domestic order purposes represents a triumph of American democracy not often recognized as such.

## IMPLICATIONS FOR POLICY

This survey of the historical continuity of the U.S. reserve system from its English medieval roots to the present has illustrated one aspect of the fact that a nation's military manpower system reflects its entire history, culture, and especially its geographical and strategic circumstances. Economists and quantitative analysis specialists, who dominate the ranks of military manpower analysts and policymakers in the United States (especially within the Department of Defense and particularly in the Office of the Secretary of Defense), repeatedly fail to take this into account in their work and policy proposals. This is especially true in the case of the reserves, an area of military manpower policy where the military interacts very closely with the civilian population and civilian ideas. Thus, in the name of efficiency, there have been proposals within the past two decades to merge the National Guard and Reserves;[48] insert large numbers of active-duty military personnel into the reserves as cadres; limit the higher echelons of reserve leadership to active military officers detailed from the active force for that purpose; and, in general, reduce or abolish the local, autonomous nature of the reserve components.[49]

These proposals have generally received short shrift because we have not had to adopt them in the past in order to survive and because the pressure to do so is not compelling in the national consciousness. Implementation of any of them, no matter how desirable from the point of view of technical efficiency and readiness for war, will continue to be possible only on the most painstakingly slow and incremental basis, if at all, for the same reason. If U.S. military manpower analysts and policymakers kept their eyes on the more intangible disciplines of history, philosophy, and politics, as well as the comparatively concrete ones of management, administration, and finance, they would have a better grasp of the unpredictability, seeming irrationality, and always emotional roots of how a country raises and uses its armed forces.[50] Until then, numerous administrative measures and legislative proposals from an historically-ignorant Pentagon will founder on the rocks of the American military tradition, using up much political capital and energy that policymakers can ill afford to lose.

## NOTES

1. A description of this system in action can be found in Michael Prestwich, *War, Politics, and Finance under Edward I* (Totowa, N.J.: Rowman and Littlefield, 1972), pp. 41-113 (hereafter cited at Prestwich, *Edward I*).
2. Correlli Barnett, *Britain and Her Army, 1509-1970: A Military, Political, and Social Survey* (Bungay, Suffolk, Great Britain: Penguin Books, 1974), pp. 3-50; C. G. Cruickshank, *Elizabeth's Army*, (2nd ed. (New York: Oxford University Press, Oxford Paperbacks 1966), pp. 1-40; A. L. Rowse, *The Expansion of Elizabethan England* (London: Sphere Books, Ltd., Cardinal Editions, 1973), pp. 373-86 (hereafter cited as Rowse, *Elizabethan England*).
3. The principles of voluntarism and localism applied to freemen possessing full civil and political rights. If persons were excluded due to their inferior socioeconomic status, it merely limited the applicability of the principles, rather than their philosophical soundness as viewed by the mass of Englishmen.

    It is also important to note that the two systems described here existed side by side for a long period of time, applying as they did to two different segments of society. In the late thirteenth century, for example, mounted knights under feudal or quasi-feudal obligation formed the majority of the cavalry, while most of the infantry were conscripts from local militia. (Prestwich, *Edward I*, pp. 91, 99-105). In general, the decline of cavalry in the fifteenth and sixteenth centuries hastened the decline of the traditional royal summons of great feudal nobles and their personal retinues, as the nobility's advantage of being mounted became less important. The direct responsibility of the nobility to bring their own vassals and subjects into the military service to the Crown appears to have been shifted into a more diffuse responsibility to lead the popular militia, resulting in a blending of the two military service traditions—that of nobles for service of the Crown and that of the people to defend the homeland. In particular, "The equation of military responsibility and socioeconomic status encouraged the belief that military talents were inherent in the well-to-do classes. Although the feudal array was in the early seventeenth century and before a military anachronism, romantic chivalric myths and hierarchical ideas about military responsibility remained." (Lois G. Schwoerer, *"No Standing Armies!" The Antiarmy Ideology in Seventeenth Century England*, Baltimore: The Johns Hopkins University Press, 1974, p. 13). In the face of the obsolescence of the feudal system, therefore, leadership of the popular militia provided an outlet for the "romantic chivalric myths and hierarchical ideas about military responsibility" which still existed in the minds of the upper classes.
4. Rowse, *Elizabethan England*, pp. 374-75, 380-81 makes this quite clear.
5. Barnett, *Britain and Her Army*, pp. 30, 36, 50.
6. Schwoerer, *"No Standing Armies!"*, provides a detailed dissection of the roots of English antimilitary attitudes.
7. Barnett, *Britain and Her Army*, pp. 36-37.
8. Cyril Falls, *Elizabeth's Irish Wars* (London: Methuen 1950), *passim*, but especially pp. 35-66.
9. Barnett, *Britain and Her Army*, pp. 71-76; C. V. Wedgwood, *the King's Peace, 1637-1641*, 5th Fontana Library ed. (London: William Collins Sons, May 1972), pp. 297-326.
10. Barnett, *Britain and Her Army*, pp. 31-37.
11. Fully 25 percent of the white population of Virginia was killed during Opechancanough's Rebellion of 1622. Casualties were similar during that chief's second attack in 1644 and Kieft's War in the Hudson Valley in 1642-45 (Douglas Edward Leach, *Arms for Empire: A Military History of the British Colonies in North America, 1607-1763*, New York: Macmillan, 1973, pp. 42-77; Russell F. Weigley, *History of the United States Army* (New York: Macmillan, 1967), p. 9. Weigley's work, it should be noted, is an absolute must for anyone examining any aspects of the history of U.S. military manpower policy.
12. Weigley, *History of the United States Army*, p. 8; pp. 4-12 summarize these characteristics of the militia.

13. Leach, *Arms for Empire,* p. 65.,
14. Ibid.
15. For example, in *Arms for Empire,* p. 69, Leach estimates that over 1,000 colonial soldiers and civilians died in King Philip's War. If the "worst Indian war of the seventeenth century" could result in the death of less than one percent of the estimated 1675 colonial population of 125,000, the population balance had clearly turned decisively against the Indians.
16. See Leach, *Arms for Empire,* pp. 80-510, *passim,* for a history of the wars of 1689-1763.
17. Don Higginbotham, *The War of American Independence: Military Attitudes, Policies, and Practice, 1763-1789* (Bloomington, Indiana: Indiana University Press by arrangement with Macmillan, 1977), pp. 11-12, contains an excellent discussion of the transmutation of European ideals of military service to the American context.
18. For Indian wars from the Revolution through the War of 1812, see Francis Paul Prucha, *The Sword of the Republic: The United States Army on the Frontier, 1783-1846* (Bloomington, Indiana: Indiana University Press by arrangement with Macmillan, 1977), pp. 1-118.
19. Weigley, *History of the United States Army,* pp. 86-87.
20. Ibid., pp. 93-94; Maurice Matloff, ed., *American Military History* 1st ed., rev. (Washington: Office of the Chief of Military History, United States Army, 1973), pp. 108-09.
21. An outstanding discussion of the militia—unorganized mass and organized volunteers—can be found in Marcus Cunliffe, *Soldiers and Civilians: The Martial Spirit in America, 1775-1865* (New York, The Free Press, 1973), pp. 179-254.
22. Weigley, *History of the United States Army,* pp. 94.
23. R. Arthur Bowler, *Logistics and the Failure of the British Army in America, 1775-1783* (Princeton: Princeton University Press, 1975); Higginbotham, *War of American Independence;* Matloff, *American Military History,* pp. 58-60, provides a good short discussion of British logistical and administrative problems in waging transoceanic war in the eighteenth century.
24. John Shy, *Toward Lexington: The Role of The British Army in the Coming of the American Revolution* (Princeton: Princeton University Press, 1965), is an extraordinarily acute examination of the many reasons for growing colonial antimilitary sentiments resulting from the British Army's actions between the Seven Years War and the beginning of the Revolution.
25. Higginbotham, *War of American Independence,* pp. 392-93; and Weigley, *History of the United States Army,* pp. 41-42.
26. John Shy, in his "American Strategy: Charles Lee and the Radical Alternative," has argued that conscription of the militia amidst such a revolutionary situation was feared by the American political and military leadership, who had no desire to "change the war for independence into a genuine civil war with all its grisly attendants—ambush, reprisal, counter-reprisal. It would tear the fabric of American life to pieces. It might even undermine the political process, and throw power to a junta . . ." (*A People Numerous and Armed: Reflections on the Military Struggle for American Independence,* New York: Oxford University Press, 1976, pp. 132-62). Higginbotham, *War for American Independence,* pp. 93-94, 432, makes the same point.
27. Weigley, *History of the United States Army,* p. 126.
28. Richard H. Kohn, *Eagle and Sword: The Beginnings of the Military Establishment in America, 1783-1802* (New York, The Free Press, 1975), pp. 286-88.
29. Ibid, pp. 277-303, has a good summary of the tensions and birth pangs of American military institutions during the 20 years immediately following the Revolution.
30. Prucha, *Sword of the Republic,* pp. 118-231, 249-318.
31. Ibid., pp. 139-92, 233-48, 339-95; Robert M. Utley, *Frontiersmen in Blue: The United States Army and the Indian, 1848-1865* (New York, Macmillan, 1967); Robert M. Utley, *Frontier Regulars: The United States Army and the Indian, 1866-1890* (New York, Macmillan, 1973).
32. There are concise descriptions of the post-War of 1812 Army reforms at Matloff, *American*

*Military History*, pp. 148-51; and Weigley, *History of the United States Army*, pp. 138-43. For the steady growth in Army-Indian fighting capability during the nineteenth century, despite numerous problems and chronic personnel shortages, see Prucha, *Sword of the Republic*, pp. 169-92, 319-37; Utley, *Frontiersmen in Blue*, pp. 18-58, 341-59; and Utley, *Frontier Regulars*, pp. 10-92.

33. Keneneth Bourne, *Britain and the Balance of Power in North America* (London: Longmans, Green, 1967) is an authoritative discussion of this issue. A whole body of literature has grown up refuting the popular conventional wisdom that American-Canadian relations have always been sweetness and light, of which the most notable is probably Charles P. Stacey's legendary "The Myth of the Unguarded Frontier, 1815-1871," *American Historical Review* (1950-51); 1-18. As Bourne's study makes clear, however, contingency plans and occasional war scares do not mask the obvious if slow growth of mutual Canadian-American accommodation throughout the nineteenth century, and the progressive relegation of serious plans for war to the backs of file drawers.
34. The reasons why the Civil War had so little fundamental impact on American military institutions are explored in Cunliffe, *Soldiers and Civilians*, pp. 427-35; and Shy, *A People Numerous and Armed*, pp. 242-45.
35. This is exactly what happened with those militia volunteer units that were in existence before the Civil War.
36. These ideologies found more explicit expression in naval and maritime writings, led by those of Mahan, and seconded by those persons in and out of government pressing the late nineteenth and early twentieth century revitalization of U.S. naval power. For an example of popular writing incorporating these concepts and demonstrating amazing predictive capacity for strategic and geopolitical analysis as well, see Homer Lea's two books: *The Valor of Ignorance* (New York: Harper and Brothers, 1909), and *The Day of the Saxon* (New York: Harper and Brothers, 1912).
37. Weigley, *History of the United States Army*, p. 309.
38. For a representative collection of such proposals, see Walter Millis, ed., *American Military Thought* (Indianapolis: Bobbs-Merrill, 1966), pp. 179-92, 240-61, 273-303, 342-49.
39. The Department of Defense has prepared an official memorandum on the dual state-Federal status of the National Guard, discussing both its history and current statutory basis. U.S. Congress, House, Committee on Armed Services, *Hearing on H.R. 871 . . . S.3906 . . . H.R. 1201 . . . H.R. 5056 . . . H.R. 12860* before Subcommittee No. 4 of the Committee on Armed Services, 93rd Congress, 2nd session, 1974, pp. 9-13.
40. The militia/reserve reforms of the 1898-1920 period are summarized in Weigley, *History of the United States Army*, pp. 320-22, 335-50, 396-400.
41. The reserves of the Navy and Marine Corps are wholly Federal in nature, as might be expected in a service (with its land arm) whose very nature makes it a centralized institution from the moment of its inception, rather than one capable of being broken down into local subunits. That an Air National Guard exists at all is almost certainly due to the comparatively late date (1947) at which the Air Force became a separate service; it is likely that the establishment of an independent Air Force in the infant days of military aviation (as happened with the Royal Air Force) would have precluded the Air National Guard from even coming into existence, and would have ensured a wholly Federal Air Force reserve component.
42. I have discussed the distinction between this system and more traditional conscription-based reserve systems in two official publications: Robert L. Goldich, "The Applicability of Selected Foreign Mlitary Reserve Practices to the U.S. Reserves: Proposals Based on the Reserve Forces of the United Kingdom, Federal Republic of Germany, Israel, and the U.S.S.R.," in U.S. Congress, House, Committee on Armed Services, *Military Posture and H.R. 5068 [H.R. 5970], Department of Defense Authorization for Appropriations for Fiscal Year 1979, Hearings*, 95th Congress, 2nd session, Part 5 of 7 Parts, Military Personnel, 1978 pp. 1437-

1604; and U.S. Library of Congress, Congressional Research Service, *Military Manpower Policy and the All-Volunteer Force,* Issue Brief 77032, March 12, 1979, pp. 11-12.

43. The system itself, by sustaining an independent reserve structure staffed by reserve officers with little if any recent active duty experience (rather than the Continental European system of cadred active units, commanded and staffed by active force officers, filled with prior service reservists upon mobilization), was the main reason for this latter problem. For a survey of the extent to which this situation still exists today, see Irving Heymont, *Demographic Characteristics of Selected Reserve Components and Active Army Commanders,* report no. CR-187, prepared for Office of the Director for Planning and Evaluation, Department of Defense (McLean, Virginia: General Research Corporation, May 1977).

    A second reason for this problem was the lack of a ruthless up-or-out personnel management system which regularly pruned the ranks of both regular and reserve forces of the professionally unfit, particularly those men lacking in mental and physical drive, stamina, and endurance (often through no lack of motivation on their part). For an illuminating discussion of the latter problem during the open phases of the World War II mobilization, see Mark Skinner Watson, *Chief of Staff: Prewar Plans and Preparations,* The War Department, United States Army in World War II (Washington: Historical Division, Department of the Army, 1950), pp. 241-69.

    For an excellent general summary of U.S. Army reserve mobilizations from World War II through Vietnam, see I. Heymont and E. W. McGregor, *Review and Analysis of Recent Mobilizations and Deployments of US Army Reserve Components,* report no. RAC-CR-67, prepared for the Department of the Army (McLean, Virginia: Research Analysis Corporation, October 1972).

44. A comprehensive discussion of NATO and the Warsaw Pact is found in John M. Collins, *American and Soviet Military Trends Since the Cuban Missile Crisis* (Washington: Center for Strategic and International Studies, Georgetown University, 1978), *passim,* but especially pp. 321-79.

45. The most recent statements to this effect can be found in U.S. Department of Defense, *Annual Report, Fiscal Year 1980, Secretary of Defense Harold Brown* (Washington: n.p., January 25, 1979), pp. 100-04, 284-90.

46. For two studies of the continuing vitality of the independent political and social base of the reserves, one academic and the other popular, see William F. Levantrosser, *Congress and the Citizen-Soldier: Legislative Policy-making for the Federal Armed Forces Reserve* (Columbus, Ohio: Ohio State University Press, 1967); and Jim Dan Hill, *The Minute Man in Peace and War: A History of the National Guard* (Harrisburg, Pa.: The Stockpole Company, 1964). See also Martha Derthick, *The National Guard in Politics* (Cambridge, Mass: Harvard University Press, 1965).

47. A concise summary of many of these programs is in U.S. Department of Defense, Office of the Assistant Secretary of Defense (Manpower, Reserve Affairs, and Logistics), *Manpower Requirements Report for FY 1980* (Washington: n.p., February 1979), pp. IX-8/9.

48. In 1965, Secretary of Defense Robert S. McNamara proposed merging the Army Reserve into the Army National Guard. See U.S. Congress, Senate, Committee on Armed Services, *Proposals to Realine the Army National Guard and the Army Reserve Forces, Parts 1 and 2, Hearings,* 89th Congress, 1st session, 1965. In 1973, an amendment to the FY 1974 Department of Defense Appropriation Authorization Act (Public Law 93-155, section 810) required DoD to study the possibility of merging the Air Force and Air National Guard. See U.S. Department of Defense, *A Report on the Merger of the Air Force Reserve and Air National Guard* (Washington: n.p., January 1975). Nothing came of either proposal. The General Accounting Office is currently attempting yet another resuscitation of the concept. See Larry Carney, "NG, Reserve Merger Recommended Again," *Army Times,* April 9, 1979, p. 6.

49. For a discussion of such proposals, noting their desirability in purely technical military terms,

## 132  Defense Manpower Planning

see my study for the House Armed Services Committee. Goldich, "The Applicability of Selected Foreign Military Reserve Practices to the U.S. Reserves," pp. 1469-80.

50. I have expanded on this theme at slightly greater length in Office of the Director of Net Assessment, Office of the Secretary of Defense; Directorate of Concepts, Headquarters U.S. Air Force, and Defense Studies Institute, University of Edinburgh, "Method and Mystique in Military Manpower Analysis," in *Final Report of the Seminar on Soviet Military Manpower: A Focus on the Soviet Military District,* Seminar held at the University of Edinburgh, Scotland, April 5-7, 1978, Appendix C.

Chapter 8

# U.S. Army Selected Reserves: Incentives/Disincentives to Join/Remain

William J. Taylor, Jr.

## INTRODUCTION

There are seven fundamental considerations that should serve as the backdrop for understanding the behavior of people in relation to the Army Reserves.
1. The active duty army components of the All-Volunteer Force have problems recruiting and retaining enough quality soldiers. On balance, the nation's 16½ active divisions are neither as bad as some critics claim nor as good as some proponents assert they are. Some are better than others. Most of the better units are overseas.[1] In any case, army unit commanders are "coping."
2. Army reserve components (Army Reserve and National Guard) are vitally important for national security. Under the "Total Force" concept, current plans call for Army Reserve Forces to constitute almost half the U.S. general purpose land forces (12 of 25½ division force equivalents) required for wartime mobilization under a major land war scenario.
3. Current shortages of airlift and sealift capabilities aside, most likely war scenarios envision a "come-as-you-are" effort with little or no time available for drafting and training soldiers.
4. The strength of Army Reserve components has fallen to levels which must be considered dangerous under conditions of major land warfare in Europe. Referring to shortages in the Army Reserves, General Bernard W. Rogers, Supreme Allied Commander in Europe, testified in the spring 1980:

"I don't have a very high sense of confidence that I can accomplish my mission—as far as U.S. forces go."[2]
5. There is a shortfall in the Individual Ready Reserve (IRR), the pool of pretrained reservists not in organized units who would be called as individual replacements for combat losses. There is a personnel shortage in the Selected Reserve (SR), the organized army units which are designed to be committed intact during wartime, and in Army National Guard units. The total shortfall for the reserve components is measured most importantly in terms of requirements for soldiers to fight a major land war in Europe. Some estimate the shortfall to be about 250,000;[3] others think the shortage could reach 500,000 depending upon the intensity of conflict.[4]
6. Alternative proposals notwithstanding, the status quo method for acquiring and retaining people in all components is volunteerism. Each of the major alternatives—selective service, universal military training/service, universal national service, a smaller volunteer force, and variants of each—are replete with problems which make their adoption by Congress unlikely in the foreseeble future.[5]
7. The population from which most volunteers must come, 18-year-old males, is projected to decline by 24 percent between 1979 and 1993. This is certain to affect Army Reserve accessions negatively.

The purpose of this study is to address the question of why young people do or do not join Army SR units and why they do or do not stay in the SR. It is a stark fact that "more reservists are going out the back door than are coming in the front, despite the fact that recruiting incentives and service-related benefits have been expanded significantly in recent years."[6] Although there are several economic models and surveys which purport to provide answers to the question, it is sometimes not a bad idea to go talk with the human beings who are the objects of analysis, and observe them in their own environments to find out first hand what they think about various things and why.

As part of an overall research program on factors affecting Army Reserve accession and retention, Harold W. Chase, OSD Deputy Assistant Secretary of Defense for Reserve Affairs, established a team of seven officers from the U.S. Military Academy who visited Army Reserve units in the summer 1979 using nonsurvey techniques to determine attitudes of reservists and of people in their surrounding communities. Prior to field work, these officers were trained in nonsurvey techniques at the University of Virginia. The project itself was one more manifestation of a growing awareness in official circles since 1978 that the Army Reserve components are in trouble.

Fully aware of the shortfalls in the SR and IRR, the Office of the Secretary of Defense (Manpower, Reserve Affairs and Logistics), the Army Staff, and the Office of the Chief of the Army Reserves have instituted a host of programs to provide incentives for Selected Reserve recruitment. The DOD Annual Report for FY 1981 summarizes these:[7]

- Enlistment and reenlistment bonuses and educational assistance incentives for all DOD Selected Reserve Components, though aimed primarily at the Army;
- The consolidation of responsibility for recruiting functions for the U.S. Army Recruiting Command (USAREC);
- Optional enlistment term in Selected Reserve of three, four, or five years, with the balance to be a total of six years in the Individual Ready Reserve;
- Optional initial training programs, such as:

    Split-training where initial active duty may be taken in two increments, the first being basic military training of approximately eight weeks, and the second being military occupational specialty training of at least 20 days;

    A test of a military careers (VOTEC) program where high school seniors taking a vocational course which can be transferred to qualification in a military occupational skill are only required to attend eight weeks of basic military training;

    A test of a Civilian Acquired Skill Program (CASP) where enlistees with a civilian skill which can be transferred to military occupational skill qualification will only be required to attend eight weeks of basic military training.

Many other proposals designed to provide recruitment incentives require legislation and have been introduced in Congress.[8] Many of these are financial incentives such as bonuses or provisions to reservists of limited shopping privileges at post exchanges and commissaries. (The latter has been passed.)

## SOCIAL CHANGE AND INCENTIVES

The most fundamental, if only the most recent, change reflective of American social values is the All-Volunteer Force system itself which simply provides the option of avoiding any kind of military service if one wishes and, except for the lowest income groups, most do. The sociologists and social psychologists have been trying to tell us for some time that the attitudes of Americans toward organizations and work have been changing. Clearly, plans, policies, and programs for the Army Reserves must take these changes into account.

First, there has been change in attitudes toward authority. The most fundamental aspect of the "youth revolution" of the late 1960s was a shift in approach to authority ("the Establishment") in both its governmental and private sector managerial forms. Many have assumed that "rebellion" against authority would disappear with age and the acceptance of responsibility for making a living wage, and they appear to have been correct. Others predicted that the youth revolution would join other factors of social change with durable impact. For example, the new generation of employees "will expect their immediate supervisor to recognize their individual talents and to challenge these talents in an atmosphere that allows them as much freedom as possible to 'do their own thing.' "[9] By 1970, the approach to organization itself was changing:

> Thus we find the emergence of a new kind of organization man—a man who, despite his many affiliations, remains basically uncommitted to any organization. He is willing to employ his skills and creative energies to solve problems with equipment provided by the organizaton, and within temporary groups established by it. But he does so only so long as the problems interest him. He is committed to his own career, his own self-fulfillment.[10]

There are many reasons (e.g., the education revolution and the information revolution) for such a widespread shift in mass psychology, all of which are too complex for treatment here (as well as being imperfectly understood by the author). But the fact is that employees seem to have become just as interested in personal dignity and "fate control" as they are in wages and benefits, even if one concludes that the latter requirements are being satisfied to such an extent that fulfillment of the former becomes predominant simply by default. The drive for personal dignity in the work environment manifests itself in many ways, one of which is the movement toward "codetermination," or worker participation in management decisions which both condition one's everyday life and shape the organizational mission.[11]

Second, there has been change related to work. Social psychologists tell us that "There is an ideological movement afoot among the industrial, democratic nations of the Western world to enhance the quality of work life."[12] This movement is referred to variously as "industrial democracy," "codetermination," or "worker democracy." Trends in this direction are not new; their underpinning is the general historical shift in the West toward democratic and egalitarian principles. Made possible in large part by the trade union movement which preceded it, the movement has accelerated over the past 15 to 20 years, manifesting itself in growing employee perceptions of arbitrary treatment at the hands of management, and discontent with dehumanizing working conditions and meaningless work.[13]

All these changes led to the brief "movement" toward military unions begun in 1975 and stopped by legislation in 1978.[14] And these changes were, in part, the basis of Charles Moskos' thesis that the American military has been moving away from an institutional format where motivation for "service" was based upon perceptions of profession or calling to a format that increasingly resembles an occupation.

The third change which has already emerged clearly among middle class managers is that, among employment incentives, money has become less important. Alvin Toffler explains:

> No one suggests those workers don't want money. They certainly do. But once a certain income level is reached, they vary widely in what else they want. Additional increments of money no longer have their former impact on behavior.[15]

Individuals, especially the young in low income groups, place increasing employment emphasis on acquisition of marketable skills and recognition. "Moonlighting" as a part of the American life-style for the lower-income strata is just beginning to fade as increasing numbers of people place less emphasis on material "things" they have and more on leisure time, with proximity to home becoming increasingly necessary due to gasoline-induced increases in travel costs. Having the weekend off is of far greater significance to more and more people. As we shall see later, people do not join the Reserves primarily to acquire additional income.

However, the general trend notwithstanding, Reserve participation is a form of "second job" and has been considered by some to be a form of moonlighting. According to the analysis in a well-known study of moonlighting,[16] the supply of labor for second jobs (or, for the willingness of someone to join and remain in the Army Reserves) will increase if:

1. wages in the Reserves increase significantly.
2. the person is black.
3. the person is nonurban.
4. wages in the primary job decrease significantly.
5. the person is not a high school graduate.
6. the number of hours required for the primary job decrease.
7. the person's spouse is not working or quits working.
8. the person's nonlabor income (interest, dividends, etc.) decreases or is nonexistent.

Keep this study in mind as we address below the issue of pay as an incentive or disincentive to join or remain in Army SR units.

Reserve recruitment and retention programs must work against great odds. Recruitment may be viewed as the easier task because many of the young will not know what they are getting into. Retention must be based upon the individual's judgment whether the ideal of reserve membership is matched by the realities of reserve service. In far too many cases, the two do not square, explaining why more reservists are going out the back door than are coming in the front.

## INCENTIVES/DISINCENTIVES TO JOIN

For the IRR, the problem of incentives has been different from other Reserve Components because its members previously have been those who complete active duty service and serve the remainder of their obligation on the IRR roles. Thus, the task has been to retain, not recruit. However, a new program being tested does provide for direct enlistment into the Army IRR where the challenge of providing incentives will apply.

The major shortfall in SR strength is in the grades E-4 and below and in medical personnel. The question is why so few enlist in SR units. At a high level of generalization, there are five basic reasons.

First, upper and middle income families in the communities surveyed do not think about, do not know anything about, and consider that they have no need for anything the Army Reserves have to offer. The Army Reserves are absent from the hearts and minds of the more affluent; middle class America is missing from the enlisted ranks of Army Reserves.

Second, in "The Community" writ large, community leaders, especially corporate executives, know very little about, feel no particular responsibility for, and are curious why anyone would ask them questions about the Army Reserves in their area. Even community leaders whose civic responsibilities might be served by SR unit resources generally do not feel any responsibility for helping in SR unit recruiting. This attitude is shared by first-line supervisors in both large and small community businesses. The nature of the community from which SR units draw enlistees makes this phenomenon understandable. SR units draw from a community circumscribed by travel time from the Reserve Center facility. Thus, an encompassing city is not the SR unit's community. Rather, especially for the younger population without automobiles and with little or no job income, the relevant community is a much smaller neighborhood. Another factor is that community leaders are busy people who have more immediate demands on their time from other civic functions such as United Way, Red Cross, Community Chest, YMCA, Boy Scouts, Jaycees, church functions, and disaster relief (a National Guard function from which SR units are generally precluded). Although there is wide variance between the attitudes of high school supervisors and educators toward recruiting efforts (e.g., passive support in the midwest, to avoidance or antipathy in the northeast), few feel any responsibility for active support of Reserve recruiting. In brief, there are few incentives for community support of SR recruiting efforts.[17]

Third, the potential of SR units to enhance their profiles for community service is circumscribed by Army regulations and sharply diminished by the paperwork and lead-time requirements for permission from higher headquarters to do something considered socially useful.

Fourth, lower-ranking members of SR units generally do not recommend their units to friends and acquaintances in the communities for a variety of reasons to be explained below.

Fifth, although recent initiatives in advertising may have a measurable, positive impact, most of the young people in SR unit communities who were not in the Army Reserves did not recall in the summer 1979 anything from television or other forms of advertising which impressed them about the Army Reserves.

An increasing proportion of the individuals who, by whatever means, came in contact with local Reserve recruiters were 17 years old, black, female, had a 10th grade education, were loners, lived at home, had parents who were divorced or separated, were unemployed, and had prior histories of menial jobs. They were seeking a civilian-transferable skill, group identity, recognition, and pay. In some cases, the incentive to join was a means of entry into the Active Army otherwise denied by mental, physical, or previous record disqualifications. Enlistment in the Reserves followed by basic and advanced individual training constitutes a form of "prior service" which can contribute toward waiver of Active Army enlistment disqualification.

## INCENTIVES/DISINCENTIVES TO REMAIN

It is important to remember that "incentives" have meaning primarily as individual perceptions. Whether or not a factor *should* be or is reported to be positive or negative as a unit phenomenon matters less than what individuals say. The following represents a consensus in what most respondents told interviewers in one-on-one or small group sessions in the summer 1979.

### Training and Skill Acquisition

The search for training in a skill which is transferable to the civilian job market is the first and foremost reason given by non-prior-service (NPS) individuals who join SR units. The skill transferability theme is accordingly now significant in Army advertising and, much more importantly, in recruiters' approaches. Most of the recruits do acquire expected skills in basic and advanced training for the 12 weeks after enlistment. The problem comes in weekend training with the SR unit.

To the extent that SR units provide relevant training, the incentive to remain is reinforced. Unfortunately, in large numbers of cases, relevant training is limited. The reasons are several. First, in those SR units organized as combat arms units (e.g., infantry, armor, artillery), positions requiring military occupational specialties (MOSs) with civilian occupation transferability are limited. Most of the positions require training in small unit tactics, gunnery, and other military-oriented skills. The number of positions for mechanics, clerks, carpenters, cooks, etc. are few. Second, training time in an SR unit is limited by a number of factors. SR units train only one weekend per month and during a two-week period, normally held in the summer. Much of the weekend training time scheduled for sixteen hours over a Saturday and Sunday is used for administration, minireorganizations, and briefings on what has transpired during the month since the last weekend training session. Much of the time scheduled for training is taken up with inspections or preparing for inspections. Much of the training actually conducted is poorly organized or the instructors are insufficiently prepared. Much of the instruction is just plain boring, the result of an officer or noncommissioned officer (NCO) reading from a lesson plan. Training aids or equipment required for proper "hands-on" training, especially for medical units, often is not available because supply requests are unfilled or unit leadership is apprehensive that equipment used for training will not be in condition for inspection by higher headquarters. The net result is skill transferable training which either does not exist or is done poorly. Junior reservists find little of appeal in such units; they are absent from drill a great deal and they leave the Reserves as soon as possible. Clearly, there are units where training is excellent and where individual perceptions differ from the above; but, based on interviews, such units constitute the exception, not the rule.

## Group Identification and Recognition

Large numbers of junior reservists (out of school, out of work, and unlikely to be members of familiar social organizations based on middle class values) joined the Reserves out of a need to "belong." They express a need to establish an identity with others organized for a purpose and to fill a void in their lives. They seek the recognition and status that are perceived to come with wearing the Army uniform and acquiring rank, and recognition of excellent performance. Many are sadly disappointed as their needs and expectations clash with the SR unit's organizational process and the modus operandi of more senior NCOs and officers.

Confronted by administrative requirements and performance objectives set by higher headquarters (principally by active Army officers) and perceived as unrealistic and unwarranted, the senior SR unit leadership has little time to devote to the young reservists they are supposed to lead. Typically, the majority of the unit officers and NCOs spend a large part of their single monthly training weekend closeted together in meetings or filling out forms and reports—not because they want to but because Army regulations require it. A form of priority inversion ensues; there is little time for training or for interacting in leadership functions with the young reservist. Too often, the lower ranking enlisted people are left to themselves with tasks vaguely defined or undefined and without priorities. It was all too common to find small groups of young people sitting around with time on their hands—the last thing they needed, wanted, or expected when they enlisted.

The attitudes of many of the senior NCOs and officers, many with prior active Army service, toward the younger reservists generally were in direct conflict with the needs and expectations of the latter. Not unrepresentative was the comment of one officer that "they ask me to develop soldiers and they send me the bum of the week." Senior personnel, almost all employed in the civilian sector and established in middle to lower-middle class suburbia, have very little in common with the type individuals being recruited. They do not socialize with them outside the Reserve Center and would prefer to avoid any semblance of identity with them during training. They have low regard for high school dropouts and do not consider them "trainable." The older officers and NCOs did not receive "bonuses" to join the Reserves and they resent the idea of "paying money to get bums." Given such a stratified background in personal and group relationships, where the most basic of the young reservists' perceived needs are not met, it is little wonder that there is extraordinary difficulty in socializing them into the SR unit and in developing organizational commitment.

Even if there were a predisposition among NCOs and officers to socialize with their junior reservists, and even if the demands were not so heavy on the short time available one weekend per month, the opportunities to make the reserve unit experience "fun" are circumscribed by regulations. Reserve Center facilities can be used only for specific purposes. For example, having a "beer party" at the Reserve Center near the end of, but during, the training day is prohibited. Such restrictions are counterproductive to unit morale and cohesion. In any case, the local commander should have greater authority over unit matters. Less attention should be paid by higher headquarters to how the unit is run and more to results.

Acquisiton of rank brings recognition and status (and more pay). The junior reservists perceive the rank of sergeant (in any pay grade) to have special status. Yet, in each unit there are only so many NCO positions authorized. These positions are held by the more senior reservists who have been in the SR unit longest and who remain there. A new program (CASP) based upon civilian acquired skill permits direct entry into the Reserves with rank higher than private. This program also blocks promotion of many of the new reservists. Thus, promotion often is blocked and many of the younger soldiers learn early that, no matter how quickly they learn or how well they perform their jobs, they are not likely to be promoted. If they can, they seek reclassification into an MOS which is not blocked in the SR unit. The problem here is that the MOS probably will require skills for which they are not trained and, given a shortage of Reserves quotas for active Army schools, they may not be able to get the required training.

Other forms of recognition, such as Army awards, are few. For the right reasons, the active Army normally reduces the number of awards given in peacetime. Even the Army Commendation medal, the lowest order decoration for achievement or service, must be approved by active Army commanders.[18] The net result is that very few awards are approved for reservists. Too often, the recognition and status the young reservists seek are not realized—and they grow to resent it.

## Pay, Benefits, Retirement

It was a rare exception when young reservists, no matter how the question was put and regardless of their civilian employment status, stated that pay, benefits, or future security in reserve retirement had been important in their reasons for enlistment. Almost all E-3s agreed that their reserve pay (above the minimum wage) was fair and reasonable. This finding is supported by other survey and broad-based interview results.[19]

Admittedly the finding is contradicted by existing macroeconomic studies. For example, one study concludes that "the implications of this work are that the persons who are less competitive in the labor market are far more sensitive to reserve wage differentials." Another short study done in 1980 by Thomas W. Fagan relies in part on the moonlighting study referred to earlier (see also note 16), concluding that: 1) reservists (moonlighters) are motivated by pay; and 2) that the shortfalls in Reserve strength over the 1970s are attributable to inadequate pay. He looks at real private nonagricultural weekly wages in the civilian sector between 1973 and 1979, noting that the former fell by 7 percent and the latter by 17 percent. His data and analysis are worth examination in detail (see table 8.1).

> Note that Reserve pay is linked to active duty pay. The "capped" pay increases which were given to the active Army during the late 1970's were distributed disproportionately to allowances other than base pay. Consequently, the base pay portion, which is the portion that the Reservist actually receives, fell even more dramatically that the Active Force's RMC.
>
> There are two parts to the "relative wage" argument. One is the level of wages; the other is the relative increase or decrease in wages. The "level" of wages continues to be a major concern in the Active Force . . . $55.19 for a Private First Class as compared to $96.24 for the private nonmanufacturing weekly wage in 1976 dollars (if these were 1979 dollars, the numbers would be PFC-$120.00/private employment-$219.91). Hence, the Active Force emphasizes "benefits" and a Madison Avenue Tune in an effort to attract recruits. Because the reserves do not have benefits to proffer, their method of "keeping-even" is the double-drill-pay ruse. In essence, a Reservist receives four days pay for two days work. For example, the PFC's weekly wage in 1978 was $112.10; hence his monthly salary was $112.10 × 4.33 weeks in a

**Table 8.1.** Comparative Nominal and Real Wages Between an Average Nonagricultural Weekly Wage Earner and a Private-First-Class in the Reserve Forces

| Year | Nonagricultural Weekly Wage | PFC Weekly Wage | (1967 = 100) CPI | Real Nonagricultural Weekly Wage | Real PFC Weekly Wage |
|---|---|---|---|---|---|
| 1969 | $114.61 | $ 28.47 | 108.8 | $105.34 | $26.16 |
| 1970 | 119.83 | 38.72 | 116.3 | 104.47 | 33.29 |
| 1971 | 127.31 | 71.84 | 121.3 | 107.61 | 59.22 |
| 1972 | 136.90 | 77.04 | 125.3 | 111.12 | 61.48 |
| 1973 | 145.39 | 86.30 | 133.1 | 104.22 | 64.83 |
| 1974 | 154.76 | 92.00 | 147.7 | 97.51 | 62.28 |
| 1975 | 163.53 | 96.58 | 161.2 | 95.02 | 59.91 |
| 1976 | 175.45 | 100.04 | 170.5 | 98.90 | 58.67 |
| 1977 | 189.00 | 106.28 | 181.5 | 100.53 | 58.55 |
| 1978 | 203.70 | 112.10 | 195.3 | 98.76 | 57.39 |
| 1979 | 219.91 | 120.00 | 217.4 | 96.24 | 55.19 |

Source: Thomas W. Fagan, "The Reserve Forces of the United States: The Incentives and Disincentives to Join and to Remain," paper presented at the 21st Annual Convention of the International Studies Association, Los Angeles, Calif., March 18-22, 1980, pp. 11-13.

month = $485.40. For a weekend (two days) drill, a Reservist receives pay for four Drills (four days). Because there are thirty days in a month, the Reservist receives four-thirtieths of $485.40+ = $64.72 . . . which is the amount reported in the 1979 Reserve Forces Almanac. Hence, beware when "Softees" [sociologists or social psychologists to Fagan] conclude that "money doesn't matter." I believe that it does matter, but because of the necesary ruse, Reserve Compensation is roughly equivalent to alternative moonlighting wages.

Arguing that the "level" of wages is comparable does not defeat the argument that the trends are adverse. As long as military pay is both "capped" and distributed disproportionately to benefits, relative wages in the Reserves will fall faster or increase more slowly than wages in the private sector. This will cause recruiting shortfalls and retention problems.[20]

Fagan's analysis makes sense. Unfortunately, what he says *should* happen is not *what does* happen. That is, the Private First Class thought before he enlisted and continued to think that Reserve pay is "sufficient." Pay "issues" simply are not on the minds of young reservists or potential reservists. Of course, if Fagan is right, and assuming no significant change in civil-sector employment opportunities, inflation, or current reserve programs, the problems of the Army Reserves should be solved in the near future by the 11.7 percent military pay increase starting October 1980, and subsequent proposals by the Reagan Administration. I would not bet my first monthly pay increase on it for the reasons stated throughout this chapter.

Many included "military benefits" among their reasons for enlisting, speaking of such perceived incentives as travel away from home for two weeks of summer training or post exchange (PX) shopping privileges while on active duty for training. But in the summer 1979, there was a great deal of dissatisfaction in perceptions of "Mickey Mouse" regulations which prevented adequate realization of such benefits. The reservists' expectation was that they would be able to travel to summer training at Army posts in their private automobiles with payment for mileage driven. However, they were ordered to travel by commercial carrier, no doubt for reasons of fuel economy. This meant, of course, that married reservists would be able to take their spouses and families with them only at extraordinary expense—and many stated that their spouses were "mad as hell" because they could not go.

Many commented that their dependents were irritated by the fact that they could not shop at Army PX's unless accompanied by the reservist. There was considerable resentment, too, over the fact that reservists on summer duty at Army posts were not permitted to shop at commissaries (Army "grocery stores" with prices below the retail market) while on active duty for summer training. In fact, these complaints often were linked to other untoward experiences on Army posts which were perceived as making reservists "second-class citizens" in what was supposed to be "one army."

Unlike the more senior NCOs and officers who were familiar with the complex formulas for computing Reserve "retirement points," the younger enlisted knew hardly anything about or had thought much about Reserve retirement which comes at age 60. This is hardly surprising; few 18-year-olds ever think about anything so far over their horizons.

## INCENTIVES/DISINCENTIVES REVIEWED

Based not upon macroeconomic studies or survey results, but upon what hundreds of reservists said in face-to-face conversations where they could be drawn out in formal dialogue in Reserve centers—at a diner for lunch, in a bar after weekend drill, or in their families' homes—one might conceptualize retention identification as depicted in figure 8.1.

Two members of our study group explained the retention identification concept as follows:

> Generally assumed to be the most common factor in recruiting, monetary remuneration is found to be important only in terms of fairness; by itself, it is not a significant factor in accession or first term retention. Only after an establishment of vestiture, does one start to find an increase in the importance of money. In short, pay is seen as adequate, and of secondary importance; given a lower salary, the young reservist would still join. Retirement has little meaning during the initial years.

## U.S. Army Selected Reserves

[Figure: Retention Identification chart with axes "High/Medium/Low" vs "Years of Service" (0, 6, 13, 20), showing curves labeled Retirement, Recognition, Money, and Skills]

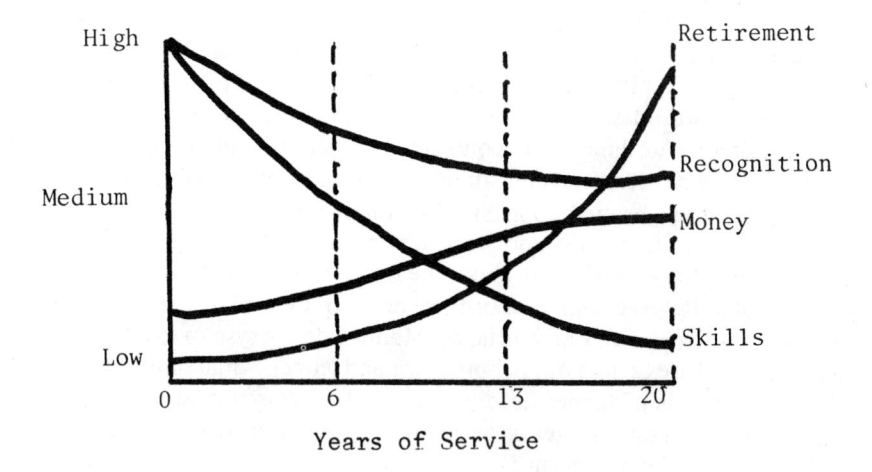

**Figure 8.1** Retention Identification

As the individual stays in the unit, the positive motivator for continued retention changes from skill, to recognition and esteem, and later to security and benefits. . . . The importance of this concept is in the defining of all the various influence curves and then noting the slope, direction and amount at each year of service. Accession and retention should be oriented to the year group from which the impact makeup is then determined. This procedure is illustrated showing that the needs of the first termer approaching reenlistment are significantly different from those of a reservist in the latter years of service. Around the twelfth year, commitment and the significance of retirement benefits begin to increase. Remuneration and bonuses are seen as secondary income and are sometimes used as a justification to the spouse for continuation in the program; the existence of the remuneration, as opposed to the amount, is more important.[21]

## CONCLUSIONS

The views expressed in this chapter are not totally new. The findings of the study group do, however, reinforce the position that, although money matters in recruitment and retention for Selected Reserve units, it matters less than other factors and a great deal less than some—especially the economists—claim.

In these times of escalating manpower costs, money for manpower is hard to acquire in defense budgets. However, it is an easier variable to manipulate than the intangibles surfaced in this chapter. Acquiring in some fashion the active support of communities in which Reserve units are located is a monumental task, and it is primarily a local task difficult to influence from offices in Washington, D.C. "Progress" in this respect is also difficult to measure. Changing the attitudes of the senior NCOs and officers who lead, plan, organize, direct, coordinate, and control SR units is difficult at best.

Changing the burdensome and stultifying administrative requirements and detailed regulations heaped upon SR unit commanders and sunk in the concrete of bureaucratic process and standing operating procedures is far from easy. Educating the Active Army about the Reserves and changing attitudes to permit greater Reserve unit authority over their own plans, policies, and programs is both necessary and difficult. Monitoring the system to ensure that changes ordered are carried out in both spirit and letter—while simultaneously easing the demands of higher headquarters—requires exemplary leadership. These are the toughest long-term tasks, but they are value-oriented steps that could be taken in the near term.[22]

The importance of the Army Reserves was stated at the outset. Army SR units are undermanned.[23] This chapter purports to provide some major reasons why this is so. However, there are combat-ready units which appear to be able to overcome the problems cited. Future research might look at only the "best" SR units, in this case those which acquire and retain people at 100 percent unit strength, and focus on the reasons for their success.

# NOTES

1. See Richard Halloran, "Army Rates Six of Ten Divisions Unready to Fight," *The New York Times,* September 9, 1980, p. 1.
2. General Bernard W. Rogers, quoted in *The Army Times,* March 3, 1980, p. 1.
3. Ibid.
4. See Kenneth J. Coffey, "To Draft or Not to Draft: The Approaching Decision," paper presented to the Comptroller General's Consultant Panel, Washington, D.C., July 25, 1980, p. 7.
5. See *Defense Management Planning: Final Report of the U.S. Military Academy Senior Conference,* 1980 (West Point, N.Y.: September 1980), *passim.*
6. See Colonel James R. Compton, USAR, "Army Reserve Components: Some Additional Suggestions for Enhancing Retention Rates," unpublished paper at the Army War College, 1979, p. 3.
7. See Secretary of Defense Harold Brown *Department of Defense Annual Report, Fiscal Year 1981,* pp. 272-73.
8. See Honorable Harold W. Chase, Statement of Deputy Assistant Secretary of Defense (Reserve Affairs), "Hearings Before the Subcommittee on Military Personnel, House Armed Services Committee," February 27, 1980, pp. 20-24.
9. Eugene Koprowski, "The Generation Gap, From Both Sides Now," in *Optimizing Human Resources: Readings in Individual and Organization Development,* edited by Gordon L. Lippitt, Leslie E. This, and Robert G. Bidwell, Jr. (Reading, Mass.: Addison-Wesley, 1971), pp. 287-88.

10. Alvin Toffler, *Future Shock* (New York: Random House, 1970), p. 149. A decade later, Toffler validates and extends this thesis in *The Third Wave* (New York: William Morrow, 1980), especially Chapters 18 and 19.
11. The Army's "organizational effectiveness" programs are fully cognizant of this; so were similar corporate programs which, incidentally, failed in some of the socialist countries.
12. Lauri A. Broedling, "Industrial Democracy and the Future Management of the United States Armed Forces," paper presented at the Annual Convention of the International Studies Association, St. Louis, Mo. March 16-20, 1978, p. 1.
13. See ibid., pp. 2-4; and David G. Bowers, "Work Related Attitudes of Military Personnel," in *The Social Psychology of Military Service,* edited by Nancy L. Goldman and David R. Segal (Beverly Hills: Sage Publications, 1976), pp. 91-99.
14. William J. Taylor, Jr., Roger J. Arango, and Robert S. Lockwood, eds., *Military Unions: U.S. Trends and Issues* (Beverly Hills: Sage Publications, 1977), *passim;* see also Alan Ned Sabrosky, ed., *Blue Collar Soldiers? Unionization and the U.S. Military* (Philadelphia: The Foreign Policy Research Institute, 1977), *passim.*
15. Alvin Toffler, "A New Kind of Man in the Making," *New York Times Magazine,* March 9, 1980, p. 25. Toffler's view is substantiated in *The Economic Report of the President,* January 1978, p. 298. The data show clearly that, as their income goes up, people are working less.
16. See Compton, "Army Reserve Components," p. 9.
17. The Assistant Secretary of Defense for Manpower, Reserve Affairs and Logistics is aware of this problem and has instituted The Employer Support Program in conjunction with The Advertising Council. The mission of the Program "is to build a spirit of cooperation among employees and their Reservist employees." See John R. Brinkerhoff, "Future of the Army Reserves: Plans, Policies, and Programs," *Final Report of the U.S. Military Academy Senior Conference,* p. 181. The program involves advertising, for example, this self-adhering stamp (which does not adhere very well):

**ESGR**
**EMPLOYERS SUPPORT**
**THE GUARD & RESERVE**

18. See Lowndes F. Stephens, "To Get Citizen Soldiers," *The New York Times,* March 7, 1980, p. A27; and Colonel James R. Compton, "Retention in the Reserves: The Motivation Factor," *Parameters* 9 (March 1979): 33-34.
19. See Karen Cleary Alderman, "Selected Reservists' Labor Market Characteristics and Supply Elasticities: A Review of Recent Evidence," Office of the Secretary of Defense (Manpower, Reserve Affairs and Logistics), November 8, 1979, p. 10.
20. See Thomas W. Fagan, "The Reserve Forces of the United States: The Incentives and Disincentives to Join and to Remain," paper presented at the 21st Annual Convention of the International Studies Association, Los Angeles, California, March 18-22, 1980 pp. 11-13.
21. See Captain Herbert F. Harback and Captain Daniel J. Cox, Jr. "Research Report on the Accession and Retention of Individual Reservists," unpublished report in the Department of Social Sciences, U.S. Military Academy, August 1, 1979, p. A5.
22. For sixteen specific recommendations, see Compton "Army Reserve Components," pp. 6-9.
23. SR units were manned at less than 70 percent at the time of this study. A year later, in the summer 1980, SR strengths had increased significantly to approximately 76 percent.

Chapter 9

# Are We Really Serious? A Critical Assessment of Manpower Policies in the Army Reserve Forces

Kenneth J. Coffey

The message from the Pentagon in 1980 concerning the health of the army reserve forces is clear: thanks to innovative new policies and programs, the problems which have plagued these forces since the advent of the all-volunteer force (AVF) in 1973 are being resolved; further, that by 1985 the reserves should be able to meet their mobilization and war-fighting commitments.

There is no disagreement between the Pentagon and "we" critics over the increased role of the Army Reserve Forces in national defense, or over the manpower, equipment, and other factors of readiness which are critical to the accomplishment of their mission. Nor is there any major disagreement over the fact that improvements have been made during 1978 and 1979 and that further improvements will be made in 1980 and beyond. There remains, however, a reasonable difference of opinion concerning whether the new policies and programs will accomplish the Army's goal or, in contrast, whether they will provide only incremental "band-aid" fixes to much deeper problems.

It is the purpose of this chapter, then, to critically analyze the current state of reserve affairs in relation to the ongoing and planned improvements. By assuming this devil's advocate role, it is contended that the extent of the problems can be more clearly defined, that the impact of the new policies and programs can be more accurately weighted, and that a clearer understanding of the remaining issues can be developed.

## WHAT ARE OUR STANDARDS OF SERIOUSNESS?

Since the advent of the AVF, the Army Reserve forces have assumed a mobilization and war-fighting responsibility of far greater magnitude than in the draft years. Due to major reductions in the size of the active Army, increasing commitments for deployment to Europe in support of NATO or to the Middle East, compression of the allowable time for delivering reserve reinforcements, higher expected casualty rates, and a reduction in the expected warning time for any conflict, the reserves have been given responsibilities that, while not equal to, are as nearly demanding as those of the active army.

The seriousness of the commitment to provide reserve forces the necessary capabilities should be measured by those criteria normally applied to the active forces. Specifically, I submit that a mark of serious commitment should be planned or ongoing programs instituted to ensure (1) that the Reserves reach a manning level near to their wartime manpower requirements; (2) that the quality of Reserve forces personnel be maintained at a level close to that of the active Army; and (3) that the personnel recruited and retained be the right people in the right jobs who are well trained and ready to perform their mobilization roles. Against these measures, then, how are the Reserves doing? How are they likely to be doing by the mid-1980s?

## WILL THE RESERVES HAVE ENOUGH PEOPLE?

The Army Reserve Forces consist of three major components: the Army National Guard, the Army Reserve, and the Army Individual Ready Reserve (IRR), and the manning levels of all three components have fallen dramatically since the end of the draft. Due to a variety of reasons, their combined loss reached almost 400,000 from the manpower levels which had been maintained in the pre-Vietnam peacetime years. Whereas there were enough trained reservists during those years to meet mobilization and war-fighting demands, the manpower resources of the Reserves in 1980 would be far from adequate.[1]

Nevertheless, the policy changes and new programs which were designed to improve the recruiting and retention of personnel in the key reserve forces components have prompted small incremental improvements.[2] For example, as noted in table 9.1, the National Guard was able to increase its strength from 341,000 in FY 1978 to 345,500 by the end of FY 1979.

The gains registered by the Guard, Reserve, and IRR were the first since the end of draft calls in 1972. The gains in the IRR were, in large measure, one-time-only gains, prompted by the stopping of automatic transfers to the Standby Reserve (which has ceased to be a major source of mobilization manpower).

Will the gains that should accrue from the new policies and programs be

Table 9.1. Army Reserve Forces Components: Manning Level Changes

| Component | End FY 1978 Strength | End FY 1979 Strength | Gain or Loss |
|---|---|---|---|
| National Guard | 341,000 | 345,500 | +4,500 |
| Reserve | 185,800 | 190,000 | +4,200 |
| IRR | 177,200 | 206,300 | +29,100 |

enough to meet the Army's 1985 requirements? The Pentagon believes so, but the magnitude of the tasks remaining casts a large shadow of doubt on this position.

The basis for this doubt is multifold, and concerns not only the large number of additional personnel that must be recruited and retained, but also a variety of yet-to-be-discussed weaknesses in the current posture and in several of the ongoing corrective programs.

Concerning the attainment of manning level objectives, it should be noted that the stated peacetime objectives are far above the current levels for all components. As table 9.2 illustrates, the challenges of increasing the size of the three major components will be formidable.

Table 9.2. Contrasts Between FY 1979 and Peacetime Manning Level Objectives

| Component | End FY 1979 Manning Level | Peacetime Objective | Shortfall |
|---|---|---|---|
| National Guard | 345,500 | 418,000 | 72,500 |
| Reserve | 190,000 | 252,400 | 62,400 |
| IRR | 206,300 | 400,000 | 197,700 |

Even if these peacetime objectives are attained, both the National Guard and the Reserve still would be some 50,000 personnel below their wartime manning needs. Yet, there would be enough trained personnel in the IRR not only to fill out the National Guard and Reserve Units, but also to fill out all active Army units and provide casualty replacements during the early months of a conflict.

Compounding the problem, however, is the recent decision of the Army to expand its mobilization manpower requirements by 60,000 over the next six years.[3] Whereas some of this increase will be met by planned increases in the active Army, the bulk of the added manpower (40,000 or so) will have to come from the Reserves. Thus, it is likely that the current FY 1985 manning level objectives will have to be raised even further. There are also various weaknesses which merit discussion in the current posture of the Reserves and in several of their new programs.

First, Pentagon statements and releases concerning the Guard and Reserve often overstate strength by including men and women in their totals who have enlisted but have not as yet completed basic military training. Such personnel—who numbered 25,253 in the Guard and 10,017 in the Reserve at the end of FY 1979—will, at some point, be usable assets.[4] Until they complete their training, however, it is misleading to include them in overall strength figures. Though the Reserves categorize such personnel as members of a training pipeline, this distinction is seldom cited in official presentations.

Second, as a result of a detailed audit by the General Accounting Office (GAO) of the Army's system of keeping track of unit strength totals in the guard and reserve, several reporting and administrative errors have come to light. The net result, according to GAO, is that the Army Guard and Reserve are overreporting their on-board strength by almost four percent, a disparity of some 20,000 personnel.[5]

Third, an Army Audit Agency (AAA) report issued in late 1979 identified more than 34,000 Guardsmen and 15,800 Reservists who had missed half or more of their drills during the first half of FY 1979, a level of training far below the standards of acceptability set by the Department of the Army. These unsatisfactory performers amounted to about 10 percent of the Guard and 8.5 percent of the Reserve strength totals.[6] In total, then, some 105,000 (20 percent) of the personnel in the Guard and Reserve at the end of FY 1979 were questionable assets.

Moreover, among those men being released from active duty and transferred to the IRR are some who are being released for reasons of bad attitude and other motivational problems; and there are serious reservations concerning the usefulness of these personnel in a mobilization effort. The usefulness of those people being transferred to the IRR from Guard and Reserve units is further suspect because they are not fulfilling their obligations to attend drills and summer camps. Many of these men have not been seen by their unit commanders for many months and, in my view, it would be folly to say that we could find them quickly in the event of a military emergency.

## QUALITY OF GUARD AND RESERVE RECRUITS

Quality performance is difficult to assess and even more difficult to predict. Impacting upon it are a myriad of individual traits—honesty, integrity, skill, loyalty, commitment, and motivation. It also is a product of situational variables—the work environment, unit esprit, training, and leadership. Consequently, it is next to impossible for the armed forces or any other large employer to effectively select the right people for all of their positions. At best, efforts are made to select those with the highest potential. At worst, because of the time and cost factors associated with even a basic selection program, choices are made on the basis of impressions, work history, and other subjective judgments.

The two attributes principally used by the armed forces to describe and measure the quality of their new recruits are level of education and mental aptitude. Possession of a high school diploma has proven to be a sound indicator of capacity to adjust to the discipline of a military environment, while the scores attained by potential recruits on the three-hour Armed Services Vocational Aptitude Battery (ASVAB) have proven to be good indicators of potential success in training. More sophisticated methods of measuring quality exist; yet, their implementation would appear to be remote due to very high costs. As a result, it is likely that both the active Army and the Reserve forces will contiunue to use the two traditional methods of measuring quality.

In the case of high school diploma graduates, then, how did the recruits for the National Guard and reserve in FY 1979 compare with those for the active Army? The answer to this question cannot be accurately determined until all the young men recruited by the Guard and Reserve while they were still in high school finish their high school programs or drop out. Nevertheless, by giving "credit" to the Guard and Reserve for such students, a reasonable comparison can be made, though weighted slightly in favor of the Reserves.

The proportions of male high school diploma graduates among the new recruits in FY 1979 differed markedly among the three components. As table 9.3 highlights, the Guard achieved a high school diploma rate somewhat above the rate for the active Army (which was the lowest of the four active services) while the Reserve rate was substantially lower.[7]

Table 9.3. Proportion of High School Diploma Graduates in FY 1979 Male Recruit Groups

| Component | Percent of Diploma Grads | Percent of Non-Diploma Grads |
| --- | --- | --- |
| Active Army | 59 | 41 |
| National Guard | 65 | 35 |
| Reserve | 30 | 70 |

By including the statistics for women high school diploma graduates, the proportions of such quality recruits improve slightly for all components, due to the universally high qualifications of their women recruits. The relative positions of the three components, however, do not change.

The same disparities between the Reserve and the active Army/National Guard appear when statistics for mental categories are examined. As table 9.4

Table 9.4. Proportion of Mental Categories in Male Recruit Groups, FY 1979

| Component | I & II | III | IV |
|---|---|---|---|
| Active Army |  | 89% | 11% |
| National Guard | 20% | 69% | 11% |
| Reserve | 12% | 68% | 20% |

shows, the proportions of Mental Category IV personnel in the Reserve (those least desired) was about double the proportion in the active Army and the National Guard.[8]

The bleak status of quality recruiting in the Reserve is clouded further by the probability that the mental test system being utilized by the Active and Reserve Forces has been inflating Mental Category rankings by a significant amount. Such inflation has been suspected by many analysts for some time, but it was not confirmed by the Department of Defense until early 1980. At that time, Assistant Secretary of Defense for Manpower, Reserve Affairs and Logistics Robert B. Pirie told members that "statistical sampling suggests that a sizable fraction (less than one half but probably more than one quarter) of FY 1978 male recruits labeled as Mental Category III should have been labeled as Mental Category IV."[9] (FY 1979 data are now being analyzed.)

If Pirie's conclusion is extended to the FY 1979 group (and every indication supports this), then the inabilities of the Reserve to recruit quality personnel during FY 1979 was even greater than indicated. At worst, if 50 percent of those labeled as Mental Group III were actually Mental Group IV's or lower, then somewhat more than one-half of men recruited by the Army Reserve were in Mental Group IV and V, or the lower 30 percent of the World War II-era standard population which is used as a base reference for testing purposes. In addition, in all probability, most of the men identified as Mental Group IV's were Mental Group V's (the lowest 10 percent who are excluded by statute from service). Thus, if correct test scoring procedures had been in effect during FY 1979, the Army Reserve would have been precluded from enlisting some 20 percent of their accessions (the Active Army and the Army National Guard would have been precluded from enlisting some 10 percent). Such actions, of course, would have impacted heavily on the overall recruiting programs and on unit manning levels and it is likely that instead of registering small manning level gains, major force level reductions would have occurred.

Compounding this problem is a recognized level of recruiting malpractice, actions which also inflate the quality measures of new recruits. During FY 1979, the Active Army conducted an extensive investigation of test compromise and other forms of irregularities within the Active Army and Army Reserve recruiting programs. Their efforts concluded that some two-to-three percent of those enlisting had participated in some malpractice, including many who had received improper coaching or other help on the ASVAB test.

## DO THE RESERVES HAVE THE RIGHT PEOPLE IN THE RIGHT JOBS, TRAINED AND READY?

Beyond the questions of whether the Reserve Forces can reach their desired levels of manning or whether their quality can equal that of the Active Army is—perhaps—a more critical question of whether they are recruiting and retaining the right personnel.

In order to provide the Reserves with the right mix of younger, more energetic and junior personnel in the lower ranks and older, more expeienced veterans in the NCO positions, the Reserves have determined that they want a yearly input mix of about 60 percent non-prior service (NPS) personnel and 40 percent veterans. This determination, however, is not based on an extensive force structure analysis. Nevertheless, the 60-40 split was about the level maintained during the draft years.

Since the end of the draft, neither the National Guard nor the reserve has been able to attain its desired level non-prior service (NPS) accessions. As a consequence, their recruitment of more than enough veterans may be having a negative impact on their effectiveness, as well as on the strength level of the IRR.

If the Guard and Reserve were to attain their desired strength levels and also attain their desired levels of NPS accessions, then the Guard each year would need to recruit some 60,000 such men and the Reserve would need to recruit some 52,000. Clearly, the achievement of this goal has been beyond the current capabilities of either component, though the Guard has done far better than the Reserve. Nonetheless, the Guard's input of male NPS recruits in FY 1979 of some 42,000 would have to be increased by 18,000, while the Reserve's input of 22,000 would have to be more than doubled. While each of the components in recent years has made incremental improvements in their recruitment of NPS personnel, it is doubtful that the combined impact of their new policies and programs will allow them to reach the desired levels.

An examination of the distribution of personnel within the enlisted grades of the Guard and Reserve illustrates this problem. Within the Guard, at the end of FY 1979, there were some 160,000 E-1 to E-4 personnel, or some 62 percent of their wartime manning requirements. At the same time, the 150,000 E-5 to E-9 personnel were already some 11,000 more than needed for the wartime structure. Within the Reserve, the 71,000 E-1 to E-4 personnel would have filled only 61 percent of their wartime requirements, while their more than 81,000 E-5 to E-9 personnel represented 86 percent of their needs. Despite this disproportionate ratio, however, and perhaps due to a serious rethinking of their prior-service needs, the Reserve hopes to increase their numbers of such personnel.

Beyond the problems concerning shortages of junior personnel are many other manpower problems, including disproportionate shortages of personnel in the combat career fields (infantry, combat engineering, field artillery, air defense artillery, and armor). Whereas the Guard overall is short some 20 percent of the personnel needed for their wartime manning, the shortages in the five combat skill areas are almost double, with the highest shortages in the infantry and air defense artillery. In sum, as the General Accounting Office recently concluded, the five combat-type career management fields numerically represent about 70 percent of the total enlisted shortages.[10] Within the Reserve, similar shortages exist though, since the Reserve consists predominantly of combat support and combat service support units, the shortage skills are somewhat different from those of the Guard. In the Reserve, the major shortage skill areas are combat engineers with only 63 percent of their wartime strength, field artillery with only 48 percent; and medical personnel with only 65 percent.

The shortage problems within the critical skill groups in the Guard and Reserve are heightened by a relatively high percent of assigned personnel who are not qualified for their jobs. As the GAO also has noted, within the five critical combat skill areas in the Guard, only some 78 percent of the personnel onhand are qualified to serve in their positions. In total, then, the Guard has only slightly more than half of the qualified personnel it needs in its combat jobs. Within the Reserve, the combination of manning level shortfalls and unqualified personnel results in an even grimmer situation. For the three skill areas of combat engineers, field artillery, and medical, the numbers of trained personnel in FY 1979 represented only 43 percent, 35 percent, and 47 percent respectively of their wartime manning requirements.[11]

These shortage problems would be compounded upon mobilization for contrary to policy, it would be likely that some members of the various Reserve forces components would not report immediately for active service. The reasons for this would be many—health, personal business or family problems, or inadequate Army records, among others. As a recognition of this, the Secretary of Defense in 1978 developed "yield rates" for each category of manpower resource.[12] Whereas the Army subsequently has been directed to improve the rates, little evidence can be located that supports positive movement, though the army has been improving its record-keeping procedures. In contrast, however, recent mobilization exercises illustrated that the rates—particularly for the IRR—may be optimistic. On the one hand, in total, there are enough pretrained personnel in the various categories to meet the army's needs, if Retired Personnel are included. On the other hand, however, if the expected losses from these sources are understated, the Army's problems would be even greater.

A variety of factors would influence the validity of the "yield" rates. For example, the willingness of Americans to serve would vary considerably between a politically inspired mobilization in response to an insurgency in a Third World oil-producing country and a call-up in response to a major Warsaw Pact attack in Central Europe. In addition, there would certainly be a different response rate from personnel of different grades, skills, ages, and obligations for recall.

Another problem concerns the matching of the Army's specific manning needs with available personnel. While some 70 percent of the IRR (perhaps more) would be likely to report on mobilization, few efforts have been made to match these personnel with specific jobs or to provide them with needed retraining or new skills. While 75 percent of the Army's filler and replacement needs would be in combat arms, medical, combat engineering, and other direct support fields, only about 25 percent of the IRR personnel possessed these skills in FY 1979.

A serious question also arises as to whether the manpower available upon mobilization would be ready in time to play a useful role in the critical early weeks. The Army has concentrated on developing new programs and policies aimed at increasing the strength levels of the Guard and Reserve as well as the IRR, but it has given far less attention to time-related problems. In fact, however, most of the personnel needed to boost the wartime force to its peak level would be needed in the first few weeks, and it would be unlikely that the reporting and deployment schedules called for in current plans could be met, particularly by those in the IRR. In such cases, initial ordering and administrative processing would take time. Many personnel would require refresher training before they could function effectively in operating units; those assigned to new specialties would require even longer periods of training. Though such personnel might eventually fill units to their wartime levels, enough of them would be delayed in reporting to their units to cause major manning problems.

## HOW SERIOUS ARE WE ABOUT THE ARMY RESERVE FORCES?

As our examination of the measurement criteria illustrated, the Army Reserve forces, the Reserve in particular, have not been nearly as successful as the active Army in meeting manning level, manpower quality, and personnel effectiveness goals. But is this the result of deliberate or unconscious inattention, or is it the result of different and apparently unsurmountable recruiting, training, and retention problems unique to the Reserve forces?

Whereas some positive changes have taken place, the weight of evidence supports the conclusion that the leadership elements within the Army and the Office of the Secretary of Defense have not as yet fully matched their repeated statements of concern over the problems in the Reserve forces with appropriate action, management attention, and resources.

Decisions reflected in the budgetary process provide a clear indication of this. For example, in his official guidance to the armed forces issued during

1979 for the preparation of the FY 1981 budget, the Secretary of Defense made a sharp distinction between his concern for the active forces and his concern for the Reserves. While spelling out in great detail desired manning levels, numbers of high school diploma graduates and women, attrition rates, and other goals for the active forces, his directions for funding the Reserves were limited to broad statements such as "peacetime manning should be increased where it is lower than authorized, and particular emphasis should be placed on the early deploying units." And in terms of the high school diploma graduate marketplace, he created what could be considered as a second class citizenship for the Reserves by directing them to minimize competition with the active forces among high school seniors by concentrating on labor force participants, postsecondary students, and individuals with low propensity to enlist in the active forces.[13] Though the stated purpose was to penetrate an unused market, many active Army recruiters have said to Guard and Reserve recruiters: "Stay away from the prime recruiting area!"

There are those within the Pentagon that say that the lack of definite goals for the Reserves in the Budget Guidance was not due to lack of concern, but rather to an acceptance of the fact that the Reserves, particularly the Army Reserve forces, could not control and manage their recruiting and retention programs to the level of sophistication attained by the active forces and necessary for the establishment of more definitive goals. Nevertheless, the Guidance did not allow each branch of service to set its own goals for its reserves. Consequently, in their subsequent budget process, the Army not only established end strength goals far below peacetime manning objectives, it also set quality standards lower than those set for its active personnel. Further, the army did not request the Reserve pay changes, increased bonus funds, improved training facilities and programs, increased recruiting forces, and other resources that would have provided the means for the Army Reserve forces to make a serious and substantial movement toward greater parity with the active Army.

In defense of the Army's failure to fully support its Reserve forces, it should be pointed out that Congress in recent years has not been favorably inclined to major and revolutionary changes in Reserve pay and other policies, though they recently initiated and funded a needed enlistment/reenlistment bonus program. They have not, however, seriously supported the major departures from current policy (such as unlinking active and Reserve pay and making major increases in Reserve incentives) which would be necessary to fully resolve the manpower problems. In any case, it is clear that the Army's position on setting less-than-optimum goals for the Reserve has been influenced by what they believed they could get (rather than by what they needed) in order to make significant and continuing improvements. The absence of a strong commitment on the part of Reserve organizations and leaders to major departures from current policy also has impacted on the Army's decisions.

What are the major reasons why the Army has been less than fully serious about its Reserve forces?

First, the Army has been preoccupied since the end of draft calls with the problems of manning the all-volunteer active Army. With continuing difficulties in finding and keeping enough quality personnel, particularly for the combat arms, active Army managers have been hard-pressed to retain even a slowly shrinking force. Consequently, in an era of limited resources and management skills, priority has been given to countering the problems of the active Army.

Second, there is a large body of opinion within the Army and elsewhere which is increasingly questioning the necessity for a large Reserve force in a period of history which they believe will be characterized by short, violent confrontations, with premiums on ready forces and mobility. Whereas certain of the Guard and Reserve units earmarked for early deployment could play a role in such short-war scenarios, the bulk of the Reserve forces would not be ready for deployment until weeks or even months after the outbreak of a crisis, and they would have little impact on the eventual outcome. As a result, these critics argue there is little justification for expending resources or management expertise for forces of such marginal value.

Third, there is the realistic view of many in the Army establishment and elsewhere that the role of the Reserves is being severely limited by equipment, supply, war reserves, and strategic mobility weaknesses.[14]

A variety of statistics and testimony could be presented on our current inabilities to deliver and support massive reinforcements in the event of a crisis in Europe or the Middle East. Whereas there is a lack of agreement on our exact capabilities, most experts agree that the United States could not deploy the bulk of its stateside active Army units, much less many of the Reserves, in a time frame which was close to that called for in contingency plans.[15] Accordingly, it can be argued that, until we begin to have the capability to equip, transport, and support massive reinforcements, the commitment of added resources to the Reserves would only sidetrack monies and management attention that could be better utilized in areas of more critical importance.

## WHAT CHOICES ARE OPEN?

I suggest three alternative courses of action to be considered by Pentagon decision makers in the early 1980s: (1) maintaining the current degree of commitment and resources; (2) becoming fully committed to bringing the reserve forces up to the hoped-for levels of strength and effectivenss; or (3) redirecting Reserve forces assets and management attention to the critical early deploying units, with the remaining units being assigned to cadre status.

The continuation of the status quo policies and programs for the Guard and

Reserve no doubt would result in a steady slow improvement over the next few years. Such incremental gains, however, could not be expected to bring the two components up to the desired levels of readiness and manning; and, at least in the late 1980s, many of the gains could be offset by major recruiting difficulties, prompted by the shrinking pool of eligible enlistment candidates.[16]

While some gains would be realized in the IRR from the various programs already initiated or being planned, this manpower resource still would be inadequate to meet wartime requirements, if not in terms of gross numbers, then at least in terms of skilled and ready personnel.

The second alternative would be the most expensive and difficult to achieve. Failing a return to Selective Service or the adoption of a special IRR draft—highly unlikely events—major changes would have to be made in the attractions of Reserve forces service. Pay would have to be decoupled from active Army pay rates and substantial increases would be necessary. A myriad of new enlistment and reenlistment bonuses also would be required, as well as major increases in the recruiting forces and their supporting personnel and facilities. In addition, there would have to be improvements in Reserve training programs so that more of those enticed to Reserve forces service would remain. And in this regard, more and better equipment, training facilities, and funds, and greater active Army affiliations and supervision would be needed. The price tag for such a commitment cannot be determined without detailed additional research, though it probably would require several billions of dollars. Yet, as the draft for the active forces was ended on the basis of the work of the Gates Commission in 1969-1970 and the subsequent commitment of added funds, there can be no doubt that a similar effort and commitment in 1980 and 1981 could achieve the same result for the Reserves. In short, as Martin Anderson urged in a recent op-ed piece in the *Washington Post:* "We should announce that from now on the Reserves are serious business, not a paid routine gambol."[17]

Some may argue that the stronger position of the Carter Administration on national security matters, which resulted from the Iran and Afghanistan crises, will be the first serious step on the path toward buidling such fully ready reserves. Indeed, a 3.2 percent real growth objective was included in the President's FY 1981 budget. Unfortunately, however, a close examination of the budget highlights serious weaknesses in this position; specifically, it is based on assumptions about inflation that are not likely to turn out to be true. One only has to remember that President Carter also made a "real increase proposal" in 1979 and that this projected gain turned into a loss because of the unexpectedly high inflation. Neither does the FY 1981 Budget, as proposed, add much to the sorely underfunded Reserves or to manpower programs overall.[18] Indeed, even if inflation allows "real" increases to take place, the gains will be in weapons systems development and procurement, which are admittedly needy areas but not exclusively so.

Perhaps, then, the most realistic course of action would be to accept the fact that the problems of the Reserves will not be fully corrected in the near future and that whatever assets are available should be concentrated in the units designated for early deployment. To a great extent, such concentration already is taking place. Such units are receiving more management attention than their later deploying counterparts. Full-time manning is at higher levels. Enlistment and reenlistment incentives are targeted at personnel in these units, and the units are receiving priority for new equipment and better training. At the same time, however, many resources and attention still are being directed elsewhere.

The adoption of a cadre manning policy would free full-time manning personnel, equipment, training, and personnel funds for use with the early deploying units; and there is little doubt that these added resources would prompt improved recruitment and retention of more high quality personnel and a higher level of unit effectiveness and readiness. Under such a cadre concept, the later deploying Guard and Reserve units would maintain their officers and senior NCOs (as well as their junior personnel already on the rolls), but they would be relieved of responsibility for recruiting and training new, nonprior service personnel. Such a fall-off in strength would deter traditional training and require massive fills of new people upon mobilization. At the same time, however, it would not be necessary to strip the few remaining junior personnel from these units upon mobilization for use as fillers, a policy which though not popular has nevertheless been advanced by the leadership in the Pentagon.[19] Instead, the early deploying units could be manned at higher levels while the later deploying units in cadre status could amend their training programs to foster the skills necessary for forming units and leading personnel fresh from the training base.

Whether the status quo is maintained or a cadre policy is adopted, it is clear that upon mobilization the available combat arms and other shortage skill personnel in the IRR would have to be assigned to early deploying units; and the later deploying units would have to be filled with retrained individual reservists or newly trained conscripts, personnel who would not be ready for assignment until several months after mobilization. Thus, whether or not such units are allowed to continue their recruitment and retention of junior personnel, they would not be ready for deployment at an early date. Due to limitations on strategic mobility, war reserves, and our capcity to continously supply an overseas force, however, such longer-than-expected delays in achieving readiness for deployment would not be the Army's most critical weakness.

In a recent article in *Army* magazine, Thomas D. Slear, a West Pointer and a former Army officer, reported that the Reserve infantry company which he observed was authorized 155 personnel, that 55 people were on the rolls, but that only 25, almost all officers and senior NCOs, had shown up for weekend training. Of the remaining 30 or so personnel, 11 had not been seen for upwards of five months while the others, almost all E-1s to E-3s in their initial terms of service, had called in with such excuses as marital problems, bad colds, and car troubles. On the positive side of the ledger, however, Slear noted that "the unit's enthusiasm, competence and esprit in their field training bespoke the existence of a strong cadre of leadership that a mobilizing Army would welcome."[20] Such are the strengths and weaknesses of many Reserve units today. And whether formalized or not, it is clear that units such as that visited by Slear already have evolved to a cadre status.

Of the three alternative courses of action, there is no doubt that national defense would be best served by a more serious commitment on the part of the Army and the Department of Defense to the resolution of the many Army Reserve forces manpower problems. Failing this, however, the Army must make the best use of the available resources and the formalization of a cadre policy for the majority of the Army Guard and Reserve would be a positive step in this direction.

# NOTES

1. Estimates of the extent of the shortfall vary. One of the more optimistic (270,000) was made by a top Pentagon official in early 1980. See Statement of Assistant Secretary of Defense for Manpower, Reserve Affairs and Logistics, Robert B. Pirie, *Hearings Before the Military Personnel Subcommittee of the House Armed Services Committee,* February 19, 1980, p. 28.
2. For a summary of the new policies and programs, see Office of the Assistant Secretary of Defense (Public Affairs), "Status of the Individual Ready Reserve (IRR): Strength and Initiatives, Fiscal Years 1978-1979," January 30, 1980; and "Selected Reserve Manpower Strength Assessment and Recruiting Results for Fiscal Year 1979," December 31, 1979.
3. Pirie, *Hearings Before the Military Personnel Subcommittee,* p. 28.
4. See Office of Deputy Assistant Secretary of Defense (Reserve Affairs), "Official Guard and Reserve Manpower Strengths and Statistics," September 30, 1979, for a display of all Army Reserve Forces strength and quality data used herein.
5. General Accounting Office, General Accounting Office Report to the Secretary of the Army, *Army Guard and Reserve Pay and Personnel Systems are Unreliable and Susceptible to Waste and Abuse,* January 28, 1980, p. 28.
6. Ibid., pp. 24, 31.
7. Despite the fact that the Guard was able to recruit more than twice the proportion of high school diploma grads than the Reserve, both components were able to attract about equal proportions of black and white quality recruits. For example, within the Guard, 61.5 percent of the white recruits were high school diploma grads compared with 64 percent of the black recruits. In the Reserve, 30 percent of both the white and black recruits were high school diploma grads.
8. Unlike the nearly equal proportions of blacks and whites with high school diplomas, there was a far greater proportion of blacks in Mental Category IV than whites. For example, in the Guard, 19.2 percent of black male enlistees in FY 1979 were ranked as Category IV's, while only 8.2 percent of the whites were so-classified. In the Reserve, 31 percent of the blacks were ranked in Category IV, compared with 13.6 percent of the whites.
9. Pirie, *Hearings Before the Military Personnel Subcommittee,* p. 11.
10. General Accounting Office, Comptroller General's Report to the Congress, *Critical Manpower Problems Restrict the Use of National Guard and Reserve Forces,* July 11, 1979, pp. 34, 50.

## 162  Defense Manpower Planning

11. Ibid., pp. 36-37, 51-52.
12. The Secretary of Defense has provided the following "yields" for use in mobilization planning: Selected Reserve (Guard and Reserve units), 95 percent; IRR, 70 percent; Standby Reserve, 50 percent. See *Consolidated Guidance,* March 7, 1978, p. 0-8 (unclassified).
13. Secretary of Defense Harold Brown, *Consolidated Guidance,* April 12, 1979, p. N-8 (unclassified).
14. Concerning these limitations, the Secretary of Defense had this to say to Congress in early 1980: "We have economized (some would say skimped) on the nuts and bolts needed to sustain a non-nuclear conflict in a particular theater for more than a relatively short time." See *Report of Secretary of Defense Harold Brown to the Congress on the FY 1981 Budget, FY 1982 Authorization Request and FY 1981-1985 Defense Programs,* January, 29, 1980, p. 99.
15. The Army's plans for deployment of reinforcements from the United States for a major conflict in Europe include most of the Guard and Reserve units, as well as the Active Army divisions not currently assigned overseas. And in order to meet the Army's deployment schedule, the movement of all of these units would have to be completed in 90 days or less. See *Fiscal Year 1978 Authorization for Military Procurement, Research and Development, and Active Duty, Selected Reserve, and Civilian Personnel Strengths,* Hearings before the Senate Committee on Armed Services, March-April 1977, p. 2436.
16. By 1986, the number of 18 year old males will be only 1,839,000, a reduction of 324,000 from the 1979 level. There also will be corresponding reductions in the number of male high school diploma graduates and increased competition for such youth from educational institutions and civilian employers.
17. Martin Anderson, "Build the Reserves, Not Lists," *Washington Post,* February 3, 1980, p. C-1.
18. A recent Department of Defense study documented that the "real" expenditures for the Guard and Reserve (all four Services) actually decreased by about 10 percent from FY 1978 to FY 1980. See Office of the Deputy Assistant Secretary of Defense (Reserve Affairs), *Review of the Guard and Reserve,* December 26, 1979.
19. As a top Pentagon official told Congress in early 1980: "We would borrow people in shortage skills from late deploying units, accepting the fact that the units that are reduced may not be able to deploy when scheduled." See Pirie, *Hearings Before the Military Personnel Subcommittee,* p. 35.
20. Thomas D. Slear, "The Men of Company A," *Army,* January 1980, pp. 40-41.

## Chapter 10
# Future of the Army Reserves: Plans, Policies, and Programs
### John R. Brinkerhoff

The Army Guard and Reserve are better than most people believe, but they still are not yet good enough. The combined strength of the Army Guard and Reserve together is about 120,000 below the peacetime objective strength. The Army's Individual Ready Reserve (IRR) would be insufficient, even when supplemented by recalled retired personnel, to meet the demands for fillers and initial replacements in a full mobilization. Army Guard and Reserve units have well over three-quarters of the equipment needed to go to war, but there are some shortages of critical equipment. Training problems occur, and participation in training is less than fully satisfactory. The system for mobilizing the IRR is outmoded and may not work very well. It is fair to say that the United States has a major problem in the present unsatisfactory condition of reserve forces. On the other hand, it is also fair to say that the United States has a considerable asset in the 540,000 Army Guardsmen and Reservists who train each month.

What should be done about this situation? I will consider four basic courses of action. Although other options are possible, these four are most often suggested:

1. Increase the active forces and eliminate the Reserves.
2. Adopt a different (and better) reserve system.
3. Draft people for the Reserves.
4. Build up the Reserves through volunteerism.

# INCREASE THE ACTIVE FORCES AND ELIMINATE THE RESERVES

Some people suggest that it would be good to increase active forces so that reliance on reserve forces would be obviated or diminished. Many more people believe this proposition but hesitate to say it out loud. This idea is particularly prevalent among older regular officers brought up on a diet of disdain for the militia.

It is a peculiar characteristic of our American military tradition that the two major themes are contradictory. On the one hand, there is the tradition of the citizen-soldier—the Minuteman who drops his plow and picks up his musket to defend his home as a member of the militia. On the other hand, there is an institutionalized feeling of contempt on the part of the regulars for the militia. This disdain is capsulized in a familiar illustration of the Battle of Chippewa, in the War of 1812, showing Winfield Scott's Brigade of Infantry advancing on the British. The caption reads: "Those are Regulars, by God."

One of the major problems of our national military policy is how to reconcile these opposing viewpoints into a worthwhile product. It is a fact that attitudes of regulars toward reserves are a major factor in the effectiveness of the reserves. Regulars who despise the reserves tend to create reserves worthy of their contempt. Conversely, the more understanding and acceptance there is on the part of the regulars, the better the reserves tend to be. A worthwhile synergism of active and reserve forces exists in the Air Force, where the regular elements accept, appreciate, and give recognition to the reserves, resulting in an outstanding total Air Force system.

Nevertheless, it is true that, other things being equal, active units are better than reserve units. This does not imply that all active units are better than all reserve units. On the contrary, the evidence is that some reserve units are much better than similar active units. For one thing, reservists tend to be more experienced than regulars in technical areas. Active units may train for over 200 days each year, while reserve units may train no more than 40 days each year (with a few exceptions). It would be good, from a national security viewpoint, to have in the active forces all of the units needed to execute our national military strategy—if we could afford it.

The overwhelming advantage of reserve units is that they cost less than corresponding active units. The cost differential stems from the fact that all active personnel are paid for every day of service (whether they train or not) while reservists are paid only for the training or work that they do. The difference is between full-time workers and part-time workers. The cost of equipment is the same (provided the reserve units are issued combat-worthy gear), but the cost of people is different. Reserve units cost from one-third to two-thirds as much to operate as active units, depending on how many of the reserve unit personnel are on a full-time basis. This cost differential means that, for the same amount of money, we can keep more units in the total force by maintaining some of them in the reserves. The offsetting consideration is that the reserve units are, in general, less ready, less well trained, and less capable of rapid movement in a mobilization than are active units.

An additional factor is that the size of the active Army is today limited by the number of volunteers it attracts. It is possible that more money spent on advertising, recruiting, and incentives could induce more people to join the active Army; but, in this case, the cost advantage of reserve units over active units would be increased. It is also true that active Army strength could be increased by conscription, but that would entail other problems. Unless there is a draft, it does not appear possible to increase the active Army substantially at any cost. An active duty draft, moreover, would cause a rapid increase in Guard and Reserve strength and would eliminate that reason for having a draft.

The cost and supply constraints involved in increasing the active forces to compensate for reserve shortages make this option considerably less attractive than it appears at first glance. The Guard and Reserve contain half of the Army's infantry, tank and artillery battalions. About two-thirds of the service support units for the total Army are in the Guard and Reserve. At present, there are about 540,000 Army Guard and Reserve personnel training in units and another 200,000 pretrained individuals in the Inactive National Guard and Individual Ready Reserve. Assuming some manpower economies because of more training for active personnel, it still would take about 500,000 additional active Army soldiers to allow us to eliminate the Guard and Reserve completely. It would take at least 100,000 active soldiers just to compensate for the current shortfall in Guard and Reserve strength.

However, any sizable increase in active strength would require more money and more volunteers. Neither is likely to be forthcoming. If the supply of willing volunteers were plentiful enough to increase the Active forces substantially, it is likely that the Guard and Reserve also would be up to strength and, therefore, in condition to augment the active Army immediately upon mobilization. The $3 billion the Army spends on its Guard and Reserve personnel would buy only 200,000 more active-duty personnel. This would add about 80 combat battalions (infantry, tank, artillery, combat engineers) to active strength and capability but would delete 400 combat battalions presently in the Guard and Reserve. On balance, it does not make sense to increase the active forces substantially at the expense of the Army Guard and Reserve.

## ADOPT A DIFFERENT RESERVE SYSTEM

Another common suggestion is that the United States should adopt a different system because of the inadequacy of our present system. It is true that we inherited the system from our British and colonial forefathers and have had relatively little to say about it. It is also true that the system has produced somewhat mixed results in our previous wars. However, there is no evidence that another system would do as well or better, and there is considerable evidence that our present system does work well.

Critics of our current system often urge us to adopt their favorite scheme, implying all will be well if we follow their advice, but seldom facing up to the potential problems of their proposed system. Some advocate we adopt the Dutch system, which essentially takes a conscript battalion after 14 months of active service and transfers it intact to inactive status for another 20 months. Others advocate the classical conscription-based system which generates large numbers of trained individual reservists but does not form them into reserve units. Upon mobilization, the individual reservists augment active units and provide replacements. A variation of this proposal retains small reserve units—up to battalion size—but does not permit higher levels of reserve organization or high-ranking reserve officers. This classical conscription-based model of reserve utilization exists now in several West European nations. Many people would like us to adopt the Soviet system, not only for our reserve but for our active forces as well. (There is an irresistible attraction in some intellectual circles for the systems, techniques, and organizational structures of our potential adversaries.) The Soviets have cadre-strength active divisions which, upon mobilization, are brought to full strength by recall of preassigned individual reservists. The Soviets recently used reservists to bring several of these active cadre divisions to wartime strength and used them to invade Afghanistan.

We would take these suggestions more seriously if there were no evidence that our present system can do the job and meet the demanding response times required by the national military strategy. Fortunately, we have good evidence that our system does work.

Often overlooked in the debate over the Army Guard and Reserve is the fact that the Naval Reserve, the Marine Corps Reserve, the Coast Guard Reserve, the Air National Guard, and the Air Force Reserve all are up to strength and all are ready to perform their mobilization missions. Our National Guard and Air Force Reserve fighter aircraft can be flying sorties in Europe within 72 hours after mobilization. The Naval Reserve can meet its deployment schedules. The Marine Corps Reserve will provide a complete fourth Marine division and air wing when needed. The existence of these Reserve components which do make the present system work well proves that there is no fundamental defect in our system. It leads us to believe that, if the Army Guard and Reserve were up to strength and manned and equipped more like the Air Guard and Reserve, it could perform just as well.

This belief is reinforced by two more points. First, the French are moving toward a system which is very similar to our own. The French have organized three reserve divisions and plan to organize more. These reserve divisions will be combat organizations manned entirely and commanded by reservists up to the regimental level. This is a sharp departure from previous French doctrine. Second, the Army Guard and Reserve are not uniformly poor. There are many units within that formidable force that are up to strength and are ready to perform their wartime missions well. Even the units that are below strength have more capability than is generally recognized. With 540,000 personnel in units, the Army Guard and Reserve is a formidable and highly capable military force.

## DRAFT PEOPLE FOR THE RESERVES

A common proposal these days is that we should solve the manpower shortages in the Army Guard and Reserve by drafting for these components. Many people believe that we should eliminate the shortfall in the Army's IRR by drafting people directly into this component. One proposal would induct 200,000 young people selected by chance for four to six months of initial training on active duty, followed by five and a half years in the IRR. Some versions require annual refresher training; others do not.

It is true that a large-scale IRR draft would provide large numbers of IRR personnel in relatively short order. However, these people would be neither well-trained nor reliable assets for a mobilization. The Army states that a graduate of basic training and advanced infantry training has mastered only half the skills needed to be an effective combat infantryman. The young soldiers who go on to serve in active or reserve units complete the other half of their individual training in their units where they also learn to operate as members of teams. The individual who receives only initial training is half-trained and has never had the socializing experience gained by serving in a unit. Upon mobilization, the person who had served only in the IRR would not be able to perform well without further individual and unit training. This training deficiency is compounded by the fact that persons compelled to serve in the IRR would be far less likely than volunteers to report promptly or even to report at all in the event of mobilization. An IRR draft would place large numbers of personnel on the books and create the illusion of having solved the problem, but the IRR members who are drafted would be only half-trained and unreliable. Because of this, we do not favor a draft for the IRR.

Another suggestion, though less prevalent than the IRR draft, is to draft for the Selected Reserve. This also is a bad idea. Volunteerism is the essence of Guard and Reserve membership. The active forces are not so bound to voluntary participation. It is possible to compel a draftee to perform in the active forces because the active forces are in business 24 hours a day, each day, and can provide a highly structured operational environment. There are rewards and sanctions to entice and enforce compliance. For most people on active duty, including draftees, it is easier to go along with the system than not, and it takes a conscious effort to rebel against the system.

It is quite different in the reserve forces. The environment is not very structured, rewards exist, but sanctions are ineffective. It takes a conscious act of will to get up at six o'clock on Saturday morning to go to the armory to attend training. It is a voluntary act. The reservist is still primarily a civilian and must make a conscious effort to go along with the reserve system. It is very difficult to compel people to participate meaningfully in reserve training. The point is made by that old adage: "You can lead a horse to water, but you can't make him drink." Well, you can draft a person into the Reserve, but you can't make him participate.

The best way, if not the only way, to use conscription to help build up the strength of the Guard and Reserve is to draft people for active service. After two years of active service, these draftees will still have four years to serve in the Ready Reserve to satisfy their military service obligation. These people will be fully trained and will have served in active units. Many will choose to affiliate with a reserve unit. Strength would increase simply because more people would be obligated to serve in the Ready Reserve upon release from active duty.

Another, and perhaps more significant, source of additional strength would be from persons joining the Army Guard and Reserve to avoid serving on active duty. This would happen if members of the Guard and Reserve were exempt from the active duty draft. This did happen during the recent peacetime drafts for the Korean and Vietnam wars. At that time, the Guard and Reserve were up to strength, and there were waiting lists.

In retrospect however, those were not the "good old days" for the Guard and Reserve. Too many bad habits were learned then that are proving to be hard to unlearn. In an era of excess manpower supply, it was not necessary to lead well or provide good training to maintain strength. The threat of the active duty draft kept people in despite poor treatment and poor training. Policies were established that were designed to push people out and make it hard to get in. (We are suffering today from the continued enforcement of some of these policies.) The people who joined were not really volunteers, and many of them were not interested in serving their country. On the contrary, many joined the Guard and Reserve to avoid serving their country. A great many members of the Guard and Reserve were college students who were completely unsympathetic with the aims and methods of the Guard and Reserve, and who fought the system that gave them shelter. The Guard and Reserve, in the recent draft era, may have been large in strength, but were composed of people who had less interest and motivation than today's Guardsmen and Reservists—all of whom are true volunteers.

An active duty draft would not be a panacea for the problems of the Army Guard and Reserve. A draft for the reserves alone would cause more problems than it would solve. A draft for the active force would lead to an increase in strength, but it would also cause other problems.

In any event, it is not useful to count on having an active duty draft. Having a draft depends on the will of the nation. There is no indication that the nation wants a peacetime draft. The President has not advocated a peacetime draft, neither has the Secretary of Defense. Many groups oppose not only a draft, but the less burdensome step of registration. Congress does not appear to favor resumption of the draft at this time. So, the practical manager has to rule out the draft at this time, and proceed to get the job done without it.

## BUILD UP THE GUARD AND RESERVE THROUGH VOLUNTEERISM

The solution that the Office of the Secretary of Defense (OSD) is pursuing is to get the Army Guard and Reserve up to strength and ready to go to war through volunteerism. We see no possibility of increasing the active force enough to be able to do without a reserve, or even enough to offset existing reserve strength shortages. We reject the idea that our situation would be improved by adopting some different scheme for reserve organization; we still would face the essential choice between voluntary membership or compulsion under any system. We do not believe that a draft will be resumed in the near future; and we realize that, even if a draft were resumed, all of our problems would not be solved.

At present, there is no choice but to get the Army Guard and Reserve up to strength within the context of the All-Volunteer Force. This can be done, if we try. Until two years ago, we were not even trying. The measures adopted in 1973 to ease the transition from draft to voluntary enlistment for the active force were not put into effect for the Guard and Reserve at that time. Much was done in 1973 in raising pay, setting up bonuses, and improving quality of life to attract young people to the active Army. Much money was spent to build better barracks and to improve the attractiveness of active Army service. None of this was done for the Guard and Reserve. There were no bonuses for the Reserves. There were no major policy changes. Those who then were in charge of the All-Volunteer Force concentrated solely on the active forces.

Five years later, in 1978, it became apparent that the major problem in the All-Volunteer Force was the Army Guard and Reserve. By this time, the Army Guard and Reserve unit strength was about 135,000 below the peacetime objective and about 180,000 below wartime strength. The IRR had shrunk in size to the point where it could no longer provide sufficient fillers and replacements to sustain the Army during the initial few months of a major conventional war. By mid-1978, the strength of the Reserve components was recognized as a major problem.

It was at this time that some of the same kinds of management programs which had proven successful for the All-Volunteer Force in the active forces

**Table 10.1.** Army Guard and Reserve Strength as of September 30 (thousands)

| 1974 | 1975 | 1976 | 1977 | 1978 | 1979 | 1980 |
|------|------|------|------|------|------|------|
| 638  | 620  | 557  | 544  | 526  | 536  |      |

were applied to the Reserves. Instead of policies designed to repel recruits and force members out, new policies and programs to attract people to the Guard and Reserve and make them want to stay in were adopted. Most of these new programs were initiated in late 1978; they took full effect in 1979. By and large, they have been successful. During fiscal year 1979, the strength of the Army Guard and Reserve increased for the first time in five years. Table 10.1 shows the strengths of the Army Guard and Reserve on September 30, of the years shown. The strength increase resulted primarily as a result of applying to the Reserves the same kind of all-volunteer management programs which had been applied five years earlier to the active Army.

There are two major aspects to strength: recruitment and retention. During FY 1978 and FY 1979, we emphasized programs to improve recruiting. In the past two years, we have improved our advertising program, established enlistment bonuses and educational assistance, provided initial training options to make it more convenient for young men and women to receive initial active duty training, offered a three-year initial enlistment, and created a full-time professional recruiting force. These efforts have paid off. We have met our recruitment goals. However, we still have not increased strength sufficiently because we are still experiencing too much attrition.

Our major effort during FY 1980 will be to decrease attrition. There are two aspects to attrition management: increasing reenlistments and reducing unprogrammed losses. We want to increase the number of good people who reenlist upon successful completion of their term of enlistment. To do this, we are offering a reenlistment bonus designed to retain persons with critical skills. We also are attempting to promote more flexible career management policies to facilitate upward progression and development of promising reservists. Many of our present personnel policies were put into effect in an era of manpower plenty, and they were designed to force people out and make it difficult to get in. We are suffering today from continued application at the working level of these outmoded policies. We are publishing new policies designed to be more appropriate for an era of manpower scarcity, but it takes time to get the word and the new approach down to the working level. Our new policies are designed to make it easy to join and hard to get out.

Far more serious than insufficient reenlistments, however, is the large number of unprogrammed losses. These are people who drop out even before completing their term of enlistment. About 40 percent of our young men and women simply quit. This is too many. This is not uncommon in the United States today. Young people quit high school, college, industry, the active armed forces, and the Guard and Reserve in about the same proportions. We are instituting several programs to reduce these unprogrammed losses substantially in the immediate future. These programs are of three general types: administrative actions, removal of obstacles to membership, and creation of a positive organizational environment.

Administrative actions include such items as writing more definite contractual agreements with IRR personnel, making it harder to obtain a discharge simply by refusing to participate in training, and inducing commanders to exercise more care before getting rid of young people. The net effect of these actions is to provide a climate in which there is more incentive to fulfill the period of service to which the individual agreed originally.

Our research indicates that there are three major obstacles to continued service in the guard and reserve: conflicts with family, conflicts with employers, and poor training. We are working to improve all three of these areas. The impact of family attitudes is direct, powerful, and difficult to modify. The spouses and children of reservists are asked to support an activity that makes the member unavailable to them one weekend a month and two weeks each summer. Reserve participation normally is in addition to a full-time job, and the deprivation is considerable. We want the families of guardsmen and reservists to consider themselves as members of the team and to feel a part of the reserve community. Our inability to provide much in the way of tangible benefits hampers these efforts. However, we are continuing our efforts to build support among these families.

Lack of employer support for membership in the Guard and Reserve by their employees is a major problem. While most employers are supportive of the Guard and Reserve, too many are not. Although the law is clear that the reservist shall not be discriminated against on account of his reserve membership, such discrimination does occur. It is difficult for a young man or woman to retain membership in the Reserve and participate enthusiastically in the face of threats of firing or blocked promotion on his full-time job. When put in the middle between an uncooperative employer and the reserve unit, the young person most often chooses to leave the reserve unit. The young person cannot be blamed for protecting his livelihood. It is necessary to create a cooperative attitude between employers and reservist employees that facilitates both activities. The existence of the law helps, but compliance with the law must be based essentially on voluntary assent. We have a major program to build employer support. It relies upon voluntary participation in state and local committees by local businessmen and labor leaders, as well as reservists. The mission of the committees is to build a spirit of cooperation among employers and their reservist employees. To support the local efforts, there is a national public relations program, including an extensive public service advertising campaign sponsored by the Advertising Council. The Employer Support Program has been very successful, and we need to continue it and expand it in the future.

The third major obstacle to retention is poor training. We hear sometimes about training "horror stories." While most Guard and Reserve training is reasonably good, there is sufficient truth to the reports of bad training to warrant our serious attention. We are placing major emphasis on improving reserve training, not only to eliminate the "horror stories" but, more importantly, to make that training a positive influence in convincing unit members to stay in and to participate. Young people today do not want their time wasted. They like to feel that they are doing something worthwhile. Impromptu training conducted sloppily turns them off, and so do make-work projects. However, effective and realistic training, no matter how difficult, turns them on. We believe that performing actual work—that is, producing a useful product—is a highly effective and attractive kind of training.

We are devising policies and programs that will allow unit commanders at the lower levels the flexibility and the resources they need to plan and conduct good training. One important element of this is to remove regulatory constraints which prescribe too much activity and result in too little training. Another important element is to provide full-time personnel in the units to prepare and conduct the training and also to perform the administrative work on nontraining time so that valuable training hours are not spent in routine paperwork. It is not easy to prepare and deliver 16 hours of effective training each month, and we need to support well those unit commanders who actually have to do this.

In addition to family support, employer support, and good training, there is also the matter of the general organizational environment. Human beings like to socialize. They like to gather to get things done or to participate in pleasurable activities. Much more than active military units, the Guard and Reserve units take on the characteristics of social organizations. Guard and Reserve units are rooted in the community. They mean more than just a job for most of their members. Many of these members know and relate to each other in the community outside the context of their reserve units. In this respect, Guard and Reserve units are similar to the clubs and fraternal organizations that are so popular in American society. While mobility and the great distances that some reservists travel to train with their units lessen the importance of this social factor, it is still an important element of retention for many reservists. We are seeking ways to understand and to enhance this organizational empathy.

Finally, the Guard and Reserve program depends ultimately on the support of the communities in which the units are located. Local support is the deciding factor in determining whether a Guard or Reserve unit will be a good one or a bad one. The National Guards of some states are always overstrength, well trained, and ready. In other states, the units are understrength, poorly trained, and unready. The difference is in the amount of public support for the Guard in each state. It is true that a nation gets the kind of armed forces it deserves, and it is particularly true for the Guard and Reserve.

None of the programs and policies discussed above will work in the absence of community support. Throwing more money at the problem will not solve it without community support. Management actions are ineffective without community support. We can make it easy to join the Guard and Reserve and hard to get out, and we can make the Guard and Reserve service more attractive and satisfying, but we cannot have a good Ready Reserve if the American people do not want a good Ready Reserve.

It is really up to the people to decide. We who are charged with improving the state of the Army Guard and Reserve cannot do the job alone. Only when it becomes the right thing, the accepted thing, and the responsible thing to belong to a Guard or Reserve unit will we have a truly "Ready" Reserve. Only when America accepts the need for an effective reserve force and is willing to allow—even encourage—young men and women to belong, will we get up to strength. Only when the men and women of America put service before self will we have the military force and the will to defend our freedom.

# Part III:
# Alternatives

# Introduction to Part III

To the extent that defense manpower problems exist, alternative solutions are in order. Some of the alternatives offered by the authors are attempts to make the present AVF system, including both active duty forces and reserve forces, work better through such programs as higher pay at the margin to compete for labor in the civilian market or a GI Bill of such magnitude that middle-class Americans would be attracted to military service. Other alternatives presented in Part III assume that the AVF is simply unworkable, that marginal programs offer inadequate improvements, and that fundamental changes must be made to acquire the kinds of military forces that will be necessary to accomplish the nation's likely national security tasks for the foreseeable future.

Even if it were politically feasible, should the nation return to a conscription system? Would the draft be significantly less expensive? Would it be socially equitable? Or, should the nation adopt some variant of national service, given the experience of smaller state or local programs which capitalize on a volunteer ethic? Would people volunteer, and how many people of what qualifications would choose to serve in the military? How much would a national service program cost? Does the apparent success of selective service registration in the early 1980s imply a greater willingness among America's youth to serve in the military if called?

In addition to the program alternatives offered here is Robert C. Kelly's alternative model of analysis which claims that defense analysts cannot even understand, much less solve, the manpower problems of the AVF using their current analytical models. He urges adoption of the substitute model he has developed.

Understanding the alternatives in Part III will be important for the decade ahead. There are many signs that most, if not all, of these approaches will be debated in many forums, including the Congress of the United States.

Chapter 11
# Selective Service Program Overview and Results of the 1980 Registration
Bernard D. Rostker

On the evening of Wednesday, January 23, 1980, President Jimmy Carter stepped before the Congress and, as part of his assessment of the State of the Union, called for a resumption of draft registration and a revitalization of the Selective Service System. Six months later, on July 21, 1980, Selective Service, with the help of several governmental agencies, started the first mass registration since World War II. The following describes the events leading up to the registration; other steps taken to revitalize the Selective Service System; the results of the 1980 registration in terms of both the registration process and improved capability; as well as future plans for Selective Service.

## BACKGROUND

### The Selective Service and the All-Volunteer Force

In 1970, the President's Commission on an All-Volunteer Armed Force (AVF) reported a unanimous belief "that the nation's interest will be [best] served by an all-volunteer force, supported by an effective standby draft."[1] The Commission also recommended that Selective Service maintain:

1. a register of all males who might be conscripted when essential for national security;
2. a system for selection of inductees;

3. specific procedures for the notification, examination, and induction of those to be conscripted;
4. an organization to maintain the register and administer the procedures for induction; and
5. that a standby draft system can be invoked only by resolution of Congress at the request of the president.[2]

Anticipating the advent of the AVF, the Congress, in 1971, amended the Military Selective Service Act (MSSA) to provide that:.

> The Selective Service System . . . shall . . . be maintained as an active standby organization with (1) a complete registration and classification structure capable of immediate operations in the event of a national emergency and (2) personnel adequate to reinstate immediately the full operation of the system . . . in the event of a national emergency.

In FY 1973, the AVF became a reality. The last draft calls were issued in December 1972; statutory authority to induct expired in June 1973. On April 1, 1975, President Ford suspended the requirement that those subject to the MSSA register with the Selective Service System. Classification actions were terminated and local boards, state headquarters, and appeal boards were closed in FY 1976.

## The Standby Selective Service System

Under the AVF concept, the Selective Service is to provide a "standby" system to support a military mobilization. The system must be ready, without notice, to provide the untrained manpower that will be required to staff our armed services during a military emergency, while protecting individual rights through a fully developed system of administrative due process. The specific requirements—numbers of people and delivery schedule—are established by the secretary of defense.

In the mid 1970s, the secretary of defense established an induction requirement which Selective Service believed could be met without difficulty. In October 1977, however, the Department of Defense increased the requirement. The requirement was again increased in November 1980. Table 11.1 contrasts the 1975, 1977, and 1980 induction schedules.

Between 1977 and 1979, the ability of the Selective Service to meet the revised schedule was the subject of a number of critical reviews, including a report by the Congressional Budget Office, the General Accounting Office, and the President's Reorganization Project.[3] Each study concluded, as did the then Acting Director of Selective Service in a report to the Congress (March 1979), that Selective Service does "not presently have the capability to meet the

Table 11.1. DOD Induction Schedule

|  | First Inductions (days) | 100,000 Inductions (days) | Total Inductions in Six Months |
|---|---|---|---|
| 1975 | M + 110 | M + 150 | |
| 1977 | M + 30 | M + 60 | 650,000 |
| 1980 | M + 13 | M + 29 | |

M = Mobilization Day

Department of Defense wartime manpower requirements from our 'deep standby' status."[4]

In the summer of 1979, President Carter nominated a new Director of Selective Service with the task of building a new system which could meet the mobilization requirements of the Department of Defense, in support of the all-volunteer force. This effort had just begun when, in late December 1979, the Soviet Union invaded Afghanistan.

## The President's Decision.

The administration considered the invasion of Afghanistan a serious threat to the peace in an area of the world where we have vital interests. As a result, in his 1980 State of the Union address, President Carter, while reiterating his support of the AVF, said:

> The men and women of America's armed forces are on duty tonight in many parts of the world. I am proud of the job they are doing and I know you share that pride. I believe that our volunteer forces are adequate for current defense needs and I hope that it will not become necessary to impose a draft. However, we must be prepared for that possibility. For this reason, I have determined that the Selective Service System must now be revitalized. I will send legislation and budget proposals to the Congress next month so that we can begin registration and then meet future mobilization needs rapidly if they arise.[5]

While the call for peacetime registration was a shift in administration policy,[6] the administration felt that the change was justified since registration would "increase our preparedness, assure our ability to respond and demonstrate our resolve."[7] The president's decision substituted an operating system for a not-fully-developed and untested contingency plan and, in so doing, assured Selective Service's ability to respond in an emergency. An independent study by the General Accounting Office confirmed the administration's contention and stated that, "The President's recent decision to resume peacetime registration will enhance [Selective Service] operations and improve national defense capabilities. . . . With an ongoing program of registration, system weaknesses can be identified and corrected before mobilization occurs rather than after mobilization."[8]

## Congressional Action

On February 11, 1980, the president submitted a report to the Congress conveying his recommendations for Selective Service reform. The report highlighted a number of key elements of the registration, induction, and claims processing system which had to be rebuilt if Selective Service was to meet its mission.[9] Specifically, the report called for:

- A registration process that is reliable and efficient.
- A nationwide public information campaign to publicize the registration.
- An automated data processing system that can handle the pre and postmobilization data management requirements.
- A system for the promulgation and distribution of orders for induction.
- A claims process that can quickly insure all registrants' rights to due process are protected.
- A field structure that can be quickly reconstituted and provide timely support for the claims process.
- A new training and testing program for Selective Service Reserve Officers.
- A revitalization of the national headquarters in order to manage the system.

On April 22, 1980, the United States House of Representatives passed House Joint Resolution 521 that transferred $13,295,000 from the Department of Defense to Selective Serivce to enable the revitalization and registration to go forward. On June 12, 1980, the United States Senate passed a slightly different version of the resolution, On June 25, 1980, the House of Representatives agreed to the Senate version and, on June 27, 1980, the president signed House Joint Resolution 521.

## Political Support

While there was a great deal of vocal opposition to the president's decision to resume registration and some active opposition in the Congress, including a filibuster in the Senate led by Senator Mark Hatfield, the American people strongly supported registration. On April 29, 1980, George Gallup released the results of a survey based upon personal interviews with 1,541 adults, 18 years of age or older, conducted in 300 select localities during the period March 2-5, 1980. Table 11.2 shows the results of Gallup's survey.

Table 11.2. Gallup Poll - March 1980

"Would you favor or oppose the registration of the names of all young men so that in the event of an emergency the time needed to call up men for a draft would be reduced?"

|  | Yes | No | No Opinion |
|---|---|---|---|
|  |  | (percent) |  |
| National | 76 | 17 | 7 |
| Young Adults (18-24) | 73 | 20 | 7 |
| Men (all ages) | 79 | 15 | 6 |
| Women (all ages) | 74 | 18 | 8 |

# REGISTRATION

## Who Must Register

One of the first decisions which had to be made was who would be asked to register. While some saw a conspiracy in limiting the initial registration to 19 and 20 year olds, the decision was made on the basis of the operational needs of Selective Service.[10]

When the draft was suspended in 1973, Selective Service was operating under a series of legal and regulatory reforms designed to correct the inequities of the draft during the Vietnam period. Specifically, the lottery was instituted in 1969, occupational deferments were eliminated in 1970, and student deferments were eliminated in 1971. Regulatory reforms canceled the "oldest first" policy and replaced it with the policy of prime year of vulnerability/youngest first, thus reducing the years of uncertainty which characterized earlier drafts. It was the president's intent to carry out these reforms and, thus, to register only sufficient year of birth groups to ensure that Selective Service could meet the initial emergency needs of our armed services.

Presidential Proclamation 4771 of July 2, 1980, sets forth the requirement for persons to register.[11] Basically, young men born in 1960 and 1961 were to register between July 21 and August 2, 1980. Those born in 1962 would register during the week of January 5, 1981. Continuous registration of 18 year olds was initiated in 1981. If it ever becomes necessary to draft anyone, Selective Service would operate under the concept of random selection based on year and date of birth, i.e., the prime age groups are those who reach age 20 in the year of the draft. In the unlikely event that it becomes necessary to increase the size of the pool, Selective Service is prepared to undertake supplemental registrations of those born in or before 1959, who are subject to the MSSA. The size of the pool will, however, increase over time as 18 years olds register each year, and Selective Service keeps current the records of those previously registered until each reaches his 26th birthday.

## Planning for the 1980 National Registration

The president's call to resume peacetime registration did not change the basic mission of the system as a backup to the AVF during a national emergency. Thus, we did not want to build a large and costly bureaucratic structure with almost 2,000 local offices simply to register. Selective Service considered a number of plans to meet the registration requirements. Studies by the Congressional Budget Office, the General Accounting Office, the President's Reorganization Project, and our own analysis pointed up the need for a fast and efficient registration plan. The unique attributes of the United States Postal Service (USPS) made it an ideal choice to accomplish the registration. The USPS has an existing command, communication, and transportation network which includes more than 34,500 local post offices in many convenient locations throughout the United States. Most registrants are well aware of the locations, and a short trip to the post office to register is of minimal inconvenience.

The 1980 registration was an outstanding example of cooperation among government agencies. Selective Service, the Postal Service, and the Government Printing Office jointly developed plans for printing, packing, and distributing registration forms, information brochures, poster and counter cards, and other materials to be used during the registration. In all, more than 18 different items were distributed to 34,500 post offices and 252 embassies and consulates in quantities needed to accommodate the registrants expected at each registration site. In addition, bulk quantities of each item were available as backup supplies at USPS Management Sectional Centers. Selective Service also provided other items for use in registration, including posters and brochures in Spanish, posters for those few post offices not participating in registration, items for use by the State Department overseas, and labels for use in shipping and returning completed forms to the Selective Service.

The actual registration process, as worked out by Selective Service and the USPS, is simple. A registrant fills out a form in the post office. He signs it in front of a postal clerk who acknowledges the registrant's identification and date-stamps the completed registration form. The cards are batched and sent by registered mail to Internal Revenue Service or Social Security Administration data entry facilities. The postal clerks are not required to provide any information to the registrant other than that necessary to complete the registration form. Brochures, prepared by Selective Service and given to each registrant at the time he registers, advise him of his rights, provide answers to the most common questions, and inform him to contact Selective Service if he has additional questions. The postal clerks were instructed to refer questions from registrants directly to Selective Service.

The Selective Service and USPS planned to register one year of birth group per week so as not to interrupt or place an unusual burden on postal operations, nor to unduly inconvenience postal patrons. This meant that an average of approximately 108 young men would register at each post office between July 21 and August 2, 1980. If a majority of the registrants followed publicized schedules and registered on specific days according to their month of birth, the average daily transactions would increase by nine at each post office during the registration period. This was approximately a 4.6 percent increase in the number of daily window customers. Since certain post offices were expected to experience a higher number of registrants (for example, post offices at popular resorts and college towns), Selective Service worked closely with the USPS to identify potential trouble spots and provided them additional registration materials. Additionally, in a few locations, local postmasters were directed to open a dedicated window or staff alternate registration sites, i.e., a fire or police station.[12]

## Public Affairs

As noted, Selective Service registration was terminated in 1975. With the reinstatement of registration in 1980, it was critical that young men obligated to register be properly informed of the specific provisions of the registration. Unlike previous registrations, the 1980 program was limited to 19 and 20 year olds (those born in 1960 and 1961), young men were being asked to register on a specific schedule, and registrations would be taken only at post offices. Selective Service faced unique problems since the funds needed to fully develop a public service announcement program were not available until the Joint Resolution passed the Congress. Once approved, Selective Service had only four weeks to implement its public affairs program.

After obtaining the funds from Congress, Selective Service produced ten radio and television public service spot announcements ranging in length from 10 to 60 seconds. In the weeks before registration, broadcast quality tapes were distributed to 7,000 radio stations and 750 TV stations. In addition, print media announcements were mailed to 2,500 newspapers throughout the United States.

The effectiveness of the public service program is illustrated by the following comparison to the number of spots broadcast between July 14 and August 3 in the three largest TV markets:

- Six New York TV stations broadcast 74 spots, with an estimated commercial value of $15,270.
- Five Chicago TV stations broadcast 36 spots, with an estimated commercial value of $5,113.
- One Los Angeles TV station broadcast 3 spots, with an estimated commercial value of $4,075.[13]

The estimated commercial value nationwide of all spots broadcast was approximately $1 million for TV alone. The commercial value of individual airings ranged from a high of $85,000 for a prime-time network spot to a low of $25 for off-hours, small market exposure.

The varied use of the spots appears to be related to three factors. First, given the unfortunately short lead time, many stations were reluctant to change established public service schedules. Similar efforts in support of government programs provided stations with considerably longer than one week's notice to schedule public service announcements. Second, the ruling by the Federal District Court in Philadelphia, that an all-male registration was unconstitutional, only 72 hours before the registration was to begin resulted in the cancellation of many of the scheduled spot announcements. (However, the publicity surrounding the Philadelphia case was a net addition to the public affairs program since it gave regular news programming a dramatic story upon which to focus public awareness.) Third, specific groups determined to discredit the registration program threatened TV stations that they would file Fairness Doctrine complaints asking for equal time for opponents to draft registration. Even though a clarifying ruling by the Federal Communications Commission was made on July 17th and distributed by mailgram to major TV stations,[14] the threat of legal action appeared to be the major reason so few Selective Service spots were aired in Los Angeles.

As it turned out, spot announcements were less important than regular news coverage or appearances by Selective Service officials on local or national interview shows. Clearly, in the period between the two political conventions, the registration was one of the biggest news stories. The ruling by the Philadelphia Federal District Court and the rapid stay by Supreme Court Justice William Brennan provided a focal point for news coverage all through the weekend preceding registration. The beginning of registration was also widely covered. On July 21st, the ABC-TV network had the registration as the lead story on "Good Morning America," the "Evening News," and "Nightline." Other networks provided similar exposure, with local stations following up with public interest stories featuring registration in their own communities. More thorough exposure was provided when the Director was a guest on "The MacNeil/Lehrer Report" on July 22nd. A particularly useful forum was the "Donahue Show" which devoted a full hour to registration on 210 TV stations, mostly during the first or second week of registration.

## Data Management

The face-to-face registration is only half of the registration-to-induction process. The registration, by itself, is of no value until the data is put into a form which allows Selective Service to establish a lawful order of induction. In fact, this process of "managing" the registration data is the most costly and time consuming part of the process. A failure to appreciate the critical need to establish registration files from completed registration forms has led to the erroneous analogy between current Department of Defense mobilization schedules and World War I and II experiences. During both world wars, it was approximately four months after registration when the 100,000th person was inducted. Current plans require Selective Service to be prepared to deliver the 100,000th inductee in 29 days.

At the beginning of 1979, Selective Service owned two obsolete computers which were not capable of supporting a mass registration, or the maintenance of registration files, or an emergency conscription program. While Selective Service developed the long-term (two year) plan to support an automated registration-to-induction process including claims processing, it was faced with the immediate problem of acquiring the computer hardware and of designing the software necessary to process approximately 4 million registrant records in July 1980, 2 million in January 1981, and 1.2 million from January through July 1981. Specifically, data entry and data processing equipment were needed, as well as the programs required to create, correct, and maintain up-to-date, error-free registrant files indexed by birthdate. Because the short-term plan had to be implemented long before the permanent computer facility or programs were completed, the following organizations provided temporary ADP support:

- The U.S. Internal Revenue Service, for data entry/key punch in July 1980.
- The U.S. Social Security Administration, for data entry in January 1981.
- The U.S. Department of the Interior, for computer capacity.
- A private contractor, Science Management Corporation, provided error correction and data management services.
- Government Printing Office for printing acknowledgment letters.

In addition, programs and procedures were developed which enabled Selective Service to exert positive controls over registration forms from the time they left the Postal Service until they were microfilmed and safely stored in the Federal Records Center, e.g., completed registration forms were sent from post offices to key punch sites by official and registered mail. At the key punch site, registration forms were batched and numbered to make them identifiable and retrievable. Audit procedures were established to ensure complete accountability.

Programs were also written to audit the interface as key punched data were entered onto registration files. Data edit routines and special error correction procedures such as letters to registrants who provide incomplete or inconsistent information and procedures to generate "acknowledgment letters" to all registrants were also developed. In addition, while the automated system, especially the claims processing, is not completed, the induction programs were updated to ensure that Selective Service could effectively use the new registration files.

## Registration: July 21-August 3, 1980

With the passage of HJR 571 on July 27 and the issuance of Presidential Proclamation 4771 on July 2, 1980, Selective Service undertook an intensive effort to put its registration plans into effect. During the four weeks before the start of registration, Selective Service distributed millions of registration forms, brochures, change of address cards, thousands of posters, and other registration material to every post office in the United States. Public service announcements were duplicated and distributed. Postal clerks and their supervisors were trained, and final procedures were tested at the IRS data entry sites, the DOI computer center, and the contract data management center. It is not exaggeration to say that, even after months of planning with the final registration date known for over a month, Selective Service used every bit of the time available to it to prepare for the registration.

In order to ensure that the registration would go smoothly and as planned, National Headquarters monitored daily every aspect of the preparation as well as the registration itself. It was decided well before the registration that we would not tabulate the number of registrations per day by post office, state, or region. To do so would be meaningless. We could not project the distribution of potential registrants by post office. Young people are especially mobile in the summer. They could register where they chose—near home, at work, or on vacation. Thus, no goal or quota could apply to any individual post office. While individual post offices did forward registration reports (Form 6) to Selective Service, the built-in delay in reporting and the burden of tabulating over 400,000 separate reports during the actual registration would have slowed the process, loosened controls, and provided numbers which were meaningless. As a result, a quantitative assessment was not planned until the actual registrations and Form 6 reports were keypunched.

Immediately before and during the registration, our concern was how well the system was working. To this end, we used Selective Service Headquarters personnel to contact by telephone all 285 MSC Postal Coordinators, nearly 300 local post offices, and 40 embassies during the two weeks before registration to determine that all had either received their registration materials or taken the appropriate steps to acquire the necessary items. In some cases, clarifying action was taken by USPS and the Department of State. By July 21st, all indications were that the system was ready.

During the registration, Selective Service monitored progress by on-site visits to 125 post offices and consulates, daily phone calls to MSC coordinators in 13 select cities, and reports from Federal Regional Councils and Executive Boards in 25 major cities. By all indications, the system worked smoothly.

In a summary report, the monitoring team noted that telephone calls and visits revealed that demonstrations against registration were limited generally to the first few days of the registration effort, but that leafletting continued in many areas for the entire two-week period. Supplies proved adequate for the entire period although one MSC required resupply near the end of the first week. None of the MSC's reported any difficulties with the registration or any interference with regular postal business. No unusual queues were reported anywhere. The number of telephone calls received by local post offices and MSC coordinators was considered quite heavy. The amount of time spent by clerks with a registrant averaged about one minute nationwide. MSC coordinators believed this time was so short because registrant's questions often had been answered in advance through telephone calls to the post office.

The incidence of irregularities such as obviously phony names, failure to present indentification, notations of desire to register as a conscientious objector, women attempting to register, theft of blank forms, or defacing of posters was quite low in each case. The only irregularity reported with any frequency was failure of personnel in individual post offices to follow instruction for completion of the SSS Form 6. Reports of such irregularities declined significantly after the Postal Service Headquarters sent a message to all post offices emphasizing the importance of proper completion of these forms.

## How Many Registered?

Subsequent to the two-week registration period, public attention centered on two questions: How many were supposed to register, and how many registrations did Selective Service receive? Subject to final publication of the 1980 Census, Selective Service estimated the registrant population at 3.88 million, as shown in table 11.3. Other estimates place the registrant population at 3.8 million. In testimony before the House Judiciary Committee on May 22, 1980, the Chairman of the Committee Against Registration and the Draft (CARD)

Table 11.3. Estimated 1980 Registration Population

| | |
|---|---:|
| Population of males born in 1960 or 1961 (According to "Estimates of the Population of the United States," Bureau of the Census, Jan. 1980) | 4,310,000 |
| Institutionalized (Bureau of the Census, April 1978: ratios of institutionalized population by age) | (60,000) |
| Armed Forces active duty | (370,000) |
| Total estimated registrant population | 3,880,000 |

said, "The acid test of peacetime registration, of course, may come this summer. . . . So if registration occurs in July, there are 3.8 million men out there who are supposed to trudge off to the post office."

As of November 28, 1980, Selective Service had received 3,677,887 registrations, with more arriving each week. We estimate that approximately 3,375,000 registered during the official two-week period, with the balance as late registrations. The Presidential Proclamation, Section 1-109, provided that registrants could register after the specified two-week period if prevented from on-time registration because of "some condition beyond their control."

## Comparison: 1973-1980

The current compliance rate is substantially higher than that for 1973, the only year we have comparable data, as seen in table 11.4.

Between August 4 and December 4, 1980, approximately 330,800 late registration forms were delivered to Selective Service, adding nearly 8 percent to the number of on-time registrations. As of this writing, the most recent estimates show that nearly 95 percent of the estimated eligible population have been registered. This is only about 4.5 percent lower than the historical rate of 99.5 percent registrations in a single age group, but it covers far less time than the historical records, which included late registrations submitted over a period of two years.

## Constructing the Registration File

As noted, there is a distinction between receiving a registration and processing the information into a registration file which can be used to initiate a lawful

Table 11.4. Comparative Registration Results: 1973-1980

|  | 1973 | 1980 |
|---|---|---|
| On Time Registrations | 77% (within 30 days of 18th birthday) | 87% (during 2-week registration period) |
| First month late registrations | 6% | 7% |
| Additional late registrations through fourth month | 7% | 1% |
| Final total | 99.5% | 94.8% (as of 15 Feb '81) |

induction. The "raw" registations were scanned by computer to identify missing or inconsistent information. We initially set aside registrations with incomplete addresses, those for people not born in 1960 or 1961, and the registraion of females. As of November 28, 1980, over 20,000 phone calls were made to verify and correct incomplete addresses. We sent out 96,000 letters asking for clarification of either birth date or sex and, as a result, are prepared to void 22,000 registrations with 42,000 record errors still outstanding. We mailed about 3.65 million confirmation letters with all but 59,000 delivered to registrants. These letters also act as change of address forms and are part of our program to keep registrations current. As a result of the registration, Selective Service now has a file which can be used to start a rapid, orderly induction process.

## The Impact of Registration: Proud Spirit 1980

In 1978, the National Mobilization Exercise "Nifty Nugget" reported that the Selective Service System was not able to deliver manpower to the Department of Defense on a timely basis. In November 1980, Selective Service, as part of the 1980 mobilization exercise "Proud Spirit," demonstrated its ability to mobilize the nation's manpower. The ability to meet assigned delivery schedules was made possible by reinstituting registration. The Organization of the Joint Chiefs of Staff, at their First Impressions Conference for Proud Spirit reported that:

> Selective Service objectives in REX 80 BRAVO/PROUD SPIRIT 80 were to exercise and evaluate Selective Service induction procedures, field reconstruction and mobilization interfaces with DOD, FEMA, and other civil agencies.
>
> Selective Service successfully exercised its emergency induction procedures by performing, in real time, required induction functions. This included conducting a lottery, developing induction legislation, running the computerized induction programs, producing induction orders, transmitting induction orders via Western Union Mailgram to the home addresses of 700 Selective Service reservists who acted as registrants, transmitting computerized induction data to and from MEPCOM, and testing the new Selective Service induction order.
>
> Selective Service field reconstitution was also successfully exercised. . . . With the present registrant data base on hand, the Selective Service computer can start issuing induction orders from a cold start, but the standby field structure must be reconstituted to handle claims. The reconstitution portion of the exercise involved physically reestablishing the 55 Selective Service State Headquarters, 434 Area Offices, and performing AFEES liaison functions.

Selective Service reservists performed this activity during their annual two week training period.

Exercise results indicate Selective Service successfully achieved its exercise objectives. Most important, Selective Service demonstrated that Selective Service can provide DoD the required manpower under the most demanding DoD requirements.

# NOTES

1. The Report of the President's Commission on an All-Volunteer Armed Force, (Washington: Government Printing Office, 1970), pp. 5-6.
2. Ibid., p. 119.
3. The Congressional Budget Office found that Selective Service could not meet DOD's wartime induction schedule because it did not have a reliable plan for a quick, mass registration; the ADP support was neither adequate or appropriate; and the field structure was too complex and cumbersome (See Congressional Budget Office, *The Selective Service System: Mobilization Capabilities & Option for Improvement,* Washington: Government Printing Office, 1978, p. 23).
    Similarly, the General Accounting Office found that, "The Selective Service System, under its current procedures, does not have the capability to respond to the Department of Defense's needs. . . . In our opinion, the key to a shorter delivery time lies in having an existing list of eligibles to be drafted in the case of mobilization." (Comptroller General, *What are the Capabilities of the Selective Service System?* Washington: General Accounting Office, 1978, p. 13). Also see, President's Reorganization Project, *Selective Service System Reorganization Study—Final Report* (Washington: Office of Management and Budget, 1978).
4. Director of Selective Service, *Semiannual Report of the Director of Selective Service: Oct. 1, 1978—Mar 1, 1979* (Washington: Government Printing Office, 1979), p. 1.
5. 1980 State of the Union Address.
6. "When the issue of peacetime registration was raised last September [1979] during the debate on the Defense Authorization Act in the House of Representatives, the Secretary of Defense and the Director of OMB said that registration was not necessary (and I highlight) *at that time.* There was no crisis that had the potential for an imminent threat to the vital interests of the United States. The situation is different now, and so is our position on the issue of peacetime registration. The Administration's position before this crisis in Southwestern Asia was that the *President would not hesitate to use his present authority to require registration at any time he sees it as a necessary step to preserving or enhancing our national security interests.* He is convinced that time has come." John P. White, *Military Draft Registration,* Special Hearing before the Senate Appropriations Committee, (Washington: Government Printing Office, 1980), p. 18.
7. Ibid., p. 17.
8. Letter from the Comptroller General to the Director of Selective Service (July 22, 1980) accompanying *Actions to Improve Parts of the Military Manpower Mobilization System are Underway* (Washington: General Accounting Office, 1980).
9. *Presidential Recommendations for Selective Service Reform: A Report to the Congress,* prepared pursuant to P.L. 96-107, February 11, 1980.
10. See "The Young Should Register Twice," *New York Times* Editorial, July 2, 1980; and "A Key Element of Preparedness" by Bernard Rostker, Director of Selective Service, *New York Times*

# Selective Service Program Overview and Results of the 1980 Registration 193

      Letter to the Editor, July 13, 1980.
11. Registration regulations were published in the *Federal Registry,* Vol. 45, No. 140, July 18, 1980, pp. 48130-31.
12. See *USPS Role in Registering Male Citizens,* Hearings before the House Subcommittee on Postal Operations and Services of the Committee on Post Offices and Civil Service, July 24, 1980, Serial No. 96-101.
13. Selective Service public service spot TV announcements were monitored for one week each in 44 markets, and for the full two week period in New York, Chicago, and Los Angeles by Broadcast Advertisers Reports, Inc.
14. In Report No. 17587, the FCC found that "announcements (which) only explain a law to the public, without presenting supporting or opposing views on that law, did not present one side of a controversial issue of public importance. . . ." The Commission emphasized that "a station is free to broadcast an announcement even if it presents one side of a controverisal issue of public importance. Such announcement . . . would only trigger an obligation to afford reasonable opportunity for the presentation of contrasting viewpoints in the station's overall programming."

Chapter 12

# The Market Model of Military Labor Procurement: A Survey of Current Issues

Robert C. Kelly

## INTRODUCTION

### Scope

In examining the market model, a number of studies on the economic aspects of military manpower have been reviewed. To adequately cover the subject, the scope of this study has been narrowed in several respects. First, the literature cited concerning the market approach has generally been confined to the period from the Gates Commission (1970) to the present (1980). Secondly, the analysis of the market approach has generally been restricted to the problem of active and reserve force accessions. While a number of other critical issues relating to the volunteer force concept center around the problems of retention and management of the career force, the need to keep the analysis manageable restricted the discussion in this chapter to accessions. Aspects of retention and career force management which relate to the accession issue, however, are dealt with in the analysis. Lastly, the study deals primarily with the issue of enlisted accessions and sidesteps the problems of officer accession programs.

### Method

The following section overviews trends in manpower data and examines recent divergent views on the ability of the volunteer system to achieve national military manpower objectives. The third section outlines the market model of military recruiting with emphasis on those aspects of the military labor market relevant to the current debate on the volunteer force. In the course of developing the market model, a brief review of the empirical literature relevant to enlisted accessions is presented. The fourth section reviews the current debate on the market method in the context of the market model. Finally, some conclusions are offered.

# DIVERGENT VIEWS ON THE VOLUNTEER SYSTEM

## Overview: Key Trends in Manpower Data

Individuals inquiring about the status of America's volunteer forces are faced with a bewildering amount of data on military personnel and personnel costs. Table 12.1 gives an overview of the trends in several key indices which are often cited in the debate on the volunteer force. The data gives trends in total strengths, accession entry level characteristics, and military compensation. The years covered include 1964, the last year of the pre-Vietnam draft military, and fiscal years 1974 through 1979 which were all in the volunteer era.

Table 12.1. Key Trends in Manpower Data
Selected Years
FY 1964-1979

|  | FY 64 | 74 | 76 | 78 | 79 |
|---|---|---|---|---|---|
| **Strength Data (1000s)** |  |  |  |  |  |
| Active | 2,687 | 2,161 | 2,081 | 2,061 | 2,025 |
| Selected Reserve | 827 | 809 | 708 | 788 | 798 |
| IRR | 846 | 931 | 485 | 356 | 396 |
| **Accession Data** |  |  |  |  |  |
| % HSDG | 68 | 61 | 69 | 77 | 73 |
| % MC I & II | 38 | 340 | 34 | 34 | 29 |
| **Military Compensation Active Personnel** |  |  |  |  |  |
| ($ × 10⁹) | 12.3 | 22.1 | 23.3 | 25.1 | 26.3 |
| % Defense Budget | 25 | 28 | 27 | 24 | 23 |
| % GNP | 1.9 | 1.6 | 1.4 | 1.2 | 1.1 |
| Per Capita (1967 $) | 4,927 | 6,924 | 6,567 | 6,233 | 5,974 |

Sources: *Annual Report of the Secretary of Defense FY 78, 81 America's Volunteers: A Report on the All-Volunteer Armed Forces Economic Report of the President,* January 1980 *Military Manpower Statistics,* July 1979

See text for a description of the data.

The first set of data give the fiscal year end-strength totals for the active forces, the selected reserve, and the individual ready reserve (IRR). As the data indicate, active duty end-strength in FY 1974 was 526,000 below pre-Vietnam draft levels, and dropped an additional 136,000 between FY 1974 and FY 1979. In the area of the selected reserve, however, the end-strength dropped substantially in the first years of the all-volunteer force (AVF) but turned around in 1976 and, in 1979, was within 4 percent of the pre-Vietnam draft levels. Lastly, the IRR has experienced significant declines since the end of the Vietnam conflict and has remained at levels substantially below those of both the pre-Vietnam draft force and those attained in the first few years of the volunteer era.

The second set of data shows two entry-level characteristics of active duty nonprior service (NPS) enlisted accessions. The first series cited gives the percentage of NPS enlisted accessions possessing a high school diploma. As the data indicate, the percentage of high school diploma graduates entering on active duty has remained relatively stable in the volunteer era and is not significantly different from the pre-Vietnam figures. As Moskos and Janowitz note, however, the aggregate data may mask significant compositional shifts within the force whereby the proportion of high school diploma graduates within the combat arms of the army may be lower than the military-wide average.[1] Moskos and Janowitz also note that the relatively stable percentage of accessions with high school diplomas has occurred during a period in which the proportion of high school graduates in the total population is increasing.[2]

The second series of entry level characteristic data gives the proportion of NPS accessions coming from the upper two mental categories as measured by Armed Services Vocational Aptitude Battery (ASVAB) test scores. The upper two mental categories generally indicate the top third of the distribution of individuals arranged by ASVAB scores. As the figures show, the percentage of NPS accessions from MC I and II actually increased in the early period of the volunteer force, but have declined since 1976.

The compensation measure shown reflects solely the active military personnel appropriations portion of manpower costs. This amount reflects total direct compensation to active duty military personnel, or the active military wage bill. While this figure in nominal aggregate terms has increased substantially over 1964 levels, much of the increase has been due to the effects of inflation. When viewed in relation to the defense budget and to the gross national product (GNP), total current wage payments for active duty personnel have experienced a secular decline since the beginning of the AVF. The percent of GNP spent on active wages has even declined relative to the 1964 level. These percentages are somewhat misleading, however, in that the budget and gross national product have increased while the number of personnel on active duty has declined. A more relevant measure of the trend in wage payments is the last measure shown, the value of the wage bill expressed in constant dollars per active duty service member. This figure was arrived at by deflating the nominal wage bill for active force personnel by the consumer price index and dividing the result by active force strength. As the figures show, between 1964 and 1974, real wages per capita in the military increased substantially, increasing at a compound rate of approximately 3.4 percent in real terms per year. Between 1974 and 1979, however, the opposite trend occurred and military wages per capita in 1979 stood at 86 percent of their 1974 value, an average compound decrease in real terms of 3 percent per year over the volunteer period. In contrast, as shown in table 12.2, between 1964 and 1974 real wages per workers grew at a rate of 1.4 percent and decreased between 1974 and 1979 at a rate of 0.2 percent. Over the entire period, real wages per worker grew at a rate of about 0.9 percent while military real wages grew at 1.3 percent.

Thus, while real military wages per capita experienced a modest increase between 1964 and 1979, most of the increase occurred in that portion of the 15 years during which the draft was in effect. During the volunteer period, real military wages per capita have declined, and declined substantially relative to real wages per worker.

The data presented here are not intended to support a normative viewpoint on whether or not the AVF has proved successful. The purpose of providing these trends is to allow the reader to put in perspective the views that are summarized in the following sections.

Table 12.2. Real Wages Per Worker
Selected Years
1964 - 1979

|  | 1964 | 1974 | 1976 | 1978 | 1979 |
|---|---|---|---|---|---|
| Wages ($ × 10$^9$)* | 404.1 | 906.5 | 1056.7 | 1326.6 | 1480.3 |
| Consumer Price Index (1967 = 100) | 92.9 | 147.7 | 170.5 | 195.4 | 217.4 |
| Real Wages (1967$ × 10$^9$) | 435.0 | 613.7 | 619.8 | 678.9 | 680.9 |
| Employment (10$^6$) | 72.044 | 88.164 | 89.629 | 96.490 | 99.033 |
| Real Wage Per Worker (1967 $1000s) | 6038 | 6961 | 6915 | 7031 | 6875 |

*Includes wages, other labor income, and proprietor's income.

**Source:** *Economic Report of President,* January 1980, pp., 226, 234, 262

## Alternative Views on the AVF

Although there are a myriad of opinions on military manpower management, three sets of views have appeared to predominate in the late 1970s concerning the efficacy of the market approach to military manpower management. These include the current position of the Department of Defense—the market view; the views put forth by various critics of the AVF who lean toward a nonvolunteer solution to the manpower management problem—the nonmarket view; and the view which rejects the current form of the volunteer concept but retains elements of the volunteer approach in the alternative—the Janowitz/Moskos view.

**The Market Views.** In the debate on the success of the volunteer force, the general position of the Department of Defense is best summarized by the following excerpts from the conclusions of a December 1978 internal Department of Defense study on the volunteer concept:

> The AVF has provided the military services with a full-strength active force of a quality equal to or superior to that achieved under the draft. The cost of this policy has been close to that projected in 1970 by the Gates Commission. . . .
>
> Although Navy, Marine Corps, and Air Force Reserve Components have been able to meet Congressionally authorized strengths, the Army National Guard and Reserve have sagged. A number of programs are being tested or have been adopted to increase both the strength and readiness of Army reserve components. . . .
>
> Current levels of the IRR and other pools such as military retirees are probably not sufficient to meet immediate requirements for individual replacements in a major war. A variety of programs are under active consideration that would increase the level of resources in this particular area. . . .
>
> The results of this study do not support a return of peacetime conscription for either the active force or the reserves.[3]

The DOD view, thus, essentially supports the general intellectual arguments made in the conclusions of the Gates Commission Report[4] and later by Cooper[5] in support of the volunteer system. Although recognizing areas of concern in the management of the reserves, DOD maintains that, with sufficient resources devoted to problem areas, the volunteer approach can continue to be effectively used as a system of military manpower management in a peacetime environment.

**The Non-Market View.** Several critics of the DOD positions contend that the volunteer method, as currently employed, has not been successful in developing a manpower base which can meet national security requirements. In particular, studies on the AVF by King[6] and Reed[7] reach an opposite conclusion to that of the DOD study and recommend examination of nonmarket-oriented solutions to the manpower problem. In particular, King notes high manpower costs associated with the AVF, attrition, and representativeness as problems with the current volunteer approach. Reed specifically notes:

> The U.S. Army total force is a failure due to major losses in Reserve force strength. In the event of wartime mobilization to support NATO forces the Army will be deficient by at least 500,000 personnel within 60 days after the beginning of hostilities. The Active force has been successful in recruiting adequate numbers of individuals to meet peacetime force strength levels; however, the Army has continued to decline in Active strength during the past 5 years. Active forces are 80,000 personnel short of wartime needs and the Reserves and National Guard are 180,000 short of wartime strength. The Individual Ready Reserve (IRR) are badly depleted in numbers and skills (aviators, doctors, combat arms, etc.). The Selective Service System machinery does not exist to recruit adequate manpower for wartime mobilization.
> All of the deficiencies listed above are a direct consequence of stopping the draft and moving to the use of volunteer labor.[8]

In considering alternatives to the AVF, both King and Reed recommend, among other alternatives, a review of national service programs where all persons within a given age cohort are given a responsibility of some form of government service, to include the military. While granting that peacetime conscription may not be politically feasible in the near term, both studies argue that policymakers should carefully examine national service and other nonmarket alternatives to the AVF.

**The Janowitz/Moskos View.** The third view to be discussed is that espoused by Janowitz and Moskos.[9] Janowitz and Moskos conclude that the current methods of managing military manpower is ineffective because it fails to bring the mainstream of American society through the military institution. The current AVF, they contend, as a result of the economic incentives offered, is made up of an unrepresentative segment of American youth. The measures that are used to define representativeness include education, income of parents, and racial composition. In all of these areas, Janowitz and Moskos contend that the military, and particularly the combat branches of the military, are, as a result of the market orientation of the volunteer concept, becoming socially unrepresentative. The implications of this problem are noted in the following passage:

> Our policy perspective . . . includes the belief that a broadly representative and integrated military is both a more effective armed force and one more

compatible with the value of a democratic society. . . . The burdens of military service and sacrifice cannot fall disproportionately on any particular group, especially those that are socially deprived.[10]

As a solution to the problem of an unrepresentative force, Janowitz and Moskos reject both conscription and coercive types of national service programs. These, they argue, lack political support and could be organizationally counterproductive.

The market or expenditure solution is also rejected. As Janowitz and Moskos note:

> increased economic expenditures will not solve the issues confronting the all-volunteer force. . . . In short, we believe, as we have in the past and continue to do after this assessment, that a marketplace model is not an adequate rationale for managing the military establishment and for strengthening civilian control.[11]

In general, Janowitz and Moskos propose a restructured manpower system as a solution to the problem. Their solution includes the following elements:

1. a two year enlistment option for the combat arms with a comprehensive educational package as a benefit,
2. offering technical specialties to those who first serve in the combat arms,
3. reducing permanent change of station moves,
4. making Federal Civil Service contingent on military service,
5. tying Federal education benefits to military service.

As Janowitz and Moskos note in conclusion to their proposals:

> The grand design is to keep alive and update the citizen soldier concept in the all-volunteer context by emphasizing the idea that military service is a period through which a significant number of persons will and ought to pass enroute to their adult or second careers. On balance we are certain that such arrangement will "civilianize" the military rather than "militarize" civilian society. It will at the same time contribute to the solution of the personnel problem and the dilemmas of the all-volunteer force.[12]

## THE NATURE OF THE MARKET MODEL

### Overview

The opposing viewpoints discussed above have centered around the effectiveness of the market as a method of attaining enlisted manpower. In this section, we discuss the nature of the market system, the mechanics of the market model, and some of the empirical literature on the characteristics of the military labor market.

## The Nature of the Market

The market mechanism is essentially a social organization which coordinates the economic activities and transactions of large numbers of people through the concept of voluntary exchange.

The coordination function of the market is accomplished through the forces of supply and demand which translate the desires of seller and buyer into the market. In the most libertarian view of the market, the role of the government in such a process is to enforce contracts; to demand those goods for which no markets can be formed, i.e., public goods, such as national defense; to regulate monopolies; and to regulate those industries where externalities exist, such as in the case of pollution.

## The Market Model

The market model of military recruiting can be best summarized by the supply and demand curves shown in figure 12.1. The Supply Curve, $SS^1$, indicates the number of individuals that would be willing to offer their services per period to the military at various wage rates. The supply curve is upward sloping to reflect the assumption that increased wages will induce more individuals to join the military relative to the number that would join at lower wage rates. The steepness of the supply curve is an indicator of the "pay elasticity." The pay elasticity is defined as the percentage change in military labor supplied, as a result of a percentage change in the military wage. A very steep (i.e., nearly vertical) supply curve would reflect a very inelastic supply, or that changes in the wage would have little effect on the quantity of labor supplied. The opposite would be true for a more horizontal supply curve.

The supply curve essentially reflects the value that individuals place on the use of their time. A variety of alternatives to military service are available to most individuals including alternative civilian employment, leisure, production of consumption services in the household, or further education. Associated with each one of these choices is a monetary as well as nonmonetary return. The wage rate associated with each point on the supply curve shown in figure 12.1 reflects the individual's supply price, or that amount which the military services must offer to make monetary and nonmonetary returns to the individual greater than those for the best available alternative.

The area under the supply curve is a conventional method of measuring the total economic cost of utilizing a given amount of military labor. Total economic cost reflects the foregone opportunity, in terms of monetary and

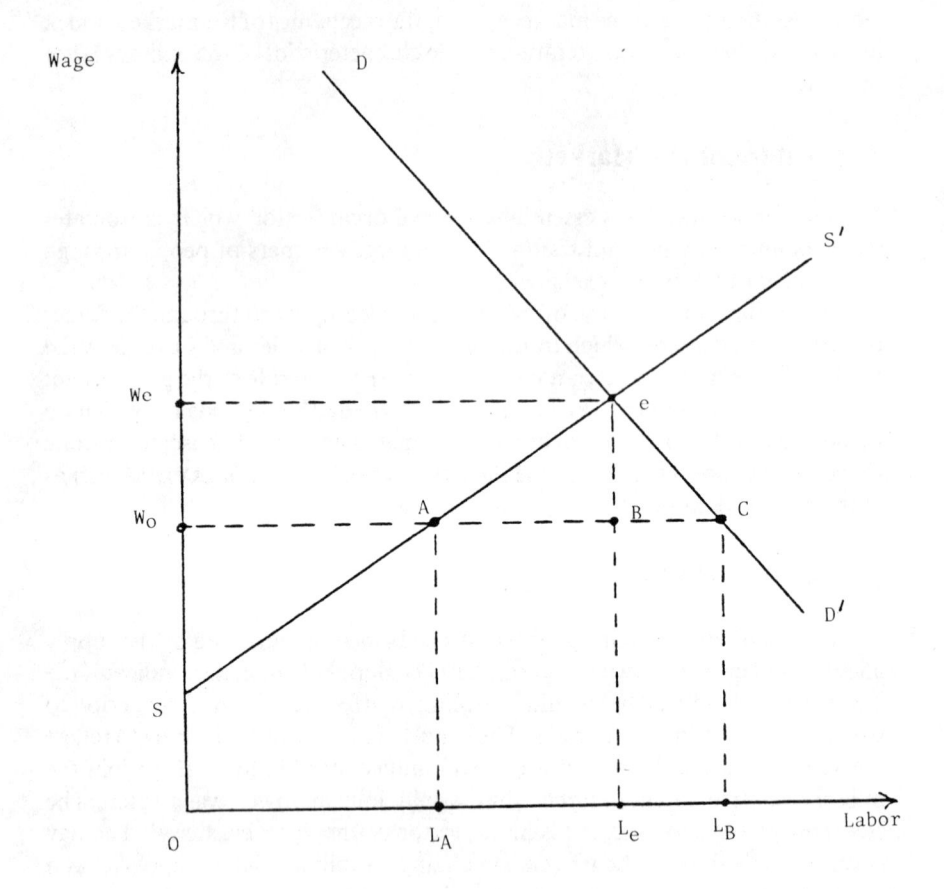

**Figure 12.1.** The Military Labor Market

nonmonetary returns, to all individuals employed in the military. Thus, by adding up the supply prices for all those serving in the military, we can obtain an estimate of the economic cost of utilizing the military labor force. For example, the economic cost of utilizing $L_e$ individuals in figure 12.1 would be approximated by area $OSeL_e$.

The demand curve for military labor is given by $DD^1$ and is downward sloping to reflect the assumption that the military will utilize less labor at higher wage rates. The rationale for the downward sloping demand curve is two-fold. First, as the price of labor increases relative to other types of resources that the military can employ to produce defense output, the military can and does substitute these other factors, such as capital, for labor in order to provide national defense at least cost. Additionally, as the price of military manpower increases, the government, in response to the higher price of defense services, may also substitute nondefense for defense goods and, hence, reduce the quantity of defense output demanded in order to utilize scarce government revenues in a socially optimal fashion. The second reason for the downward sloping demand curve is that a higher price of labor essentially reduces the real income of the government and, consequently, results in a general reduction in the overall expenditure on goods and services, one of which being national defense.

The steepness of the demand curve reflects the elasticity of demand or the percentage change in military labor demanded, as a result of a percentage change in the military wage. A very steep (i.e., nearly vertical) demand curve would reflect a very inelastic demand, or that changes in wage rates would have very little effect on the quantity of labor demanded. The opposite would be true for a more horizontal demand curve.

The demand curve for military labor represents essentially the benefit measured in money terms resulting from the employment of the marginal enlistee. The total benefit resulting from the employment of a given amount of labor is conventionally assumed to be given by the area under the demand curve.

The method by which the market works to determine the quantity of labor enlisted by the military can be demonstrated by referring to figure 12.1. If we assume that the military wage rate is set at $w_o$ by the government, then $L_A$ volunteers will offer to enlist but the military will desire $L_B$. The result will be a shortage of enlistees given by the difference between the two, $L_B - L_A$. To eliminate the shortage using the simplest variant of the market approach, the wage rate is allowed to rise to $w_e$ where the quantity of labor demanded by the services is equal to the quantity supplied.

As the wage rate increases, two separate effects occur which eliminate the shortage of enlisted manpower. The first is the supply response, or that increase in enlistments from $L_A$ to $L_e$ which is induced by the increased return to military service. The magnitude of the supply response is, *ceteris paribus,* dependent on the pay elasticity of the supply curve. If the supply curve is very inelastic, the percent wage increase required to increase enlistments to $L_e$ will be larger than the percentage increase in enlistments required. If the supply curve is elastic, however, the opposite is true.

The second effect which eliminates the shortage is the demand response, or that decrease in the demand for enlistments brought about by the higher price of military labor. In the example shown in figure 12.1, the demand response to higher wage rates is the reduction in the quantity of labor demanded, shown as $L_B - L_e$. As in the case of the supply response, the magnitude of the demand response depends on the elasticity of the demand curve. For an inelastic demand curve, the percent reduction in demand is less than the percentage change in the wage while, for an elastic demand curve, the opposite is true.

## Some Complexities in the Model

The model described above essentially simplifies the complexities involved in interpreting the military labor market by assuming that there is a single homogeneous quantity which is called military labor, and that the price which is paid and received for the voluntary exchange of labor services is a simple wage. In reality, these concepts are much more complex.

The military labor market is actually not a single market, but a market for a number of different types of labor, each with differing entry-level characteristics. Thus, to accurately describe the problems of accession in the enlisted force, it is necessary to specify which entry-level characteristics are desired before analyzing the market. Thus, the market for non-high school graduates is different than the market for high school graduates, and each should be described using a separate market model.

The price of labor is almost much more complex than depicted in the simple model above. The wage rate employed in the simple model essentially reflects the monetary return per period perceived by the individual enlisting and the government. Thus, an accurate description of the price of labor should include not only direct payments, but also the current monetary value of expected in-kind benefits and deferred compensation prorated over the life of the enlistment contract. From a rational perspective, the enlistee would view his wage as not only the direct compensation received for enlisting, i.e., basic pay, quarters, and subsistence, but also place some evaluation on such in-kind returns as medical, dental, and educational benefits as well as tax advantages and the expected value of the retirement fund.

## Shifts in Supply and Demand

We have assumed, thus far, that the supply and demand curves for labor are fixed, or that all factors that affect the supply and demand for military labor, other than price, were held constant. In this section, we relax this assumption and discuss those factors which result in shifts in the supply and demand curves.

Most of the literature on the supply of enlisted accessions has identified several key factors which may result in a shift in the supply curve. These factors and their presumed effect on supply are shown in table 12.3.

Increases in civilian wages generally increase the attractiveness of the civilian occupational alternative for those considering military service. Increases in unemployment, however, generally reduce the earnings which the individual can expect to receive by going into the civilian job market and, therefore, make the military occupational alternative more attractive.

The population variable represents the population qualified and available for military service. Most studies on enlisted supply generally perceive this

Table 12.3. Factors Shifting the Supply Curve

| Factor | Effect on Supply of Increases in The Factor |
|---|---|
| Civilian Wages | Decrease |
| Unemployment | Increase |
| Population | Increase |
| Recruiting Resources | Increase |
| Draft Pressure | Increase |

group to be the 17-21 year old age cohorts, excluding those mentally, medically, and physically unqualified.

Recruiting resources generally refer to the recruiting force as well as to expenditures on media advertising.

Draft pressure is the effect that the threat to the individual of being drafted has on the supply curve. Empirical studies conducted using data from periods when conscription was in effect generally defined the draft pressure variable as the ratio of inductees to the population. As inductions relative to the population size increased, most studies conducted using the draft pressure variable tended to show increases in the supply of voluntary, but draft-induced, enlistments.

On the demand side, the factors that are assumed to shift the demand curve are shown in table 12.4, along with the presumed effect of increases in each of the factors on demand.

National preference for defense reflects the effect of the public's taste for defense services. If the taste for defense services increases due to exogenous factors such as wars or increased international tensions, then the demand for defense services will increase and along with it, the demand for military labor.

If national defense services are normal goods, then increases in national income will generally result in increasing expenditures on defense.

Table 12.4. Factors Shifting the Demand Curve

| Factor | Effect on Demand of Increase in The Factor |
|---|---|
| National Preference | Increase |
| National Income | Increase |
| Prices of Complements | Decrease |
| Prices of Substitutes | Increase |
| Technological Change | Decrease |

The price of complements refers to goods or services which are generally required to be utilized along with military labor. An example would be medical services. Increases in the price of medical services would raise the combined price of an enlistee and the associated medical treatment and tend to reduce the combined demand for both services.

Substitutes for military labor of a specified type would include other types of military labor (i.e., substituting career for noncareer military personnel), civilians, and capital. If the price of a substitute declines relative to the price of the labor in question, then the demand for military labor of the type concerned would be reduced.

Technological change may affect the demand for military labor in a number of ways. For example, technological advance in a field related to military equipment may allow for a reduction in the size of crews required to operate certain weapons systems, thus reducing the overall demand for military manpower.

The effect of changes in a shift variable on the labor market is shown in figure 12.2. To illustrate the point, it is assumed that the national preference for defense increases resulting in a shift in the demand curve to the right. The effect of the shift is to initially create a shortage of military labor equal to $L_B - L_e$. The market response to the shortage would be to allow the wage rate to rise to $W^*$. As wages increase, the shortage is eliminated by the increase in supply brought forth at the higher wage, $L_A - L_e$, as well as the reduction in demand resulting from income and price effects of higher wage rates, $L_B - L_A$. The magnitude of the wage rate required to bring the market into equilibrium and to eliminate the shortage depends on the elasticities of supply and demand.

The following section describes some of the empirical literature on the elasticities involved and their implications for the market model.

## Supply and Demand Literature

The literature on the characteristics of the supply curve for enlisted accessions is voluminous. The seminal article in the literature, which developed the basic supply model and provided econometric estimates of the pay and unemployment elasticities, is the 1969 study by Fisher.[13] Other articles appearing at the same time which also dealt with enlisted accessions include those of Altman[14] and Klotz.[15] One year later, the Gates Commission Report and Background Papers provided still more estimates of the enlisted supply curve by Fechter, Gray, Cook, and White.[16] A survey of the econometric work in the area of enlisted supply up to and following the Gates Commission is found in reviews by Grissmer et al.,[17] and Amey et al.[18] One of the latest published works in the field is that of Cooper.[19]

In general, the results of the various studies tend to confirm the basic hypotheses of economic behavior assumed in the market model. The supply of

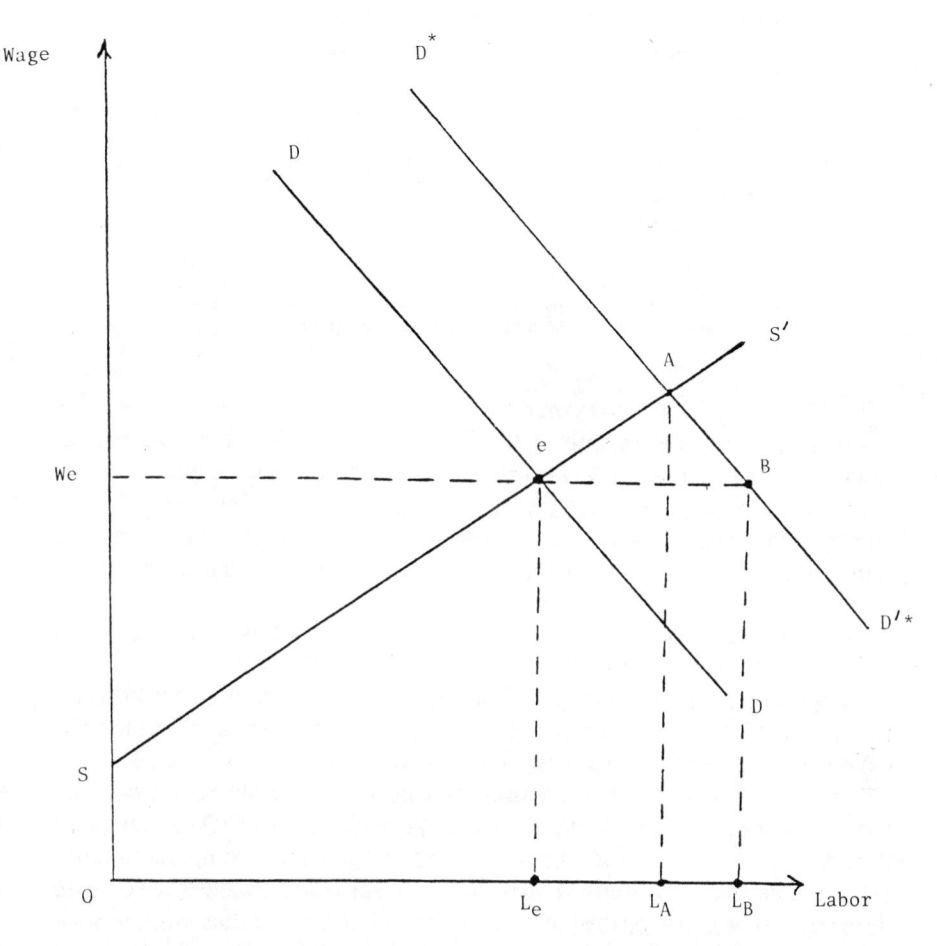

**Figure 12.2.** Effect of an Increase in Demand on The Military Labor Market

enlistees tends to behave as described in the market model above, although the range of estimates in the literature varies widely depending on the type of model used, the market studied (i.e., entry-level characteristics of the enlistee under consideration), and the data base. Table 12.5 provides the estimates obtained by Cooper for pay, unemployment, and recruiting resource elasticities. Cooper's analysis examined the market for active force high school diploma graduates in the upper three mental categories, and used data from 1971 to 1976 to obtain the estimates.

There are very few studies on the supply elasticities for selected reserve forces. A 1974 study by Rostker[20] on the Air Force Reserve and a 1979 study by Kelly[21] on aggregate DOD selected reserve accessions are the only two studies

**Table 12.5.** Supply Elasticities: High School Diploma Graduates in Mental Categories I-III Active Force Accessions

| Factor | Elasticity |
| --- | --- |
| Pay | 1.21 |
| Unemployment | .19 |
| Recruiting Resource | .30 |

Source: R.V.L. Cooper, *Military Manpower and the All-Volunteer Force* (Santa Monica, California, 1977), p. 168. Elasticities shown are evaluated at mean AVF pay, AVF recruiting resources, and for an unemployment rate of 13.5 percent for 18-19 year old males.

currently available which examine selected reserve supply elasticities. The Rostker study found the supply of Air Force reservists to be elastic with respect to pay, with a zero draft pay elasticity of 1.3. Kelly found the supply of DOD reservists to be pay inelastic, with a pay elasticity of .2, but responsive to employment conditions with an employment elasticity of -3.4. Given the importance attached to improving the strength of the selected reserves, this is an area where more research is warranted.

Because the IRR in the past has served generally without pay, there have been no published studies on the supply of individuals to the IRR.

On the demand side, the empirical literature has concentrated on substitutes for first-term NPS male enlistees. The prime candidates here include the substitution of capital, careerists, and women for NPS males.

In the area of capital labor substitution, Cooper[22] and Roll[23] have examined the relative price of capital and labor and the response of DOD to changes in the relative price. In general, they conclude that, given the rising cost of labor relative to capital, substitutions of capital for labor would enable given defense objectives to be accomplished at a smaller total budget cost than without such substitutions. Along the same lines, a study by Kelly[24] of the capital intensity of the armies in NATO countries shows that, in the long run, policymakers tend to make such substitutions in response to changes in the relative price of labor and capital.

Another area of the demand for labor examined by Cooper is the substitution of career for noncareer labor. In examining the price of careerists relative to noncareerists, Cooper concludes that significant cost savings can be obtained by reducing the demand for first-term accessions by shifting the force mix in favor of careerists.[25]

The use of women in the military has been the subject of increased attention in the military manpower literature in the past several years. A compendium of studies edited by Hoiberg,[26] and studies by Binkin and Bach[27] as well as by DOD[28] have outlined a number of relevant issues. While many analyses have concluded that the increasing use of women can ease recruiting problems, questions on the numbers of women available as well as on the effect of women on the organization continue to be studied.

## DIVERGENT VIEWS FROM THE MARKET PERSPECTIVE

### The Market View

The DOD view outlined above essentially takes a straight market approach to managing the force. Given the wage rate determined by the executive branch and Congress, DOD essentially attempts to fill accession requirements by using bonuses to increase the wage rate in those particular markets where there are shortages. DOD also utilizes a combination of advertising expenditures and recruiters to shift the supply curve to eliminate shortages.

The major problem with this approach is that DOD, in the face of relatively fixed accession requirements and changing economic and demographic conditions, does not directly control the general military wage rate or the resources that are spent on recruiting or advertising. Wages, bonuses, and recruiting expenses are determined by Congress. Without this flexibility, DOD must either suffer shortfalls or substitute individuals with less desirable entry-level characteristics during periods when economic and demographic conditions are unfavorable for recruiting.

In the upcoming years, this problem will have significant short-run and long-run consequences. The short-run consequences result from the cyclical variations in the unemployment rate, while the long-run problem centers around the youth demographic situation.

In the short-run, the problem with the volunteer system is to recruit during periods of low unemployment. While the unemployment supply elasticity, as measured by Cooper, is low, (.2) swings in the unemployment rate for teenagers during changes in the business cycle tend to be very large and result in significant shifts in the supply curve. During the period from 1969 to 1979, for example, the unemployment rate for white males aged 16 to 19 varied between 10 and 18.3 percent.[29] Furthermore, these unemployment swings can occur very rapidly. In 1974, the unemployment rate averaged 13.5 percent but jumped to 18.3 percent in the next year, a change of 35 percent.[30] Given Cooper's unemployment elasticity, this would result in a reduction in enlistments of 7 percent over the period of a year if all other factors remained the same.

One area in which factors are not remaining the same is in the area of demographics. Table 12.6 shows the Department of Commerce projections for the male population aged 17-21 for the rest of the twentieth century. As the population figures indicate, the pool of young people will decline significantly

Table 12.6.  Projected Population Estimates
(Millions)

| Year | Males Age 17 | Males Ages 17-21 |
|---|---|---|
| 1980 | 2.093 | 10.740 |
| 1985 | 1.780 | 9.593 |
| 1990 | 1.640 | 9.005 |
| 1995 | 1.849 | 8.565 |
| 2000 | 2.115 | 10.253 |

Source: *Current Population Reports,* U.S. Department of Commerce, Bureau of the Census, Series P-25, No. 601, October 1975. Series II projections.

until the 1990s and intensify competition for these age groups in the labor market. The result will be that the armed forces can expect significant recruiting problems in the 1980s and 1990s unless the demand is reduced or other factors affecting the supply curve change in ways favorably affecting enlistments.

Overriding all these considerations is the fact that, during the entire period of the volunteer force, average wages in the military have been falling relative to average wages in the rest of the economy. Thus, in terms of pure wage incentives, the military has become less competitive for the past several years. A similar trend on top of the demographic trend shown in table 12.6 will exacerbate the problems of recruiting in the 1980s.

## The Nonmarket View

The effect of a nonmarket solution is illustrated in this section by considering the economic effects of a draft.[31] The effects of a national service program would be equivalent to a draft of the entire age cohort under consideration.

The effects of a draft from the market perspective are shown in figure 12.3. With the wage rate at W*, a shortage of enlistments would result. The shortage is given by the difference between $L_B$ and $L_A$. To make up the shortfall, the military would induct $L_B - L_A$ individuals. This method of providing manpower ensures the military of a given quantity of individuals with given entry-level characteristics. It is this feature of the draft which its proponents argue is worth the cost.

The problems with this approach are threefold. First, it tends to be inefficient in an economic sense in that it tends to use scarce resources which have a greater social benefit elsewhere. A measure of this inefficiency is shown by the cross-hatched area in figure 12.3 which represents the difference between the social cost of the labor used (the point on the supply curve) and the social

## The Market Model of Military Labor Procurement     211

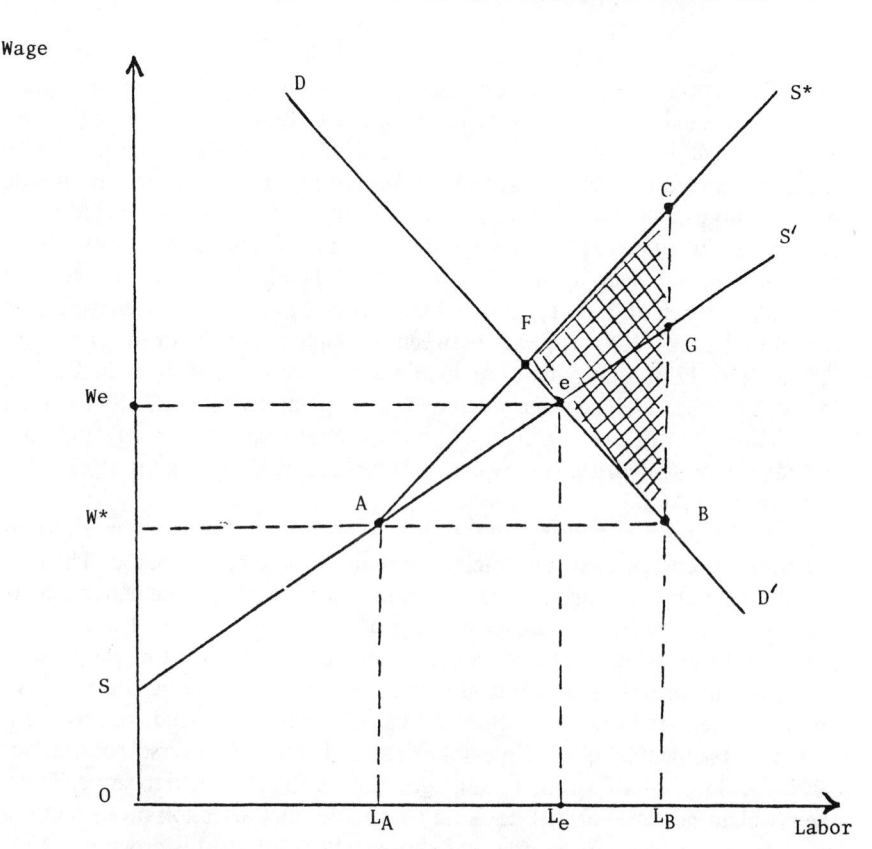

**Figure 12.3.** The Effects of the Draft on the Military Labor Market

benefit in the military (given by the demand curve). Note that the supply curve used to calculate the economic cost of the draft differs from the original supply curve shown in figure 12.1 to the right of point A. The reason for this is that the original supply curve, SS', orders individuals from left to right along the horizontal axis by increasing supply price. The supply curve used to calculate the economic cost of the draft, SAS*, however, orders only those who are drafted by supply price to the right of point A. In the case of a perfect draft, i.e., where those who are drafted lie along the original supply curve from point A to point G, the draft supply curve and the nondraft supply curve would be the same. In the more likely case where those who are drafted would randomly lie along the supply curve to the right of point A, some individuals to the right of point G on the original supply curve would be drafted. These individuals would tend to raise the draft supply curve and account for the greater slope between points A and S*.

A second problem with the draft is the fact that the economic cost of the draft is not explicitly reported in the budget while the cost of a purely volunteer force is reported as a budget cost. The individuals that are drafted do have an economic cost, however, and that cost should be measured and compared with the cost of a volunteer force before any claims are made as to the relative merits of either approach. The economic cost of those that are drafted includes not only the arbitrary wage that is paid to draftees, but also the opportunity cost to the individual of being drafted as opposed to being able to accept the best alternative in lieu of military service. One measure of this cost, often called the conscription tax is the difference between the wage which the draftee receives, W* in figure 12.3, and that wage which would have induced the individual to join voluntarily, i.e., the wage given by the draft supply curve, SAS* in figure 12.3. Thus, the true cost of drafting $L_B$ individuals in figure 12.3 would not only include the budget cost given by area OW*B$L_B$, but also the conscription tax given by area ACB.

In addition to comparing the amounts resulting from each method of taxation, the cost of collecting each type of tax should be compared. The cost of collecting taxes to support the volunteer system includes the general costs associated with the income tax system. The costs of the conscription tax include not only the costs associated with the income tax system for the budget cost aspect of the draftee force, but also the cost of administering the Selective Service System and the costs which individuals expend to avoid conscription.

A third problem is equity. Unless the draft is a form of universal service, not all eligible individuals within a given age cohort will be selected to serve. Thus, the problem becomes one of devising a nonvoluntary selection process in the absence of a market. As Cooper has shown, the result of this process in 1970 appeared to be that those with the least ability to pay were taxed proportionately higher than those with a greater ability to pay, or that the conscription tax was regressive.[32] Although this may not always be the case, it is certainly more difficult to devise a progressive tax based on post-high school socioeconomic indicators than it would be to use the current income tax schedule.

### Janowitz/Moskos View

If the basic underlying characteristics of a market is voluntary exchange, then Janowitz and Moskos retain a market approach to manpower management in their solution to the manpower problem. Instead of using pure cash on the purchasing side of the transaction, however, Janowitz and Moskos use a combination of cash and in-kind benefits (education, preferences, etc.). Thus, an individual contemplating an enlistment must convert the combined cash and in-kind payment to a single wage to evaluate the military with other alternatives and make a choice.

In the end, however, it still must hold that the evaluation the individual places on the combined cash and in-kind supplements must be greater than or equal to his supply price. If not, the individual will not enlist. Thus, a key question in this approach is whether the government will be able to secure the types of individuals that Janowitz and Moskos desire more efficiently with the cash plus in-kind approach or with a pure cash approach similar to the policies followed under the current version of the AVF.

Some economic theory suggests that the pure cash approach would require less expenditure to obtain the same individual. (See the Appendix to this chapter.) The reason for this is that individuals place a premium on the ability to reallocate resources they possess to maximize their satisfactions. On the other hand, the offer of a large education benefit to individuals who desire to go to college may be a form of advertising which is effective in reaching those with the entry-level characteristics that Janowitz and Moskos argue are vital to the force.

The interesting and innovative aspect of the Janowitz and Moskos approach to the problem, however, is the use of currently existing and funded programs and employment requirements to increase the incentive for individuals to join the military and, specifically, the combat arms. These suggestions essentially provide the military with increased resources without a major restructuring of the organization or social policies and at the same time retain the voluntary aspect of the force.

## CONCLUSIONS

The alternative views and approaches to manpower management examined in this chapter have advantages and disadvantages. The current DOD approach has the advantage of being voluntary as well as generally efficient. The inability to know with certainty employment conditions and to control funding, however, may cause the military to either substitute individuals with entry-level characteristics less than those desired or to suffer shortages during certain periods. These effects will be especially severe when there is a desire to restrain wages, in periods of low unemployment, and when the recruiting age population is declining.

The draft or national service approach has the significant advantage of certainty about the quantity and entry-level characteristics of the force. If a draft is efficiently administered, the military would be able to obtain large supplies of labor and to reduce recruiting efforts and costs. The major disadvantages here, however, are inefficiency and the cost and equity of the conscription tax. This approach also calls for major social change which may create substantial political upheaval and unrest.

The Janowitz and Moskos approach redirects the efforts of the manpower program in an attempt to obtain individuals with more education and those from a more representative socioeconomic background. The advantages of their approach are that it is voluntary; it would utilize currently existing federal programs to increase resources in the manpower area; and, if successful, it would also improve the efficiency of the force. The major problem with the approach is that it may be more costly than other voluntary programs which achieve the same result.

The choice among these alternatives will be made by the president and Congress. Any of the above approaches can be made to work with sufficient resources. The choice selected, however, should achieve the nation's national security objectives at the least social, economic, and political cost.

One final point should be made about the criticism of the market approach in the King/Reed and Janowitz/Moskos views of the AVF. The market is composed of individuals and agencies that make decisions and execute those decisions through voluntary exchange. Credit for the success or failure of the market approach should not be placed on the market per se, but on the decisions made by those individuals who participate in the market. It is difficult to see how the market system can provide the nation with an upwardly mobile and representative enlisted force when real military wages have declined significantly relative to average civilian wages throughout the volunteer period. The market process should not be used as a scapegoat to mask the failure of the nation to bid for talent in the labor market. Regardless of which method the nation chooses for management of military manpower in the future, without sufficient recourses, our military manpower objectives will not be attained.

## NOTES

1. Morris Janowitz and Charles Moskos, "Five Years of the All-Volunteer Force: 1973-1978," *Armed Forces and Society* 5 (Winter 1979): 171-218.
2. Ibid.
3. Office of the Assistant Secretary of Defense (Manpower, Reserve Affairs and Logistics), *America's Volunteers: A Report on the All-Volunteer Armed Forces,* December 31, 1978, pp. 186-87.
4. *The Report of the Presidents Commission on an All-Volunteer Force* (Washington, D.C.: U.S. Government Printing Office, 1970).
5. Richard V. L. Cooper, *Military Manpower and the All-Volunteer Force* (Santa Monica, California: Rand, 1977).
6. William R. King, *Achieving America's Goal: The All-Volunteer Armed Force or National Service?* Committee on Armed Services, U.S. Senate 95th Congress (Washington, D.C.: U.S. Government Printing Office, 1977).
7. Jerry L. Reed, *An Analysis and Evaluation of the United States Army, The Beard Study in Hearings The Status of the All Volunteer Force,* Subcommittee on Manpower and Personnel, Committee of the Armed Services, U.S. Senate, 95th Congress, (Washington, D.C.: U.S. Government Printing Office, 1978), pp. 129-266.
8. Ibid., p. 257.
9. Janowitz and Moskos, "Five Years of the All-Volunteer Force: 1973-1978."
10. Ibid., p. 209.

11. Ibid., pp. 208-09.
12. Ibid., p. 209.
13. Anthony C. Fisher, "The Cost of the Draft and the Cost of Ending the Draft," *American Economic Review* 59 (June 1969): 239-54.
14. Stuart Altman, "Earnings, Unemployment, and the Supply of Enlisted Volunteers," *Journal of Human Resources*, 4 (Winter 1969): 38-59.
15. Benjamin Klotz, "The Cost of Ending the Draft: Comment," *American Economic Review* 60 (December 1970); 970-79.
16. See *Studies Prepared For The President's Commission on an All-Volunteer Armed Force*, Volume 1, (Washington D.C.: U.S. Government Printing Office, 1970).
17. David Grissmer, et al. *An Econometric Analysis of Volunteer Enlistments by Service and Cost Effectiveness Comparison of Service Incentive Programs*, (McLean, Virginia: General Research Corporation, 1974).
18. Dorothy Amey and others, "Econometric Models of Armed Forced Enlistment Levels," mimeographed, General Research Corporation, October 1976.
19. Cooper, *Military Manpower and the All-Volunteer Force*.
20. Bernard Rostker, *Air Reserve Personnel Study: Volume III Total Force Planning, Personnel Costs, and the Supply of New Reservists* (Santa Monica: Rand, 1974), p. 22.
21. Robert C. Kelly, "The Supply of Volunteers to the Selected Reserve," mimeographed, Department of Social Sciences, U.S. Military Academy, May 1979, p. 14.
22. Cooper, *Military Manpower and the All-Volunteer Force*, pp. 277-290.
23. Charles R. Roll, "Potential for Capital-Labor Substitution." Paper prepared for the U.S. Air Force Academy Rand Conference on the Economics of National Security, August 1979.
24. Robert Kelly, "Military Manpower Costs and Manpower Policy: An Economic Assessment" in *Military Unions: U.S. Trends and Issues*, edited by William J. Taylor, Robert J. Arango, and Robert S. Lockwood, (Beverly Hills, California: Sage, 1977), pp. 792-304.
25. Cooper, *Military Manpower and the All-Volunteer Force*, pp. 303-18. See also Martin Binkin and Irene Kyriakopoulos, *Youth or Experience? Manning the Modern Military* (Washington, D.C.: Brookings, 1979).
26. Anne Hoiberg, ed., "Women as New 'Manpower'," *Armed Forces and Society* 4 (Summer 1978).
27. Martin Binkin and Shirley Bach, *Women in the Military* (Washington, D.C.: Brookings, 1977).
28. *Use of Women in the Military: DOD Background Study*, Office of the Assistant Secretary of Defense (Manpower, Reserve Affairs, and Logistics) May 1977.
29. *Economic Report of the President, January 1980* (Washington, D.C.: U.S. Government Printing Office, 1980), p. 238.
30. Ibid.
31. See Cooper, *Military Manpower and the All-Volunteer Force* pp. 66-101 for an in-depth study of the economics of conscription. This section uses many of the ideas on conscription developed by Cooper.
32. Ibid., p. 88.

# APPENDIX
# Is an Education Approach Less or More Costly Than Pure Cash?

Assume the government offers a lump sum educational benefit plus cash, or a pure cash income to individuals with the characteristics desired by Janowitz and Moskos. Let E* represent the quantity of education offered, E the actual

**216**   **Defense Manpower Planning**

All Other Goods, X

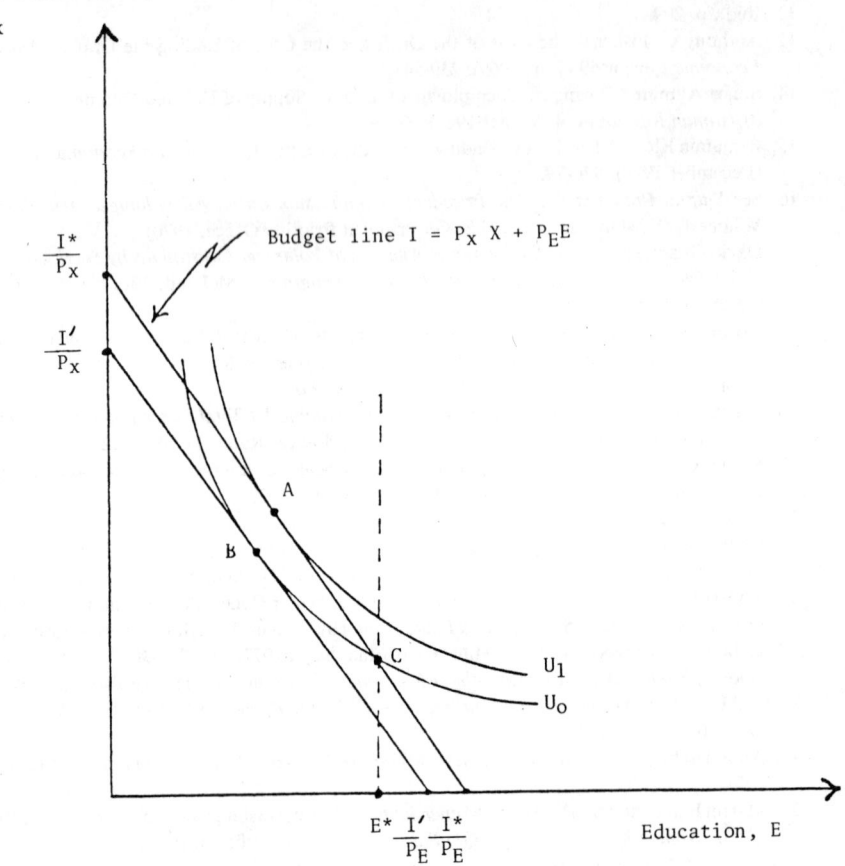

[Figure: Graph with vertical axis "All Other Goods, X" and horizontal axis "Education, E". Shows budget line $I = P_X X + P_E E$, points A, B, C, and indifference curves $U_1$ and $U_0$. Vertical axis intercepts labeled $\frac{I^*}{P_X}$ and $\frac{I'}{P_X}$. Horizontal axis points labeled $E^*$, $\frac{I'}{P_E}$, $\frac{I^*}{P_E}$.]

**Figure 12.A.**   The Income Evaluation of Janowitz-Moskos Plan

amount of education consumed, X represents all other goods, $P_E$ the price of education, and $P_X$ the price of all other goods. Let the individuals' preferences for education and all other goods be given by the indifference curves shows in figure 12.A. The amount of cash income the individual is given is equivalent to $I^* - P_E E^*$. If the individual had the preferences shown and could convert his educational benefits to cash, he would end up at A. But, given the fixed educational grant, he ends up at C on indifference curve $U_o$. The government could alternatively provide a pure cash income equal to $I^1$ which would leave the individual equally satisfied. But since $I^* > I^1$ and the government must provide either, it is less costly for the government to use the pure cash approach than the educational benefit. If the individual's preferences are such that his utility maximizing bundle of goods lies between $I^*$ and C, then the education plan and the cash plan would be equally costly.

Chapter 13
# National Service: An Alternative to the All-Volunteer Military
William R. King

For most of its history, the United States has supported its peacetime defense establishment on a volunteer basis. However, within much of the lifetime of many living Americans, peacetime military conscription has been the accepted practice.[1] The United States returned to its traditional peacetime practice when, on January 27, 1973, Secretary of Defense Melvin R. Laird announced that the armed forces would henceforth depend exclusively on volunteer soldiers, sailors, airmen, and marines. This termination of more than three decades of military conscription in the United States came after nearly a decade of study by the Department of Defense and other interested parties.

The decision to move to an all-volunteer force was made prior to March 27, 1969, when President Nixon appointed an Advisory Commission on an All-Volunteer Armed Force under the chairmanship of The Honorable Thomas S. Gates, Jr., formerly Secretary of Defense. The president's statement announcing the formation of the commission charged it with developing "... a comprehensive plan eliminating conscription and moving toward an all-volunteer armed force."[2] Although the decision to move to an AVF had already been made, as this charge makes clear, the Gates' Commission chose to look into both the feasibility and desirability of the move to an AVF. In early 1970, they reported favorably on both counts and made many recommendations—foremost among them being significant military pay increases—that they believed necessary to make the all-volunteer concept a success.

The essence of the Commission's findings is summed up in two paragraphs from Secretary Gates' letter of transmittal:

> We unanimously believe that the nation's interests will be better served by an all-volunteer force, supported by an effective stand-by draft, than by a mixed force of volunteers and conscripts; that steps should be taken promptly to move in this direction; and that the first indispensable step is to remove the present inequity in the pay of men serving their first term in the armed forces.
>
> We have satisfied ourselves that a volunteer force will not jeopardize national security, and we believe it will have a beneficial effect on the military as well as the rest of our society.[3]

The administration accepted the commission's recommendation in principle, but extended their recommended timetable for two years until July 1, 1973. Congress approved a two-year extension of induction authority until that date, thus creating a "transition period" extending from 1970 until January 1973 when the draft was actually ended.

The transition period, during which the military was still supported by a draft while knowing that it faced a 1973 termination of induction authority, was one of planning and experimentation for DOD. During that uncertain period, many officials and laymen were doubtful that the Gates' Commission's conclusions were valid. The fact that the draft was ended six months ahead of schedule, in January 1973, undoubtedly reflected both effective planning and the influence of uncontrollable factors such as the economy and declines in the magnitude of the war-stimulated need for large military forces. However, as Binkin and Johnston state in their 1973 study of the transitional achievements in preparing for the AVF: "Taken together, these achievements suggest that this nation can accomplish what no other nation has ever attempted—to maintain an active armed force of over two million men and women on a voluntary basis."[4]

Since the AVF was fully instituted in 1973, some skeptics appear to have been converted. The AVF is in existence and statistics are routinely produced by the Department of Defense which demonstrate that the military forces are generally meeting quantity targets, that the "quality" of accessions is acceptable, and, generally, that the concept is working.

However, disquieting rumors, magazine and newspaper articles,[5] and study results[6] that had circulated widely concerning the status, viability, and effectiveness of the AVF were given greater credibility in 1976 by a report of the Defense Manpower Commission which concluded that:

> The sustainability of the All Volunteer Force during peacetime will depend upon the economic situation and other interrelated factors, some of which—such as public attitudes toward the armed forces—cannot be predicted with any certainty.[7]

Thus, for most of the 1970s and into the 1980s, we have had an all-volunteer military which is the direct result of a political campaign promise to end the draft. The motivation for the promise was clearly the campus riots, draft protests, draft-board break-ins, and draft-card burnings of the Vietnam era.

Our nation has moved to a radically different approach to raising military manpower than the one that served since the early 1940s. In doing so, there is evidence to suggest that we may have created impacts on the military and on the fabric of American society that were unintended. And, despite the Gates' Commission report, study of the relevant documents shows that we made this change without careful thought and analysis of other alternatives to the draft which might have been, and still may be, more beneficial to the nation than the AVF.

## THE PERFORMANCE OF THE AVF

The performance of the AVF has been a varied one. Much like an on-again off-again baseball team, the AVF has met and failed to meet recruiting quotas in various time periods. Often, the failure to meet quotas has come at surprising times—as in the last quarter of 1976 when both the Army and Marine Corps failed to meet quotas that had been established at levels significantly below those of the previous year. The surprising thing about this shortfall was that it occurred just before the end of the GI Bill—a time when there should have been a rush to get into the service in order to qualify for benefits.

During periods when recruiting quotas were generally met by the services, a significantly lower percentage of high school graduates were recruited in order to accomplish the goal.

The AVF is apparently a sometimes thing, constantly operating at the ragged edge of viability. Even in terms of the aggregate statistical indicators that DOD chooses as measures of success—recruiting results matched against self-determined quotas; "quality" of recruits as measured by high school graduation and scores on the Armed Services Vocational Aptitude Battery (ASVAB); and "representativeness" as measured by racial, sex, and educational distributions—it is clearly a matter of opinion as to whether or not the AVF is a success.

## Crucial Questions Concerning the AVF

Despite the apparent general viability of the AVF,[8] its ragged performance serves to motivate serious questions concerning its future viability, the quality of the defense that we are buying, and the AVF's effect on our nation and society. Among the most crucial issues concerning the AVF are:

- Is the AVF solely a peacetime concept, and does it therefore fail to achieve some basic national security objectives?

- Does the AVF unfairly distribute the burdens of defense to various segments of the population?
- Will the AVF ultimately undermine the nation's defense capability through an erosion of public confidence in the military which leads to decreasing support for defense expenditures?
- Will the AVF ultimately undermine the level of patriotism in the American public?
- Will the AVF lead to greater isolation of the military from the rest of society?
- Does the nature of the AVF restrict the range of policy choices available to our leaders in using military forces to achieve national objectives?

If the answer to any of these questions is negative in terms of the AVF's overall impact on the nation, an even broader question is naturally suggested—is there an alternative to the AVF which would help the nation to achieve its goals without detracting from defense capabilities?

A variety of studies have been performed that suggest that many of these answers may, indeed, be negative.[9] It is not the purpose of this chapter, however, to repeat those arguments. Rather, here we presume, as even its most ardent proponents would agree, that the AVF has been less than an unqualified success. As a result, we pose the issue: Are their viable alternatives to it that might benefit the nation more?

## ALTERNATIVES TO THE AVF

Since the performance of the AVF presents a "mixed picture," it is wise for us to look into AVF alternatives. Among those which might be considered are:

1. A Return to the Draft
2. A "Reserve-Only" Draft
3. A "Better Managed" AVF
4. Universal Military Training
5. National Service
   (a) Compulsory
   (b) Voluntary

### Return to the Draft

A "natural" alternative to the AVF is a return to the practice of conscripting recruits into the military. This is the system with which we are most familiar and it would necessarily avoid many of the problems associated with the present and future AVF. However, the draft alternative cannot be justified on the basis of sigificant cost savings unless dramatic pay decreases in the lower ranks are undertaken. Even then, the savings would not be as great as have been the budget costs of the AVF since many of the benefits which were offered to military personnel under the AVF have been institutionalized.

The annual savings to accrue from a return to the draft have been estimated between $325 million and $2.8 billion—the former figure being that of no pay decreases and the latter being the extreme case involving the institution of poverty-level compensation level for recruits.[10]

One of the factors mitigating against the draft is public attitudes. In 1973, nearly 79 percent of Americans favored the abolition of the draft; and, since many of the AVF's problems are not well known by the public, there is no reason to believe that the draft has wider public support now.[11]

Despite the fact that registration has been reintroduced, the draft would probably operate effectively and with benefit to the nation only in the case of a clearly-perceived threat to national security. In an era in which threats are subtle and ambiguous, this is not the most likely circumstance. Therefore, the draft does not seem to be an alternative to the AVF that would benefit the nation, except in the most severe circumstance.

## Reserve-Only Draft

A "mixture" of the draft and AVF which would vitiate some, but not all, of the AVF problems is a "reserve only" draft. Under such a plan, individuals would be drafted—probably on a lottery bases—into the individual ready reserve (IRR), given the essential training, and after some period, assume only the modest military responsibilities of a member of the IRR.

This alternative would directly resolve many of the problems which currently exist for the reserves under the AVF, and it would provide a modest "draft inducement" to enlistment in the active or reserve forces. It would not be inordinately costly, but it would require the reinstitution of a selective service system—something that we will probably do eventually to provide us with a "backup" draft capability.

The primary disadvantages of such a system are the "hidden" economic and social costs of any draft, the geographic problems if reservists were to be drafted into reserve units, and the fact that the plan does not directly address the broad range of problems which are facing the AVF.

One of the difficulties with the AVF is its unintended and sometimes unperceived impacts on our nation. These impacts certainly extend into our society far beyond its military domain. A reserve-only draft, as with any "patchwork" solution to the AVF's problems, will not significantly alter those effects.

## A "Better Managed" AVF

One of the alternatives to the current system is a "better managed" AVF. This does not imply that the AVF has been mismanaged. Indeed, the DOD has done a commendable job of instituting a radically-new system into a huge organization. However, an awareness of the current AVF problems and a commitment to improve them is an essential prerequisite to the development of a comprehensive plan for the attainment of a better managed force. Some of the elements of such a plan should be:

1. Demand reduction programs—such as capital substitution for labor, increased utilization of women, increased overhead reductions, civilianization, greater use of contractor support, and the encouragement of higher reenlistment rates.
2. Supply enhancement programs—such as those that will attract older recruits, prior-service persons, and individuals possessing civilian-acquired skills, decreased quality standards, increased paid advertising, and educational incentive programs.
3. Improvements in the quality of military life—to assure the fulfillment of recruiting promises and to improve the attitudes of enlisted personnel.
4. Enlisted attrition reduction programs.

Such programs represent the strategy that has already been adopted to remedy the AVF's deficiencies. This is a proper course of action since no rational person, however much opposed to the AVF he may be, would argue that we should do less than our best with the AVF while it is our only means of national defense. However, these programs represent another "patchwork" solution to a series of problems that many consider to be so general that they cannot be resolved in any way other than a structurally different approach to the military manpower system.

## Universal Military Training

Universal military training (UMT) in the generic term used to describe various plans under which "everyone" would be given at least a minimum amount of military training on a compulsory basis. Such systems are now in existence in countries such as Israel, Sweden, Switzerland, and the USSR (although it is not officially recognized as such there).

Support for the UMT concept is apparently surprisingly strong among young people. However, it is interesting to note that the concept receives much higher support than does any of the several specific UMT plans which respondents were queried about in a 1965 survey.[12]

High military training costs per recruit would make the UMT concept a costly one.[13] The additional cost would be at least $20 billion annually, and possibly much more depending on the necessity for increasing physical facilities, weapons, etc. If the military could significantly reduce its recruit training costs through increased class size or other means, the UMT concept might be less costly than it is generally perceived to be.

While the UMT alternative is a structurally different one that might indeed directly remedy some of the negative impacts of the AVF, its compulsory nature is anathema to some who consider compulsion to be inconsistent with our principles of a free society. Certainly, UMT would meet with many objections if it were seriously to be considered by the Congress. Moreover, while it would address many of our military objectives and needs, it would also have nonmilitary second-order society consequences, as does the AVF. Some of these would undoubtedly be so negative that we might find ourself in an "AVF-like" position after having instituted UMT.

## National Service

"National Service" is another generic term which is used to describe a variety of plans having the common element of service in a variety of military and nonmilitary fields which are deemed to be in the nation's best interests. A number of varieties of national service may be usefully distinguished:

1. Compulsory national service—in which all are required to serve in some military or nonmilitary capacity.
2. Alternative national service—in which all would be required to serve, but those choosing nonmilitary service would be exempted from a military obligation.
3. "Voluntary" national service—in which nonmilitary service is encouraged, but it does not exempt one from a military obligation.
4. "Minimally-Coercive" national service—in which everyone is required to register and be evaluated, but there is no service commitment.
5. "Pure" Voluntary national service—in which no commitment for service (military or nonmilitary) exists, but such service is encouraged and facilitated.

The United States today has a "purely voluntary" system of the latter variety since both military and nonmilitary service programs, such as the Peace Corps, are encouraged but not required by anyone. The "voluntary" system, (#3), is something of a misnomer since it is the system which existed in the United States during the draft era.

The other options are of greater interest.

**Minimally-Coercive National Service.** Under minimally-coercive national services all young Americans would be required to register, to take medical and aptitude tests, and to be counseled concerning the various military and nonmilitary service options available. Diagnosis of physical and educational problems would also be provided, so that, even if the individual did not choose to serve, he or she could be referred to the most appropriate medical care or educational programs. Such a system might include a backup draft to accommodate military requirements should the voluntary choice process not fulfill them. However, there is evidence to suggest that defense personnel requirements might be met without resort to a draft. This is so because a registration system would increase the "pool" of potential recruits available to the military in the sense that more individuals will be provided with substantive information and placed in the position of making a conscious and enlightened choice concerning military service.

More than 55 percent of male junior and senior high school students surveyed in 1965 (before large military pay increases had taken place) said that they would choose a military option under a national service program as compared to 26 percent who said that they would choose a nonmilitary option.[14] If these intentions are fulfilled, the military would obtain more than its "fair share" of youths.

These data can, in part, be explained by the fact that the military would probably be the only national service alternative which involves, in and of itself, substantial career opportunity. Thus, it would have a built-in attractiveness relative to the other service options. Moreover, the national service system can be designed so that pay, benefits, and service durations can be adjusted among the service alternatives to make military service relatively more attractive, as necessary to obtain adequate numbers of recruits. It may not even be as necessary to do this as some might imagine. This is so because even minimally-coercive voluntary national service would give the military the opportunity to provide substantive information about military careers to all prospective recruits—not just those who they reach with their advertising effort with its minimal information content. Survey evidence suggests that this would be advantageous in obtaining recruits, since the potential recruits—young men (under 20)—their parents, and educators (who influence the enlistment decision) are all positively influenced in their views toward military service when they are given factual information about the military.[15]

**Alternative National Service.** The alternative national service concept would involve a commitment on the part of everyone to serve in some capacity. Those who chose to enter nonmilitary service would be exempted from military service. However, quotas or a draft for the military would be required to ensure the achievement of military requirements.

**Compulsory National Service.** Compulsory national service is the most coercive form of national service. It would involve a "draft" and assignments into various services being determined "by the system" largely on the basis of national goals and priorities rather than as a matter of individual preference.

## THE BENEFITS OF NATIONAL SERVICE

All of the various forms of national service have the advantage of enabling the nation to pursue national goals with greater effectiveness. Moreover, even the least coercive option should serve to resolve many of the current problems of the AVF because it would require registration for service and, hence, facilitate the use of a draft in emergencies; and provide a greater number of youths with information about military life and, thereby, increase their likelihood of enlisting.[16]

Additionally, such systems directly address the severe youth unemployment problem[17] through providing vocational testing and counseling for all, and job training and experience for those who participate.

The registration, evaluation, and counseling elements of even the "minimally coercive" national service alternative would also serve to:

- identify and assess the skills and deficiencies of young Americans,
- prescribe remedial or skill-enhancing activities which the individual may wish to consider,
- offer factual information concerning a wide range of service and training opportunities for which the individual may be suited,
- facilitate the channeling of resources into critical areas of national need.

For the nation, even such a minimal national service system would provide the registration system which is the basis for a backup draft and a mechanism for performing public service work (such as civil defense preparation, public facilities construction, and nursing care for the elderly) which will otherwise go undone. It would also alleviate the substantial problems of youth unemployment and some of the negative attitudinal and behavioral consequences, such as crime and welfare dependence. Perhaps more significant than any of these benefits is that a well-run program of national service should serve to develop an overall attitude and spirit among American youth that cannot but benefit the nation.

Of course, the cost of any national service program would be high—although it could be accomplished for much less than many believe through the cooperation of existing private service and volunteer agencies, and through the use of volunteers as leaders and trainers. The benefits to the nation from such a system—in terms of work accomplished in our cities, parks, waterways, and shores—as well as in benefits to the people who participate, are potentially enormous.

## THE FEASIBILITY OF NATIONAL SERVICE

The feasibility of national service is always one of those things that is called into question when the topic is raised. In answer to this, one need look only at the Depression-era WPA and CCC programs and the present-day employment and training program of our federal government to realize that we have successfully operated, and are operating, programs of a nature and magnitude similar to that of national service. If a national service alternative to the AVF is carefully designed and implemented to utilize the tremendous reservoir of volunteer talent which exists in the nation, to serve local, national, and individual needs, and to avoid excess bureaucratic control, it can be cost-effective to the nation.

## SUMMARY

The current AVF has produced many actual and potential undesirable and unintended consequences. Further problems can be foreseen that will reduce the AVF to a peacetime activity that can be prepared to cope with significant emergencies only at great cost and with great delays. Such a force reduces our international credibility as well as our ability to defend ourselves and to meet our worldwide commitments.

We must look at the AVF realistically, rather than through the rose-colored glasses of those draft opponents who see the draft as the only feasible, and undesirable, alternative, or those defense officials who have dedicated themselves to making it a success, despite their underlying doubts. The time has come to conduct a searching and candid evaluation of the AVF, its effectiveness, its costs, and its impact on our society. In doing so, we should examine various alternatives to the AVF from the overall perspective of our national goals. Only through such an analysis of alternatives will we be able to choose that overall system which will best serve us in both peace and war.

## NOTES

1. With the exception of a brief period in 1947-48, conscription into the military had been continuously practiced since 1940.
2. Statement of President Richard M. Nixon, March 27, 1969.
3. "The Report of the President's Commission on an All-Volunteer Armed Force," February 20, 1970, p. iii.

4. Martin Binkin, and John D. Johnston, "All-Volunteer Armed Forces: Progress, Problems and Prospects," Report of the Committee on Armed Services, United States Senate, June 1, 1973, p. 25.
5. For instance, see A. DeStefano, "Is All Well With the Volunteer Military?", *Intellect*, May-June, 1976, pp. 560-62; and D. Cortwright, "Our Volunteer Army: Can a Democracy Stand It?", *The Nation,* October 16, 1976, pp. 357-62.
6. For instance, see A. N. Sabrosky, "The First Two Years of the Modern Volunteer Army: A Preliminary Assessment," paper delivered at the 1975 Biennial Conference of the Inter-University Seminar on Armed Forces and Society, Chicago, October 16-18, 1975.
7. "Defense Manpower: The Keystone of National Security," Report to the President and the Congress, Defense Manpower Commission, April 1976.
8. For example, see Binkin and Johnston, "All-Volunteer Armed Forces"; and "The All-Volunteer Armed Force: Current Status and Prospects," Department of Defense, December 17, 1976.
9. See, for example, W. R. King, "Achieving America's Goals: National Service or The All-Volunteer Armed Force?" U.S. Senate Committee on Armed Services, U.S. Government Printing Office, 1977; and Charles C. Moskos, Jr., "The Enlisted Ranks in the All-Volunteer Army," Northwestern University, January 1978.
10. "Fact Sheet: The Cost of Defense Manpower and the Volunteer Force," Department of Defense, February 1975.
11. D. R. Segal, "Civil-Military Relations in the Mass Public," *Armed Forces and Society,* February 1975, pp. 215-29.
12. L. Bramson, "The High School Student, The Draft, and Voluntary National Service Alternatives," in *The Draft: A Handbook of Facts and Alternatives,* edited by S. Tax (Chicago, Ill.: University of Chicago Press, 1967), pp. 177-87.
13. "Military Manpower Training Report for FY 1977," Department of Defense, March 1976.
14. See: Bramson, "The High School Student, the Draft and Voluntary National Service Alternatives".
15. "Attitudes and Motivations Toward Enlistment in the U.S. Army," Opinion Research Corporation, April 1974, pp. xi-xix.
16. Ibid.
17. "Policy Options for the Teenage Unemployment Problem," Congressional Budget Office, Background Paper #3, September 21, 1976.

## Chapter 14
# Making the All-Volunteer Force Work
### Charles C. Moskos

Is the all-volunteer force working? Look at the evidence in several official and semi-official statements: from the *Defense Manpower Commission Report of 1976,* "There is no evidence to suggest that the armed forces are now or are in danger of becoming a poor man's army"; from *Military Manpower and the All-Volunteer Force, 1977,* "The evidence presented here shows that the military has not been nor is it becoming an army of the poor or of the black"; from *America's Volunteers,* the DOD White Paper on the force published in late 1978, "The quality of the active force is comparable with that of the draft era. Concerns that the active force would not be representative of the society at large have not materialized"; from the *Secretary of Defense's Report for 1979,* "Current mental standards for both enlistment and reenlistment are higher now than during the draft or the early days of the AVF." Should one conclude that conditions in the AVF are good and getting better?

There can be no question that the enlisted ranks of the army have undergone a tremendous social metamorphosis during the all-volunteer era. The only question is, how can high-powered commissions and DOD studies come up with the opposite conclusion? A large part of *the problem* concerning the all-volunteer force is the failure of the Defense Department to "fess up" to its problems. This has caused important members of Congress and the Senate to adopt what can generously be called a skeptical, if not an antagonistic, attitude toward the personnel policies, issues, and reports presented by Defense Department officials. From the most recent Armed Forces House Committee comes a most interesting statement: "Rather than attempting to reorient the recruiting process to attract people from broader segments of the civilian population, and instead of exploring new alternatives to energize a faltering recruiting program, defense officials appear to be expending their efforts to justify the continuation of past policies."

There was a conference at the Hoover Institute in December 1979 that might be considered a Gates Commission redone. Those in attendance congratulated themselves on how well the volunteer force was working and how close the predictions of the Gates Commission had come to hitting the real targets. Then, of course, by February 1980, we start talking about draft registration and the manpower problems that had surfaced. What happened? Did everything fall apart between December 1979 and February 1980? Hardly. It is just a plain and documented fact that, ever since the ending of the draft, the level of education has declined among recruits entering the army. It speaks to the times that we are now talking about possession of a high school diploma as the *sine qua non* of quality. But even more dramatic has been the disappearance of the college educated among the people we recruit. In 1964, 15 percent of recruits, whether drafted or volunteers, had at least some college upon entering the army. In more recent years, the figures are around 3 percent. May, 1980 statistics on educational levels of the active duty army show that, of the entire combat arms of the United States Army, among first termers (which is over 100,000 men), there are 25 college graduates. In fact, there are only 276 college graduate first termers in the entire U.S. Army. One cannot gainsay such figures.

The rising proportion of black entrants has probably generated more heat than any other topic among the so-called "representativeness" issue of the all-volunteer army, but it is to be stressed that the decline in educational levels is not correlated with the rising minority content. Since the end of the draft, the proportion of blacks entering the army with a high school diploma has exceeded that of whites; and this is a trend which, at least until fiscal year 1979, has been increasing. Indeed, if you took all white recruits entering the army who are high school dropouts and painted them blue, there would be just about as many blues entering the army as there would be blacks. In other words, the army is not only attracting a disproportionate number of minorities, but also an unrepresentative segment of white youth who, if anything, are even more uncharacteristic of the broader mix than are our minority soldiers. One should add here the tremendous increase in the rise of young enlisted marrieds. The figure is now about 45 percent for E-4s, which is about double the pre-Vietnam levels. It is much more a white phenomenon than it is a black phenomenon, and it also runs contrary to national patterns which lean heavily toward later age first marriages. This is another indication of recruiting at the margins during the all-volunteer era.

It is true that the military has always recruited large numbers of youth, white and black, with limited alternative job prospects. The army will always continue to draw disproportionately from poor people and young blacks as long as they are victims of structural defects in the economy, especially the flight of manufacturing jobs from central cities. But present trends to label the army as a recourse for America's underclasses are self-defeating for the youth involved, precisely because they directly counter the premise that military participation should be one of broader-based national service. Whatever success the army has had as a remedial organization for deprived youth has been due largely to the armed forces being defined on other than welfare grounds, whether it be national defense, citizenship obligation, or even manly honor. In other words, those very conditions peculiar to the armed forces which serve to resocialize poverty youth to more productive ends depend directly upon that organization not being defined as a welfare agency or an employer of last resort.

It is also well known, of course, that we now face an attrition problem. Approximately 35 percent of our entering soldiers do not complete successfully their first tour of service. We have a new defense establishment verb now, "to attrit," which is not yet in the dictionary, but will be in the next edition. Over 600,000 young people have been returned to civilian life as attritees, that is, people who could not make it, who either dropped out or were pushed out by the military. What does this mean for recruitment, what does this mean for social imagery of the all-volunteer force? What does it mean when over 600,000 kids have been put back in society since the end of the draft, in a sense, as two time losers?

To what degree the changing racial composition of the army reflects white reluctance to join an increasingly black organization, one does not know. Surely, it is a factor, yet it is hardly clear than any significant number of middle class youth, white youth or middle class youth of any race, would be more likely to join the army under present recruitment incentives, even if the Army were overwhelmingly white. Essentially, the only real difference would be 30 percent less strength. The fact that the disproportionately white Navy and the racially-balanced Air Force also face recruitment problems indicates that there is more than racial content at work in recruiting an all-volunteer force. The distinctive quality of the enlisted experience, starting with World War II as the mixing of the classes, and starting with the Korean War as the mixing of the races, gave deprived youth an opportunity to compete, often successfully, with more privileged youth. This leveling of persons from different social backgrounds had no parallel in any other institution in American society. This state of affairs began to disappear toward the later years of the Vietnam War, when the college-educated avoided service. This is the situation that has all but disappeared in the all-volunteer army. These observations have to be placed in the context of studies which show all-volunteer soldiers displaying levels of alienation far exceeding those of the contemporary youth population. One should not argue in any sense that the military ought to be perfectly calibrated to the social composition of the larger society. But one should ask about the kind of society which makes it a matter of all but official policy to preclude its privileged from serving in the ranks of its army. It is a social reality that the combat arms will never be representative of the broader mix. It is always going to be disproportionately poorer, less educated, and of minority background. But to foster policies that accentuate that trend is perverse. If participation of people from minority or poor backgrounds is a measure of democratic representativeness at leadership positions, it is even more important that participation of advantaged groups in the rank and file also be a measure of representational democracy.

These kinds of issues that are now being raised despite the official line cited earlier have led to talk of bringing back the draft. That possibility is relatively remote. It would pose again the problem of who serves when not all serve. It is important to remember that one of the factors (and it is only one) that worked for the legitimacy of the draft during the 1950s and early 1960s was that there was a realtively small cohort maturing at age 18 and a fairly large standing force. As a matter of fact, proportionately more eligible men were drafted in the late 1950s at the height of the Vietnam War. Virtually everybody was going in during the 1950s because of the small cohort. We would not have that situation now if one considered a draft of approximately 10 to 20 percent. We are living in a fool's heaven if we think that bringing back the draft will not result in troubles on our college campuses. It is predictable that ROTC units would again become objects of attack. There would be social upheaval. Even "seemingly fair" lottery systems will define a minority as unlucky to begin with—those whose number happened to come up. What are we going to do with other kinds of problems of a draft such as conscientious objection, homosexuality, and others? Even the present registration law is, in a sense, the worst of both worlds. It neither solves any of the serious problems of the all-volunteer force nor is it much of a symbol to foreign leaders. Had the law passed overwhelmingly, this would have been one thing, but it did not. It is worth noting that one of the groups in opposition to the draft is an organization known as the Coalition Against Registration for the Draft (CARD for short) which argued that "The AVF is within ½ percent of meeting even the inflated quotas set by the Defense Department and with better educated troops than under the draft, according to studies by both the Defense Department and the Rand Corporation." We were close to being hoisted by our own petard! As one who views the draft as a moral good, I do not see it as politically feasible. The social upheaval involved would be quite severe and, as we well know, the draft would not solve many of the retention problems.

Another option that has been mentioned is to reduce the size of the force. Unless accompanied by a major retrenchment of America's defense commitments and a complete rethinking of America's international role, this will further aggravate the already hyper-like qualities of the all-volunteer force. Already, too few people are asked to do too much. In any event, whatever the size of the armed forces, one must answer the test question: Is this the best possible force that we can have?

Just grant for the moment that neither conscription nor a major reduction in the force are in the offing. What about the major management steps that could be taken to improve manpower utilization? Here, one runs into the difficulty that almost all proposals along this line do not get to the core issue, e.g., getting young men into the combat arms and aboard warships at the recruitment level. Neither lowering the physical or mental standards for men, nor increasing the number of women, nor greater reliance on civilian personnel, nor use of more older people really suit the imperatives of the combat arms. Large raises in military pay for lower enlisted personnel were the prinicipal means used to induce persons to join the all-volunteer force as set forth by the Gates Commission. Large pay increases did occur in the early 1970s, but pay rates have lost ground due to consistently high inflation rates. Youth recruiting surveys reveal a double edged sword. Cash seems to motivate less-qualified youth, defined as being high school dropouts or those of poor grades, while having much less effect on college-bound youth. There is no definitive evidence on this, but what little evidence we do have shows there is greater responsiveness from quality, college-bound youth to educational incentives over cash benefits or salary wages.

The central question is whether, without the draft, we can attract a cross section of young men to the combat arms and related tasks. Put another way, can we obtain the analog of the draftee or the draft-motivated volunteer in the all-volunteer era? I believe that there is a way, but it will not be easy. Three steps must be taken: 1) restoration of the GI Bill; 2) a linkage of present federal subsidies for college students to forms of national service; and 3) a two-track military personnel system. First to the GI Bill. I have long advocated a GI Bill along the World War II model which included tuition plus a stipend. Bills have been introduced in Congress along these lines. I think it is a sad commentary that these bills are not at the initiative of the Defense Department but have to come from independent sources. The calculations of the cost of such a generous World War II model GI Bill are hard to calculate, but preliminary evidence shows that these costs would probably be under $1 billion annually. That would be the outlay, and there would also be countervailing reductions which have to be considered in any form of calculation. There would be a reduction of recruitment outlays, the elimination of combat arms bonuses, lower attrition and, most likely, fewer young enlisted marrieds. It should be noted here that the present educational incentive packages which are allowed by the army are steps in the right direction, but they are simply too complicated to understand. There is a contributory side that can be brought in. There are different sums which one can contribute. Soldiers can put in kickers, which will help cover their share of the goal. To get the assistance, the soldier must be in Mental Category III or above. Bonuses go to certain combat arms. The soldier has to be a Philadelphia lawyer to figure out these kinds of incentives.

The second step has to do with linkage. This proposed GI Bill will be different from old GI Bills, which were a reward for past service, basically in that the new GI Bill will not be enough. The old GI Bills existed in a situation where they were the only major, federally-subsidized, college aid programs. That is no longer the case. In 1980, federal aid to college students will amount to $4.4 billion and, under the Higher Education Act Bill in Congress in 1980, between $37 and $50 billion were projected over the next five years for college aid. In effect, what we have here is a GI Bill without the GI. With the passage of the 1978 Lower Income Student Assistance Act eligibility for many of these grants was greatly expanded. The Basic Educational Opportunity Grant which is free can now go to families earning as much as $25,000. There is now a no-need requirement for the Guaranteed Student Loan Program which is a 7 percent loan program. Many young people borrow this money, invest it in a long-term security, and make a great deal of interest. The Work-Study Program at $600 million a year is now becoming a major source of graduate student support. What is more, a college student who can establish self-supporting status is eligible for all these federal assistance programs. If we want the all-volunteer force to work (and this will be a political question), the principle has to be established that no able-bodied person can be eligible for student aid unless he or she performs some form of national service, on a voluntary basis. This would include civilian options as well as reserve obligations. In point of fact, the increases alone, without working at the actual sums, projected at the minimal rate, are twice to three times as much as the cost of a GI Bill. We really have created an insane situation here where a sensible person can get more educational benefits by staying out of the military than by going into it.

A third aspect to be introduced is a two-track personnel system. This should recognize the difference between a citizen soldier and a career soldier. This citizen soldier would serve two years in the combat arms, for example, in low-skilled shipboard duty, on aircraft security guard, as a clerical worker, or some other labor-intensive position. Such a two-year volunteer would receive lower active duty pay, lower even than at present, and no entitlements, particularly no marital entitlements, except this generous GI Bill. Such benefits ought to be linked to reserve obligations following active duty because, without some greater reliance on prior service personnel, there seems to be no way to salvage the army reserve components in the all-volunteer context. Moreover, because there would be no presumption of acquiring civilian skills in the military, the terms of such service would be honest and unambiguous, thus alleviating a major source of postentry discontent in the all-volunteer force. With well-motivated reasonably-intelligent soldiers, could you get your money's worth from them in two years—like the draftees of old? Minimally, in the army, for E-4 and under, 50 percent (and that is an underestimate) of the jobs could be performed by such persons who would, in turn, be replaced by similarly qualified people. This might be a little lower in the Navy and Air Force, but even there it would be quite high.

What is more interesting is the career soldier track. These would be people who enter with longer initial enlistments of three or four years. These will be the individuals going to technical fields where lengthy training is required. The pay would be higher for them than for the two-year enlistees, even at entry level. Entitlements would be similar to those of the prevailing system, and in this the Nunn-Warner Bill is a step in the right direction. With higher compensation, which means these people receive more pay and improved entitlements, one can talk about maintaining and retaining a career force. In addition to higher pay-rated entry levels than the two-year soldier, one could consider a large raise in pay at the reenlistment level at pay grade E-5. What has happened in the services over the course of the last decade is that the E-9:E-1 pay ratio has gone down when what one really wants, of course, is for it to go up. Savings would be gained from siphoning off some of the educational benefits now provided to nonmilitary servers as well as from the lower pay provided for those in the two-year track. This probably would more than compensate for the extra cost required in higher salaries and entitlements for the career force. It is a zero sum world—the money is going to have to come from somewhere, and this proposal provides a way to get it.

Of course, the GI Bill must be available to those in the career track as well as the citizen soldier track, but the use of the GI Bill for career soldiers may be reduced by several factors, e.g., the major pay rate increase at E-5, perhaps a larger reenlistment bonus in lieu of a GI Bill, partial civilian college or technical education, or even in-service education programs.

When considering the career track and military technicians, one will always face the fact that civilian salaries are going to be hard to compete with. This is true because civilian groups and organizations that hire military-trained technicians have not paid the training costs for those technicians. It is a simple economic reality that the military is always going to have to pay them a little bit less because they are already paying for the technician's training costs as well. That is why one must talk as much as possible about rewards in kind or in the form of entitlements. Most intriguing, however, is the possible interface between this two-year, citizen-soldier track and the longer, career-soldier track. One thing that could happen might be that those in the two-year track would discover that others with the same time in grade are receiving a higher salary. Is this unfair? It is an invidious comparison with possible advantages for the AVF. If soldiers in this situation do not like it, they have a simple option. They can merely shift over into the career track and get the higher pay. There is an analogy. In the 1950s, draftees about to complete basic training were placed in a large parade ground formation where names were called out for people going to advanced individual training (AIT). A Princeton cum laude was designated for AIT in the Combat Engineers. The idiot next to him was designated for military intelligence. How could this be? There was a simple solution; all the

Princeton graduate had to do was sign up for four years like this guy next to him. This system might address yet another interesting phenomenon. It would be interesting to know how many of the senior NCOs in the army were originally draftees? One is frequently surprised by how many career military people say that they were initially draftees and later on decided to make the military a career. The German experience is relevant here. The Germans have a system of four-year volunteers and 15-month draftees who receive different pay. The question is how many of these 15-month German draftees switch over to the longer career routes, in a sense trading time for money. Unfortunately, that is a military secret in the Bundeswehr, but some observers estimate that 30 percent decide to shift over into the longer enlistment for the higher pay. That may provide some indication of what one might expect in America. Viewed another way, the long-term enlistees who find for one reason or another that they cannot conform to or do not enjoy the military might be permitted to switch to the short-term route with some type of financial penalty. The British, as another example, have a system under which a soldier can buy out of an enlistment. These are the types of concepts one should consider in addressing the attrition question. The intersection of these two types of personnel systems could be very productive.

The problems of the all-volunteer force do not reside in the end of conscription, nor in the declining youth cohort of the 1980s, nor in the efforts of service recruiters (who have really accomplished a task of immense proportions). The grievous flaw has been a redefinition of military service in terms of "economistic" models—the view that the military is to be understood as just another kind of occupation, or at least an occupation without any fundamental difference from civilian pursuits. I think that the all-volunteer force cannot survive on the premises or the kinds of initiatives that have emanated from the Defense Department. The initiatives of the 1970s have served only to move the American military away from its institutional moorings. They have eroded the idea of citizenship obligation and failed to attract or retain the necessary quality and quantity of service members. There are other nagging implications of present policy. The all-volunteer force as presently constituted has come to preclude enlisted participation of those who will become America's future leaders, whether in government, business, or the intellectual and academic communities. There is a not-so-subtle implication in the works of the occupational modelists that college educated youth are too good to serve in the ranks, particularly too good to serve in the ranks of combat arms or in jobs requiring menial tasks. We need a paradigmatic shift in our view of the all-volunteer force—a move away from the occupational model, which has been dominant since the Gates Commission, into other more institutional formats.

The definition of military service needs overhauling as badly as the machinery of recruitment and retention. It has to be recognized frontally that, in the main, military service is not like civilian pursuits. Maintaining the military is not an exercise is econometrics. Such a realization would clarify the military's role by emphasizing the higher calling of national service.

# Chapter 15
# National Service Program
## Adam Yarmolinsky

If one begins with the proposition that some of the most essential tasks in our society may need to be assigned by public authority, then it is possible to examine the future of military service in the context of a general program of compulsory national service. Such a program could avoid the difficulties of relying on volunteer military service—the disproportionate recruitment of the poor and minorities, the high and rising cost of military person-power, and the uncertainties of the voluntary recruiting process—while not singling out the military for application of the compulsory process.

A compulsory national service program could help to build better bridges between the world of education (or, for many young people, the world of being stockpiled in allegedly educational institutions) and the world of work. It could assure the performance of many socially useful functions for which the job market does not now make adequate provision. And it could help some young people find their way out of dead-end situations.

But without making a value judgment about the desirability or the undesirability of a compulsory national service program, I must begin with serious doubts about its constitutional, political, economic, and administrative feasibility.

Constitutionally, there is a serious question whether compulsory civilian service is within the powers of the United States government to impose. Such compulsion would clearly be open to constitutional attack not only under the Fifth and Thirteenth Amendments, but as beyond the enumerated and implied powers of government.

Politically, the idea of compulsory civilian service is alien to the genus of American institutions, and even compulsory military service has been resisted, except in times of national emergency. We may need to be reminded that the World War II draft was renewed by a margin of one vote in the House of Representatives, less than two months before the United States entered the war.

Economically, the cost of operating a program that enrolled the entire age-cohort of young people reaching the service age, even for a one-year term, and even without offering any service opportunities for retired people (of which more below), could amount to some $12 to $20 billion, depending on the level of stipends, and assuming, quite optimistically, that jobs could be found for all these people that did not involve significant capital costs.

Administratively, the thought of setting up the administrative machinery to find some four million job assignments every year, in non-leaf-raking jobs, is one that boggles the mind. The possibilities are frightening for waste, corruption, malfeasance, and abuse in so enormous a system, operating under the principle of compulsion, and not in a time of national emergency, as that term is generally understood.

There is another way of thinking about national service, however, as a major national program organized on a voluntary basis, involving perhaps as many as a million volunteers annually, after a phased development period, and including voluntary military service as one of its options. Such a program, if well organized and imaginatively executed, could attract large numbers of volunteers, although only a minor fraction of the age cohort. And it could attract them into military as well as civilian service, primarily through the satisfactions of public service rather than material rewards.

The military service element of a voluntary national service program should remove some of the disadvantages of the present volunteer system. By popularizing the voluntary idea it should broaden the base for military recruitment; and, by shifting the incentives, it should hold down the rising costs of the system. There is the danger that a civilian voluntary program might attract true volunteers away from military service by offering them a wide range of other volunteer opportunities. But if the military services accepted this challenge, and responded to it, they should be able to make their alternative a fully competitive one.

A voluntary national service program could have very substantial public policy benefits, if it worked. And there are good reasons to believe that it could work.

The greatest unmet needs in the United States today are for human services, delivered by relatively untrained but caring people at the local community level. Most of the human services professions—doctors, nurses, teachers, lawyers, social workers—are not in critically short supply, or would not be if they were better distributed geographically. What we lack most are people like home health care aides and classroom aides and playground counsellors and helpers in community centers. Many of these services are the kind that were provided by neighbors and friends when communities were more cohesive and more stable. Some are new services, responding to new situations like the discharge of so many mental patients into the community, or the detention, even temporarily, of increasing numbers of juveniles; and some of these services have yet to be invented.

At the same time, public facilities are deteriorating for lack of adequate maintenance, and public use of these facilities is being cut back; there are not enough attendants for the public parks or the public libraries. When public budgets are cut, it is the low-skill human services, and the maintenance services that permit human enjoyment of public facilities, that are cut first. The same thing tends to happen in private nonprofit organizations, which are in an even tighter budget squeeze.

While these things are happening, two great reservoirs of man and woman power for these essential low skilled jobs are largely untapped; the young people just entering the labor market, and older people who have just left the labor market. Young people, who have the highest ideals, also have the highest unemployment rates (almost 20 percent, and estimated at 40-60 percent for inner-city minorities) of any age group, with consequences in social disruption that are all too familiar. There are currently some 3 million unemployed young people between 16 and 24, and economists agree that high unemployment declines with age. Older people, by and large, find very limited reemployment opportunities; and, as people are leaving the job market at an earlier age, they are discovering that a pension is not a complete substitute for a job.

Very large numbers of young people, and many older people as well, are without any sense of excitement in a challenging job, the moral values in work and service, or participation in American society as a mutually rewarding enterprise. In a fundamental sense, they are not full citizens, because they lack the opportunity to make the kind of contribution to society that will be recognized and acknowledged.

The needs of young and older people to use their energies by serving their fellow citizens in a recognizable role and the need of all citizens for more adequate human services and better access to public service facilities can be met by a major voluntary service program. Such a program can also offer young people the opportunity to absorb the values and habits of work, and possibly to move into some kind of apprenticeship situation, leading to a paying job at the end of their period of voluntary service.

Federally-sponsored voluntary civilian service programs are not a new idea. The Civilian Conservation Corps (CCC) of the 1930s provided useful work and subsistence for young men in a completely disrupted private job market, and many CCC veterans remember it now as the critical first step toward responsible adulthood. The Peace Corps was one of the more successful programs of the 1960s, replicated in part in the VISTA domestic volunteer program, but the VISTA program never enrolled more than a few thousand volunteers. Under the Nixon administration, several new domestic volunteer programs were developed, and all federally-sponsored volunteer programs were combined in a single agency, ACTION. During the Carter administration, there was a further reorganization aimed at reducing the bureaucracy under which the Peace

Corps was separated from ACTION and several other programs were transferred to the Federal Business Administration. By 1980, all these programs were on too small a scale to have any significant impact—the Peace Corps was down to 5,700 from a peak of 15,000 and VISTA operated with about 4,500 volunteers.

The lineal successor of the CCC was not VISTA, but the Job Corps, a residential job training program, including urban training centers and centers for young women as well as young men; while the lineal successor of the 1930s National Youth Administration was the Neighborhood Youth Corps, a nonresident job training program, which has become essentially a temporary employment program, providing not much more than make-work, often as summer jobs.

One difficulty with all these programs is that they split their population into two groups, the middle class young people who were attracted to VISTA (and the Peace Corps), and the poor, who were recruited into the Job Corps and the Neighborhood Youth Corps. The first group was limited in size and impact; the second group was limited by motivation and public image; and there was no chance for interaction between these two groups.

The idea of a major national voluntary service program has surfaced from time to time over the last 20 years. It was put forward by Robert McNamara in his 1966 Montreal speech in which he noted that:

> As matters stand, our present Selective Service System normally draws on only a minority of eligible young men. That is an inequity and it seems to me that we could move toward remedying that inequity by asking every young person in the United States to give two years of service to his country, whether in one of the military services, in the Peace Corps or in some other volunteer developmental work at home or abroad. We could encourage other countries to do the same, and we could work out exchange programs much as the Peace Corps is already planning to do.[1]

The idea was supported by a number of public commissions in the late 1960s. The Scranton Commission on Campus Unrest recommended a national voluntary program. There have been a number of private proposals, such as the one which emerged from an Eleanor Roosevelt Foundation conference in 1976. A chart of legislative proposals before Congress in 1977 appears as table 15.1. In 1979, Representative Paul McClosky introduced a bill (HR2206) containing a provision for national service. Senator Sam Nunn, a leading critic of the All-Volunteer Force, indicated in a journal article published in 1979 that universal national service might be the best long-term solution to current problems.[2]

To develop a workable national program of major proportion would require an intensive planning effort, involving knowledgeable people from all levels of government and the nonprofit sector. At this point, it is only possible to project the rough outlines of a program, and to indicate the principal problem areas. But such a projection may still be useful.

A national program could set a goal of recruiting a million civilian volunteers a year (in addition to military volunteers), the goal to be reached over a three or four-year initial period. Any smaller number would not amount to a truly national effort. There are now more than 4 million young men and women in the 18-year-old age cohort, although that number will be decreasing by about 20 percent over the decade of the 1980s. The program might set age limits for young volunteers from 18 to 22, giving it an initial population of some 12 to 15 million to recruit from, and setting an eventual goal of about 10 percent of the number entering the age group each year. The elderly, of whom some 30 million are 60 and over, might be recruited from the age of Social Security benefits eligibility or job retirement, whichever is earlier, with an eventual goal of 2 percent of the entire elderly population.

These calculations are only illustrative, but they make the point that a million-person goal is not unreasonable. What is essential is that the program be large enough so that it will have a major impact on the American scene. People will talk about it, tell stories, and make jokes about it. It will appear on the TV screen, and not just on talking heads programs. A volunteer will be a recognizable, respected person, part of a well-known program, and his identification with the program will be at least as important as with his hometown, whether it is a central city ghetto or a middle-class suburb.

Applications for volunteers would be submitted by state and local governments and private, nonprofit organizations, based on demonstrated need, capacity to assure useful activity to volunteers assigned to them, and, wherever possible, opportunities for on-the-job training that might, for young people, lead to regular employment. Volunteers would enlist for a stated term and would be given an opportunity to express a preference for a particular type of work. They would ordinarily be assigned in their home areas, but if it turned out that higher proportions of volunteers tended to come from areas with lower need, there would have to be more assignments away from home.

Among the questions and problems that would have to be settled in the design of the program are the following.

## What is the Size and Shape of the Demand for Volunteer Service?

Estimates of the demand for volunteer services are necessarily imperfect, because it is difficult to assess the demand for services that are not now generally available.

In a nonquantitative way, we are aware that there is a general shortage of unskilled and semiskilled help in human service agencies and occupations, particularly in the public sector. It is easy to think of examples: hospital aides,

## Defense Manpower Planning

Table 15.1. Legislative Proposals Before Congress in 1977

| Title | Youth Initiatives Act of 1977 | Employment Resources Act | Young Adult Conservation Corps |
|---|---|---|---|
| House/Senate Sponsor Committee | HR20/S20 A. Young/Cranston Education/Human and Labor/Resources | /SI /Mathias /Human Resources | HR32/S249 Meeds/Jackson Education/Energy and Labor/ Natural Resources |
| Age Range | From end of compulsory education to age 22 | 16-24 | 19-24, plus 16-18 for dropouts and HS graduates |
| Maximum Size | National Youth Service: 250,000 Private Enterprise: 35,000 | National Youth Service: Open Young Adult Conservation Corps: 300,000 Wage Supplement: 500,000 | Not specified |
| Target | All youth, with at least 75% unemployed and poor | Low income youth only | All youth, with persons from high unemployment areas preferred |
| Stipend | From 100% to 125% of minimum wage | From minimum wage to prevailing wage | Minimum wage or higher |
| Activities | Community service, Housing, Conservation, Mass transit | Community service, Housing, Conservation, Transportation, Rural development | Conservation |
| Educational Linkages | Yes | Yes | Not specified |
| Grantee | State or local commission | Any public or private organization, including unions and businesses | States |
| Administering Agency | President will decide | Department of Labor | Department of Agriculture Interior |

| Comprehensive Youth Employment Act of 1977 | Youth Community Improvement Program | Youth Employment Programs |
|---|---|---|
| HR1731/S170 Simon/Humphrey-Javits Education/Human Resources/Labor | /S.306 /Stafford /Environment & Public Works | President Carter's message of March 9, 1977 (not yet in legislative form) |
| 16-21, inclusive (Conservation Corps to age 24) | 16-19, inclusive | Conservation: 16-24 Community Improvement: 16-19 Employment & Training: 16-21 |
| Youth Community Service: 1 million Private Enterprise: 500,000 Work Experience (part-time): Open National Conservation Corps: 300,000 Job Corps: About 50,000 | 200,000 plus | National Youth Conservation Corps: 35,000 Youth Community Conservation and Improvement Projects: 30,000 Comprehensive Youth Employment and Training Programs: 138,000 |
| Mostly unemployed youth | All youth | Conservation: All youth Community Improvement: Unemployment, Employment & Training: Poor & Unemployed |
| Minimum wage or higher | Minimum wage or higher | Minimum wage or higher |
| Community service, Conservation, Private Enterprise | Construction, Housing, Conservation | Conservation, Community service, Construction |
| Yes | Yes | Mostly training |
| CETA Prime Sponsors | Local nonprofit corporations | Mostly CETA Prime Sponsors. $110 million discretionary funds outside CETA |
| Department of Labor (Conservation Corps: DOA & DOI) | Department of Commerce (EDA) | Department of Labor |

## 244 Defense Manpower Planning

Table 15.2. Federal Agency Personnel Requirements: A Sample

| Agency* | Short-Term Demand | Long-Range Need |
| --- | --- | --- |
| Department of Agriculture | 20,000 | 300,000 |
| Department of Interior | 20,000 | 90,000 |
| Department of Transportation (partial) | — | 35,000 |
| Department of Health, Education and Welfare (Day Care Only) | 35,000 | 280,000 |
| Environmental Protection Agency | 77,000 | 500,000 |
| Federal Energy Administration (partial) | 2,500 | 2,500 |
| | 154,500 | 1,207,500 |

*Note that such major areas as health and education are not included in these figures.

Source: Data provided by Donald J. Eberly, Executive Director, National Service Secretariat, Washington, D.C.

schoolroom and playground aides, home visitors for old people and shut-ins (delivering "meals on wheels" for instance), library aids (to avoid increasing curtailment of library schedules), parks workers. The list can be extended almost indefinitely. In one sense, these needs are a function of the disintegration of the extended family and the erosion of a more stable society—although one should beware of the rosy glow of hindsight. By and large, the sick, the old, and the poor were even worse off in earlier periods of our history than they are today.

Any attempt to catalogue volunteer opportunities is itself a statement of preferences and priorities. Fortunately, we can bracket our target by a process of triangulation (if that's not a too-unmilitarily-mixed metaphor). There are three recent estimates, from different sources.

A miniature youth service experiment in Seattle in 1973 canvassed local agencies and, with a relatively low-profile, low-intensity effort, came up with some 1,200 volunteer opportunities in some 220 organizations over a three-month period. That figure is the equivalent of some 300,000 positions nationwide, and does not include any openings in conservation work.

An illustrative, informal survey by ACTION of six federal agencies in 1977 is reproduced in table 15.2.

Lastly, a survey of needs (and educational requirements) conducted by the Russell Sage Foundation in 1970 (table 15.3) showed an estimated need for more than 4 million participants on a one-year full-time basis.

**Table 15.3.** Estimated Needs and Educational Requirements for National Service Participants (numbers in thousands)

|  | Need | H.S. Dropout | H.S. Grad. | Some College | College Grad. |
|---|---|---|---|---|---|
| TOTAL | 4,030 | 1,340 | 1,470 | 935 | 285 |
| EDUCATIONAL SERVICES | 1,000 | 205 | 420 | 270 | 105 |
| Tutors | 600 | 100 | 300 | 180 | 20 |
| Teacher aides | 300 | 100 | 100 | 80 | 20 |
| Teachers | 60 | — | — | — | 60 |
| Public media aides | 40 | 5 | 20 | 10 | 5 |
| HEALTH SERVICES | 900 | 215 | 405 | 230 | 50 |
| Health aides | 800 | 200 | 350 | 210 | 40 |
| At hospitals | 600 | 150 | 250 | 170 | 30 |
| Outside hospitals | 200 | 50 | 100 | 40 | 10 |
| Mental health aides | 100 | 15 | 55 | 20 | 10 |
| At institutions | 50 | 10 | 25 | 10 | 5 |
| Outside institutions | 50 | 5 | 30 | 10 | 5 |
| ENVIRONMENTAL SERVICES | 800 | 600 | 110 | 50 | 40 |
| Conservation aides | 500 | 400 | 50 | 30 | 20 |
| Pollution & sanitation aides | 100 | 60 | 20 | 10 | 10 |
| Beautification aides | 100 | 70 | 20 | 5 | 5 |
| Park development aides | 100 | 70 | 20 | 5 | 5 |
| SOCIAL SERVICES | 560 | 110 | 210 | 210 | 30 |
| Day care aides | 200 | 30 | 100 | 65 | 5 |
| Welfare aides | 200 | 30 | 50 | 110 | 10 |
| Parole & Probation aides | 20 | 5 | 10 | 5 | — |
| Prison aides | 20 | 5 | 10 | 5 | — |
| Geriatric aides | 50 | 20 | 20 | 10 | — |
| Settlement house aides | 50 | 20 | 20 | 10 | — |
| Legal aides | 20 | — | — | 5 | 15 |
| PROTECTION SERVICES | 300 | 60 | 155 | 65 | 20 |
| Police aides | 200 | 25 | 120 | 45 | 10 |
| Fire aides | 50 | 20 | 15 | 10 | 5 |
| Highway safety aides | 50 | 15 | 20 | 10 | 5 |
| OTHER SERVICES | 470 | 150 | 170 | 110 | 40 |
| Public works aides | 200 | 100 | 70 | 25 | 5 |
| Recreation aides | 100 | 20 | 50 | 25 | 5 |
| Library aides | 50 | — | 15 | 30 | 5 |
| Mayor's aides | 20 | 5 | 5 | 5 | 5 |
| Others | 100 | 25 | 30 | 25 | 20 |

(Columns under Minimum Academic Background: H.S. Dropout, H.S. Grad., Some College, College Grad.)

Source: Donald J. Eberly, *The Estimated Effect of a National Service Program on Public Service Manpower Needs, Youth Employment, College Attendance and Marriage Rates,* Russell Sage Foundation, January 1970, Table A.

The overall picture, then, is one of a wide distribution of activities, most of them requiring no more than a high school education, and many (almost one-third) appropriate even for high school dropouts.

It seems reasonable to assume also that as a national program got under way, new areas of need would appear, and new ways to employ volunteers in socially useful tasks would be discovered. And in order to arrive at a total figure, one must add the number of volunteers needed for the military, giving a total more than adequate to take up the available human resources.

## Why Would Citizens Volunteer?

For a major program of national service to be successful, it must be able to attract citizens from every walk of life, from every ethnic group, from town and country, suburb and central city. The primary motivations for enlistment would be the opportunity for service to people, and the challenge of productive work. These motivations, in turn—and, indeed, the success of the program as a whole—would depend on the kind of work assignments that were generated by the program—how worthwhile, how important, how exciting, how satisfying—and on the spirit that could be developed within the program itself, by its leadership, at every level, and by the interactions among the volunteers, young and old, well-off and poor.

For young people from slums and ghettos—and for old people trying to get along on SSI—a large part of the program's appeal might be economic. If the program is dominated by these motivations, it will be a failure, for two reasons: because these low income groups will then not see themselves primarily as volunteers; and because they will turn off other groups, thus destroying the broadly representative character of the program. These developments can be avoided, however, by a carefully prepared, well-balanced recruitment program; by the selection and publicizing of challenging and rewarding assignments; by offering high school equivalency benefits and even college credits, where appropriate; and by not allowing this program to be taken as a substitute for an adequate full-employment policy.

Indeed, an eventual test of the program would be its continued success as a social institution after unemployment for young people has been substantially reduced. When the general unemployment rate declines significantly, the very high unemployment rate for young people, and especially for young males, should also begin to go down, and more young people will move directly from school to jobs. But if a national service program has caught on by that point, it could become a national transition stage between school and job, or between school and college or professional training. In this connection, Charles Moskos has advanced the interesting idea that volunteer service might be made a condition of future federal employment.[3]

Another way to emphasize the volunteer service aspect of the program is to make sure that compensation is at or close to subsistence levels, which raises the next question.

## How Much Would Volunteers Be Paid?

Volunteers could be paid at the minimum wage rate, or they could be given subsistence allowances, to include direct work-related expenses, pocket-money if they were living at home, and room and board if they were on their own, plus standard health insurance for those below the Medicare eligibility age. The second alternative might save as much as $2,000 per volunteer (or $2 billion for a million volunteers), particularly since most elderly volunteers would need only work-related expenses under a subsistence scheme. A better use for any additional funds might be to provide some GI-bill type of educational benefits for young volunteers. The subsistence alternative would also be closer to traditional ideas of volunteer service, and would reinforce the justification for the program as a way of providing important human services that our imperfect political economy is not now willing to buy in the market place. On the other hand, it might arouse more concern among labor unions in the public and nonprofit fields, that the program could be a threat to both levels of employment and wage standards. The best course here might be to discuss the program informally with national union leadership (among other groups) before it is put in final form, emphasizing that it will develop new kinds of jobs, that there will be a sharp distinction, from the outset, between volunteers and employees, and that maintenance-of-efforts agreements will be required and vigorously policed.

## How Would Projects Be Selected?

There are two basic alternatives for selecting projects: Quotas can be allocated to the states on a formula grant basis (population adjusted by some standard measure of need), and individual positions can be allotted by state agencies, under federal guidelines, to applicant institutions—state and local agencies and private nonprofit organizations. Or applicant institutions might compete directly for positions without regard to state quotas, competing for allocation of positions from the national office. Past experience suggests that the second alternative is more likely to encourage effective and innovative local programming. In either event, individuals and groups with ideas for new projects should be encouraged to apply under the sponsorship of existing institutions.

## How Would Volunteers Be Recruited, Assigned, and Trained?

A national recruiting drive seems essential in order to develop the interest and enthusiasm that is needed for the program to take off. Such a drive would have to be centrally managed, with uniform selection standards, and carefully administered, to assure a broad, varied, and balanced enrollment, particularly in the initial stages of the program. A brief (one or two-week, longer for overseas volunteers) orientation should probably be part of the recruitment process, at a regional level. Training would be the responsibility of the user agency, on the job, and would be supplemented by career counseling and, possibly, specialized job placement services.

## How Would the Program Be Managed?

Overall responsibility for the program would have to be lodged in a new national entity. Whether that entity would be a new federal agency or a public corporation seems less important than (1) that it replace the present accumulation of federally-sponsored volunteer and service programs; (2) that it have new and dynamic leadership; (3) that it involve all relevant interest groups, through broad-based advisory bodies at the national and local level; (4) that it decentralize as far as possible without relying on existing business-as-usual organizations at the state and local levels; and, (5) that it plan to maintain its own vitality by devices such as the Peace Corps "five-year flush" of management personnel. This national entity would be responsible for recruitment, selection, orientation, and, unless the state model were adopted, for placement of volunteers. It would have to monitor the actual operations of the program, and act when necessary to disqualify particular projects or to dismiss individual volunteers. A tough inspector general would be required.

## How Much Would the Program Cost?

Among those who examine national service alternatives, cost estimates vary substantially; many are higher than my own. Assuming a relatively generous set of subsistence allowances to the volunteers, the total cost of the program, at full enrollment, might be about $4 billion a year. This figure is based on an average direct payment to the volunteer of $3,000, and an estimate of $1,000 per volunteer for recruitment, selection, orientation, and assignment. If volunteers were all paid the minimum wage, the total might be nearer $6 billion. Neither sum is insubstantial, but each should produce very substantial results, and the costs of the program will vary, within broad limits, directly with the response of the volunteer participants. The first year cost should fall below $125 million, but it would be essential that there be a clear commitment to the full-scale program, or the net effect, in disappointed hopes and aspirations, would be a negative one.

## How Long Would Volunteers Serve?

Domestic volunteer programs generally require a one-year enlistment, while the Peace Corps calls for a two-year commitment. Initially at least, a one-year term would be more likely to attact volunteers for service within the United States, and ought not to prove too short for valuable service in low-skill jobs. Volunteers should be free to reenlist for an additional period, and might be encouraged to do so in certain cases, particularly in human service assignments where personal relationships may be especially important. Length of service could also be related to opportunities for on-the-job training. If the average length of service is increased, there will be a proportionate reduction in the number of new volunteers that the program can cover on the same total budget and there will be some reduction in administrative overhead.

## Should the Program Include Old People As Well As Young People?

Some proposals have been advanced for a national voluntary service program limited to young people, as a simpler effort to organize. On balance, however, it seems preferable to include the elderly, and not in a separate program, because it expands the recruiting field and leavens the loaf at the same time. The possibilities in part-time srvice, especially for the elderly, should not be excluded.

A national program of volunteer service on the scale proposed here would necessarily be a gamble. There have been no studies or experiments that have satisfactorily demonstrated the willingness of very large numbers of young people—and older citizens as well—to undertake this kind of obligation. The proponents of such a program would be leading the way with a new kind of challenge. If, and only if, they are able to formulate that challenge in exciting enough ways to capture the imagination of the young and the old, they should be able to generate a significant response, and a response that could extend to military as well as to civilian service.

## NOTES

1. Robert S. McNamara, *The Essence of Security* (New York: Harper and Row, 1968), pp. 156-57.
2. Sam Nunn, "Those Who Do Not Serve in the All-Volunteer Armed Forces," the *Journal of the Institute for Socio-Economic Studies* 4, no. 3 (Autumn 1979) p. 19.
3. See Charles C. Moskos, "Education as an Inducement to All-Volunteer Military," *The Washington Star,* April 5, 1981.

Chapter 16

# If the Draft Is Restored: Uncertainties, Not Solutions*

## Kenneth J. Coffey

The all-volunteer force (AVF) has come on hard times, with an increasing barrage of testimonies and media comments highlighting its manpower problems. We hear of recruiting shortfalls in the active forces, and massive manning level deficits in the selected reserve and the individual ready reserve. We read of too many lower quality recruits who are unable to master the complex demands of ever more sophisticated equipment, and extraordinarily high enlistment rates from black Americans with the resulting prospect of disproportionate casualties in time of war. We are told of major shortages of technically trained NCOs needed to maintain equipment and train the recruits, and of overall shortcomings in weapons development and procurement programs and Strategic Mobility and War Reserve capabilities. We listen while experts tell us that many of these problems are due to the absence of a draft and to the high manpower costs associated with attracting volunteers in the open marketplace of supply and demand, and, at the same time, we sense a growing belief in the Congress and in the countryside that a draft-supported force would be the most sensible course of action for the nation to follow for the remainder of the 1980s.

Is the wisdom of this position justified, or are there unrecognized pitfalls that have yet to surface? This is the question which must be addressed before a defensible position on the value of restoring conscription can be reached.

---

*This is a version of a paper prepared for the Working Group on Voluntary versus Non-Voluntary Military Service, a project of the Center for Philosophy and Public Policy, University of Maryland. It will appear in a volume of essays on the moral dimensions of military manpower policies, in the Maryland Public Philosophy Series published by Rowman and Littlefield, Totowa, New Jersey.

It is the purpose of this chapter, therefore, to provide insights into this issue by challenging the assumption that a restoration of the draft would necessarily counter most of the AVF manpower and manpower-related concerns. In pursuing this objective, it is contended that a return to the draft could impact greatly on some of the concerns, but that such an impact could not be guaranteed. Further, that depending upon a variety of decisions concerning the size and composition of the volunteer and conscript cohorts and the policies of the armed forces on volunteer recruiting, the degree of impact could be very limited or, at the extreme, counterproductive.

The chapter commences with a discussion of the likely deferment, exemption, and disqualification practices and their impacts on the composition of draft groups. Then, as a basis for discussing the impacts of three different draftee-volunteer mixes, the recruiting results for the army during fiscal year 1979 are documented. Thereafter, the interrelationship of the size and composition of conscript and volunteer groups are discussed in the context of the size of draft calls, their impact on the quality of recruits, and their impact on the racial balance in the recruit group. Then, in reference to different options, possible cost-savings are discussed. Finally, conclusions are offered.

In totality, the discussion will illustrate the complexities—rather than the simplicities—associated with a return to the draft. Hopefully, the discussion also will provoke further reasoned public debate on the issue.

## COMPOSITION OF DRAFT COHORT GROUPS

If the draft were restored at some time during the 1980s, the composition of the draft cohort groups would be far less than representative of America's youth population. And the degree to which this cohort would be less than representative would be determined by deferment, exemption, and disqualification policies and practices. At one extreme, if the armed forces allowed the conscription of those who met the most liberal World War II standards, up to 75 percent of all identifiable segments of the youth population would be represented. Much more likely, however, a combination of deferment and exemption policies and high disqualification rates would limit draft calls to those in groups representing no more than 50 percent of the population.

Young men were drafted into the military in all but one year in the 33 years between 1940 and 1973; and, during this period, the participation of youth never approached closer to an equitable sharing of the burden than the 75 percent level of World War II. To a great degree, at least during the 1950s, 1960s, and early 1970s, this was due to the granting of a variety of deferments and exemptions which excused or indefinitely postponed conscription of many youths with high levels of family income and education. For the most part, such deferment and exemption policies were initiated because of decisions to foster the development of more scientifically-trained youths and to provide cheap, college-trained labor for community services.

Since those days, much has changed and little evidence can be offered today to excuse youth from service on these grounds. Thus, if the draft is resumed, it is likely that the only categories of deferments and exemptions which would remain would be family hardship and conscientious objection (CO).

The number of youths excused from military service for reasons of family hardship would be very small. Though concentrated in youths from families on the lower end of the economic spectrum, the numbers involved would not significantly impact on the representational or quality levels of the conscript cohorts.

Conscientious objection could impact more. During the heyday of the Vietnam War, almost as many men were applying for CO status as were being inducted. Indeed, the rate was more than 100 times greater than the rate during World War II.[1]

The reaction of youth to induction for peacetime military service would not be the same as that of youth facing combat. Nevertheless, because of the precedent of the Vietnam War period and the broadening impact on CO eligibility of Supreme Court decisions, there is every likelihood that a substantial number of young people would seek CO status. Further, it would be likely that the types of youths which sought such status in the Vietnam War era—namely, white youth from better colleges and universities with a small sprinkling of blacks and traditional COs from the "Peace Churches"—would comprise the group. If so, the continuing provision of CO opportunities would impact on both the racial make-up and the quality of the conscript groups.

There is no doubt, however, that the greatest reason why a restored draft would never approach an equitable level of service sharing would be the unwillingness of the armed forces to accept those youth with minimal qualifications. Such disqualifications were high during the Vietnam War when avoiding the draft became a form of high art, if not science. Yet, even during the years of peace which preceded and followed the Vietnam experience, large numbers of youth were rejected.

The highest peacetime rate was achieved in 1964, when slightly more than one-half of those examined were rejected at the preinduction review, with one our of ten of those who passed the preinduction review being disqualified at the induction exam. In total, then, 57 out of every 100 men were rejected.[2]

During the Vietnam War era, the rejection rates reached higher levels, due in large measure to the sophistication of draft-avoidance programs and the antidraft sympathies of many examining officials. At its extreme, during 1971, 63 out of every 100 men were rejected.[3]

The rejection levels for 1964 and 1971 as well as for other years were influenced by service decisions to limit the number of accessions who ranked in the lower mental categories. Thus, as Bernard Karpinos has noted, the proportion of Mental Group IV candidates (those who ranked in the 10th through 29th percentile on the standard entry test) who qualified for entry into the forces varied greatly over time.[4]

The impact of a resumption of peacetime induction on the composition of the conscript groups, then, must be considered in light of these historical precedents. And their message is clear: even if we returned to the "Lottery Draft" policies, the sharing of the military service burden among eligible youth would be far from equitable. Further, as will be discussed in the following sections, if the quality or education standards for conscripts are tightened beyond those of the previous draft years in order to raise overall quality levels or more closely approach national racial distribution norms, the burdens of military service would be placed on an even smaller portion of the youth cohort.

## BASIS FOR COMPARISON: THE ARMY RECRUITING RESULTS IN FISCAL YEAR 1979

The recruiting results of the army during fiscal year 1979 provide the best basis for a discussion of the probable impact of a return to a draft. This conclusion results both from a belief that a draft would be used primarily for the army and from the fact that the army's recruiting record—to a far greater extent than the other services—could be significantly changed by draft influences in the areas of manning levels, quality of recruits, and racial make-up of the groups.

During fiscal year 1979, the army recruited 129,000 nonprior service recruits, 17,000 of whom were women. The army had hoped to recruit additional high school diploma graduates, and they were unwilling to take additional non-high school diploma graduates who were applying for enlistment in large numbers. As a result, a recruiting shortfall of some 16,000 occurred.

The relative success which leaders believed had been obtained by the army in fiscal year 1979 was abruptly challenged in the spring of 1980 when Pentagon leaders publicly admitted the probability that their methods of determining volunteer recruit quality were providing misleading data. The errors—caused by mistakes in norming the entry test results to the Standard Reference Population—were particularly evident in the ranking of applicants by the services into mental categories.[5]

Whereas the four services for fiscal year 1979 initially reported that they had recruited only 5 percent Mental Category IV's, a recalculation of the figures using the correct norming guidelines showed that 30 percent of the recruits were so categorized.[6] The most significant change occurred in the army. Initially, they had reported 9 percent Mental Category IVs in their fiscal year 1979 recruit group; under the correct norming procedures, this should have been 46 percent.

**Table 16.1.** U.S. Army—Fiscal Year 1979 Nonprior service (male and female) enlistees by Mental Categories (Using renormed criteria)

|  | High School Diploma Graduates | | | |
|---|---|---|---|---|
|  | White | Black | Other | Totals |
| Mental Category I | 2,100 | 67 | 35 | 2,202 |
| Mental Category II | 13,600 | 1,700 | 400 | 15,700 |
| Mental Category III-A | 8,100 | 3,000 | 400 | 11,500 |
| Mental Category III-B | 9,500 | 7,400 | 700 | 17,600 |
| Mental Category IV | 12,900 | 21,300 | 1,700 | 35,900 |
|  | 46,200 | 33,467 | 3,235 | 82,902 |

|  | Non-High School Diploma Graduates | | | |
|---|---|---|---|---|
|  | White | Black | Other | Totals |
| Mental Category I | 200 | 14 | 5 | 219 |
| Mental Category II | 3,800 | 400 | 100 | 4,300 |
| Mental Category III-A | 4,600 | 1,100 | 200 | 5,900 |
| Mental Category III-B | 8,600 | 3,400 | 600 | 12,600 |
| Mental Category IV | 12,700 | 9,200 | 1,500 | 23,400 |
|  | 29,900 | 14,114 | 2,405 | 46,419 |

Source: Office of the Assistant Secretary of Defense (Manpower, Reserve Affairs, and Logistics)

As of 1980, the distribution of the army's recruit group in terms of mental categories, education, and race has not been released. The preliminary totals, however, have been determined and are reflected in this chapter (table 16.1). Though unofficial and subject to amendment, the data, nevertheless, provide a basis for discussion. Care should be taken, however, to avoid using the distribution totals as other than indications of the probable outcome.

As these data illustrate, 64 percent of the Army enlistees during fiscal year 1979 were high school diploma graduates. The rates for black and white enlistees differed, however. Sixty-one percent of the white enlistees were high school diploma grads; the proportion of black enlistees with high school diplomas was 70 percent.

In terms of Mental Category IVs, however, the proportion of whites was considerably lower than that of the blacks. For example, whereas blacks overall made up 37 percent of the army total, they represented 51 percent of the Mental Category IVs. In contrast, white applicants made up 60 percent of the total, but only 43 percent of the Category IVs.[7]

In light of the significant change in the overall characteristics of the army's fiscal year 1979 recruit group which resulted from the renorming of the entry test, as well as the policy of the army in past years to disqualify many of those who inadvertently were recruited, the impact of enforcing their old standards on the fiscal year 1979 recruit group should be discussed. What, then, would have been the results for the army if they had both used the renormed test and applied their then-current entry standards?

During fiscal year 1979, when the army was using the misnormed test, their minimum entry standards precluded the enlistment of any non-high school graduates who were in Mental Category IV and limited high school diploma graduates to those who scored in the upper three-fourths of Category IV. If these standards had been applied to the army recruit group after corrections were made for the misnorming, several impacts would have become evident. First, 32,500 recruits, or fully 25 percent of the Army's input, would have been ineligible for entry. This shortfall, on top of their already recorded shortfall of 16,000 persons, would have left the Army 48,500 below their desired input of 145,000 nonprior service recruits. Second, almost half, or nearly 15,000 of the 32,500, would have been black.

Since the Pentagon surfaced the problem of test misnorming in the spring of 1980, there have been those who have questioned whether the army should discharge recruits who would have failed to meet the renormed standards. Such actions, however, would not have been possible without significantly reducing national defense capabilities, and they were never seriously considered. Further, in testimony to the Congress, the army asserted that such recruits were performing satisfactorily. Nevertheless, because of the restriction placed on the army (and the other services) by the *Department of Defense Authorization Act, 1981,* which precludes the army from recruiting more than 25 percent Mental Category IVs in fiscal year 1982 and 20 percent in the following years, such recruits may well have to be precluded from enlistment in the future.

The congressional restriction, then, must be added to the already listed concerns over manpower quality, manning levels, racial balance, and cost in order to properly assess the likelihood of a return to the draft and the impact on these factors of various volunteer-conscript mixes.

As the following sections discuss, the degree to which a restored draft could impact would be limited by the willingless of the army to restrict some volunteer recruiting and by the willingness of the American people to accept a draft which, in terms of numbers and composition, was less than equitable.

# IMPACT OF VOLUNTEER POLICIES ON THE SIZE OF DRAFT CALLS

The size of yearly draft groups could fluctuate greatly, depending upon the policies adopted by the armed forces in regard to volunteering for service.

As noted earlier, the recruiting record of the army in fiscal year 1979 can be used for comparative purposes. During fiscal year 1979, the army recruited some 129,000 nonprior service men and women and would have liked to recruit an additional 16,000 if higher quality youths had been available. Using this 145,000 goal, then, the size of conscript groups can be determined by postulating that none to some of the men and women recruited by the army in FY 1979 would have been denied entry in a draft scenario. Thus, if no enlistments were denied, the yearly draft calls would have totalled only 16,000; if enlistments were denied to all Mental Category IVs, except for those high school diploma graduates who scored in the upper one-half of the category, the yearly draft calls would have risen to 57,000; if Mental Category III-Bs and all remaining Mental Category IVs were denied entry, the yearly draft calls would have risen to 106,000.

The extension of these maximum enlistment restrictions to the Navy, Marine Corps, and Air Force would have increased yearly draft totals to more than 150,000, or about 12,500 each month. In order to induct 150,000, many additional youth would have been subject to induction processing. Using the rates of the Vietnam period as an extreme example, a total of up to 375,000 youths would have been examined for service. Such involvement would represent a participation rate among the youth cohort group of about 20 percent if the draft had been limited to men only, 10 percent if both men and women had been eligible.[8]

## IMPACT OF VOLUNTEER ENTRY STANDARDS ON RECRUIT QUALITY

The quality of entering recruit groups could be improved over those of the AVF years—but not by much—if volunteering for service was restricted to select higher mental categories and educational levels and draftees were then used to bring the yearly recruit totals up to desired levels.

In addressing this issue, the probably quality level of draftees is a necessary ingredient; and, while exact quality spreads cannot be predicted, the limitations on deferments and exemptions and the legal restriction against inducting Mental Category V personnel provide a good indication of the quality parameters. If we would use the standard World War II Reference Population as a guide, then, we could expect that any draftee group would be composed of about 75 percent high school diploma graduates (the proportion of such graduates in our society), and that the groups would comprise predictable proportions of Mental Categories I, II, III, and, perhaps IV conscripts. The degree to which public policy would support the exclusion of lower-ranked individuals from the induction process would, of course, impact on the quality distribution and the impact of the conscript groups on overall recruit quality levels.

Whereas the armed forces would like to limit conscription to those with

## If the Draft Is Restored: Uncertainties, Not Solutions 257

Table 16.2. Scenario I—16,000 Conscripts

|  | Volunteers |  | Conscripts |  | Totals |  |
|---|---|---|---|---|---|---|
| Mental Category I | 2,400 | 2% | 1,600 | 10% | 4,000 | 3% |
| Mental Category II | 19,800 | 15% | 5,600 | 35% | 25,400 | 17% |
| Mental Category III | 47,600 | 37% | 6,700 | 42% | 54,300 | 38% |
| Mental Category IV | 59,400 | 46% | 2,100 | 13% | 61,500 | 42% |
|  | 129,200 |  | 16,000 |  | 145,200 |  |

higher educational and quality rankings, it is doubtful that the political leadership would support major departures from a full range of eligibility levels. Yet, as discussed earlier, some Mental Category IVs were disqualified for military service during the period of peace between the Korean and the Vietnam Wars. Thus, at best, a draft which excluded Mental Category IVs would be possible; more likely, a draft which excluded only those in the lower half of Mental Category IV (10-19 on the ASVAB) would be a more realistic prediction. For purposes of this discussion, therefore, we are postulating that conscript groups will be comprised of 10 percent Mental Category Is, 35 percent Mental Category IIs, 42 percent Mental Category IIIs, and 13 percent Mental Category IVs.

The recruiting record of the army during fiscal year 1979 also can be used to determine the probable impact of such a draft on overall recruit quality levels. Three scenarios are offered: (1) conscripts would be used only to supplement volunteer recruiting shortfalls; (2) enlistments of Mental Category IV personnel would be limited to those high school diploma grads who score in the upper one-half of Mental Category IV; and (3) no Mental Category IV or III-B personnel would be enlisted.

In the first scenario, 16,000 conscripts would be needed. In the second scenario, 57,000 conscripts would be needed. And in the third scenario, 106,000 would be required.

Using our offered conscript quality spread, the impact of these variously-sized conscript groups on overall recruit quality is illustrated in table 16.2.

As these data illustrate, an influx of even 16,000 conscripts would reduce the proportions of Mental Category IVs and increase the Is and IIs. The profile of the force, however, still would be below that of the World War II Reference Population which consisted of 8 percent Is, 28 percent IIs, 34 percent IIIs and 21 percent IVs.

The addition of 41,000 conscripts to the 16,000 offered in Scenario I shows a marked improvement in the overall quality of the recruit group (see table 16.3). Mental Category IVs have been decreased from 42 percent to 18 percent, Mental Categories I and II have been increased to 33 percent from 20 percent. At the same time, however, the profile of the group still would be somewhat below that of the Reference Population.

## 258  Defense Manpower Planning

Table 16.3.  Scenario II—57,000 Conscripts

|  | Volunteers |  | Conscripts |  | Totals |  |
|---|---|---|---|---|---|---|
| Mental Category I | 2,400 | 3% | 5,600 | 10% | 8,000 | 6% |
| Mental Category II | 19,800 | 23% | 20,000 | 35% | 39,800 | 27% |
| Mental Category III | 47,600 | 54% | 24,000 | 42% | 71,600 | 49% |
| Mental Category IV | 18,000 | 20% | 7,400 | 13% | 25,400 | 18% |
|  | 87,800 |  | 57,000 |  | 144,800 |  |

Raising the draft totals to 106,000 while at the same time limiting volunteer enlistments to those in Mental Categories I - III-A also would have a marked impact on the overall quality, as can be seen in table 16.4. Mental Category IVs have been decreased from 18 percent to only 9 percent; Mental Category Is and Mental Category IIs have been increased from 32 to 48 percent. Further, in contrast to Scenarios I and II, the overall recruit quality levels would be higher than that of the Reference Population, though only slightly so.

In terms of planning possible future draft policies, then, it is clear that a limitation of volunteer recruiting in the army to those with higher qualifications would have an overall positive impact on the quality of recruit groups, and a continuation of the policies in effect for volunteers during fiscal year 1979 would have an adverse impact. The same arguments, although less strong, can be made for the situations in the Navy, Marine Corps, and Air Force. In the case of the Air Force, however, as their overall quality is above that of the Reference Population, an extension of the draft to the Air Force would have a negligible impact on their quality levels, though some small gains could be realized if the few Mental Category III-Bs and IVs in the Air Force were denied entry and replaced with conscripts.

Because of these inter-Service differences and the other complexities of the issue, sophisticated and flexible management by the Service leaders would be needed. Whether or not such rational management philosophies could be followed, however, would depend on the willingness of the American people and the political leadership to enforce conscription for some youths while others who desire to serve and would have met past entry standards are denied entry.

Table 16.4.  Scenario III—106,000 Conscripts

|  | Volunteers |  | Conscripts |  | Totals |  |
|---|---|---|---|---|---|---|
| Mental Category I | 2,400 | 6% | 10,600 | 10% | 13,000 | 9% |
| Mental Category II | 19,800 | 50% | 37,100 | 35% | 56,900 | 39% |
| Mental Category III | 17,400 | 44% | 44,520 | 42% | 61,920 | 43% |
| Mental Category IV | — | — | 13,780 | 13% | 13,780 | 9% |
|  | 39,600 |  | 106,000 |  | 145,600 |  |

**Table 16.5.** Scenario I—16,000 Conscripts

|  | Black Volunteers |  | Black Conscripts |  | Black Totals |  |
|---|---|---|---|---|---|---|
| Mental Category I | 100 | 1% | 190 | 10% | 290 | 1% |
| Mental Category II | 2,100 | 4% | 665 | 35% | 2,765 | 6% |
| Mental Category III | 14,900 | 31% | 798 | 42% | 15,698 | 31% |
| Mental Category IV | 30,500 | 64% | 247 | 13% | 30,747 | 62% |
|  | 47,600 |  | 1,900 |  | 49,500 |  |

# IMPACT OF THE DRAFT ON THE NUMBER OF BLACK RECRUITS

The number of blacks in yearly recruit groups also would be changed—at least in the army—upon a return to the draft. The degree of change, however, would depend upon the size of draft calls and the restrictions placed on volunteer recruiting.

In the army, blacks made up 37 percent of the enlisted nonprior service recruits in fiscal year 1979. Had a draft been in effect and had blacks made up less than 37 percent of the conscript group, then the overall black representational level would have been reduced, regardless of the number of draftees. Of course, the larger the number of draftees, the closer the overall representational level would have approached that of the conscript group.

Although current data which could be used to predict the black content of conscript groups is lacking, for purposes of this discussion it will be postulated that: (1) each conscript group will contain 12 percent blacks; and (2) the Mental Category distribution pattern of the black recruits will reflect those of the World War II Reference Population, the rates used earlier to reflect the overall quality distribution of conscripts.

As in the previous discussion on quality, the recruiting record of the army during fiscal year 1979 can be used to determine the probable impact of a return to a draft on black representation and Mental Category levels. The same three scenarios are offered.

As the figures in table 16.5 illustrate, the conscription of 1900 blacks to supplement those voluntarily enlisting would reduce the proportion of Mental Category IVs while increasing the proportion of Mental Categories I and II. At the same time, the proportion of blacks among the new accessions would be reduced from 37 percent to 34 percent.

Because of the large numbers of black Mental Category IVs in the army's fiscal year 1979 recruit group, a limitation on enlistments which impacted on the Mental Category IVs would have a marked effect. Indeed, by increasing the draft calls from 16,000 to 57,000, the proportion of black Mental Category IVs

260    Defense Manpower Planning

Table 16.6. Scenario II—57,000 Conscripts

|  | Black Volunteers |  | Black Conscripts |  | Black Totals |  |
|---|---|---|---|---|---|---|
| Mental Category I | 100 | 1% | 700 | 10% | 800 | 2% |
| Mental Category II | 2,100 | 8% | 2,400 | 35% | 4,500 | 13% |
| Mental Category III | 14,900 | 53% | 2,900 | 42% | 17,800 | 51% |
| Mental Category IV | 10,700 | 38% | 900 | 13% | 11,600 | 33% |
|  | 27,800 |  | 6,900 |  | 34,700 |  |

was reduced from 62 percent to 33 percent (see table 16.6). At the same time, the proportion of Mental Categories I and II more than doubled. Further, the overall proportion of blacks in the total number of accessions was reduced to 24 percent.

Limiting enlistment to black and white candidates who scored in Mental Categories I- III-A and then filling the recruit ranks with a 106,000 draft call would have a marked effect on both black representation and quality levels. Black Mental Category IVs would be reduced from 33 percent to 9 percent. Blacks in Mental Categories I and II would almost triple. At the same time, the overall proportion of blacks in the 145,000 accessed into the army would be reduced to 13 percent, a level equal to that of the black youth in the general population.

If a return of the draft is to be seriously considered, therefore, it is clear that the planners must recognize the probable impact of draft calls on black representation and quality levels. This would be particularly important for the army, as they are likely to continue receiving a disproportionate share of lower quality black recruits.

A limitation on the eligibility of such recruits, then, would raise quality while lowering overall representational levels. A similar argument, though less strong, could be made for the Navy, Marine Corps, and Air Force, whose proportions of blacks are less than those of the Army and whose quality distributions are closer to the norm.[9] By taking such action, however, many young men and women who desire to serve and would have met the quality entry standards of past years would be denied entry. Though some would urge

Table 16.7. Scenario III—106,000 Conscripts

|  | Black Volunteers |  | Black Conscripts |  | Black Totals |  |
|---|---|---|---|---|---|---|
| Mental Category I | 100 | 2% | 1,300 | 10% | 1,400 | 7% |
| Mental Category II | 2,100 | 33% | 4,500 | 35% | 6,600 | 34% |
| Mental Category III | 4,100 | 65% | 5,500 | 42% | 9,600 | 50% |
| Mental Category IV | — | — | 1,700 | 13% | 1,700 | 9% |
|  | 6,300 |  | 13,000 |  | 19,300 |  |

Table 16.8. Department of Defense—Fiscal Year 1979 Size and Cost of First-Term Force

| Cohort Group | Entry Size | Size at End of FY 1979 | Individual Cost | Total Cost |
|---|---|---|---|---|
| FY 1977 | 395,000 | 277,000 (30% loss) | (E-3) $9,590 | $2.7 Billion |
| FY 1978 | 332,000 | 266,000 (20% losses) | (E-2) $8,857 | $2.4 Billion |
| FY 1979 | 316,000 | 285,000 (10% loss) | (E-1) $7,992 | $2.28 Billion |
| TOTALS | 1,043,000 | 828,000 | | $7.38 Billion |

the implementation of such actions on the grounds of achieving a more racially balanced force, such actions could well be unacceptable to the American people. A draft to fill gaps in the ranks of the armed forces is one thing, using draftees to replace willing volunteers is quite another, and the level to which trade-offs could be made would depend more upon public and political emotions than pragmatic military manpower planning.

# RESTORATION OF THE DRAFT AND POSSIBLE COST SAVINGS

Mounting concerns over the manpower portion of the service budgets have focused memories on $21 a month conscripts and the potentials for significant cost savings in a return to the draft. Such expectations, of course, are far from realistic. Whereas scenarios can be offered whereby some cost savings could accrue, other scenarios—probably more likely—can be offered whereby a return to the draft would actually cost additional monies. Whether cost-saving or cost-increasing, however, it is clear that a restoration of the draft would not change the status quo of manpower expenditures to any significant degree.

The extent to which cost-savings could be realized would depend upon several decisions: (1) the size of draft calls; (2) the extent to which pay and allowances for conscripts could be reduced below that of current volunteer levels; and (3) the extent to which pay and allowances for volunteers also could be reduced.

At the extreme, pay and allowances reductions could be targeted at all youth in their first term of service. For discussion purposes, this period can be defined as the first three years. Recognizing that attrition reduces the size of each year group by about 10 percent each year, and using information recently developed by the Department of Defense on the costs of individual service personnel, an overall cost estimate for all first-termers can be developed as in table 16.8.[10]

As these data illustrate, the target population for any possible reductions in pay and allowances, though quite large, is not paid at very high rates, even under the current "high manpower cost" era of the all-volunteer force. Consequently, the potentials for cost saving by making adjustments in the rates appear to be minimal. The amounts that could be saved, however, would vary with both the size of the pay and allowances reductions and the numbers of recruits subject to the lower rates.

The 11.75 percent pay raise which was granted to all service personnel by Congress in late 1980 was thought to restore most of the parity with civilian wages which had been lost over the 1975-1979 period. Even with this raise, however, concern over the failure of the services to pay "living wages" remains. As a reasonable guideline for purposes of discussion, then, it is postulated that reductions of up to 20 percent in the pay and allowances of first-termers would be supported by the Congress, while fully recognizing the hidden or "conscription tax" costs to society of such a position.

If such a reduction were directed only for conscripts, while volunteers retained higher pay rates, the amounts saved would be directly related to the size of draft calls. With an average saving for each conscript of only $1,763 at the 20 percent reduction rate, draft calls of the sizes discussed in earlier sections (16,000, 57,000 and 106,000) would save from $67 million to $446 million. Even if the reductions were extended to all accessions, the total savings would reach only $1.5 billion. Although these funds could be used to counter some of the inequities in the pay of the career force, far greater amounts of money would be needed. And it would be extremely doubtful that a reduction of 20 percent in the pay and allowances of all first-term personnel would be possible. As a consequence, the potentials for saving monies through a return to the draft appear to be very small, if not nonexistent. Some small savings would be realized through reductions in recruiting expenses, but it would be unreasonable to expect that these amounts could be significantly increased through reductions in the pay and allowances of first-term personnel. In fact, due to the probable increases in career force personnel needs in order to provide a larger training base for the increased numbers of first-termers, overall manpower costs could even increase.

# CONCLUSION

It would be misleading to use the data and conclusions displayed herein as the basis for policy decisions or other actions, save more research; for, in order to reach a position from which we could speak with confidence, official data would need to be obtained and much more work would have to be done. With confirmed data and time, however, the characteristics and impacts of volunteer and conscript groups under different model mixes could be determined. Re-

## If the Draft Is Restored: Uncertainties, Not Solutions 263

gardless of the degree of refinement brought to this analysis, however, certain truths outlined in this chapter would remain.

First, there can be no doubt that a return to the draft would resolve the manning level problems of the active forces and would most likely prompt enough additional volunteers for the selected reserve to eliminate their shortfalls. The increased flow of young people with lingering reserve service obligations out of the active forces also would be large enough to raise the number of individual reservists to an adequate level.

Second, the degree to which the services could adjust the size and quality characteristics of conscript groups without reducing public support below the threshold level could not be determined in advance. Consequently, we would not know to what extent a restoration of the draft would counter the expressed concerns over the quality and racial make-up of the AVF recruit groups.

Third, the cost savings, if any, which could accrue upon a return to the draft would be very low, and even these savings levels would be difficult to predict.

Fourth, the degree to which the public would support a return to the draft could not be accurately estimated, for it would depend upon many variables including the size of draft calls, the composition of the conscript groups, and the limitations, if any, on volunteer recruiting. The perceptions of need for a strong military also would be a major factor.

Fifth, it is clear that a draft would not impact to any large degree on quality and racial representation unless the services were willing and able to restrict volunteer recruiting of lower quality personnel while, at the same time, limiting draft liability to those with more desired characteristics. Obviously, the case for such actions would be far less compelling than that of using the draft only to fill unmanned units, and the level of public support would be less.

Finally, there can be little doubt that a draft which inducted only a small proportion of the almost 4 million men and women who each year reach induction age would not satisfy those many citizens—young and old—who could accept a draft only if large numbers of conscripts were needed.

Beyond the equity-driven concern that draft groups represent a cross section of our society is the greater equity-driven concern that the draft experience be shared by a large portion of the youth population.

In the 1950s, draft calls reached levels more than double the highest postulated in this chapter, inducting women was not acceptable, and the number of 18 year old males was only half of today's level. As a consequence, the vast majority of eligible candidates were exposed to the draft and many served.

In the 1980s, however, within the confines of our overall peacetime military manpower needs and the constraints of our defense budgets, a participation rate like that of the 1950s would be impossible to attain. We could, of course, deny entry to those volunteering youth outside of the draft age group; we could even deny entry to all volunteers and have a totally conscript-support force. Or, we could cut conscript terms of service so that many more youths would serve.

We could even extend conscription to civilian service programs, such as the Peace Corps, reforestation, and disaster relief efforts.

Even if such actions were taken, however (and most of them would not be in the best interests of providing strong armed forces), the majority of youth still would not participate, and the uncertainty of public acceptance of the draft would remain. It is this uncertainty which is the greatest dilemma of the restore-the-draft question.

Although specific manpower problems can be identified, and the potential for resolving some of them can be seen, we have no assurance that the type and scope of draft needed to overcome the problems would be acceptable to the electorate. More than likely, this could only be determined by the trial and error of restoring a draft without specific parameters for its implementation—an action that could result in severe societal disruption and little improvement in the armed forces.

Would this degree of uncertainty be worth the potential gains of a return to the draft? Little can be offered in support and much can be offered in opposition. If serious consideration is to be given to restoring the draft, therefore, a serious and informed public debate must provide national leaders with clear justification and objectives. Failing this, there can be no doubt that expecting the restoration of conscription to eliminate many of the current manpower problems will only detract from the efforts needed now, within the all-volunteer force environment, to address and overcome them.

## NOTES

1. Kenneth J. Coffey, *Strategic Implications of the All-Volunteer Force* (Chapel Hill, N.C.: University of North Carolina Press, 1979), p. 8.
2. Selective Service System, *Annual Report of the Director of Selective Service, 1964* (Washington, D.C.: GPO, 1965), pp. 61-64.
3. During 1972 and into 1973, when draft calls were small and youth were on notice that the draft was ending, the rejection rates reached substantially higher levels. In January of 1973, the last month of large examination groups, fully 65 percent were disqualified at the preinduction review. As no formal draft calls were issued in 1973, however, few of these individuals ever entered the service. See Selective Service System, *Semi-Annual Report of the Director of Selective Service for the period January 1, 1973 to June 30, 1973* (Washington, D.C.: GPO, 1973), pp. 51-52.
4. Bernard D. Karpinos, "AFQT Historical Data (1958-1972)," Special Report prepared for the Office of the Assistant Secretary of Defense (Manpower and Reserve Affairs) by HumRRO, July 1975, p. 21.
5. Mental Categories, or Armed Forces Qualifications Test (AFQT) Groups, are expressed in percentile scores which are intended to show how a person's score compared to the scores achieved by the population that served in World War II. For example, if a recruit now receives a AFQT score of 21 (Mental Category IV), it means that his score is higher than the scores achieved by 20 percent of World War II military personnel.
6. The cataloguing or grouping of entry test scores into five mental categories has taken place for

applicants since World War II, and the distribution of service personnel in World War II is used today as the Reference Population. Thus, if an applicant's scores are in the top 8 percent (percentile range 93-100), he is classified as a Mental Category I. Mental Category IIs represent 28 percent and have percentile scores of 65 to 92. Mental Category IIIs represent 34 percent and have percentile scores of 31 to 64. Mental Category IVs represent 21 percent and have percentile scores of 10 to 30. Finally, for the 9 percent who score in the 1 to 9 percentile, Mental Category V has been established. Mental Category Vs are ineligible for enlistment or drafting.
7. The proportions of Mental Category IVs in the army's fiscal year 1979 recruit group was higher than the porportion accessed by the army in the 1950s and 1960s. During this period, the proportion of Mental Category IV enlistees ranged from a low of 17 percent in 1960, to 28 percent in 1968, to 44 percent in 1952, during the height of the Korean War induction period.
8. If the critieria for measuring involvement was extended to all of those youth who were subject to either voluntary or involuntary processing, the proportions would be substantially higher. Each year, the active and reserve forces have been recruiting in excess of 400,000 youths for voluntary service, with at least an additional 200,000 youths being rejected for enlistment.
9. Sixteen percent of the enlistees in the Air Force during fiscal year 1979 were black. This was the lowest rate among the four active services. In the selected reserve, the rates ranged from 10 percent in the navy reserve to 37 percent in the army reserve. Of all the active and reserve components, the navy reserve in fiscal year 1979 was the only one with a black enlistment rate below that of the national average.
10. The amounts cited are service averages. The rates for each service vary. Essentially, the rates are averages for all personnel in a grade and include cost elements for basic, incentive, and special pay as well as certain personnel related allowances and expenses. See Office of the Assistant Secretary of Defense (Comptroller), "Average Cost of Military and Civilian Manpower in the Department of Defense," August 1980, pp. 15-16.

## Chapter 17
# Conclusion

The preceding chapters portray a wide variety of political, social and economic factors affecting military manpower. The authors present varying interpretations of the significance or relevance of these factors; and, consequently, the book achieves little consensus in prescriptive policies or methods of analysis. In what directions, then, does this inchoate debate lead? The following distillation of the major themes in the book hopefully will serve as a useful guide and summary to future directions.

## THE CURRENT SITUATION

Military manpower must be increased just to ensure the effectiveness of the current force structure, given the deterrent and war fighting strategies advocated by the nation's leadership. Manpower shortages are all the more understated since a multitude of unmanned job requirements are excluded from the authorized force structure. Thus, additional qualified personnel must be procured to permit military commanders sufficient latitude to meet the manpower needs of a peacetime military which must also be prepared for war. Despite the possible requirement for an expanded force structure in the 1980s, the highest priority remains in filling current manpower requirements.

High first-term attrition rates exacerbate the overall manpower shortage and imply a problem, in the long term, of a lack of skilled and experienced careerists. The degradation of compensation and benefits by an inflationary economy and previous pay ceilings have only heightened this situation by causing increased careerist attrition. To fully comprehend these phenomena and their impact on readiness, data must be disaggregated and analyzed without compromise or bureaucratic deception.

Although the problems of retention may be attributed in part to mismanagement of available resources of the armed services, a number of external factors make it increasingly difficult to attract and retain personnel. Declining pay and benefits make it nearly impossible for the services to compete with the civilian sector, especially for skilled technical personnel. A rejuvenated system of bonuses and specialty pays, as seen in the Nunn-Warner Amendment of 1980, would stabilize this situation; but the long-term ability of the military to compete with the civilian economy for quality personnel is doubtful.

Defining precisely what is meant by quality personnel, and how such a characteristic is to be both measured and predicted, has assumed political as well as economic and functional aspects. Statistically, a high school diploma is a somewhat reliable indicator of retention, however, there exists no empirical evidence to link it to actual job performance. And, given the decline in literacy rates nationwide, it is no guarantee that an individual is capable of performing his job without remedial or extensive training at high cost. The inexorable drive to develop and deploy increasingly complex weapons systems in the name of efficiency demands a technical quality of personnel who are neither forthcoming nor retainable. Despite the flaws of surrogate measures, the growing, widespread assertion that the quality of the all volunteer force has declined must derive from a factual base.

The political and sociological dimensions of this issue are reflected in the growing concern of the public and the government about the trends in the minority component of the services, particularly the army. Because of apparent structural socioeconomic defects which restrict employment and educational opportunities for these groups, it is inevitable that they seek out the military as an employer of last resort. Not only are there implied questions of job performance and retention of these personnel, but there are also serious reservations about the wisdom of having combat forces that are predominantly black and Latin (led primarily by whites), that would bear the heaviest casualty burden in any future conflict. In addition, the disproportionate association of military service with lower socioeconomic groups engenders increasing disdain and avoidance of service by other groups. The dichotomous demand by minority groups that they not be restricted from enlistment by a quota system, yet not pay a disproportionate price for the nation's defense, is further exacerbated by the scarcity of minority college graduates who are willing to become professional officers. The competition with the civilian market is extremely fierce and will be resolved only when a sizable pool of minority graduates becomes available.

## WHAT CAN BE DONE?

Policy options and general solutions tend to be based on either sociological or economic perspectives. The economic approaches stress the welfare or income incentives necessary to enlist adequate numbers of people with adequate skills. This approach deals with the margin rather than the base acquisition of personnel, that is, the issue over the additional incentives needed to retain or enlist an additional increment of qualified personnel. The sociological approach includes monetary incentives as only one of several important factors inducing people to join the military. Social mobility, public service, and self-esteem must be added as motivators.

Since its inception in 1973, the AVF has been subjected to a number of demands and expectations which have effectively precluded its achievement of unquestioned success. The AVF was founded with the understanding that a competitive pay structure would attract and retain the necessary numbers of people. Thus, one could assert that the AVF has not been given a fair test unless proper pay levels are maintained. Under most economic models, the AVF becomes a costly proposal; and the problem then changes to one of continued congressional or public support for a large defense budget. On the other hand, the social and "hidden" economic costs of a conscription system are estimated by some analysts to far outweigh the budgetary costs of manning the AVF.

Too little analysis and attention has been directed at *unit* problems. However, by 1980, the Army Chief of Staff had both recognized this deficiency in public statements and put the army staff to work in search of solutions. Unit cohesiveness is a critically important and poorly understood factor in the quality of our armed forces. Through more frequent exercise of individual and unit skills and through better training facilities, job satisfaction as well as unit readiness will be enhanced. Likewise, personnel policy and management programs that are structured to meet the sociological needs of the soldier and his family, such as stabilized tours, will foster unit cohesion *and* favorable career orientations.

Other general proposals are: (1) develop pay and benefit packages and programs that enhance rather than degrade the quality of military life and extend these benefits to unmarried as well as married personnel; (2) restore the GI Bill and reduce the alternatives to subsidized education by linking a public service requirement to educational aid; (3) extend educational and quality of life benefits to reservists; (4) enhance the quality of individual and unit training programs to promote individual pride and unit morale, and to increase readiness; (5) continue to implement organizational studies and improvements (e.g., allowing commanders more flexibility and authority in personnel promotions and assignments); (6) implement some variant of a universal public service system, including one with a military option, and (7) return to a conscription system.

Proposals for higher defense budgets do not necessarily portend solutions to manpower problems. Clearly, there will always be defense budget ceilings established by the demands of competing national programs and the ever-present desire to balance the national budget. Within the ceilings established for the defense budget, there are competing demands for funds to support such critical areas as operations and maintenance; procurement; research, development, testing, and evaluation of military hardware; military construction; and military family housing.

How, then, should one view the various alternative proposals to solve the nation's military manpower problems? The editors of this volume leave it to the reader to make an informed judgment. It should be recalled from the introductory debate that the burden of proof lies with the advocate of a change to existing public policy. The burden of proof requires clear demonstration that the present system (in this case, the All Volunteer Force) is inadequate; that the AVF contains inherent, structural defects which cannot be overcome by minor repairs or "quick fixes"; and that there is an alternative which will solve the problems of the AVF, yield additional advantages unobtainable through the AVF, and will not create undesirable side effects disadvantageous for the national interest. If the analyses and prescriptions presented in this book are not persuasive, the appropriate conclusion must be that the nation must make do with the all volunteer system, making minor repairs where possible, but living with problems its critics assert with increasing frequency.

# EPILOGUE

While it is possible that some of the above proposals may ameliorate the current situation in manpower acquisition and retention there is also a need for future planning. Solutions to manpower problems typically take a long time to formulate and implement. Now is the time to work on the manpower problems of the late 1980s and 1990s. Undoubtedly, monetary incentives will effect a short-term improvement. But, ultimately, the United States must somehow recapture its "martial spirit" and give its military personnel esteem and understanding equivalent to their grave responsibility in defending the nation. With the recession of 1980, passage of a registration law, and pay increases, one could anticipate an increase in recruitment for 1981. The latest danger is that this "windfall" increase will gloss over the underlying problems and reduce the government's sense of urgency. Failure to act decisively could be critical, not only to the success of the military establishment but also, and more importantly, to the survival of the United States.

# Glossary

1. active duty—Full-time duty in the active military service of the United States. A general term applied to all active military service with the active force without regard to duration or purpose.
2. AFQT—Armed Forces Qualification Test, used to determine mental qualification for enlistment and induction into the armed services.
3. ASVAB—Armed Services Vocational Aptitude Battery, used to determine vocational abilities of inductees to the armed services.
4. full mobilization—Expansion of the active armed forces resulting from action by Congress and the president to mobilize all reserve component units in the existing approved force structure, all individual reservists, and the materiel resources needed for their support.
5. individual ready reservist—A member of the ready reserve not assigned to the selected reserve and not on active duty.
6. mobilization—1. The act of preparing for war or other emergencies through assembling and organizing national resources. 2. The process by which the armed forces or part of them are brought to a state of readiness for war or other national emergency. This includes assembling and organizing personnel, supplies, and materiel for active military service.
7. partial mobilization—Expansion of the active armed forces (short of full mobilization) resulting from action by Congress or the president to mobilize reserve component units and/or individual reservists to meet all or part of the requirements of a particular contingency, operational war plans, or to meet requirements incident to hostilities.
8. ready reserve—The selected reserve and individual ready reserve liable for active duty as prescribed by law.
9. reserve components—Reserve components of the armed forces of the United States are: a. the Army National Guard of the United States; b. the Army Reserve; c. the Naval Reserve; d. the Marine Corps Reserve; e. the Air National Guard of the United States; f. the Air Force Reserve; and g. the Coast Guard Reserve. In each reserve component there are three reserve categories, namely: a ready reserve, a standby reserve, and a retired reserve. Each reservist shall be placed in one of these categories.

10. selected reserve—That portion of the ready reserve consisting of units and, as designated by the Secretary concerned, of individual reservists required to participate in inactive duty training periods and annual training, both of which are in a pay status. The selected reserve also includes persons performing initial active duty for training.
11. selective mobilization—Expansion of the active armed forces by mobilization of reserve component units and/or individual reservists, by authority of Congress or the president, to satisfy an emergency requirement for a force tailored to meet that requirement, e.g., mobilization for domestic emergencies, such as civil disturbances or instances where federal armed forces may be used to protect life or federal property and functions or to prevent disruption of federal activities. Selective mobilization differs from partial mobilization in that it would not normally be associated with requirements for contingency plans involving external threats to the national security.
12. standby reserve—Those units and members of the reserve components (other than those in the ready reserve or retired reserve) who are liable for active duty as provided in 10 U.S.C. 273 and 674.
13. SQT—Skill Qualification Test, administered to determine proficiency in a particular military operational specialty.
14. total mobilization—Expansion of the active armed forces by the organization and/or generation of additional units or personnel beyond the existing approved active and reserve structures to respond to the requirement generated by the contingency, including mobilization of all national resources needed to create and sustain such forces.

# INDEX

Attrition, xv-xvi, 48, 64, 103, 230, 266.
Benefits/incentives of AVF, 11, 71-73, 77-78, 95, 212-213, 215-216, 232-234, 266,
   in reserves, 139-140, 142-145, 169-170.
   Compensation/wages, xiv, 12, 24, 28, 67-78, 196-197, 209, 234, 266.
   in reserves, 142-145, 159.
Conscription/Draft, xvii, 89, 95, 179-192, 210-212, 220-221, 250-264.
   equity, 57, 91-92, 100-101.
   history, 22-23, 31, 119, 122, 124.
   reserves, 100, 102, 106, 167-169, 221
   legislation, 22-23, 180
   selective service, 62, 66, 99-102
   standby system, 180-181
   as tax, 13-14
   reform, 182
Costs/Budget, 78, 85
   of registration, 182
Demography/Manpower entry poll/age cohorts, xiii, xv, 10, 79, 93, 104, 134, 241, 251, 253.
   and registration, 183, 189-190.
Desertion, 24-25, 28-29.
Education
   benefits, xvi, 215-216, 232-234
   BSEP (See training)
   colleges, 99
   high school graduates, (also see quality) 8, 12, 24, 49, 64.

   in reserves, 52, 195-196, 267.
Gates Commission, 61, 179-180, 217-218, 195, 229.
Leadership
   cadre system, 160-161
   and morale, 25-26
   NCOs, 49-50
   in reserves, 127, 141
   officers, 49-50
Manpower/strength goals/ levels,
   in reserves, xiii, 7-8, 65-66, 90, 96-97, 104, 131-134, 149-151, 154, 155-156, 163, 165, 169.
   related to technology, xvi, 169
   general determination of level, 11, 30, 48, 63, 90.
   and the draft, 255-256
   use of civilians, 104-105
   careerists, 65, 105, 154
   market view, 201-209
   National Guard, 149, 154
Militia, (See chapter 7)
Militia Act of 1792, 117-119
Minorities,
   Blacks, 9-10, 14-15, 49, 52, 54, 103, 229, 230, 259-261
   Hispanic, 9, 49, 52
   Women, 34-36, 38-39, 40-49, 53-58, 104
   sexual harassment, 53-55
   pregnancy, 47-58
National Defense Act of 1920, 123-124
National Guard, 123, 126-127, 133, 149, 154
'Nifty Nugget,' 65-66, 191

Quality/mental category, xiii, 7-9,
    12-13, 29, 64, 103, 195-196,
    253-255, 256-258
  accuracy, 7, 153
  in reserves, 152-153, 155, 157
  relation to technology, 80-87
  women, 48
  blacks, 259-261
Recruiting/enlistment
  history, 25-32
  goals, xiii, 63
  malpractice, 153
  organiztion, 25, 27-30
  in reserves, 157
  social changes, 135-139
  women, 35
Registration for selective service, 57, 66,
    88-89, 179-192, 221, 231
  1980 implementation, 184-191
  'Operation Proud Spirit,' 191
Retention,
  of skilled personnel, 14, 25-27, 48,
    64-65
  in reserves, 139-146, 171-173, 230
  and women, 48
Socio-economic
  background/representativeness,
    10, 24, 42, 92, 97-98, 101-103,
    229-231
  and marriage, 30

historical, of reserves, 111-113, 115
and reserves, 140-41 (group
    identification)
Training
  Basic Skills Education Program
    (BSEP), 48-49
  of individuals, 8-9
  and weapons, 82-85
  in reserves, 135, 139-140, 151,
    155-156
  SQT, 9, 48
  and women, 38-39
Units/Organizations
  reserve deployments, 125-126, 133,
    158, 160
  organizational
    effectiveness/models, 35-38,
    44-46
  and cohesion, 43, 49
  and combat, 38-43, 50-51
Universal Military Training (UMT), 94,
    96-97, 222-223
Universal Military Service (UMS), 94,
    96-97
Universal National Service (UNS), 62,
    94, 97-98, 223-226, 237-249
Vietnam, 10, 43, 196
  and draft, 14, 23
  and quality, 103
  effect on Reserve Policy, 169-170

# About the Authors and Editors

**Captain Bruce E. Arlinghaus,** U.S. Army, is currently assistant professor of anthropology in the Department of Social Sciences at the U.S. Military Academy, West Point, New York. After commissioning through ROTC at Ohio State University, he was named a University Fellow at Indiana University, receiving his M.A. (1973) and Ph.D. (1981) in anthropology and African studies. While assigned to the Third Infantry Division in Europe (1974-78), he served as the antitank platoon leader (14 months) and as a rifle company commander (22 months) in a TOW and DRAGON equipped mechanized infantry battalion. He is currently engaged in research on the impact of high technology arms transfers on economic development and political stability in Subsaharan Africa.

**John R. Brinkerhoff** is the Special Assistant to the Deputy Assistant Secretary of Defense for Reserve Affairs. He is a 1950 graduate of the United States Military Academy and has earned graduate degrees in civil engineering, geography, and operations research. He served 24 years on active duty and retired in 1974 as a colonel. Subsequently, Mr. Brinkerhoff joined the Office of the Secretary of Defense as a civil servant. He has worked in the areas of manpower programming, intergovernmental affairs, congressional relations, strategic planning, and resource allocation. He was assigned to his present position in the Reserve Affairs Office in May 1978. Mr. Brinkerhoff is involved in the preparation of plans, policies, and progrms to assure the readiness of the guard and reserve.

**Kenneth J. Coffey** (Ph.D., University of London) is the Defense Manpower Management Expert for the General Accounting Office. He previously directed all-volunteer force research for the Defense Manpower Commission, served as one of the key officials of the Selective Service System, and provided consultant services to the Office of the Secretary of Defense, the Congressional Budget Office, the General Accounting Office, and the National Security Council. He is the author of two recent books on military manpower problems, *Strategic Implications of the All-Volunteer Force,* (1979), and *Manpower for Military Mobilization* (1978), as well as many articles and professional papers.

**Dr. Richard V. L. Cooper** is Director of Policy Analysis and Industry Studies for Coopers & Lybrand. He received his Ph.D. in economics from the University of Chicago in 1971, and his B.A. and M.A. degrees, also in economics, from U.C.L.A. in 1967. Formerly with the Rand Corporation, where he was Director of Defense Manpower Studies from 1972 until 1979, Dr. Cooper has published widely in the area of defense manpower.

**Robert L. Goldich** is a specialist in national defense in the Foreign Affairs and National Defense Division, Congressional Research Service, Library of Congress, Washington, D.C., and has been a CRS analyst in defense manpower and personnel issues since 1972. He holds a B.A. in political science and history, Claremont Men's College, Claremont, California, and a M.A. in international affairs, George Washington University, Washington, D.C. 1977. He is author of articles on defense manpower and personnel topics in *Armed Forces and Society, Army,* and *Military Review,* of numerous studies published for congressional use or in congressional documents, and is Contributing Editor, Annual Edition, *Reserve Forces Almanac,* 1975-1981.

**Major William J. Gregor,** a 1969 graduate of the U.S. Military Academy, currently teaches comparative and American politics in the Department of Social Sciences at West Point. Major Gregor did his graduate study in political science at Yale University where he earned a Ph.D. His military experience includes combat service in Vietnam and service in platoon, company, and battalion staff levels in Mechanized Infantry, Cavalry, and Armor Units. He is a graduate of the Armor Advanced Course and has been selected to attend the Army Command and General Staff College.

**Major Robert K. Griffith Jr.** is a teaching fellow with the Combat Studies Institute of the U.S. Army Command and General Staff College at Fort Leavenworth, Kansas. A 1967 graduate of West Point, he received his M.A. and Ph.D. degrees in history from Brown University in 1974 and 1979. In previous assignments he has served in leadership and staff positions in armored and armored cavalry units in the United States, Vietnam, and Germany. From 1974 to 1979, he was Assistant Professor of History at West Point. His first book, *Men Wanted for the U.S. Army: The Volunteer Army and American Society, 1919-1940,* is forthcoming.

**Robert C. Kelly,** a corporate development planner with Continental Resources Company, Winter Park, Florida, holds a Ph.D. in economics from Harvard, and is a consultant to the U.S. Office of Management and Budget. Among his publications is a coauthored text, *Economics of National Security,* Avery Press, 1981.

## About the Authors and Editors

**William R. King** is professor of business administration in the Graduate School of Business at the University of Pittsburgh. He is the author of ten books and more than 100 technical papers in the areas of policy analysis, information systems, and strategic planning. Military manpower policy has been one of his major areas of research and consulting. During 1976, he conducted a major study of the all-volunteer armed forces for the United States Senate Budget Committee.

**Melvin R. Laird** is the Senior Counselor for National and International Affairs for the Reader's Digest Association. He was Secretary of Defense from 1969 to 1973, Counselor for Domestic Affairs to the President of the United States from 1973 to 1974, and a legislator from 1946 to 1969. Mr. Laird graduated from Carlton College before serving in the Navy from 1942 to 1946 where he was awarded the Purple Heart.

**Charles C. Moskos** is a professor of sociology at Northwestern University. He is the author of numerous studies on armed forces and society, and testifies frequently before Congress on all issues of the all-volunteer force.

**Captain Eric T. Olson** is an instructor in the Department of Social Sciences at the United States Military Academy. He is a 1972 graduate of the United States Military Academy. He was awarded the M.A. from Johns Hopkins School of Advanced International Studies in 1979. He has served in staff and command positions with the U.S. Army at Fort Carson, Colorado.

**Robert B. Pirie, Jr.** served as Assistant Secretary of Defense (Manpower, Reserve Affairs and Logistics) from 1979 to 1981. He attended Princeton University and graduated from the U.S. Naval Academy. He received a B.A. and M.A. from Oxford University, England, as a Rhodes Scholar. From 1955 to 1975, he served in various capacities on nuclear submarines, culminating his service as Commanding Officer of the *U.S.S. Skipjack*. From 1966 to 1969 and from 1973 to 1975, he served on the staff of the Secretary of Defense. In 1972 and 1973, he was on the staff of the National Secruity Council. In 1975, Mr. Pirie became the first Deputy Assistant Director for National Security of the new Congressional Budget Office where he served until June 1977, when he accepted the post of Principal Deputy Assistant Secretary of Defense (Manpower, Reserve Affairs and Logistics) with the Office of the Secretary of Defense. Mr. Pirie is a recipient of the Legion of Merit and the Meritorious Service Medal.

**Dr. Bernard D. Rostker** assumed the position of Director of the Selective Service in November 1979. He attended New York City public schools, received his B.A. in economics from New York University in 1964, where he was a

Regent's Scholar, and continued his study of economics at Syracuse University, where he was awarded the M.A. in 1966 and Ph.D. in 1970. From 1968 to 1970, he served as a captain in the Army and was assigned as a staff economist in the Office of the Assistant Secretary of Defense (Systems Analysis). In 1970, he joined the Rand Corporation; and, in 1977, became Principal Deputy Assistant Secretary of the Navy for Manpower and Reserve Affairs.

**Captain Richard A. Schrader** is currently an Instructor in the Department of Social Sciences at the United States Military Academy. He is a 1972 graduate of the United States Military Academy and was awarded the M.A. from the School of Advanced International Studies, the Johns Hopkins University, in 1976. He has served in staff and command positions in West Germany and Hawaii.

**Dr. William J. Taylor, Jr.** is Director of Political-Military Studies at the Center for Strategic and International Studies, Georgetown University. He is a former professor at West Point where he served as Director of the National Security Studies program and the West Point Debate Council and Forum. A frequent contributor to various books and journals, his most recent articles appear in *American Defense Policy, The Eagle's Brood, Public Administration Review,* and *Air University Review*. He recently coauthored (with Amos A. Jordan and associates) *American National Security: Policy and Process* (The Johns Hopkins University Press, forthcoming, 1981). His institutional memberships include The Council on Foreign Relations and the International Institute for Strategic Studies.

**Adam Yarmolinsky** served in the Kennedy, Johnson, and Carter administrations in the Pentagon, the White House, and the Arms Control and Disarmament Agency. He has taught law and public policy at Harvard and the University of Massachusetts and currently practices law in Washington, D.C.